GENERAL HENRY LEWIS BENNING

"This was a man"

A Biography of Georgia's
Supreme Court Justice and
Confederate General

J. David Dameron

HERITAGE BOOKS
2008

HERITAGE BOOKS
AN IMPRINT OF HERITAGE BOOKS, INC.

Books, CDs, and more—Worldwide

For our listing of thousands of titles see our website
at
www.HeritageBooks.com

Published 2008 by
HERITAGE BOOKS, INC.
Publishing Division
100 Railroad Ave. #104
Westminster, Maryland 21157

Other books by the author:

Benning's Brigade: Volume 1, A History and Roster of the Fifteenth Georgia

Benning's Brigade: Volume 2, A History and Roster of the Second, Seventeenth, and Twentieth Georgia Volunteer Infantry Regiments

Women Airforce Service Pilots of World War II: The WASP

Front Cover: General Henry Lewis Benning. Portrait commissioned by his grandsons, Henry Benning Spencer, Henry Benning Crawford, and Benning Hull. The artist was Ms. Kate Edwards of Atlanta, Georgia. Courtesy of the National Infantry Museum, Fort Benning, Georgia.

International Standard Book Numbers
Paperbound: 978-0-7884-2444-1
Clothbound: 978-0-7884-7042-4

General Henry Lewis Benning

To my wife Pamela.

Acknowledgments

General Henry Lewis Benning

Acknowledgments:

Exploring the life of Henry L. Benning was an adventure filled with intrigue. He lived well over a century ago, thus events that shaped his life are obscured by myths, distortions, and long-forgotten or overlooked facts. Collecting relevant data was an awesome task, yet rewarding and laden with revelations about a man who, in his time, was widely and genuinely admired. Once these valuable elements of information were compiled, evaluated and integrated, the myriad pieces of Benning's life gradually formed an accurate and transparent view of the past. Therefore, without the generous assistance of many people, the story of Henry Benning would still be fragmented and filed amidst a multitude of archival sources. It is within this realm that I am personally indebted to so many people, and I genuinely thank them all for their kind and valuable assistance.

Dr. Richard Shrader, Archivist of the Southern Historical Society Collection at the University of North Carolina assisted me in uncovering the connections between Henry Benning, John Bratton, Edward P. Alexander, and Benjamin Yancey. Their letters yielded valuable information and I sincerely appreciate Dr. Shrader's professional and eager assistance. Ms. Mary Ellen Brooks, Archivist of the Hargrett Rare Book and Manuscript Library Collection at the University of Georgia graciously supplied her assistance to my numerous requests. The letters, documents and pictures housed in the vast collections of Howell Cobb and Judge Joseph Lumpkin contributed greatly to my research. These important collections contain numerous personal letters of Henry Benning. Ms. Brooks and her staff helped me immeasurably with their expertise in locating the appropriate sources. Dr. Craig Lloyd, Professor of History, Archivist and Director of the Chattahoochee Valley Historical Collection at Columbus State University energetically rendered his time and professional assistance in several aspects of this project. His archival organization and vast knowledge of the extensive documents related to Henry Benning and Seaborn Jones made my research more refined, efficient and rewarding. He also guided me to peripheral sources within the collection, which contained many useful documents and provided me with

Acknowledgments

valuable insight concerning local Columbus history. Finally, and most importantly, he unselfishly reviewed and provided valuable comments concerning the draft manuscript of this biography and I am genuinely grateful. Dr. Lloyd's assistant, Mr. Adalbelio Garcia helped me when Dr. Lloyd was unavailable, and I genuinely appreciate his research assistance too. Also at Columbus State University, I extend my heartfelt thanks to the Director of the Simon Schwob Library, Ms. Callie McGinnis for her generous assistance and professional help in locating useful sources. I also appreciate her valuable contributions to *Muscogiana*, a local genealogy and history journal, which lists source material applicable to the Chattahoochee Valley region. The archival staffs at Duke and Emory Universities helped me locate and exploit the few primary sources connected with Henry Benning in their collections, and for their helpful assistance, I thank them too.

Most of the judicial and military documents concerning Henry L. Benning are maintained by the National Archives and the Georgia Department of Archives and History. While several professional archivist assisted me with numerous requests, I am particularly appreciative of the professional assistance rendered by Ms. Gail Miller DeLoach of the Georgia Archives and Ms. Dorothy Olson of the Georgia State Capitol, Secretary of State's Office. Mr. Randy Hackenburg, Assistant Curator at the U.S. Army Military History Institute eagerly assisted me in conducting research at that office, and I genuinely appreciate his professional assistance. I also appreciate the assistance provided by the respective staffs of the following institutions and organizations: Virginia Historical Society; Virginia State Library and Archives; Museum of the Confederacy; Georgia Historical Society; Robert Toombs House and Museum; Washington-Wilkes (Georgia) Museum; Margaret Mitchell Museum; Columbus (Georgia) Historical Foundation; Historic Linwood Foundation; Muscogee County (Georgia) Genealogical Society; Columbus Government Center; Library of the *Columbus Ledger-Enquirer*; the ladies of the Lizzie Rutherford Chapter (Columbus) of the United Daughters of the Confederacy; the officers and men of the present-day *Columbus Guards*; and Mr. Edward Annable Jr., Registrar of the U.S. Army National Infantry Museum, Fort Benning, Georgia. Additionally, I sincerely appreciate the historical preservation efforts and assistance rendered by the Marshall Autry family of Columbus, Georgia. Delores, Marshall and their daughter Tracy, have created a beautiful legacy through their unselfish contributions to the preservation, research and recording of local Columbus history.

General Henry Lewis Benning

Their work in maintaining the beauty and dignity of Linwood Cemetery is a labor of love and exemplary in the annals of historic preservation.

I am particularly grateful to the descendants of the family and friends of Henry Benning, whose generous contributions to my research made this book a reality. Mrs. Patti Andrews, whose husband Mote Andrews Jr. is a great-great-grandson of Pleasant Moon Benning, assisted me immensely with photographs, genealogical notes, maps of old homesteads and valuable Benning family lore. Mr. William Pease, a descendant of John A. Jones (Benning's brother-in-law) conducted extensive genealogical research concerning the Benning and Jones families, and I sincerely appreciate his endeavors. Mrs. Mimi Pease Childs, another descendant of John A. Jones provided me with extensive data concerning the Benning and Jones connections, valuable genealogical details, as well as fascinating photographs and paintings of the family. Her kind and generous assistance was the epitome of Southern hospitality. Mr. and Mrs. Leonard Garrard, whose family created the " Wildwood" estate, and were kin to the Benning and Jones families, provided me with exceptionally courteous assistance. Mrs. Garrard made me feel at home (and made numerous copies of material), while Mr. Garrard provided me with the most insightful information one can share- his cherished memories. From long walks and talks through the environs of " Wildwood," I gained the most valuable insight an author can achieve, and I sincerely thank the Garrards for their friendship and generosity. Mr. Henry Benning Spencer, a great great grandson of Henry Benning, provided me with letters, portraits and insightful information about the Bennings. His assistance and consideration coupled with his wife's expertise in photography is truly appreciated. Mr. Larry Russell DeLapp helped me to fill in several gaps concerning the Benning genealogy and to him, I extend my gratitude also.

Many people willingly answered my requests for photographs, letters and pertinent information concerning men that served in Benning's brigade during the Civil War. I wish to thank the following people for their contributions to my research: Judge George Green, Mr. David Cress; Mr. George Dudley; Mrs. Patricia Langford Parrish; Mr. Blaine Walker; Mrs. Diane Andrews, Mr. Ray Lokey; Mrs. Betty Slaton; Mr. Mel Middlebrooks; Mr. Ken Norton; Mr. Thomas Buffington; Ms. Vernice Harvey, Mr. John R. Fortson; and Ms. Philippa Denny.

For their professional advice and editorial reviews of the draft manuscript I thank Mr. Theodore Savas, Mr. William C. Davis and Mr. Robert Krick. Their contributions to this project are greatly appreciated and it was a pleasure working with historians of such high merit.

Finally, my deepest appreciation is reserved for my wife of twenty-four years, Pamela Gail. Her ability to transcribe difficult nineteenth

Acknowledgments

century penmanship proved to be a very critical skill and her efforts
contributed greatly to my comprehension of several key events.
Additionally, she read and commented on each and every chapter and
consequently she knows at least as much about Henry Benning as I do. Her
ability to recall distant genealogical connections within the Benning family
continues to amaze me and without her, this project would have been much
more difficult. I cherish our times working together on this book and love
her even more for sharing the journey with me.

CONTENTS

Introduction

On July 10, 1875, along the banks of the Chattahoochee River, the town of Columbus, Georgia baked beneath the heat of the summer sun. The sweltering weather made life especially difficult for the elderly and amidst the oppressive heat an old male Negro suddenly fainted. The afflicted man was known as " Old Billie," a stalwart survivor of an arduous life of slavery and hard work. He was one of many people bred and bound in antebellum America to bear the rigors of servitude and manual labor. Those who knew " Old Billie" realized that it would take much more than harsh weather and old age to fell such a man of fortitude, and in fact, his sudden weakness was aggravated by a sudden shock. Tragic news was being relayed throughout town that during the pre-dawn hours, Columbus had lost one of her finest sons. Eventually, someone told " Old Billie" and upon hearing it, grief overwhelmed him and his body collapsed under the strain. As he regained consciousness, the old man wrestled with the heart-wrenching pain that his former master, General "Old Rock" Henry Benning was dead.

    " Old Billie" had served Benning as a slave and cook throughout the war, and afterwards as a free man, he remained devoted to his former master. It is natural to question why a man held in bondage, when freed, would continue his devotion to the man that bound him. Yet, Old Billie's motivation is not so surprising when you consider that the man he honored was described as " a towering figure... of absolutely crystal truth and a braver more chivalrous spirit never breathed." 1

    As General Benning, commander of a Confederate brigade in Lee's Army of Northern Virginia, he earned the sobriquet," Old Rock." This affectionate and honorable name was bestowed upon Benning by the men that served in his command, which reflects the admiration and respect afforded him. During the epic struggle for Southern independence, Benning's men proudly followed him into the mortal hell of battle, repeatedly and with great distinction. Against overwhelming odds, Benning's brigade contributed greatly to Confederate victories in both the eastern and western theaters. Their deeds at Burnside's Bridge during the Battle of Sharpsburg and at the Devil's Den during the Battle of Gettysburg are just two examples of the tenacity with which Benning and his men waged war. While Benning excelled as a military leader, his skills in the arena of law are legendary as well. Prior to the war, Benning served his home state as a Solicitor General and as a Justice of the Supreme Court. His life-long career as a successful attorney earned him an enviable reputation as a champion of truth and justice. Henry Benning was also a devoted husband, a loving father, a generous friend, and according to his hometown newspaper," No man in our city is loved like he." 2 The Atlanta Herald recorded that:

General Benning's life was no ordinary life; his death is no ordinary loss. It is a public calamity; for he was a full grown man, who walked conspicuously in the public eye and filled a large space in the public heart. Georgia has given to the century no man who commanded in a greater measure the confidence, respect and esteem of the people, or to whom those who knew him best in the relations of personal friendship were more devotedly attached. 3

" Old Billie" was representative of the town, as the citizens of Columbus were all shocked by the sudden loss of " Old Rock" Benning. The Columbus Bar Association reported that," The sad news like an electric current, was conveyed from mouth to mouth throughout the city and surrounding countryside that General Benning was dead." Just the morning before, he had been seen in his usual stride walking briskly from his home to the courthouse " with his books and brief in hand." Benning focused his energies intently on all matters of the court. Additionally, Benning was his family's sole breadwinner, impoverished by the war, and he was struggling to care for both his immediate and extended family. Yet, throughout the night before his death, Benning labored intently in preparation of an impending legal brief. A close friend, James D. Waddell commented that Benning " never allowed the morrow's sun to rise on unfinished work, if it was in his power to complete it today." In spite of Benning's physical and moral strengths, the stress of work, his age, his many burdens and numerous sorrows, all combined and destroyed his health.

On the morning of July 9, while passing through Brook's drug store on his way to the courthouse, Benning suddenly staggered against a barrel, and collapsed to the floor. Mr. John W. Brooks, druggist and proprietor of the store, as well as a gathering crowd of concerned citizens, immediately went to his aid. At first, struggling with a severe chill, pain, and confusion,

Benning urged his friends to send word to the court that he " would be there after a little." It was obvious that Benning was seriously ill and his condition worsened rapidly. He was placed in a carriage and brought to his home, just down the street on Broad, the main avenue in downtown Columbus. Doctors Francis Stanford and Eugene J. Colzey, both prominent local physicians, examined Benning and gave what little aid nineteenth century medicine could muster. Facing the realization that " Old Rock" suffered from acute apoplexy, the doctors knew that Benning's condition and prognosis was poor. Henry Benning's affliction is known today as a massive stroke, and his daughters, Mary, Anna Caroline, and Sallie, all looked on in helpless disbelief. Benning's last few years had been filled with stress and pain, leaving him physically broken and his spirit shattered. That evening, Benning slipped into unconsciousness, and " Old Rock," stalwart as always, silently fought his ultimate battle with the specter of death. " His appointed time had come. In the midst of family and friends, and in the shadows and stillness of the midnight hour, and without pain and without struggle, he quietly and peacefully passed away." 4

Henry Benning was survived by his five loving daughters, Mary, Anna," Sallie," and the twins, Augusta and Louisa. These refined ladies ranged in age from 20 to 34. Benning's only son, Seaborn, suffered greatly from the effects of his severe war wounds and he had preceded his father in death. Henry's beautiful wife, Mary Jones Benning, also died before Henry, and she was the foundation of his happiness and success. Mary's father was the former U.S. Representative, pioneer, soldier and successful lawyer, Colonel Seaborn Jones. While Henry Benning found genuine love with Mary Jones, he also gained financial success. Mary Jones Benning enjoyed a full life complete with a mansion, wealth, and all the trappings of an aristocratic, antebellum lady. Moreover, her life mirrored the fictional characters depicted by the leading ladies in *Gone with the Wind*. Mary's personality displayed the tenacity of Scarlet O'Hara coupled with the virtues of Melanie Hamilton amidst a violent and chaotic time. While war forced most Southern women to face severe adversity, Mary's burdens were many, and during the 1860s, her world simply collapsed. During the war, Mary shouldered the many burdens of sole parenthood while Henry and her son Seaborn, served the Confederacy. From 1861 until she died, Mary fought her own civil war and in her own unique ways. In the local Confederate hospitals, she cared for the wounded, while at home, she struggled to maintain two plantations and care for her large family. She also assisted the local widows and orphans of Columbus, and she worked diligently to assist " the cause" in every way that she could. Mary's son, Seaborn was horribly wounded in battle, and she went to Virginia twice and nursed him back to health. During the war, Mary also lost her father,

her mother-in-law, her wealth, and life as she knew it. After the war, impoverished and broken, she died, leaving Henry Benning to carry on without her. 5

After the war, Henry's immediate need was to care for his family, and true to his character, he did. Benning supported his five daughters, the widow of his brother-in-law, and her five children, as well as his mother-in-law, Mary Howard Jones, then in her eighties. To provide for his large family, Henry Benning returned to the profession of law. Benning was well on his way to regained wealth, when he was suddenly struck down. The love and affection Henry's girls had for their father was deep and abiding. Henry's home reflected their femininity and charm. It was adorned with white Damask linens and drapes, marble topped mahogany furnishings, gilded china, and fine silverware. These items were cherished heirlooms and the few remnants salvaged from the war. Yet, on the beautiful Sabbath morning of July 11, 1875, the Benning home was filled with melancholy and draped in black. The body of Henry Benning was prepared for burial and his coffin was placed in the family's parlor. Benning's daughters spent their final moments with their father and the local community prepared for his funeral. 6 The *Columbus Sunday Enquirer* informed the citizens of the details concerning the funeral procession:

> The funeral of General Benning will take place this morning at nine o'clock from the late residence on upper Broad Street. Reverend W. C. Hunter, at the house, will read the Episcopal ceremony, when the column will be formed and marched to the cemetery. It is hoped that every Confederate soldier in the city will be in the line. The following is the order of the procession.
> 1. Military companies.
> 2. Confederate soldiers without regard to rank who are willing to honor the dead hero.
> 3. Fire Company No. 5.
> 4. Officiating clergymen.
> 5. The hearse with the remains.
> 6. The General's horse with military trappings, led by "Old Billie."
> 7. The family of the deceased.
> 8. Pall bearers in carriages.
> 9. The Judge, members of the Bar and officers of the court.
> 10. Citizens generally.

As the procession lined up on Broad Street, the sun gently rose behind the two-story white frame home of Henry Benning. The rising warmth of the summer sun bathed the town of Columbus in an early morning glow of genuine serenity. Inside, Benning's daughters donned in their mourning gowns gazed upon the face of their father one final time. This lion of a man, his face outlined with distinguished white hair and beard," seemed to be sleeping sweetly, and his face was very natural." In tribute to his military service, draped across the foot of the coffin lay a bullet riddled battle flag of the Confederacy. W. C. Hunter, the rector of Trinity Episcopal Church, delivered Benning's eulogy. As the weeping family departed the home and entered their place in the procession, the fantastic display of respect could not be overlooked. A multitude of people had assembled to pay their genuine respects and escort Benning to his final place of rest. 7

At the lead of the funeral procession was Colonel William Shepherd. During the war, Shepherd served under Benning as the respected and heroic commander of the 2nd Infantry Regiment. Behind their commander, sharply formed for the march, stood the proud military columns of the " Light Guards" and the " Columbus Guards." Most of these veterans had marched many miles and fought numerous battles under General Benning's command. Behind the military companies, in " caps and belts," stood the 32 members of Fire Company Number 5. Behind them, hundreds of former Confederate soldiers formed in a column of fours. Following the soldiers were the carriages of the clergymen, and the attending physicians. Next, the two-horse hearse in which Benning's coffin was carried was covered in flowers. Directly behind " Old Rock" stood the ever faithful," Old Billie." Resplendent in his Confederate gray coat, and highly polished accouterments, the old man had meticulously groomed Benning's horse, which was adorned with sword and military trappings. Next were the pall-bearers (all distinguished gentlemen): Mr. John Peabody; Judge Porter Ingram; Mr. G. DeLaunay, Judge Martin J. Crawford; Colonel W. A. Barden; Captain Thomas Chaffin; Colonel M. H. Bland; and Major R. J. Moses. Next, came the carriages of the Benning family, followed by the Mayor, City Council, the Columbus Bar Association, dozens of carriages filled with friends, and finally hundreds and hundreds of people on foot. The local newspaper also noted that," The colored people were out in force." The editor of the *Columbus Enquirer* eloquently summed up the funeral procession with:

Columbus, in all its history, has never witnessed such a numerous multitude of sorrowing citizens in the funeral train of any of its dead. The grief was universal. The high and the low, the rich and the poor, black and white, all denominations and associations, religious, social, and military-all with heartfelt sorrow joined the solemn train as it moved towards the final resting place of their friend.

The funeral train slowly traversed the eight-block route, winding gently up hill, to its ultimate destination of Linwood Cemetery. The muffled military drums accompanied the solemn procession, finally reaching the Benning section, near the center of the cemetery. With the sun now glowing with full intensity, a graveside service was read, and the Columbus Guards rendered the final military salute for General Henry Lewis Benning. Henry was laid to rest beside his dear wife, Mary. The town of Columbus rendered their final respects, and returned to their lives with " a void no one can fill." 8 A prominent Georgian, Judge Logan E. Bleckley was so moved by the loss of Henry Benning, that he honored him with this poem:

On General Henry L. Benning

Poor Southern eyes, already red
With weeping for your noble dead,
If tears are left you yet to shed,
Give some to soothe this latest woe-
For gallant Benning let them flow.

Ah, death that spared him in the fight,
Has struck, in peace, a Georgia knight-
As knightly as the proudest lord
That ever lifted lance or sword;
No truer, braver chief than he
Adorned the ancient chivalry.

For firmness in the battle shock,
His comrades said he was a rock;
Old Rock, they said, and his command
(Whoever fled) were sure to stand;
And never was that hope betrayed
By Rock himself, or his brigade.

The tricks of war he did not learn;
In stubborn valor, grim and stern,
He trusted as the pious priest
Reposeth in the blood of Christ;
To him it seemed no fight could fail
If not a single heart would quail.

When vainer warriors would assume
The wreath, the star, the sash, and plume,
He moved among his soldiers gray,
As plain and unadorned as they;
Nor cared to shine, or to excel,
Except in doing duty well.

Additionally, in a touching tribute published by the Supreme Court of Georgia, the question was asked what manner of a monument should be erected for Benning? The esteemed gentlemen recorded that:

> Brass is not durable enough; marble is not white enough! Let the sterling traits of his character, as stamped upon the memory of his countrymen, stand as his monument. Truth, integrity, courage, moral and physical, unimpeachable veracity, honor and honesty untarnished, all these were eminently his, and these will endure forever; and let them stand as an imperishable monument to the memory of an honest man. 9

As the judges declared, Benning's reputation will " endure forever." Yet, while many people readily connect Henry Benning with the U.S. Army installation, Fort Benning, the deeds and details of his life have slipped into obscurity. Even in his hometown, the historical marker that once pointed to the location of his home and briefly described him is no longer there. His home, and that entire city block on Broad Street, has been demolished. Today, Benning's old neighborhood has been replaced by a modern corporate office facility. In Linwood Cemetery, Benning's daughters placed a remarkably descriptive tombstone on their father's grave. Its simplistic form and brief remarks provide us with a graphic reminder of a genuinely honorable and well-loved man.

The headstone directly reflects the character of Benning. It commandingly faces the eastern sky. It is simple, yet stately. It is tall and prominent, but not obnoxious. It is solid and thick, yet clean edged, smoothly polished, and geometrically proportionate. It is a single monolith of Confederate gray granite, which rises above all others in its immediate vicinity. In the center is etched his name, his military rank and his sobriquet," Old Rock." Below, a slab covers the tomb, which states, his name, his parents, dates of his birth and death, and finally the statement," THIS WAS A MAN." Certainly, Benning was a man among men. He is justly included in Northern's *Men of Mark in Georgia*. A federal military installation is named for the man. Yet, why is so little known about him? Why did Negroes, formerly enslaved by him, openly adore and respect him? Just what, exactly, did this man do to receive such admiration, and from such a diverse multitude of people? Answering these questions is the purpose of this book. 10

From an early age, Henry L. Benning was a man of achievement. Today, these achievements are generally overlooked, but Benning's record cannot be ignored. Benning's family was not exorbitantly wealthy; however, his roots were well entrenched in the periphery of planter aristocracy. Moreover, he was not " born with a silver spoon," but he was provided with opportunities to excel. He received a disciplined upbringing and then admitted to Franklin College (now the University of Georgia), at Athens. Benning graduated first in his class, amongst a virtual " Who's Who of Georgia." His classmates included (his cousin) Howell Cobb (governor of Georgia: 1851-1853, U. S. Secretary of the Treasury: 1857-1860), and Herschel V. Johnson (governor of Georgia: 1853-1857). Upon graduation, he immediately began the study of law under George W. Towns (governor of Georgia: 1847-1851). Benning then achieved acceptance to the bar in Columbus, Georgia. He also served as a soldier during the Creek Indian uprising of 1836, gaining valuable first-hand military experience. These relations and achievements, secured early in his life, provided Benning with exceptional opportunities. 11

In 1837, Benning was appointed by Governor McDonald as the Solicitor General of the Chattahoochee circuit, and the next year, the Georgia legislature elected that he maintain that post. In 1839, Benning married Mary Howard Jones, the beautiful daughter of Seaborn Jones, a prominent lawyer and former U.S. Representative. At the ripe old age of 25, Benning resigned from his public office, and joined the practice of law with his father-in-law, forming the successful firm of Jones, Benning and Jones. In 1853, at the age of 39, Benning was elected to the Georgia Supreme Court. At that time, he was the youngest man to achieve such an honor. His record on the bench is immaculate and Benning excelled in preparing and presenting the opinions of the court. The case of *Padelford v. Savannah, 1852,* provided Judge Benning with the opportunity to address an issue, which would soon rise to the forefront of constitutional interpretation. 12

In this case, Benning presented an 82-page document, which challenged the supremacy of the federal court in state matters. He argued that the Supreme Court of Georgia was " co-equal and co-ordinate" with the U.S. Supreme Court. " This expression has never been overruled, but simply ignored... regarded now from a practical standpoint [it] seems visionary." 13 Benning's fear of federalism was publicly expressed in 1840, and his fervent belief in states' rights was apparent as early as 1849. Throughout his life, Benning maintained correspondence with Howell Cobb, where he expressed the details of his concern for states' rights, and the inevitability of southern secession. Again, Benning's visionary predictions concerning the constitutional supremacy of federal versus states' rights exploded in the question of slavery. 14

This book draws liberally from the life-long letters exchanged between Henry Benning and Howell Cobb. Housed in the University of Georgia Archives, these letters provide valuable insight into why and how Benning, Cobb and the Southern states chose to separate from the united bonds of our republic. In 1860, Benning worked feverishly, throughout the South, as a delegate to the many conventions debating secession. For many historians, it is within this forum that Benning has been framed as a radical " fire-eating" extremist and hell-bent on Negro oppression. While Benning was certainly an advocate for secession, he was not an oppressive slavemaster. Today, many people relate the term slavemaster with the cruel and abusive archetypical villain portrayed in Harriet Beecher Stowe's *Uncle Tom's Cabin.* Throughout the South, incidents of oppressive cruelty and outright inhumanity undoubtedly occurred, however, Benning, like most educated slave owners, treated their slaves with great concern.

Additionally, while Benning was certainly an ambitious young power seeker as defined in William Barney's book, *The Road to Secession,* it must be remembered that Benning was also striving to attain success as defined by the standards of the era in which he lived. 15 Moreover, in contrast to the theory as expressed by some historians, Benning did not support planter " slaveocracy" merely to safeguard his own personal economics. While Benning did achieve profits from planting, his work as an attorney and judge, secured his wealth. 16 Benning's primary concerns regarding slavery were based firmly on established legal interpretations and a fervent belief in states' rights. Furthermore, Benning's advocacy of a strict constructionist view of the U.S. Constitution was founded upon years of personal research, conservative jurisprudence and its application in the Georgia Supreme Court. He adamantly rejected a liberal viewpoint of constitutional interpretation and he fought in the courts and on the battlefield for his beliefs.

Henry L. Benning was a wise, prudent and selfless servant of causes he felt were just. To fully comprehend Benning and his actions, one must examine his behavior in the context of nineteenth century life. The norms and social values of a given era shape and define its unique and complex nature. Benning lived in a time wrought with complexities and his reactions to them deserve more than simple presumptions. Recall that many of our well-respected " founding fathers," Washington and Jefferson for example, were slave owners. While these great men literally built a nation, their legacy included the difficult dilemma of slavery. Henry Benning and his generation inherited this problem, and they tore our nation apart as they argued the issues of slavery, states' rights, and constitutional interpretation.

Throughout his life, Benning was committed to the study and application of the law. As a successful lawyer and state Supreme Court justice, Henry Benning applied wise jurist logic to the issues of the courts and his opinions were well respected. For decades he was a member of the Georgia bar, and for six years, he served as a member of the ultimate authority with dignity and honor. In 1860 and 1861, as a skillful speaker, delegate and diplomat, Benning energetically served the Democratic Party throughout the presidential election, the pro-secession movement, and the formation of the Confederacy. As a leader in the forum of debate, Benning experienced first-hand the frustrations of his generation as heated arguments turned into hostilities, and ultimately a bloody civil war. Under the flag of the Confederate States of America, Benning laid down his pen and took up the sword. Benning's devotion to his chosen cause coupled with a high intellect and physical prowess combined to forge a warrior and battlefield commander of the highest caliber. As one of Robert E. Lee's finest generals, Benning led his units with great skill and distinction. Yet, when the war ended in favor of his foe, Benning honorably surrendered his sword and urged his fellow Southerners " to acquiesce." 17 In the post-war era of Reconstruction, with many of his friends and family but cherished memories, Benning returned to the arena of law and a successful practice in his hometown of Columbus, Georgia. Quietly he expended the final decade of his life as a respectable attorney and a model citizen.

Henry Benning devoted the bulk of his life to serving his community in peace and war. As you read the story of this man, consider also that during Benning's life and times, the legal standards of our nation were literally in a state of flux. In 1858, the State of Georgia (while Benning served as a Supreme Court Justice) addressed difficult legal issues and became the first " English speaking commonwealth to codify the whole body of the law in force." 18 This act of legal codification set the standard for legal references in our nation. It also resulted in the creation of the first complete, condensed and annotated Code of Law, which pointed to the source of the law, be it common law, the Constitutions, the State Statutes, decisions of the Supreme Court, or the Statutes of England.

In the courtroom and on the field of battle, Henry Benning fought diligently for his beliefs. To comprehend the thoughts and actions of Henry L. Benning, we must get to know the man. We must examine his known strengths and experiences as well as his intricate complexities and human shortcomings inherent in all men. His story reflects a man whose devotion to causes, selfless service, upright morals, traits and values are worthy of admiration. Throughout the life of Henry Lewis Benning, his letters, speeches, opinions and deeds, reflect the characteristics of an honorable and remarkable man.

In a touching tribute to Benning's character, his family and friends recorded an eternal complement on his tombstone. The phrase is a simple but eloquent remark derived from the ending line in William Shakespeare's *Julius Caesar*, which states:

His life was gentle, and the elements
So mixed in him that Nature might stand up
And say to all the world," This Was a Man!"

Chapter 1

Beginnings

In origin, the Benning (Benin) ancestry is French. The lineage of
Henry Lewis Benning is traced to a family of Benins, which fled France in
the pursuit of religious freedom. During the sixteenth and seventeenth
centuries, France was embroiled with revolution and war. The names of
Joan of Arc, Cardinal Richelieu, and King Louis are important figures in
this era of French history. After the Hundred Years War, France entered
into a period known as the Reformation, a time when Protestants were
slaughtered by the thousands at the hands of the French Roman Catholic
Church. These persecuted French Protestants were known as *Huguenots*.
After decades of bloody civil war, the Huguenots achieved a short period
of religious freedom. Then, in 1685 the absolute monarch of France, King
Louis XIV, began another era of savage persecution, forcing thousands of
Huguenots to flee their nation. Amongst those fleeing France were Francis
Benning (Francois Benin) and his wife, Ann de Bonette. Originally from
Tarrigny Parish in southern France, they fled their homeland traveling to
Holland, and then to Bristol, England.

With the promise of religious freedom in the New World colony of
Virginia, the Benins accepted the exchange of religious freedom in the
Virginia colony for allegiance to the King of England. Arriving in
Virginia, in October of 1700, the Benins settled in the Huguenot village of
Monacan Towne, King William Parish, and Henrico County (presently
known as Manakin, Virginia). The village and lands were previously
inhabited by the local Indians, which had been ushered westward by the
encroaching colonists. Located near the James River, approximately
seventeen miles northwest of Richmond, Monacan Towne was established
as a refuge for the Huguenot colonists, where each family was provided
with generous tracts of free land. The Benins had an only son, (Antoine
Benin) Anthony Benning. Anthony Benning married Elizabeth Jounay.
Anthony became a large landowner and planter. In Albemarle County,
Anthony Benning established a 400-acre estate, and he served as a church

Ann had five children, the youngest being John Benning (Jean Benin),
born on December 10, 1737. **1**

Several years before the Revolutionary War, John Benning migrated
westward and settled in the piedmont region of Goochland County,
Virginia. When Virginia and the other colonies revolted against England,
John joined the patriots and became an officer in the local Virginia militia.
In the midst of the Revolutionary War, July 20, 1775, Captain John
Benning married the only daughter of Colonel Thomas Cobbs (the "s" was
later dropped), Sarah "Sally" Cobbs. After achieving victory and winning
independence from England, our young nation was free to expand beyond
the established borders of the former colonies. John Benning was among
the many hardy veterans who could not overlook the many opportunities
that freedom provided. With the promise of vast rich lands and the
elimination of English colonial restrictions, our new nation was destined to
grow. A postwar expansion into thinly populated and former Indian
territories was soon underway, and the State of Georgia provided eager
pioneers with many unique opportunities.

To encourage growth in Georgia, extensive land bounty grants, land
lotteries and simply cheap land sales spurred many Carolinians and
Virginians to migrate there. Among the Virginians, who took advantage of
the enticing opportunities in Georgia were both the Benning and Cobb
families. John and Sally Benning purchased a 640-acre tract of land in the
Savannah River valley region of Columbia County, Georgia. Located just
north of Augusta, Georgia and located along the banks of a mighty river,
the rich soil enticed the Bennings and they moved. Along the way, in
Buckingham County, Virginia, Sarah Benning delivered her fifth child, and
third son. Born on October 3, 1783, they named the child Pleasant Moon
Benning. Later in his life, Pleasant Moon Benning would become the
father of several children, and one of his sons was Henry L. Benning. **2**

Pleasant Moon Benning may seem like a flowery name, however,
Pleasant was a popular name in the early nineteenth century, and the name
Moon is derived from the family of Moon, which was a part of the Cobb
family. Sarah (Cobb) Benning 's grandmother was Susannah (Moon)
Cobbs. Thus, the connections between the Cobb, Benning and Moon
families extended through several generations. The children of John
Benning were the first generation of Bennings to drop their French spelling
of the name, thus changing it from Benin to Benning. Pleasant Benning
had four elder siblings, Thomas, Joseph, Elizabeth, and Roane.
Additionally, he had three younger sisters, Susannah, Martha and Nancy. **3**

Another family that played an essential role in the Benning history,
were the Whites. The White family was the origin of Henry Benning's
maternal lineage. After the Revolutionary War, the White family had

followed the same migration as the Benning family, and moved from the
piedmont region of Virginia to the Savannah River valley of Columbia
County, Georgia. On August 18, 1882, Captain Richard P. White, a veteran
of the Revolutionary War married Mary Meriwether. Mary was a daughter
of the Lewis and Meriwether clan, whom were a proud and prominent
family of Virginia. Mary's family was well renowned for their
contributions to our young nation, including the courageous exploits of the
famous explorer, Meriwether Lewis. Thus, the Benning and White families
shared much in common. They were all originally from Virginia, they had
fought for their independence and they had contributed to the birth of their
nation. On their homesteads, both families quickly established their roots
in the soil of Georgia. Both families established farms, cleared their land,
and planted cotton. Enjoying the fruits of liberty, Richard and Mary White
worked their farm and raised a family. On April 18, 1789, the White family
had a beautiful daughter, and they named her Malinda. Malinda Lewis
White grew up on her parent's plantation, where she was raised to be a
refined and elegant young lady, yet armed with an independent, frontier
spirit. Malinda was also destined to be the mother of Henry Lewis
Benning. 4

Malinda was the " light of the house" and " the belle of the county." At
the top of her tall, stately frame, Malinda had long flowing locks of dark
brown hair and beautiful blue eyes. She had " soft, white hands, and a still
softer voice, albeit one to command. " To honor " Miss Malindy," the slave
girls made up a little chant they sang. Within a ring of hands, a girl would
enter the center of the ring, shuffling slowly and chanting the following
tune:

> Come 'er trippin' downstairs, Miss Malindy,
> Come 'er trippin' downstairs, Miss Malindy,
> Come 'er trippin' downstairs, wid yer true love by yer side,
> You on your way ter Shiloh. * (country church)
> Oh fare you well, Miss Malindy,
> Oh fare you well, Miss Malindy,
> Oh fare you well, an' er, do fare you well,
> You on your way ter Shiloh.
> What you reckon your mother say, Miss Malindy ?
> What you reckon your mother say, Miss Malindy ?
> What you reckon your mother say, wid yer true love by yer side?
> You on your way ter Shiloh.
> Oh fare you well, Miss Malindy,

Oh fare you well, Miss Malindy,
Oh fare you well, an' er, do fare you well,
You on your way ter Shiloh.
Contrary to the jest of the song, however, Malinda and Pleasant did
not elope. 5 Pleasant Benning wooed the young maiden, and they were
properly married on June 8, 1809. Upon their marriage, Pleasant was
twenty-five years of age, while Malinda was age twenty. Pleasant Benning
is best characterized by his virtues. He was highly respected and
considered one of the most generous and compassionate men of the
community. A planter by profession, Pleasant also served as a Captain in
the local militia. His father, John Benning had died just three months
before Pleasant and Malinda were married and he and his brothers had
assumed the operation of their father's plantation. Pleasant and his elder
brothers, Joseph and Thomas, jointly owned and operated their father's
estate, which totaled 1,100 acres and 110 slaves. 6
    The marriage of Pleasant Benning and Malinda White was a beautiful
union revered not only by their families, but also by their slaves. Along
with their family silver, both families had migrated to Georgia with their
ebony treasures as well. In the early nineteenth century, the institution of
slavery extended throughout the nation. White indenturement and black
enslavement were norms of the society in which they lived. Practiced
throughout the world, privileged caste and working class were enforced, by
law. However, this is where the Benning family differed from the evil
stereotypical slaveowners of Southern lore. The Bennings were a very
religious family and they held the word of God close to their hearts. As
with most antebellum Southerners, the Bennings' religious beliefs
provided them with guidance for their daily lives. While the *Holy Bible*
taught them to love their brothers, it also provided them with supportive
passages concerning the institution of slavery. Within the Bible, believers
found solace that slavery was an historical institution, and according to the
Bible, masters should care for the needs of their slaves. For example, a
passage from the book of Colossians states, "Masters, give unto your
servants that which is just and equal; knowing that ye also have a Master in
heaven." 7 Like most Southern slaveholders, they highly valued and cared
for all of their property, including their slaves.
    This regard for life, of all races, was handed down through
subsequent generations. Furthermore, while the Benning family embraced
slave labor, they and many Christians throughout the south were beginning
to question the " peculiar institution. " The founding fathers of these United
States, whom so diligently fought for what was just and true, managed to
formally avoid the dilemma of slavery. Pleasant Benning 's generation
inherited not only freedom and opportunity, but also the question of

enslavement and what was right concerning their black brethren. Thomas Jefferson eloquently noted in 1814, "The hour of emancipation is advancing, in the march of time. It will come; and whether brought on by the generous energy of our own minds; or the bloody process of St. Domingo." **8**

During this era of the early nineteenth century, events occurring throughout the world influenced many new beginnings. In a time wrought with apprehension and repression, western civilization was on the verge of a vast transition. In Europe, the rule of Napoleon Bonaparte came to end. Crushed by the Russians, led by Alexander I, Napoleon abdicated control of France to King Louis XVIII, and he was exiled to the island of Elba. In South America, Simon Bolivar led the epic struggle to gain independence from Spain. Since 1812, Great Britain was again at war with her former colony, the United States of America. James Madison, the fourth president, was forced to flee the White House, as British forces attacked and destroyed the capital of the young nation. The British forces burned the White House and the Capitol building. In Baltimore Harbor, Francis Scott Key witnessing the siege of Fort McHenry was inspired to write a song, which later became our national anthem, *The Star Spangled Banner*. Ending in the Treaty of Ghent, the War of 1812 resolved nothing but the validity of the United States as a permanent nation that Europe could not ignore. However, more importantly, the end of the war marked the beginning of a new era. In U.S. military history, the era is known as the " Thirty Years' Peace," which provided our nation an unobstructed time for growth and expansion. Moreover, the world was transitioning into an era known as the "Industrial Revolution," and the "Era of Good Feeling." Marked by a time of peace, unity, and optimism, cotton grown in the United States was being consumed by European markets, where mass production of textiles was rapidly being mastered.

The State of Georgia mirrored the changing times as well. In Savannah, Eli Whitney's cotton gin had revolutionized the removal of cottonseeds from the cash-producing fiber. This invention made it possible for one person to do the work of what formerly required fifty laborers. Known throughout the land as "King Cotton," the combination of the cotton gin and slave labor transitioned a lucrative market into a booming economic giant. Yet, Georgia was encumbered in her cotton production efforts because of population and physical size. Blessed with fertile, virgin soil, Georgia was destined for expansion; however, the state's inhabitancy was restricted within the region of the coastal plain. With only eighteen states in the union, Georgia was the most southern state, and one of the least inhabited by the white man. White settlements extended to the north along the Dahlonega plateau and to the west and south along the Ocmulgee River, whereupon the Creek, Cherokee and Seminole Indians occupied the remainder of Georgia. To stimulate regional expansion, the federal government promised to remove the Indians from the state. Over the next several decades, white men slowly negotiated their western expansion until it became necessary to physically expunge the native races from the land. **9**

During this time, Pleasant and Malinda Benning began a family. In May of 1810, Malinda gave birth to a son, John Anthony, and the next year, yet another son was born. On November 25, 1811, Malinda gave birth to Pleasant Melvin. As so often occurred in the nineteenth century, within just a few years, both of the Benning sons died prematurely. However, their third child was truly a charm. The Bennings were blessed with their third son, which became the couples' pride and joy. On April 2, in the tumultuous year of 1814, Malinda delivered another son, Henry Lewis Benning. Baby Henry was nursed by his mother's personal servant, Queen. Queen was a slave of strong stock and devoted to a lifetime of servitude and loyalty to the Benning family. Henry quickly grew into a healthy and happy child. Sadly however, in that same year, Malinda's father passed away, and while serving his country in the War of 1812, her brother Clement was killed in battle, just three weeks before the war ended. Thus, for the Benning family, the year 1814, was certainly a time of both happy and sad occasions. For our nation and for the world of that year, 1814 marked the end of an era and the beginning of another. As previously stated, the " Era of Good Feelings," the " Industrial Revolution," and the Thirty Years Peace," all new beginnings, commenced with the year 1815. **10**

Over the next few years, the Bennings prospered. Their plantation was situated along the Savannah River, between Keg and Kiohee Creeks. Located in the upper northeastern corner of Columbia County, the virgin fields were rich with vibrant soil, and yielded abundant crops. The little family of Pleasant and Malinda Benning was growing too. Malinda again delivered a son, this time on July 4, 1816. They named the child Columbus Washington Benning, but within a year, he too, succumbed to ill health, and died on October 17, 1817. The next year however, Malinda gave birth to another son, Richard Edwin, on December 15, 1818. Richard was healthy and strong, rapidly maturing into a fine young man. Following his father's example, Richard would become a life-long Georgia planter. Adding to this brood of young men, Malinda began giving birth to girls. In October 1820, Mary Louise was born, followed by Caroline Matilda, born on September 28, 1824. Then, two stillborn twins were born in June of

1826, and finally, Augusta Palmyra on August 18, 1827. Of all these girls, only Caroline Matilda and Augusta Palmyra survived their early childhood years. For the surviving children, education became the focus of their lives. **11**

The eldest Benning child, young master Henry Lewis Benning required a formal education. In rural Columbia County of the nineteenth century, there were very few private institutions and no public schools. However, in neighboring Hancock County, the Mt. Zion Academy, run by Carlisle and Nathan Beman, was one of the finest private boarding schools in Georgia. The Bennings decided that Henry should attend and they sent him into the private tutelage of the Beman brothers. The school was administered by Reverend Nathan S. S. Beman, who also pastored the Mt. Zion Church, while the younger Carlisle Pollock Beman provided instruction and discipline for the male students. Reverend Nathan Beman instructed the female students, and Sunday worship services for all of the pupils, as well as the local community members of the church. In those days, Carlisle Beman was considered the " Nestor of Education throughout the South." **12**

Beman's educational methodology was thorough and direct. Known as a strict disciplinarian, no erring pupil escaped his wrath or rod. While the use of a cane today would not be tolerated, in those days, rules were enforced with biblical consequences. Students were compelled to study, recite and perform to exacting standards, lest punishment be rendered. While Beman was harsh, he was also fair, and he distributed immediate justice to students of varying ages and sizes. Although he was short, he was very strong and he energetically administered as he saw fit. Physically strong, mentally sharp, and spiritually clean, Beman instilled these values upon his pupils. Students that failed his exams were caned, but he did not have many failures. Perform as stated, or Beman would issue his standard threat, "I'll whip the very filling out of your shirt." **13** Charged with positively shaping young men's lives, Beman excelled in his mission. Many men of worth, in Georgia, received their education at the Mt. Zion Academy. Young Henry Benning excelled under Beman's tutelage. Benning had studied the basics of math, science and English, and now he hungered for more. In 1831, at the age of seventeen, Benning applied and was accepted to Franklin College (now the University of Georgia).

Entering college as a sophomore, Benning was accustomed to and well prepared for a rigorous academic environment. When Benning entered, Franklin College was busy establishing itself as a respectable

institution, gaining strength, influence and public favor. The institution
admitted males only, and the administration was all-male, as well. In those
days, each class only contained from thirteen to twenty-six students. Most
of the graduates of the school became important men of mark in Georgia
and several achieved noted prominence for their unique contributions.
Among them were George F. Pierce (later the President of Emory
University and a Bishop, Methodist Episcopal Church); Nathaniel G.
Foster (later U.S. Congressman and Supreme Court Justice); and numerous
doctors, lawyers, legislators, judges, and professors. Among the seniors,
the year Benning entered the college, were Alexander H. Stephens (later
U.S. Congressman, Vice-President of the Confederacy, and Governor of
Georgia) and James Johnson (later a U.S. Congressman, Superior Court
Justice, and Provisional Governor of Georgia). Among Benning's
classmates (and his close friends) were: Howell Cobb (later U.S.
Congressman, Speaker of the House of Representatives, U.S. Secretary of
the Treasury, and Governor of Georgia); and Herschel V. Johnson (later
U.S. Congressman, Superior Court Justice, and Governor of Georgia). 14
     While most of the students were earnest, hard-working pupils, a few
achieved notoriety through their impetuous behavior. One of these was
Robert Toombs (later U.S. Congressman and Confederate Secretary of
State). When Toombs was young, his father died, and Thomas W. Cobb
became his guardian. 15 Young Master Toombs behaved as he pleased.
While Toombs was a brilliant student and incessant reader, he was
eccentric, belligerent, quick-tempered and prone to act impulsively. The
following incident (unedited report) reflects Toombs behavior and the
primary reason he was discharged from the school in his senior year:

> R. Toombs called J. H. a shameful name, which he
> acknowledged to the faculty, and the said H. attacked him and
> beat him on Friday night. Toombs went to H.'s room with bowie
> knife and pistol, threw the knife at G. H. and pointed the pistol
> at J. H., which another student wrested from him. Afterwards,
> Toombs attacked J. H. with a knife and hatchet, but the students
> interfered, preventing injury. Saturday morning, Toombs
> waylaid the H.'s on their return to college, attacking J. H. with a
> club and pistol. 16 (The initials listed in the report refer to
> brothers, Junius and Granby Hillyer)

Toombs left Franklin College and went on to graduate from Union
College, in Schenectady, New York, and then he studied law at the
University of Virginia, however, myths still circulate concerning Robert
Toombs and his college activities. However, Toombs dearly loved the

school, and in his latter years, he served on the Board of Trustees and
energetically supported the institution.

Fortunately for Toombs, Mr. Cobb was able to absorb the cost. Lesser
financially sound families could ill-afford such serious mistakes. At
Franklin College, a state sponsored institution; tuition was thirty-seven
dollars per year. The college encouraged parents to send their sons and
wards with as little money as necessary to preclude distractions. According
to the administrators:

> Almost all the misconduct of students at college may be traced
> either directly or indirectly to the imprudent use of money. The
> less money they have beyond the necessary expenses, the more
> secure will their characters be, and the more will they be
> guarded against useless extravagance, self-sufficiency and vice.
> It is also earnestly recommended to parents and guardians to
> allow their sons and wards in no instance to run in debt, as a
> credit which can always be obtained, is equally as pernicious as
> too much money. 17

Too much money was not one of Benning's problems. Moreover, the
financial disparity between Henry Benning and Howell Cobb, for example,
provided Benning an advantage over his peers. The Cobbs were distant
cousins of the Bennings. While both families were plantation owners, the
Benning's net worth pales in comparison with the Cobbs. 18 The Cobbs
were not only prominent members of the local Athens and Clarke County
community, they were socially affluent and powerful as well. The Cobbs
had vast wealth, huge plantations and hundreds of slaves. While the
Bennings owned slaves, they were actually median income farmers from a
rural county, struggling to send their first-born son to college. Henry
Benning was raised in a lifestyle filled with hard work and discipline, first
on his father's farm, and then under the rigid rule of Carlisle Beman. All
the while, Howell Cobb, known as "Fatty" by his friends, enjoyed "every
advantage that could come from wealth and culture." 19 Howell's father
moved his family to Athens seeking the best educational opportunities for
his children. The Cobb family roots were deeply entrenched in Georgia
soil. Nearby Cobb County was named for his father's cousin, Thomas W.
Cobb, an early Congressman and U.S. Senator from Georgia. While
Benning's grandmother, Sarah (Cobb) Benning was part of the Cobb
family ; the link was too distant to create favor for young Henry. In spite of

their differences, young Howell Cobb and Henry Benning forged a
relationship that would span their lives. While they were close friends,
Benning seemed to gauge his life, his achievements and his goals upon the
accomplishments of Cobb, which for Benning, proved to be a challenge of
overwhelming odds.

Most of the young men attending Franklin College came from
wealthy families, which obviously provided the college trustees great
concern for potential vices. As part of the overall college experience, the
school not only provided academics, but also enforced mandatory militia
and religious services. Naturally, the young men rebelled against such
repressive tactics. Mandatory classes, morning and evening prayers, drills
and recitations, were simply too much for spoiled young men to bear. Rule
infractions carried fines, admonitions, suspensions, and possible
expulsions. The harshest disciplinarian and most feared by the disorderly
students was Dr. Alonzo Church. A former professor of mathematics, he
also served the college as president and the leader of the evening prayer
services. Dr. Church was tall and fearless, quick-tempered, but controlled.
One evening the campus exploded in riotous behavior, and Dr. Church
sweepingly expelled eleven students. Among the lot was Howell Cobb,
whose mother promptly intervened, declaring that she had " seen him
asleep in bed on the very night of the riot." Other students suggested that
perhaps, Howell slipped out after Mrs. Cobb had visited his dorm.
Nonetheless, Howell was reinstated. "The college student of the Old South
was a happy creature; he had so many rules to disobey and did it so
effectively." **20**

"Fatty" Howell Cobb was certainly a " happy creature." Popular
amongst his peers, Cobb's jovial nature reflected his physical disposition.
Cobb " weighed about 200, and when he laughed, every particle of his
avoirdupois shook like a jelly bag." **21** While Henry Benning enjoyed
having fun too, he could ill afford to take college in such a leisurely
fashion as Howell Cobb. While many of the students' parents could easily
afford their sons' indiscretions, this is where Benning's discipline provided
him with an edge. Ever conscious of proper behavior and academic
diligence, Benning bested his peers. Moreover, Benning enjoyed college.
The curriculum included Astronomy, Political Economy, Moral and
Mental Philosophy, Natural History, Chemistry, and Composition. In
addition to these subjects, the students were also graded on the areas of
industry, behavior, and punctuality. Benning excelled in them all, but what
he enjoyed the most was his extra-curricular activities in the Phi Kappa
Society. The two Greek letters represented *Philo Kosmean*. Formed in
1820 by Joseph Henry Lumpkin, as an alternative to the *Demosthenians*,
these societies forged factions amongst the student body, albeit an overall

healthy distraction from the repressive college curriculum. While the faculty despised the secret meetings and their associated vices, the students loved their literary societies, and their antics flourished throughout the campus. **22**

The Phi Kappas were a secretive organization, and it provided a forum for young men to formulate and apply oratorical skills, to subjects they desired to address. The absence of fraternities and athletics created a void that the students filled themselves, by mocking what the great men of their day engaged in-politics. Discussions and speeches concerning important topics such as slavery created an indelible mark upon the character and values of these young men. Moreover, the skills they polished in debate and oral presentation served them well throughout their futures. It was within these societies that the study of the arts and sciences blended with shared experiences to forge deep, long-lasting relationships and shared ideologies amongst the future great minds of Georgia. Years later, reflecting on their time at Franklin College, Benjamin H. Hill referred to it as being the " sweetest haunt of memory," and Alexander H. Stephens referred to his college experience as the " happiest days of my life." **23**

Meanwhile, back home, on the Benning plantation , changes were underway. In order to spur growth in Georgia and specifically to encourage westward expansion, the state held land lotteries. In the western regions of Georgia, the lands previously occupied by the Creek and Cherokee Indians were offered for settlement. Treaties had recently been negotiated with the Indians, and they agreed to allow the " white man" to have their lands. Georgia quickly surveyed and divided the region into counties, plats and lots. Additional incentives were provided for Revolutionary War veterans and their families. Based on his father's military service, Pleasant entered the final land lottery, known as the "Gold Lottery," in 1832. Pleasant was fortunate and won land in Harris County, located along the Chattahoochee River (border between Alabama and Georgia), it was just north of the newly formed town of Columbus and just to the west of Talbotton. Pleasant paid the State of Georgia his $18.00 grant fee for a 202 1/2 acre plot of prime Georgia property and prepared his family to move. **24**

While Pleasant and Malinda Benning had won a unique opportunity, their relocation to Harris County would geographically sever familial ties in Columbia County. Between Pleasant and Malinda, their only surviving parent was Malinda's mother, Mary (Meriwether) White. Mary was a sixty-nine year-old widow whose family now consisted of her daughter

Malinda, and so, she chose to move with them. With Henry away at
school, many responsibilities devolved to Richard, then age fourteen, to
assist his father. The other Benning children were all girls, ranging in ages
from six to ten. Whether it was a matter of ideology or logistics, Pleasant
brought with him very few slaves, and the bulk of slave ownership passed
to his brothers, however, the Bennings did bring with them at least one
entire slave family, consisting of Primus, Queen and their three children.
Queen had nursed the Benning children and throughout their lives, there
was a genuine mutual respect and cordial master-slave relationship
between Queen and the Bennings.

Pleasant Benning's new land was located in a fertile valley, just
below Pine and Oak Mountains, and to the east of the tiny hamlet of
Waverly Hall, Georgia. Fully forested, with gently rolling terrain, for the
next few years, Pleasant would literally have to carve out a new life for his
family.

Back in Athens, at college, Henry continued to excel scholastically.
Finally, in the summer of 1834, Henry L. Benning was declared the
valedictorian of the senior class. Achieving "first honors," he led the
commencement in a virtual "Who's who of Georgia." All receiving a
Bachelor of Arts degree, the class consisted of:

Moses L. Barron	Crawford W. Long
Henry L. Benning	William H. McBride
Edwin Cater	Charles J. McKinley
Howell Cobb	William H. Meriwether
Thomas M. Cobb	John T. Milledge
John R. Dyer	Augustus Reese
James F. Gilbert	James H. Saye
Henry S. Glover	M. C. Summerlin
Henry M. C. Jackson	Francis Walker
John O. H. Lillibridge	Herschel V. Johnson 25

Destined to achieve success, these young men now embarked on
separate journeys. Howell Cobb remained at home where he began to study
law and woe the beautiful Mary Ann Lamar. For Howell Cobb, the latter
affair took precedence and he pursued her with zeal. Always striving to
achieve, Henry Benning also pursued a career in law. In those days, with
no formal law schools available, prospective lawyers entered the study of
law under the private tutelage of a licensed attorney. In this capacity,
prospective lawyers engaged in a form of apprenticeship and independent
study until they were able to pass the local bar examination. In a move to

study law and be close to his family, Henry Benning accepted an offer to practice law with George W. Towns of Talbotton, Georgia.

Henry's mentor, George W. Towns, was a prominent lawyer and had previously served in the state legislature. Towns was a Democrat and an ardent defender of states' rights. Towns is described as "a man of suavity of disposition and ease of manner." 26 He also had a natural politeness and was very popular. A genuine Southern gentleman, Towns provided an excellent example for young Henry to model. Studying the law under Towns had profound effects upon Henry throughout his life. Under Towns, Benning learned not only the law, but also a deep-rooted sense of Southern politics and a firm belief in states' rights. Additionally, Towns moved in high societal circuits, which provided Henry Benning with opportunities he eagerly sought.

While Benning studied feverishly, the young man excitedly corresponded with his college friends, eliciting their thoughts and news of their activities. Upon graduation, the Class of 1834 began their separate lives and their own unique adventures. While Benning was excited to be preparing for his future career, he certainly missed his college chums, their exploits, and their close relationships. His old friends Howell and Tom Cobb, Herschel Johnson, and John Milledge remained in close proximity, while Benning had removed to the western part of the state, and he missed them. During this time, Henry Benning began a correspondence with Howell Cobb that lasted throughout their lives. During the course of the following four decades, their letters reflect the times and sentiments of the "Old South." However, they also reflect the diversity of their backgrounds and diverging ideologies. Intermingled amongst the reminiscences, congratulatory remarks, and genuinely happy thoughts concerning kith and kin, the great wedge of secession slowly severed their friendship.

Thus, in September of 1834, the young men were still holding onto their recent past and their cherished college memories. Eager to achieve, yet hesitant to surrender their innocence, Henry writes to Howell stating:

> I can enter into your feelings with regard to the changes which have come over the spot where we spent some of our happiest moments, for before I left Athens, it had been deserted by all the class save those you mention, and therefore, none to me an air of peculiar gloom. But fond memory brings the light of other days around me and brightens my darkest hours by the bright tablet, which she presents of things that were. 27

Henry continues his letter, jealously noting that Howell's father is now a member of the Senate. "But alas! I shall be the first of the family to promoted to that high honor, and that will be in God's good pleasure." Henry then states that he is reading Blackstone (antebellum law guide), and invites Howell to come to his office, where he will be "pursuing his studies of the law. Come and let's talk and drink and smoke and live." **28** Obviously enjoying the freedom and pursuit of happiness in adulthood, Henry nonetheless focused on his immediate goal- to become an attorney.

Howell Cobb was in no hurry to study law, he had fallen deeply in love with Mary Ann Lamar, and the study of law was suspended for amorous endeavors. Henry, however, could ill afford distractions in pursuit of his goal, and he frequently chided Howell for doing so. In November of 1834, writing to his old classmate, Henry asks Howell if he has begun the study of law or is he still "chasing petticoats." Henry states that he has nearly finished reading Blackstone, and plans to take his bar exams in April. Henry was obviously ambitious and hungered to achieve success as defined by antebellum standards. He continues with:

> How would you like to be a twenty-five or thirty-year-old
> esquire at this session of the legislature when judgeships and
> soliticorships were distributed so profusely... my bowels yearn
> for one of those fat places. But I extract some comfort knowing
> that I am studying law with a great man and therefore can enjoy
> his society sometimes. **29**

Over the course of the next few months, as Henry continues to study the law, several of his friends decide to get married. Then, Howell Cobb formally announces his engagement to Mary Ann Lamar. With a slight hint of jealousy, Henry sternly rebukes him with:

> You must all be possessed... wedding after wedding, courtship
> after courtship, in quick and abiding succession. Why are things
> so? Is it so dear as to be purchased at the price of chains and
> slavery ? Verily, verily there must be a matrimonial revival
> amongst you. I wash my hands of the matter. Your blood is
> upon your own hand, and you in the anxious class! Who would
> have thought it after hearing your oathy resolves. In regards to
> Miss L., she is a young lady of worth and accomplishments, not
> to mention other properties of a highly attractive character.
> Marry and have a young brood of Cobbs around you. They will
> help to wipe away the wrinkles from the brow of old age.

Besides it is the way to make Presidents and heroes and how delightful that will be. Go old fellow, I should like to be able to echo. And maybe I shall in the course of time.

Henry then retreats from his rebuke and says that if he can he will come to the wedding, but right now, he must keep "aloof from womanhood and like a good boy get my lessons and my license." Furthermore, he adds that he thinks that the marriage will be great. Ending the letter, Henry notes that all Talbotton can afford him in the way of amusements is a candy pulling. **30**

Over the course of the next few months, Henry continued his study of the law, while Towns and his partner Joseph Sturgis, explored the idea of opening a law office in nearby Columbus. Howell pleaded with Henry to serve as his attendant for the wedding. Henry wanted to oblige his dear friend but he could not because of the urgency Towns had placed in opening the law firm in Columbus. Meanwhile, Henry poked fun at his old friends for being "shackled and wived, and well wived. No tag-nag and bobtail women, but the real grit. Stuff to make presidents out of." Henry reminded Howell that he had promised to name his first born after him, but there was really no need to remind Howell, because people " naturally name their children after the greatest men of the ages." **31**

Henry was admitted to the bar on April 26, 1835, and he accepted the offer to begin the practice of law with Towns and Sturgis, in Columbus, Georgia. Opening their offices in May, Henry began the transition from studious college stripling to Henry Lewis Benning, Esquire. It was impossible for Henry to attend his best friend's wedding, and Howell Cobb and Mary Ann Lamar were wed on May 26, 1835. **32** Meanwhile, Henry's arrival in Columbus social circles as a lawyer and country gentleman was delayed for his first few weeks in town. Henry wrestled with what he described as a terrible bout of the " most indecent diarrhea," which rendered him " unfit for anything... coupled with the doctors and their infernal prescriptions, prostrates me." Thus, Henry marked his arrival in Columbus, a " city" which he described as " nearly deserving" the title. It was true, in 1835; Columbus was not much of a city; however, during the course of the next few decades it would explode in population and economic growth. Both Henry and the city of Columbus were on a parallel course of continuing success and remarkable achievements. **33**

Chapter 2

Benning and Columbus, 1835

Henry L. Benning, Esquire, began the practice of law in a virtual frontier town. Barely a city, the Creek Indians lived just across the Chattahoochee River. The Indians had ceded their claim to western Georgia with the *Treaty of Indian Springs of 1825*, and slowly, they were being pushed to the west. The territory addressed in the treaty extended from the Flint River in the east, to the Chattahoochee River in the west. The town of Columbus was created in the county of Muscogee, which was one of several counties formed within the former Indian lands. Muscogee County was organized as a 2,000 square mile county, named Muscogee in honor of a local band of Creek Indians. Over the next few years, the county was further divided into Harris, Talbot, Marion and Chattahoochee Counties as well. 1

It was within Columbus and the surrounding counties that Henry Benning began to establish his mark. Complete with Indians and pioneers, the region contained all the trappings of the " Old West." The enforcement of the law and the pursuit of justice were paramount to the establishment of the city of Columbus. Thus, the need for lawyers provided many opportunities for Henry Benning. When the counties were organized, the legislature also formed the Chattahoochee Circuit of the superior court consisting of Muscogee, Lee, Troup, Coweta, Carroll, DeKalb, and Fayette Counties. This Circuit would soon become a very large part of Benning's life.

When Benning arrived, in 1835, the town of Columbus, Georgia had only been in existence for seven full years. In December of 1827, the Georgia General Assembly enacted " to lay out a trading town and to dispose of all the lands reserved for the use of the state near Coweta Falls on the Chattahoochee River and to name the same." 2 The placement of a city at this location was a wise choice. The region provided settlers with an abundance of water, fertile soil, and room for expansion. Additionally, the river also served as a natural barrier to retain the Indians west of the Chattahoochee. The city of Columbus was well organized. With great forethought, the state appointed commissioners who laid out the city in organized blocks and lots with designated sectors for government, education, religion and cemeteries. The central road through the downtown sector, Broad Street was created with a width of 165 feet, and the town was officially incorporated in December of 1828. 3

The city of Columbus grew rapidly. By May of 1828, the *Columbus Enquirer* was distributing news, stagecoaches and mail routes were established, and riverboats steamed upriver from ports in the gulf. Coupled with a constant flow of settlers and speculators pouring in from the east, the city " never had an infancy." 4 The opportunities presented to the settlers were very unique. The people migrating into the former Indian lands were generally well refined and they simply established new towns and communities, which mirrored their former homes in eastern Georgia. There were thousands of acres to clear for planting and construction of every conceivable type, including homes, churches, and businesses. From its inception, Columbus was planned to accommodate rapid growth and commerce, and the town prospered.

Meanwhile, for Henry Benning, Esquire, the thriving city of Columbus, Georgia presented him with a wealth of personal opportunities and he was eager to exploit them all. At the age of twenty-one, with years of laborious study behind him and the attainment of a respectable and highly valued profession, Henry was now capable of achieving his desires. A former classmate and underclassman, at Franklin College, Benjamin C. Yancey, wrote to Henry in December of 1835, asking him about the town of Columbus and any advice he may have for him as he planned his future after college. Henry explained to Benjamin that Columbus was a young and thriving city filled with opportunities. Additionally, he provided the following advice, which reflect the thoughts and aspirations of young Henry Benning as well:

> Above all things, I advise if you desire ease and happiness, marry. Marry a lady of accomplishments, i.e., worth $100,000. It will be better than quibbling. I am anxious to experiment at last. 5

With his education complete and his career established, Henry frequently chided his school chums about marriage and their relations with women. However, as time went by, he began to change his tune. Henry wrote to Howell Cobb stating," I ought to marry oughtn't I? Not for the cause of being reformed- no room for that, but to be fashionable." Henry also added that:

> I could bear the galling yoke- to be in such good company as the class constitutes. It is grievous to feel however, that there is no throwing it off, not even for a moment. No, it presses and frets unceasingly, supposing you are an honest man and as faithful as I have the misfortune to be.

Henry continues this theme with:

Anything of the feminine gender of your acquaintance worth thirty or forty
thousand? Do me the kindship to make me favorably known with her
if you please and if you bring it about, why, I will give you all my
collecting for I should certainly thereupon resign the vulgar
profession and take mine elegant ease. 6

Henry had always placed his personal desires behind his professional
goals, yet it is obvious that he was now preparing to change his focus.
Working for George Towns, a dashing and accomplished bachelor,
provided Henry the opportunity to mingle with the elite of Columbus
society. One of the most important and influential men that Henry met was
the Honorable Seaborn Jones. A renowned lawyer and entrepreneur, Jones
was one of the first white visitors that traveled through the Muscogee
region. In 1814, General Andrew Jackson defeated the Creek Indians at the
Battle of Horseshoe Bend, Alabama, which opened the territory to
pioneering settlers. Seaborn Jones was eager to explore opportunities in the
former Indian lands, and he moved westward.

As a Colonel in the Georgia Militia, Jones traveled extensively
throughout the region, became acquainted with the local Indians, and he
was instrumental in the establishment of Columbus. Additionally, Jones
made important contacts with Indian leaders, while serving the state as an
investigative commissioner. Amongst the various tribes of Indians, there
were no legal landowners, and supposed " Chiefs" sold or made
arrangements for properties which had no legal basis at all. Therefore,
alleged crimes committed by Indian agents and illegal land speculators
prompted the state to launch investigations. Through these acts, Jones
contributed to the establishment of the *Treaty of Indian Springs of 1825*,
which was intended to resolve ownership and legal boundaries, however,
this task was virtually impossible, as no man really owned the former
Indian territory. Indian tribal and Chieftain ownership of vast, wild
territory was impossible to delineate. While the treaty did provide an
element of temporary resolve, eventually the region erupted in numerous
frontier disputes, litigation, and eventually, violent conflict.

Formerly a citizen of Milledgeville, Jones had also served Georgia as
a Solicitor General, Secretary of State, and as an aid to Governor Troup. At
the national level, Jones served three terms as a U.S. Representative.

Furthermore, Jones was considered one of the finest lawyers of Georgia, a respectable businessman and a friend of the Revolutionary hero, General Lafayette of France. 7 Using his knowledge of the region, coupled with his position as an essential player in the founding of the region, Seaborn Jones joined a land speculation firm. Organized in 1832, Jones, John Howard, and Edward Carey named their joint venture, the Columbus Land Company, and they invested heavily in Creek Indian lands. Jones also engaged in various entrepreneurial enterprises. He also established, owned and operated the first business on the Chattahoochee River, City Mills. In 1828, Jones harnessed the waterpower of the Chattahoochee and built a grist and flourmill at the northern end of town, on City Lot number one. Before the establishment of a bridge connecting the Alabama and Georgia shores, he also operated a ferry service. Additionally, he jointly owned and operated a warehouse with his close friend, the local Methodist minister, Reverend Samuel K. Hodges. 8 The virgin territory offered many opportunities, which were only limited by entrepreneurial spirit and capital. Jones was a dynamic man possessing plenty of spirit, money, and much more. Politically, Jones was a member of the States' Rights party and ardently fought for state supremacy in matters conflicting with the federal Supreme Court. These States' Rights victories greatly influenced the constitutional interpretation and political ideology of young Henry Benning. 9

But for Henry Benning, the most important aspect of Seaborn Jones was that he had a beautiful daughter. Mary Jones was the " belle of the county," and Henry was totally infatuated with her. Benning, the young bachelor that poked fun of his classmates for falling in love, also fell victim to the charms of an elegant Southern belle. Writing to Howell Cobb about Mary, Henry referred to her as " glorious" and that " she is the most perfect combination and condensation of mind, body and soul, beauty and truth." 10 Mary was three years younger than Henry. She was born on March 18, 1817 in Milledgeville, Georgia, which was then the State capital of Georgia. Raised in the capital cities of Milledgeville and Washington D. C., Mary Jones was the epitome of Southern charm and femininity.

Her parents, Seaborn and Mary (Howard) Jones were amongst the elite of Georgia. Her father was a powerful patriarch, highly respected and affluent. Her mother was a tall, dark-haired, captivating beauty, whose family, the Howards, was a wealthy and influential family of "Old Virginia." Mary (Howard) Jones complemented her husband, Seaborn with style and grace, making the couple one of the most attractive and affluent in Georgia.

Equally adept in Washington or Milledgeville social circles, Seaborn and Mary Jones were truly prominent members of antebellum society. The

Jones moved to Columbus in 1833, where Seaborn practiced law and
engaged in his various business enterprises, which included the
construction of the first public utility for the city of Columbus. Jones
joined with his neighbor Van Leonard in an enterprise to provide water to
the City of Columbus, below them. By constructing a system of crude
wooden pipes, which used gravity to deliver fresh water from a spring
located between the homes of Seaborn Jones and Van Leonard, the venture
established the first waterworks for the city. The resulting contract formed
between the City of Columbus and the entrepreneurs was continued for
decades thereafter. While the water supply could not possibly meet the
ever-expanding needs of the city, this primitive, yet necessary utility made
"Leonard's Spring" a local landmark and one of the first civil engineering
projects in Columbus. Seaborn Jones was a complex man with varied
interests in business, government, industry as well as education and
religion. In 1836, Jones joined with George F. Pierce, Lovick Pierce,
Samuel K. Hodges and thirteen other men to found Emory College. 11
Jones served as a trustee of the institution for many years and the college
has prospered. Today this prestigious institution is known as Emory
University, which is named for Dr. John Emory, a former Bishop of the
Methodist Episcopal Church, and the university is still affiliated with the
church. Like the Bennings, the family of Seaborn Jones was also very
religious and the church played an important role throughout their lives.
Through the church, the Jones and Benning families eagerly contributed
their time, financial and humanitarian assistance in support of educational
and religious goals throughout the community.

  For themselves, Seaborn and Mary Jones constructed a beautiful
mansion on the outskirts of Columbus. The home was situated on a ridge,
just east of the city, along the old Stagecoach Road (known today as
Talbotton and Warm Springs Road). Entitled " *El Dorado*," Seaborn
personally designed and built the home with bricks fired from the native
Georgia clay and hardwood timbers hewn from his land. Nearby was "
Wildwood," the elegant mansion of his mother-in-law, Mrs. Jane Vivian
Howard, whose husband Colonel John H. Howard, a former Indian fighter
and officer in the Georgia Militia, was also instrumental in settling the
land. Howard too, was a respected entrepreneur and owner of the Howard
Factory, a Columbus textile-manufacturing firm. An innovative
businessman, John Howard also harnessed the energy of the Chattahoochee
River, which powered the looms of his large textile mill. 12

In addition to their daughter, Mary (Howard) Jones, John and Jane Howard had another daughter, Sarah, who wed Mr. Matthew Evans, a local entrepreneur and businessman. The Evans family built a huge mansion, later known as " Sherwood Hall," but while it was under construction, the Evans lived with John and Jane Howard at " Wildwood. " On May 8, 1835, the young Evans family had a baby girl and named her Augusta Jane. Thus, the young Miss Evans was the cousin of Mary Howard Jones. The family was very close-knit and Augusta Jane Evans often stayed with her cousin Mary in the Jones mansion. Later as an adult, Augusta became one of our nation's first female authors and she wrote several best sellers, including *Beulah* and *St. Elmo*. It is said that the fictional mansion in the novel, *St. Elmo*, was modeled upon " El Dorado. " Interestingly, the actual mansion " El Dorado" was renamed by its latter day owners," St. Elmo." **13** The mansion stands today as a reminder of antebellum refinement.

Built in the image of a Greek temple, its three stories of white stucco are outlined on three sides with twelve massive (forty-foot) Doric columns. The home's graceful lines include a wrought-iron balcony of medallion design directly overhead of the main entrance, highlighted with elegant sidelights and a spectacular glass fan. Complementing the exterior of the home, the route approaching the estate was lined with roses. The grounds included several fountains, a large conservatory and a greenhouse, which contained tropical fruit trees and a plethora of beautiful flowers. An extended arbor led away to a pond filled with water lilies and bordered by oaks and cedars filled with lavender wisteria. Inside the home, imported mahogany stairways and doors complemented the other wood-works of native oak and cedar. " Everything that cultured taste and unlimited means could suggest was done to make this place one of the most elegant and luxurious in the vicinity." **14** Jones's " *El Dorado* " is a gem of an estate, which exudes the aura and romance of the antebellum south.

" A winding, sandy road, over which carriages and horses passed, driven by Negro coachmen, led up through rose gardens to the house, where many historic personages were entertained, among them President James K. Polk, President Millard Fillmore, Henry Clay, and General Winfield Scott. " **15** Roses were in such abundance that the entire neighborhood surrounding " El Dorado," was called Rose Hill. Nearly everyone on Rose Hill had roses, and one of the residents, Mrs. James C. Cook planted a bevy of them along the intersection of Talbotton and Hamilton Roads, making the neighborhood one of the regions most beautiful. **16** Until it was annexed in 1889, this affluent suburb, just several miles from downtown, was considered to be in the country. While there were only a few residences on Rose Hill, they were occupied by wealthy and influential families. In addition to the Jones family, the other mansions and their owners on Rose Hill were: " Sherwood Hall," (originally built and owned by Matthew Evans) the home of Thacker Howard's family; Senator Absalom H. Chappel's " Glen Lora " ; " Beallwood," the Italian villa of William H. Young, bank president and half owner of a textile mill; James Carter Cook's " Belmont," who in 1828, owned 4,400 acres of the land around Columbus ; Albert G. Redd, a wealthy planter; Judge Grigsby Thomas and family; William H. Hughes, director of the Georgia Home Insurance Company. On another ridge, just south of Rose Hill, Wynn Hill (Wynnton) contained beautiful homes and affluent residents too. Here lived: John and Jane Howard (the in-laws of Seaborn Jones), Matthew Evans, with his wife Sarah (Howard) Evans and their daughter Augusta Jane Evans (future author); Hines Holt, a wealthy lawyer ; the Carters, Flournoys, Garrards, Shepherds, Dr. Lovick Pierce (Methodist pastor), Bowers, Banks, Swifts, Yonges, Keys, Dawsons, Hurts, Woolfolks, Colquitts, Leonards, and many other influential members of antebellum Columbus. Further to the south, along a ridge overlooking the Chattahoochee River were the plantations of Raphael Moses, on " Esquiline Hill," and Doctor Francis O. Ticknor's home on " Torch Hill. " **17**

The countryside surrounding Columbus was dotted with beautiful homes, manicured grounds, and lifestyles that reflected the wealth and prosperity of its owner. " El Dorado," was a gem amidst the crowning glory of the Columbus elite. This elegant home in a stylish community complemented the refined beauty of the women in Jones's life. His daughter Mary was raised in a lifestyle of culture and ease. In 1825, when Lafayette visited Milledgeville, she had served as a flower girl, strewing petals along his path. Educated primarily by private tutors, Mary also attended a convent in Georgetown, while her father served in the U.S. Congress. Mary was small and delicate with long dark flowing hair, warm brown eyes and porcelain white skin. With her wispy elegance and grace combined with a sharp intellect, Mary Benning was the epitome of Southern femininity. Henry Benning was certainly captivated by Mary's charm and exquisite beauty. Known for her beauty, genuine sweetness and charitable spirit, Mary was in the words of Henry Benning," perfect." **18** But for Henry, love would have to wait. Just across the river, the people who formerly occupied the Columbus region were discontent. Cheated of their lands, restricted within ever-shrinking enclaves, and urged westward, the Creek Indians were bitter and they lashed out in violence.

The proximity of Columbus, Georgia with the Creek Nation, just across the Chattahoochee, created the need for an active militia. The Creek Nation was the name given to the territory which now includes the Alabama counties of Russell, Lee, Chambers, Macon, Tallapoosa, Calhoun, Barber and Coosa. In 1829, several militia companies were organized in Columbus, but the only military activities they performed were drill and ceremony. 19 The Indians were generally peaceful, and they occasionally wandered through the streets of Columbus. Yet, with the Indians discord and the pioneers' zealous exploitation of land, conflict was bound to arise. The *Columbus Guards* were organized as a member of the Georgia State Militia, and the government acknowledged the importance of the impending crisis. In February of 1836, rumors circulated that armed Indians had infiltrated in mass, just below Columbus. A 22-man force of concerned citizens led by Colonel J. H. Watson was hastily organized and dispatched to investigate the matter. The resulting scenario ended in an armed conflict, the deaths of two of their men, and the beginning of the Creek War of 1836. Referred to as the Battle of Hitchiti, the Indians were retreating when Colonel Watson's party fired on them, however, the Indians had a commanding position on a protected bluff and poured accurate fire into Watson's party. It was later reported that the Indians were hunting across the river, and south of Columbus, because the game was more plentiful in that region. With their great dependence upon game for subsistence, perhaps this was true. 20

The townspeople of Columbus responded with military planning, increased security patrols and additional volunteer militia organizations to protect their families and properties. In May, the crisis intensified with kidnappings, murders, and increased Indian incursions throughout the region. Additionally, the steamboat *Hyperion* was attacked on the river and stagecoaches running between Columbus and Montgomery fell victim to Indian attacks. 21 Henry Benning recorded that " for the last ten days, Columbus has been magnificent- filled with trumpet and drums and fifes and soldiers tramp." 22 Caught up in the fervor of the moment, amongst the volunteers enlisting was Henry L. Benning. Henry enlisted on May 8, 1836 as an infantry private in Company B, of the 66th Georgia Militia, which was promptly mustered into federal military service. 23 This company was known as the " *Muscogee Blues* " and it was commanded by Captain Phillip Schley, a prominent attorney of Columbus and the brother of the Governor of Georgia, William Schley. 24 Many of Henry Benning 's friends also served in the militia including Matthew Evans, Paul Semmes, John Howard, and Wesley C. Hodges. Another influential factor in Henry Benning joining the militia was Mary Jones 's brother, Lieutenant John A. Jones , eagerly joined the militia and served as a founding member of the "

Columbus Guards. " As rumors of Indian attacks spread throughout the area, Columbus served as the hub of activities. The militias organized and prepared for battle, while the civilian populace feared for their lives.

Columbus not only housed the bulk of the army, but fearful settlers and friendly Indians sought refuge there as well. The most feared Indian was a half-breed by the name of Jim Henry. He was rumored to be the leader of a bloodthirsty band of several hundred warriors, and was thought to be orchestrating many of the assaults. Just south of Columbus, massacres in the nearby villages of Roanoke and Uchee Creek were attributed to Jim Henry. Yet, the Creek War of 1836 was filled with rumors and miscommunications, which proved to be the biggest problem during this entire catastrophe. It has been suggested that the War of 1836 was cruelly instigated by wealthy land speculators who feared that investigations of their illegal and greedy exploitation of the Indians would be revealed. 25 Regardless of its causes, the conflict was raging and the entire region was fully embroiled in the chaos of war.

The Indians not only violated their treaty responsibilities; they had now committed heinous crimes against the settlers. Many of the Creek Indians remained peaceful, yet the passion of retribution spurred the settlers to hate them all. The *Columbus Enquirer* recorded this theme with," It is high time these blood-thirsty beings should be hunted up and made to suffer for their crimes." 26 The Indian chiefs reported that the young men were set on war, could not be controlled and they would " attack any troops that might march into the nation." 27 Reports were widespread concerning Indian attacks, murdering of whites, and the *Columbus Enquirer* reported:

> A large body of Indians, variously estimated at from 500 to 1,500 warriors, have congregated about twenty-five miles southeast from this city, and are scouring the country in all directions from their hiding place, or headquarters, indiscriminately butchering our neighbors, men, women and children, plundering their houses, destroying their stock, and laying waste their farms. On Monday last, this city presented a scene of confusion and distress, such as we never before witnessed. Our streets are crowded with wagons, carts, horses and footmen, flying for safety from the rifle and tomahawk of the Indians-many of them having left their earthly possessions, and some their protectors and friends, husbands, wives and

children, who had fallen before the murderous savage. We have
been unable to ascertain with any certainty the number of those
who have been murdered by these lawless savages... and the
Indians are yet pursuing their bloody work. **28**

Before reporting to Washington as a U.S. Congressman, Alexander
H. Stephens had recently traveled through the Creek Nation. Upon his
arrival he went to see President Andrew Jackson, whom with great interest
asked Stephens what was going on down there. The president had just
received a letter from Columbus, Georgia, which expressed the current
state of alarm. Jackson asked," In the name of God, where's Howard? The
Howard that President Jackson referred to was none other than Major John
H. Howard, Seaborn Jones 's brother-in-law. Howard's duty was to patrol
a very large area known as the Creek Nation. Stephens replied that he
thought Howard was at Roanoke (sight of a recent massacre). The
president asked," Why doesn't he move his forces across the river?
Stephens replied that he did not know and perhaps there was a problem
with jurisdiction. President Jackson sprang to his feet stating " Jurisdiction
by the Eternal! In the name of God, how big a place is Columbus?"
Stephens answered that the inhabitants numbered nearly three thousand.
Jackson then asked," Why don't they turn out in force and drive back the
Indians ? Here I have letters calling on me for aid, and telling me the whole
population is flying to the interior!" **29**
    It was readily apparent that the situation demanded additional troops.
The Governors of both Alabama and Georgia simultaneously increased
their militias while imploring assistance from federal authorities. Governor
William Schley wrote to General Scott :

The Creek Indians are in a state of open war, killing and
destroying everything in their way. They have crossed to the
Georgia side of the Chattahoochee and burnt Roanoke, and an
attack on Columbus is daily expected. All the white people of
the nation that have not been murdered have fled to Georgia.
The people on the frontier are in a wretched condition, their
lives and property being at the mercy of the savages. The militia
of the adjoining counties have been called out en masse and I
have been making exertions to get troops in the field, but the
want of proper organization of the militia makes this a difficult
task...If your presence is not necessary in Florida, I shall be very
glad to see you on the line of the Chattahoochee. We know little
of military matters, and the economy of an army, that your
presence will be quite acceptable. **30**

Nonetheless, events were occurring in rapid secession, but communications were too slow for a proper response. Very rapidly, the isolated incidents turned into a full-scale war between the Indians and the local settlers. Perhaps encouraged by news of the Seminole Indian resistance in Florida, the young Creeks revolted as well, organizing an estimated force of 10,000 men. Fighting the Seminoles in the low swamplands of Florida was no simple task, and the U.S. forces were under the command of General Winfield Scott. Once the violence in Georgia was evident to President Jackson, General Scott was ordered there to suppress the Indian uprising. General Scott arrived in Milledgeville on May 28, where he joined with Governor Schley and traveled on to Columbus. Scott established his headquarters in Columbus, where he organized his army, requisitioned rations and obtained additional arms and ammunition from the arsenal in Augusta. Major General Daniel McDougald was the Columbus garrison commander, which included command of the *Columbus Guards* and the *Muscogee Blues*. Private Henry Benning was appointed as an aid on the General's staff, and amongst the young soldiers were Hines Holt, Wesley Hodges and John A. Jones , all of whom played key roles throughout Benning's life. Benning's experiences and personal contacts would prove to be highly valuable in his future endeavors. 31

General Scott and his military advisors quickly formulated a plan to halt the Indian insurrection. An immediate focus on containment was required lest the insurrectionist Creeks join forces with the Seminoles to the south. Scott immediately ordered General Jesup to Montgomery, Alabama, which was located at the western border of the Creek Nation. His mission was to organize and deploy the Alabama militia in an assault sweeping up from the southwest to the northeast. This strategy was designed to envelope and force the Indians into the Georgia troops deployed as a blocking force along the Chattahoochee River. Once fully armed and equipped, Scott planned to move the bulk of his army down the east bank of the Chattahoochee, while steamships armed with men could prevent the Indians from crossing the river. Thus, the plan was devised to crush the Indians between the Alabama and Georgia militias and keep the Indians from moving to the southeast and joining forces with the Seminoles. The Governors of Georgia and Alabama accepted the plan and it was immediately put into motion. 32

The plan did not materialize as Scott envisioned it. General Jesup prematurely launched his effort shortly after taking command of the

Alabama troops because the troops were so anxious to attack. Rumors of marauding Indians, murder and pillaging was too much for them, and upon his arrival they set forth to sweep the Creek Nation. Within just a few weeks, General Jesup and the Alabama Militia had captured and killed hundreds of Indians including several of the fiercest Creek warriors, Chiefs Enea Mico and Enea Mathla . Yet, the victory was not complete as several hundred Indians escaped across the Chattahoochee River into Georgia. General Scott had not yet effected his deployment of the blocking forces. General Jesup moved to within fourteen miles of Fort Mitchell , a frontier fort located just south of Columbus. Located on the Alabama side of the Chattahoochee, the triumphant yet beleaguered forces marched proudly in triumph. General Scott was furious and he wrote the following note to General Jesup:

> Imagine my astonishment to learn that instead of marching the disposable force of Alabama troops upon Irwinton, with subsistence for at least ten or five days in advance, to hear you had come through the heart of the Indian country, seeking private adventures, which if successful, could hardly have advanced the war, and against my known plan of operations, to Fort Mitchell , forty-five miles out of position... my grief and distress are at their utmost! **33**

General Jesup defending his actions replied with:

> You have treated me with a degree of harshness, which is cruel in the extreme. You charge me with deranging your plan of campaign. I understood one part of that plan to be the protection to the frontier settlements of Alabama. I may have failed in judgement as to the proper mode of protecting it; but give me leave to say, the course I adopted has been successful. The frontier is secure... my occupation has been so incessant that I have not averaged three hours sleep in twenty-four for two weeks... If you will move today General, with your disposable force, we can end the war before tomorrow night... I am not ambitious of the honors of Indian warfare. I am content that the whole of them shall be yours; but let me entreat you to act promptly. I felt resentment this morning; I feel it no longer. By our former friendship, let me entreat you to act promptly. **34**

While General Jesup certainly upstaged his commander 's plan, General Scott could not ignore his subordinate's success. General Scott expecting to be ready for deployment the following day, ordered General Jesup to stand fast and await his orders. Disheartened, Jesup penned a letter to an editor who later showed it to President Jackson. Despite his success, for Jesup to betray his commander in such a flagrant manner was totally unethical and disloyal. Yet, General Scott had gained a reputation for moving too slowly and President Jackson, himself an old Indian fighter, ordered the Secretary of War to replace General Scott with General Jesup. Again, communications did not keep pace with the hectic pace of events, and the campaign was ended before General Scott knew of his demise. The following day, General Scott deployed his Georgia forces (2,500 men) which joined with the Alabama forces. With the exception of rounding up the few Indians in Baker County, Georgia, the war was officially terminated on June 24, 1836. 35

That same month, the volunteer militiamen were mustered out of service, and Henry Benning resumed the practice of law. With voluntary servitude as a soldier, and his capabilities as a valuable and highly capable member of Columbus, Benning established vital connections for his future. The overall effects of the war on Henry Benning and the city of Columbus were establishment and validation. Benning was a man. Columbus was a city. Their roots were firmly established within the soil of the Chattahoochee Valley. Both had ended their innocent youth and were resolved to growth and maturity. Their destinies were now entwined and they would grow, together.

Chapter 3

Attorney at Law

Henry Benning 's friends and associates regarded him with high esteem, but more importantly, Henry was rapidly gaining favor amongst the " men of mark in Georgia." His desire to obtain " one of those fat places" was achieved much sooner than he expected. Henry's former mentors and law partners, George W. Towns had recently been re-elected to Congress and Joseph L. Sturgis was elected as the Chattahoochee circuit Judge. These influential men combined with friends such as Walter T. Colquitt, Seaborn Jones, Hines Holt and Phillip Schley, young Henry Benning finally received the professional recognition he so eagerly desired. In November of 1836, the Solicitor General of the Chattahoochee Circuit, James Horne resigned his position. To fill the void, Governor Charles McDonald appointed to the post an ambitious young lawyer from Columbus, Georgia, Henry Lewis Benning. With only five full months experience as a lawyer, and only twenty-two years of age, Henry was suddenly thrust into a " do or die" situation. Entrusted with an incredible responsibility, Henry was provided many opportunities to make his own mark in Georgia. 1

In 1836, the district Judges and Solicitor Generals " rode the circuit," which required frequent travel throughout the region. Benning rode to court throughout the counties of Muscogee, Lee, Harris, Troup, Coweta, Carroll, DeKalb, Talbot, Marion, Chattahoochee and Fayette Counties. One of Benning's first major court cases involved the trial of the notorious Indian, Jim Henry. Jim Henry had surrendered to authorities in Alabama, and so he was tried there first. While Jim Henry was believed to be the leader of the murderous Indian raiders, there was not adequate evidence for a conviction. Jim Henry was then extradited to Georgia where Benning served as the prosecutor. 2 Again however, Jim Henry was acquitted. There was some controversy concerning this affair in Columbus. The defense attorney s in the Jim Henry case were Hines Holt, J.C. Alford and Walter T. Colquitt, all of who were friends of Benning. The jest of the controversy centered upon Colquitt, whom was rumored to have conspired

with Jim Henry in Alabama land speculations. Many of these illegal
transactions may have contributed to the Indian uprising; however,
Colquitt vehemently defended himself against these accusations, and later
won elections as a U.S. Congressman and Senator from Georgia. **3**

Nonetheless, Solicitor General Benning failed to achieve a conviction
in his first high-visibility trial; however, most of the cases Benning argued
did not rise to the drama of the Jim Henry affair. " In the country counties,
the court business soon took on that character which distinguished most of
the litigation in the other parts of Georgia- questions as to the winding up
of estates, land titles, trust estates, debts for slaves and supplies, etc." **4** The
term in which Benning was serving under the Governor 's appointment
expired in 1838, however, he was officially elected by the legislature to
remain at his post. **5**

While Benning spent a great deal of time riding the circuit and
performing his official duties, he also pursued personal interests close to
home. During this time, he continued his relationship with Mary Jones, and
frequently visited his family in neighboring Harris County. Additionally,
he also served on the *Columbus Literary Committee* with the future Mayor
of Columbus, Mr. Wiley Williams. Their mission was to promote literacy
and establish a public library in Columbus. The committee formulated a
plan to raise capital. For the sum of $5.00, the public could join the
Literary Society, which would provide the financial resources to build a
Library. In a plea reflecting Benning's intellectual jurist logic, he and the
Literary Committee, appealed to the citizens of Columbus, with:

> The human mind is constituted so as to require frequent and
> almost constant action... without anything to excite it, [it] is a
> continual source of inquietude and unhappiness...It is a well-
> known fact that women are great readers, and they will converse
> what they read. Gentlemen, therefore must read to maintain the
> dignity of their sex, or consent to receive information second
> handed from their female associates, and nothing in the opinion
> of the committee gives a woman a more contemptible opinion of
> a man, than a knowledge of the fact that she is superior to him in
> any one acquirement that he ought to have...Columbus, the
> beautiful but neglected daughter of Western Georgia so justly
> celebrated for deeds of charity and benevolence, without her
> resources of money and talent, be in the rear of the foremost? **6**

Eventually, as the desire spread through the community, the " daughter of Western Georgia" established a 2,500-volume public library in downtown Columbus. The *Literary Society* remained active for the next several decades promoting literacy and education. Meanwhile, several bookstores, as well as other modern businesses added to the culture of Columbus. Benning continued to move amongst the elite of Columbus society and attended important events such as the Independence Day celebrations, which in antebellum days, were very elaborate events. During the 4th of July celebration in 1837, Henry Benning served as the reader of the Declaration of Independence, along with Walter T. Colquitt as orator, and Reverend Lovick Pierce, known as the " Nestor of Southern Methodism," offered the official prayer. Again in 1838, establishing an annual event in which Benning frequently played key roles, he made a public toast to the great Southern politician, John C. Calhoun," unanswered and unanswerable." 7 Thus, Henry Benning began publicly voicing his political affiliations and beliefs.

Henry had a passion for politics, which soon overshadowed everything else in his life. Speaking in the courts as the Solicitor General combined with his associations with other public speakers and politicians, encouraged Benning to seek the limelight in other public affairs. In 1838, Henry Benning, Seaborn Jones and John H. Howard were sent as members of a delegation to attend the Commercial Convention in Milledgeville to argue Columbus 's right to the Chattahoochee River for waterpower. Specifically, sent by the City of Columbus " to obtain relinquishment from the State of Georgia to whatever rights the state had to the water," their efforts were instrumental in the growth of the city and Benning received public recognition for his service to the city. 8

Benning's relationship with the Jones family was becoming closer all the time. His affiliation with Seaborn Jones had gained great strength and proved to be a catalyst for opportunity and success. Moreover, his relationship with Mary was reaching new heights. Rumors were beginning to run their course, and Henry's old friend Howell Cobb pressed him for information concerning his intentions with Mary. Henry expressed that he was hesitant to make any public announcements concerning their love because he was uncertain about he and Mary. Henry wrote to Howell explaining that:

> I am confident the declaration when made will be well received. Whether it will or not passes my   penetration. I will say however, that I have seen nothing in any quarter to make me despair...It is common talk here that I am courting or engaged, which if then were nothing else would compel me to press

forward to the mark of her prize. It has become due to her to give her an opportunity to reject me should I ever know beforehand that to be my fate. **9**

Mary did accept Henry's offer of marriage and the wedding was planned to be held at " *El Dorado*," on Thursday, September 5, 1839. As the grand event neared, the Benning family traveled from their farm near Waverly Hall, along the Talbotton Road to the outskirts of Columbus. The journey, by carriage, was but a short jaunt. While the stage road was renowned for its difficult ruts on dry days, and its treacherous mud, when wet, nonetheless, the journey was a joyous family adventure. Their destination," El Dorado," prominently located on a ridge, overlooking Columbus from the east, was truly a magnificent home. While the awesome, pillared structure is captivating; the grounds set the mood. Surrounded by stately hardwoods, the approach to the mansion was lined with rose arbors and one can envision, the added beauty of gaily trimmed, wedding flora. With friends and family arriving, the occasion was cause for great celebration. Henry's family consisted of his parents: Pleasant and Malinda; his younger siblings, Richard, age twenty-one; and his sisters, Caroline, age fifteen; Augusta, age twelve; and Amanda, age seventeen. It must have been an exciting occasion for Pleasant and Malinda, as their eldest son was marrying " very well."

Yet, while happiness prevailed, an unexpected tragedy marred the occasion. Just like today, antebellum teens occasionally suffered overwhelming confusion and depression. Young Amanda Benning was " beloved by her acquaintances," as well as renowned for her " high intellectual endowments and accomplished education. " **10** Yet, whether it was the impending wedding, the opulent wealth of her future in-laws, or some other over blown emotion, Amanda Benning committed suicide. Lying in her bed, on the eve of the wedding, she penned a short note and ingested Hydrocyanic acid, and she died, September 5, 1839. The poison she used is also known as Prussic acid, which was used in the nineteenth century as an insecticide for fruit trees. The Jones estate had an abundance of fruit trees and apparently, insecticides as well. Suddenly, the families were wrought with grief, and the wedding was re-scheduled for the following week. The Bennings returned Amanda to her home, and buried her in the small family cemetery, on a hill, beside her grandmother, Mary Meriwether White. The following week, in a bittersweet ceremony, Henry Lewis Benning and Mary Howard Jones," the only daughter of Seaborn

Jones, and all of Muscogee County," were joined in marriage by the Reverend Samuel K. Hodges, on September 12, 1839. 11 Henry and Mary Benning moved into " *El Dorado,*" where they and the Jones would reside harmoniously for many years to come.

On October 30, 1839, Henry resigned from his position as the Solicitor General and joined his father-in -law, Seaborn Jones in the practice of law. When Mary's younger brother, John A. " Jack" Jones, graduated from Emory College, he too, joined his father and Henry Benning in the legal profession. 12 Their firm was known as *Jones, Benning and Jones,* and it proved to be a very successful venture. Henry Benning began to accumulate the wealth and stature he had so eagerly craved. Henry had followed his own advice and married very well. Seaborn Jones was one of the wealthiest and influential men of Georgia, and now Henry could pursue his growing passion with politics.

In the antebellum South, wealthy white men solely dominated politics. The landed gentry of society ruled the southern states and Henry desperately sought a higher position on the social ladder. Surpassing his parents desire to see their son succeed, Henry Benning 's obsession with achievement drove him to new heights. With his marriage to Mary, Henry had transitioned from a comfortable mediocrity to aristocracy. While his family, in neighboring, Harris County was living a simple existence, carving out a living as farmers and casting off the practice of " slaveocracy," Henry was embracing it with an unquenchable desire. His father-in-law, Seaborn Jones was a firm believer in slavery and his success validated the institution for Henry Benning.

In 1840, throughout the South, most politicians were successful lawyers, planters, and slaveowners. By joining the Jones family, Henry was now all three. In May of 1840, Henry's dreams were coming to fruition. His wife Mary was with child, his business was booming and he had time to focus on politics. Siding with the States Rights Democratic Party, Henry joined their causes with a fervor. Just as Henry joined the party, it was splitting into two factions, the followers of Martin Van Buren and William Henry Harrison. Henry pleaded with Howell Cobb to use his influence to bolster the party as Henry felt it should be. Specifically, Henry urged Howell to support specific candidates (Van Buren supporters) at a political convention to be held in Milledgeville on July the Fourth, 1840. While Howell Cobb and Henry Benning were certainly old friends, politics became a wedge that would slowly drive them apart. Since college, Howell had achieved great success as a lawyer and his family too had friends in high places. Much to the displeasure of Henry however, Howell chose a more moderate political stance, which frustrated Henry greatly.

Howell tried to ignore Henry's frequent letters urging specific political advice. Finally, in a letter to Howell in June, with the convention date rapidly approaching, Henry writes," I am so mad I can hardly write. Why do you not answer my letter?" 13 Henry desired that Howell would organize the Van Buren men in the Clarke County area and open a supportive dialog with the men of the western area of the state to promote the Van Buren cause throughout Georgia. Nevertheless, Howell Cobb had his own ideas and simply ignored Henry's repeated requests for support. Meanwhile, Mary delivered a healthy baby boy. Named in honor of her father, Seaborn Jones Benning became the first born son of Henry and Mary Benning, July 8, 1840. 14

Frustrated with Howell's lack of support, Henry thrust himself into the political arena. In a zealous effort to support the old States Rights party and ward off federalism, Henry ran as a nominee for the general assembly. Writing to Howell Cobb in September of 1840, Henry states," I am a candidate with fair prospects of success, notwithstanding formal bragging." 15 In spite of Henry's earnest effort to enter politics, he was soundly defeated by the Whig candidate. Rejected, Henry returned to the practice of law, yet he did not fully retreat from politics. Henry maintained his relationship with his old friend Howell, whose own political ambitions soon began to surface.

While Henry Benning and Howell Cobb were both Democrats, Georgia politics were in a period of transition. Henry had sided with an ultra states' rights faction that Howell and most conservative Georgians did not wholeheartedly embrace. Yet, on one issue, Howell and Henry agreed and that was the contempt they held for the Whig party. The Whig party was ultra conservative and " received a greater degree of newspaper support than did the Democratic party." 16 The Whigs were a powerful national party, best characterized as leery of factions and supporting a strong federal government. In Columbus, Georgia, the presidential election of 1840 reflected the pro-conservative sentiment that had defeated Benning at the local level, with Harrison achieving 824 electoral votes, and Van Buren 503. 17

With politics now a second thought, Henry focused his efforts close to home. Continuing to amass his own personal wealth in the legal profession, he also began to invest in land, which would eventually become his own plantation. Mary delivered a second child on November 23, 1841. This child was a daughter, and they named her Mary Howard Benning (the third " Mary Howard"). 18 During this time, on May 17,

1842, Henry Benning 's younger sister, Caroline Matilda married a close
friend of his, Mr. Benjamin Y. Martin. He, like Benning was also a lawyer.
Additionally, Martin was a respected member of the community, a
conservative gentleman, very religious, and he served as the Georgia
Supreme Court reporter. 19 Martin displayed values and traits that were
paramount to success, and he was highly regarded by both Seaborn Jones
and Henry Benning.

While it is always wise to be conservative and prudent, these traits
were especially important for the men of the early 1840s. As lawyers, both
Henry Benning and Seaborn Jones were intimately aware of the high price
of legal and financial misfortune. During a time which speculations in
land, railroads, and other " get rich" quick schemes were simultaneously
lucrative for some yet devastating for others, attorneys were intimately
aware of the consequences and risks of speculative matters. Moreover,
since 1828, when the first gold rush in the United States occurred in the
mountains of north Georgia," get rich" mining speculations extracted a
heavy toll from overly exuberant investors. Lucrative investments in gold
mines often yielded little more than a folly filled with worthless rock. Yet,
many men became obsessed with the affliction known as " gold fever," and
one of them was Benning's brother-in-law, John A. Jones . After John
graduated from college, he was eager to make his fortune, but he was also
thoroughly overcome with " gold fever." John actively investigated both
mining investments and operations in Lumpkin County, but he was
hampered by a lack of personal capital with which to invest. In a letter
dated March 30, 1842, John Jones pleaded with his father stating," send
some of your hands to Lumpkin to dig gold... pray do not neglect this
opportunity but go or send Benning... get to work as soon as you can." 20
Young Master Jones explained the details to his father, but the elder and
wiser Jones urged his son to return and focus his attention closer to home.
Still, Seaborn Jones did invest in the Pigeon Roost Mining Company, a
loss which his son-in-law, Henry Benning would be forced to settle later.

Meanwhile, Benning sought word from his old friend, Howell Cobb,
stating," Why don't you write to me sometimes, if for nothing else to let
me know how your family do and grow. Mine are well. I have a son and a
daughter." 21 Unbeknownst to Henry, his old friend was busy
contemplating his own political ambitions, and taking care of his own
family matters, which centered upon financial despair.

Howell Cobb 's parents had invested the bulk of their wealth in several of
the popular investment schemes of their day, including gold mines,
railroads, banking and insurance stocks. The economy of the latter 1830s
and early 1840s has been characterized as a depression, and the Cobbs
became one of its many victims. They were forced to the brink of

bankruptcy and the family had to sell their assets. Howell Cobb sold his own home to aid his misfortunate parents, and for the next several years, he paid the creditors of his father's debts. Additionally, Howell also paid the last two years of college tuition for his younger brother, Thomas R. R. Cobb. Yet, despite the Cobbs' losses and amidst all of the family turmoil, Howell Cobb was elected in 1842, as a Democrat, to the U.S. House of Representatives. 22

While Henry was certainly happy for his old friend's accomplishment, he certainly felt somewhat bitter as well. Writing a letter of congratulations to Howell, Henry recorded:

> Allow me to congratulate you on your honors. Hurrah for the class-seven years out of college and one member of it a congressman, beating such nags as Wilde and Chappel. But then the question naturally presents itself... if one who had a respectable place in the class- a very respectable place in the class is fit for Congress, where shall we rank on glory's page who was first? I begin to doubt whether modest merit is a virtue after all. It is certainly not appreciated in this vile world. I know you will not suppose them as anything selfish or personal in these remarks, for it was all I could do to prevent my friends from forcing me upon the ticket. 23

Henry always considered himself more capable than Howell and his words reflect that sentiment. Henry had finished first in his class and Howell was fourth. In Henry's eyes, he had been bested by his old college chum," Fatty," and obviously it hurt. Furthermore, Henry was unhappy with the currents of Georgia political affairs. The " Whiggers " were gaining ground and the old States Rights party was floundering. He considered many of the office holders as " inferior" and to Henry's disdain, the Whigs maintained a " money grip" on elections. His old classmates, Robert Toombs and Alexander Stevens also won seats in the U.S. House of Representatives. Henry maintained pressure on Howell to use his influence, particularly to assist Judge Joseph Sturgis in his re-election bid as the Judge of the Chattahoochee circuit, unless Howell was not already " under any pledge, bias or prejudice." 24 Henry was becoming very bitter concerning political matters, yet he still yearned for " one of those fat places." While Howell Cobb went on to Washington, Henry Benning continued the practice of law, building his personal wealth, and enjoying the love of his family and life in Columbus, Georgia.

These were happy days for Henry and Mary Benning, complete with friends, family, births and marriages. In 1843, Mary had another baby girl. This daughter was born on September 30, 1843, and they named her Sarah Elizabeth Benning. **25** Meanwhile, Mary's only brother, John A. Jones fell in love with Mary Louisa Leonard, the daughter of Van and Frances R. " Fanny" Leonard. The Leonards were wealthy neighbors and close friends of the Jones family. In addition to Mary Louisa, the Leonard family had two other daughters, Henrietta and Anna, and a son named Van. The Leonards were originally from Morgan County, Georgia, where Van (de Van) Leonard II had served as a State Representative from 1821 to 1831. In Columbus, the Leonards purchased and occupied the elegant mansion," Wildwood. " Van Leonard was a business associate of John H. Howard, and together they operated several successful business ventures including railroads and textile mills . While both men engaged heavily in various enterprises, Leonard's primary position was serving as the President of John Howard 's textile firm, the Howard Factory and later, the Eagle Mills. **26**

On October 5, 1843, Reverend Lovick Pierce of the Methodist Church officiated as John Abraham Jones married Mary Louisa Leonard. Seaborn Jones provided land adjacent to his estate for the newlyweds, and their place was known as " Bonnie Doone. " John A. Jones was an ambitious young attorney and he served in the state militia as an Infantry officer, and Captain of the " Crawford Guards. " Another wedding occurred in April of 1844. Henry's brother Richard, struggling to carve out a living as a farmer in Harris County, married Frances " Fanny" Simpson, the daughter of his friend and neighbor, Robert Simpson. Richard and Fanny Benning lived a simple life of farming in a peaceful valley between Pine and Oak Mountains. Their farm was located just below Shiloh, Georgia, where they lived their entire lives. Fanny's parents lived close by, while Richard's parents lived about five miles away, just outside of Waverly Hall. Richard Benning embraced the lifestyle of his father and devoted his life to farming and raising a family.

While the same humble, religious parents raised both Richard and Henry Benning, their experiences in early adulthood were very different. Henry experienced challenges and success amidst the social elite, while his brother, Richard found solace in working the land. Henry continued the course he had learned in college- achievement. After college, his desire to achieve grew stronger and it was further inflamed with political ambition. **25** Henry Benning 's passion for political affairs was expressed openly with his old friend, Howell Cobb. In frequent and candid letters, Henry provided Howell with unsolicited advice, political opinions and general comments concerning various state and national politicians. Yet, Henry's time was occupied primarily with legal cases and the courts. Many involved Creek War Indian reparation claims, and he solicited Howell's assistance in Washington. Henry used this pretense as an excuse to write to his old friend, whom he obviously missed. Henry wrote:

> I have three of the finest children you have ever seen and if you doubt it, I dare you to compare with me in Columbus...But, I never expect to see you here again...Howell write me all the interior party villainy at Washington. I'll keep it a secret. Being a Van Buren man, you are in it. What is Benton's position on Texas and otherwise? What will you do with the tariff this session and who's who with Polk, Van Buren or Calhoun? **27**

While Benning enjoyed a pleasant life in Columbus, he was highly envious of his old friend, Howell Cobb, and desired to be " in it" where politics were concerned. For now, however, he would have to put political ambitions on hold. In the town of Columbus, life was good. The city prospered and after several disastrous fires, a permanent fire-fighting company had been organized. Hines Holt was elected to the position of city attorney. Mrs. Seaborn Jones, as President of the Methodist Female Benevolent and Educational Society, petitioned the city to erect an asylum in town. The city began to install water and sewer services and the cotton fields were producing record crops. In 1844, there were 209 businesses listed for Columbus, including 34 other lawyers besides Henry Benning. On August 21, 1844, newlyweds, John and Mary Jones gave birth to their first child, a son. Named in honor of his grandfathers, his complete name was Seaborn Leonard Jones. **28**

On a final note concerning Columbus in 1844, several ominous events passed with little immediate concern. First, in a financial investment scandal that would soon prove to be the same for many others in the local area, the Phoenix Bank of Columbus closed its doors in failure. In what would later be known as the " Columbus bank cases ," Henry Benning would face a major legal and political nightmare that would haunt him for quite some time. Secondly, the expansion of the United States into the western territories would bring controversy and division concerning the issue of slavery. Texas in particular would bring not only great debate, but also war into the political arena. Henry Benning eagerly desired to enter the political fray. Finally, the local Methodist Church, of which Benning was a member, faced a major crisis. The topic of slavery in the context of religion began to split the church. Throughout the South, it was common for members of the clergy to own slaves ; however, the brethren in the northern states could no longer accept this practice. Locally, several members of the Columbus congregation, including Seaborn Jones and Van Leonard, who supported a proposition that the local Methodist Church be segregated, broadened this rift in the church. 29 Jones and Leonard were " giants" in the local community, and their Pastor was the Reverend Lovick Pierce, himself a well respected and influential leader in the Methodist Church. With his kith and kin embroiled in a bitter dispute, Henry Benning witnessed the beginning of an argument that would engulf his life and change it forever. The social foundations of the South were being shaken, and while peace was at hand, seeds of future discord had been sewn.

Chapter 4

Changes

For Henry Benning and the other citizens of Columbus , Georgia, the decade of the 1840s are best characterized as an era of transition. In the midst of technical revolutions with their potential to enhance life, dark clouds of social and institutional upheavals overshadowed the promise of a brighter day. In a local newspaper article entitled " What Next," the project of connecting Columbus, Georgia to New York and New Orleans via Morse telegraphy was questioned with," Is not the world going ahead too fast? Space is annihilated as to the transition of mind, and almost to matter, by the Telegraph and Steam." 1 The city of Columbus was on the verge of an explosion in growth and modernization. Throughout Georgia, the railroad and steam lines were choked with the importation of commercial goods and the exportation of cotton. For the people of Columbus," King Cotton " was the catalyst of transition from pioneer outpost to boom town. While bulk, baled cotton was still being exported; spinning factories were being enlarged, which forever changed the economy of Columbus. The textile mills , which brought increased wealth and opportunity to the region, are still a vital part of today's modern economy.

While the economy in Columbus and throughout the Chattahoochee region boomed, poverty remained a problem. As the wealth increased amongst the elite members of society, there were many that society ignored. With no organized social safety net, the impoverished and destitute of the region received only sympathy. In an effort to address this situation, several prominent ladies of Columbus energetically fought to assist the needy. As President of the " Methodist Female Benevolent and Educational Society " , Mrs. Seaborn Jones petitioned the city to erect an asylum in town. Originally established in 1840, the society vainly struggled for recognition and assistance in their quest. The city officials finally embraced the idea, and in 1845, joined with the ladies of the church to improve conditions of the poor. The ladies reorganized their group as the " Ladies' Education and Benevolent Society of the Methodist Episcopal Church, of the City of Columbus," which sought to improve the conditions of the needy through benefit drives, donations and direct assistance with the poor families of Columbus. 2

Mrs. Seaborn Jones, Mrs. Henry L. Benning, Mrs. Van Leonard, Mrs. John A. Jones , and Mrs. William Garrard, were among the members of this society that wisely used their husbands' legal expertise and influence, and achieved a charter granted by the General Assembly of the State of Georgia. Organized " for the purpose of educating and relieving the poor and destitute, and to build an Asylum for the orphans and poor of said city," the ladies of Columbus embarked on the first of many worthwhile, honorable, and sincere causes. The City of Columbus authorized four acres on the East Commons of Columbus for the construction of the home, and the Governor of Georgia granted the ladies the construction of the Asylum, free of expenses. A frame building was erected between Fifth and Sixth Avenues and Fourteenth and Fifteenth Streets, at the cost of $1,385.59, including furnishings. Reverends Lovick Pierce and James E. Evans dedicated the Girls' Asylum, on April 7, 1845. Within months, this building burned and a brick building replaced it that same year. 3

The ladies work was very beneficial for the poor of the city, and the school and home for orphans prospered. Many influential ladies of Columbus society joined and assisted the organization with donations and many served as officers of the society. The ladies later changed the name of their society to the " Ladies Educational and Benevolent Society of the City of Columbus," which broadened their membership, assistance, and influence. The society rapidly became a virtual " who's who" of Columbus, but despite its lofty influence it always maintained its genuine desire of providing assistance to the poor. The ladies' journal reflects that the children in their care were all females, and a genuine concern for their well being was tenderly rendered. Additionally, the society grew in financial strength through donations of cash and stocks, which provided a college education for several girls. Over the course of the years, the society has undergone changes, but it is still in existence today, as the " Anne Elizabeth Shepherd Home, Inc." 4

As illustrated by the ladies' work with the poor, religion played a large role in the betterment of Columbus society. The influence of Christianity and the importance of charity reached well beyond the church. The Bennings and Jones families were members of St. Luke Methodist Episcopal Church, and study of the scriptures was of paramount importance. As a social institution, religion served as an important foundation throughout the South, and the membership of the Methodist

Church in Columbus included many influential people. Among the congregation were the families of Colquitt, Hoxey, Urquhart, Iverson, Schley, Leonard, Howard, Hodges, Sturgis, Shivers, and the Billups. All of these families were affluent and many of their patriarchs were lawyers, judges and business tycoons. Yet, it is also noteworthy that the black membership of St. Luke Methodist Church outnumbered the whites. 5 The mission of the Southern Methodist Church was to achieve salvation for the souls of all races. " Christian churches were the only institutions in the South which could and did speak for the Negro. " 6 Upon the recommendation of bishops, white ministers and support of two-thirds of their men, Negro men were ordained as deacons. While this practice was certainly " peculiar work within the peculiar institution," religion provided the only " hope" for a hopelessly oppressed people. 7

Throughout the South, as Abolitionism spread and Northerners increasingly pointed their accusing fingers, the Southerners simply considered it heresy. In the South, slavery was simply an institution and the common way of life. Generations had flourished amidst the institution and " slavery was so interwoven into society that the Church could do nothing more than to make the master-slave relationship palatable." 8 While slavery by its general nature is cruel, at least religion provided boundaries for the treatment of slaves and common ground in the master-slave relationship. When compared with other regions where slavery was practiced, most slaves living in Columbus, Georgia were treated quite well. With an aggressive Methodist Slave Mission in Columbus, slaves were treated with special consideration, especially for their spiritual well being. There are numerous cases where former slaves of Columbus state that they were " kindly treated" by their master and " they took interest in the spiritual welfare of their slaves and that they were called in for prayer meeting regularly." 9 One slave recalled that " no darkies " that he could recall " ever went hungry or suffered for clothes until after freedom." 10

While incidents of vicious cruelty were undoubtedly committed against the slaves, the fortunate slaves of wealthy Christian owners bear a different testimony. Such was the case with Henry Benning, whom as a child had been nursed and raised with a Negro nanny, and insisted that his children treat her with respect. Yet, the " peculiar institution " created irony and confusion for Christians, north and south of the Mason-Dixon Line. Arguments pro and con can be gleamed from the scriptures and the Northern Abolitionists slowly persuaded the Methodist Episcopal leadership to raise the issue to the forefront. Amidst the numerous changes in Columbus, perhaps the most important influence on the future course of events, and upon Henry Benning, was the argument of slavery and its impact upon the Methodist Church.

In Baltimore, Maryland during the Methodist Conference of 1844, the tensions concerning slavery between Northerners and Southerners reached the boiling point. Heated speeches and debate focused upon the issues of states' rights, property rights and the laws of slavery. The Southern delegates argued that state laws determined property rights, while the northerners argued with the voice of abolitionists. Bishop Andrew of Georgia was cited by northern members of the conference as committing sins against the church for owning slaves and therefore he should resign his post. The vicious debate, which followed, reflected the impending political battles, which would arise throughout the nation concerning slavery. Dr. George F. Pierce, the son of Lovick Pierce, attempted to intervene and halt the vindictive fight stating," I do hope the brethren will pause before they drive us to the fearful catastrophe, now earnestly to be deprecated, but inevitable if they proceed." Dr. Lovick Pierce, of Columbus, defended Bishop Andrew with " Show your people that Bishop Andrew has violated any one of the established rules and regulations of the church, and that he refused to conform himself to those established laws and usages, and you put yourself in the right and us in the wrong." 11

The Northern delegates refused to withdraw their fierce unfounded attack against Bishop Andrew (no church law or rules had been broken) and they forced the issue to a vote. The Southern delegates stood by Bishop Andrew and chose to separate from the Conference, thus forming the Methodist Episcopal Church South, from which, in 1845, the Southern Methodist Church convention was formed. 12 The argument of pro-abolition complicated through a northern interpretation and distortion of church regulation lit a fire in the heart of Henry Benning. For Benning and most Southerners, their institutions were now under attack. Benning feared the Whigs and abolitionists would join forces creating an unbearable strain upon the status quo in Georgia, and throughout the South. From this point forward, Benning was a fervent pro-slaver and prophesied this single issue would became an all out Northern assault upon Southern states ' rights.

In 1845, in addition to the erosion of Southern institutions, Benning also lost his father. Captain Pleasant Moon Benning, at the age of sixty-three, died at his home, two miles north of Waverly Hall, Georgia, on October 29th. Pleasant Benning was a highly regarded member of the community, and he was buried on his land in a small family cemetery lined with a short, circular, rock wall. Pleasant was buried alongside his daughter and mother-in-law. To his right lay Malinda's mother, Mary Meriwether White, who died in 1840, and Pleasant's daughter, Sarah Amanda, who

had committed suicide in 1839. Upon his passing, his wife Malinda
remained on the farm with her daughter, Augusta, age eighteen. Malinda's
son Richard and his wife, Fanny, lived close by in a farm several miles
north near Shiloh, Georgia. Despite having a lawyer in the family, Pleasant
died without a will, which created some distress for Malinda, however,
between her sons, Henry and Richard, and family friends, most of their
belongings were recouped during the requisite estate sale. **13**

The following month, November 10, 1845, Henry's wife Mary, gave
birth to their fourth child, Caroline Matilda Benning. Born at *El Dorado*,
Caroline was named for Henry's younger sister. Tragically, the Bennings
lost a child in July of 1846. Their daughter, Sarah Elizabeth died at the age
of three of some unrecorded malady. That same month, John and Mary
Jones also lost a child. Their youngest son, Eugene, not yet six weeks old
died too. It was a common occurrence to lose children to a myriad of health
ailments in the antebellum era. Columbus and every other community
suffered outbreaks of various illnesses that swept through the populace and
took the lives of many young children. With little hope of medical
assistance, outbreaks of Smallpox, Yellow Fever, Scarlet Fever, and
Influenza were often fatal for small children. Thus many families suffered
serious illnesses and many children did not reach adulthood. When the
Jones family lost their son Eugene, Mary had to bury her son without her
husband, as John had departed for service in the Mexican War.

During the summer of 1846, the President of the United States called
for volunteers to fight against Mexico. Mexico sought to reclaim the land
that was inhabited by U.S. citizens and known as Texas. This war was our
nation's first expeditionary force to participate in land warfare on foreign
soil. Among those answering the President's call was the men of the "
Columbus Guards. " The " Columbus Guards" were joined by two other
locally formed units, the " Crawford Guards " and the " Georgia Light
Infantry. " All of these units voluntarily enlisted for Federal service in the
United States Army. Among these Columbus volunteers was Captain John
A. Jones , organizer and commander of the " Crawford Guards." On June
28, 1846, the units from Columbus combined with 7 other companies to
form a Volunteer Georgia regiment, commanded by Colonel Henry
Jackson of Savannah. An epic military parade was held, Governor
Crawford reviewed the troops, and the men departed for war. Again, the
Georgia volunteers served under General Winfield Scott and their services
rendered during the early phases of the war included victories at the battles
of Buena Vista and Cerro Gordo. After serving their voluntary 12-month

tour, the soldiers of Columbus were honorably discharged from federal service and they returned triumphantly to Georgia and reclaimed their former lives. **14**

After the Mexican War, John Jones rejoined Henry Benning and Seaborn Jones in their highly successful law firm. Before long, life for John Jones and his family returned to normal. Henry Benning's family enjoyed prosperity as well.

While illnesses took the lives of several young children of the Benning-Jones clan, the ladies continued to have more children. By 1847, Mary Benning was pregnant again and gave birth to another daughter, Anna Malinda, on March 26, 1847. The next year, on June 21, 1848, Mary gave birth to twin girls. Augusta Jones was named for Henry's sister and Mary's maiden name, while the other daughter, Louisa Vivian, was named in honor of Mary's grandmother. Two months later, on August 20, 1848, John and Mary Jones also were blessed with a new addition to their family, a son. Named in honor of John's brother-in-law, they named him Henry Benning Jones. **15**

Overall, for Henry Benning, life was good. With a successful career in law, a loving wife and burgeoning young family, Henry Benning was living the life of which he had so earnestly desired. While living with his in-laws at their estate, Benning was able to focus his earnings on personal investments and real estate. Henry Benning was beginning to amass a fortune. During the latter 1840s, Benning purchased land north of Columbus and east of the mouth of Standing Boy Creek, on which he was slowly clearing and developing a plantation. His plantation consisted primarily of lands purchased at bargain prices from his father-in-law, Seaborn Jones. **16** Like other wealthy gentleman planters of his day, Benning planted cotton. To run his plantation, Benning purchased slaves and during the next several years, he successfully entered the realm of plantation success stories.

While Benning's plantation was successful, it was actually a moderate operation. Placed in its proper context, it was more akin to a large farm. Additionally, Benning was a gentleman planter, not the stereotypical whip-yielding plantation owner expressed in latter day depictions. His lands were located about four miles northwest of *El Dorado* and he did not actually have a home on the property. Later in the 1850s, Benning purchased additional acreage and a cottage in the nearby vicinity. Benning's father-in-law, Seaborn Jones also grew crops, but on an even smaller scale than Benning and he did not plant cotton. The Jones farm was used to provide subsistence for his family and his slaves, which consisted chiefly of skilled laborers. **17** Both Benning and Jones experimented with orchards. Benning's father, Pleasant Benning, met with local acclaim for his fruit trees, especially his " Benning Apples," which were known as the best apples in the Chattahoochee Valley. The Benning's encouraged other planters and even provided grafted buds for their friends. Annual local fairs encouraged agricultural endeavors and serious competition amongst the farmers also served as a source of entertainment. **18**

Several planters in the Columbus area achieved some interesting results with fruit trees and their harvests. A friend of both Benning and Jones, Raphael Moses boasted of shipping the first commercially produced peaches to New York, where they sold for " $30 per basket... extended his orchard and... sales amounted to nearly $10,000 per annum." **19** Moses, Benning, and Jones were a unique breed of Southern gentleman planters. While these men engaged in agricultural activities, their professions as lawyers overshadowed their farming endeavors. In contrast to these men, large plantation owners relied solely upon their crops as their chief source of income.

In comparison to Benning's property, one of the large plantation owners in the region was John Woolfolk. In 1850, the Woolfolk estate was twice the size and value of Benning's, with acreage of 2,000, while Benning cultivated only 350 acres of crops. Benning's agricultural enterprise was actually a modest operation. Published antebellum statistical data reflects that in 1850, the majority of Georgia farms ranged between 100-500 acres with a median average of 441 acres. **20** Cotton was harvested and shipped in 400 lb. bales, of which Benning annually produced 35, while Woolfolk produced 300. Benning's farm produced bushels of wheat, corn, oats and peas, while Woolfolk harvested crops in thousands of bushels. Livestock and slaves also reflect that the Benning plantation was less than half the size of the Woolfolk plantation. In contrast to the planting endeavors of Benning and Jones, the Woolfolk plantation was an immense agricultural enterprise, which encompassed the majority of the lands south of Columbus, along the Chattahoochee River. At its zenith, John Woolfolk 's estate included a large villa in the fashionable Columbus suburb of Wynnton, and a country manor located on the lands south of Columbus, currently known as Fort Benning, Georgia. During the 1850s, the Woolfolk's " Cusseta " plantation consisted of most of the land along the eastern shore of the Chattahoochee River, from its northern border of Columbus southward to the present day site of Fort Benning. The Woolfolk family owned all of the land, which today comprises the main post and headquarters complex, including the commanding general's residence, known as " Riverside " plantation. **21**

 While Henry Benning embraced the lifestyles of both city lawyer and country gentleman, his passion was keenly focused on politics. Benning obviously coveted the political achievements of his old friend, Howell Cobb. Focusing on the pulse of Washington politics, Benning continued his correspondence with Cobb throughout the latter 1840s. In a letter dated, January 15, 1846, Benning provides unsolicited opinions and advice for Cobb into matters concerning U.S relations with Great Britain, territorial expansion, abolition and his disdain for political maneuvers in Congress. After providing Cobb with his thoughts, Henry again pleads with Howell stating," You promised me at Milledgeville to tell me the sign of the times at Washington as they show themselves." Benning finishes the letter by asking specific questions concerning the actions of various legislators and other political tidbits. He urges Cobb to " write freely" and " I am anxious to hear the truth." **22**

 Many of Benning's old friends and college alumni from Georgia were politically " in it." The twenty-ninth and thirtieth congress included Robert Toombs, Alexander Stephens, Herschel V. Johnson, as well as Howell Cobb. Henry Benning greatly desired to be a part of the political scene in Washington. The latter 1840s were exciting times with the dilemmas of Texas annexation, the Oregon territorial disputes, the Mexican War and U.S. expansion. Now in his mid-thirties, Benning energetically pursued his interest in politics. He felt very strongly about the changes occurring in the United States and he highly desired to be heard. Benning continued to press his old school chum for information and much to his surprise, Cobb solicited Benning for his thoughts.

 Specifically, Cobb asked for Benning's opinion of the Wilmot Proviso, which if approved by the legislature, would strike down slavery in the western territories. Congressman David Wilmot of Pennsylvania attached this amendment to numerous bills; however, it was defeated in the Senate. The Wilmot Proviso served as a source of friction and divisive legislative debate for several years, but it was never approved. Additionally, since the South was facing mounting pressures from northern politicians, Cobb solicited Benning for his vision of the ideal Southern leadership and political strategy. Benning was caught off guard by Cobb's sudden query. Benning responded with," What you require of me involves, I think, my opinion as to the course which ought to be pursued by the Democratic Party to secure the next Presidency. On a question of such magnitude I am not prepared to speak with confidence; and yet upon your invitation... I will venture a suggestion or two." **23**

Benning provided his perceptions of the political tactics of several resolutions set forth by both the Whig and Democratic parties. Furthermore, he calculated in detail for Cobb that with little effort on behalf of the Northern politicians, the new territories would be forced into pro-abolition. Benning favored the plan of Senator Lewis Cass, a Michigan Democrat, which if the people in the new territories should be allowed to practice slavery until it was officially voted out. The reverse situation needed to be avoided at all cost. Where votes were concerned, the Democratic party needed to " gain South and not lose North." 24 Benning then outlines his plan to " gain South," by explaining that the slaveholding people moving into the new territories would simply increase the voting base of pro-slavery. He summarizes his advice to Cobb and explains that either Lewis Cass, James Buchanan or George Dallas, would all suffice as nominees for President, but he adds," I care not so much for the player as the cards." Benning concludes his letter with," Write to me again. Speak out. Condemn what I have proposed if it ought to be done, tell me what's better-above all, tell me the probable " platform " as well as the man." 25

Henry Benning reveled in the fact that Representative Howell Cobb had solicited him for his personal thoughts and opinions on the important issues of the day. While Cobb was most likely placating his old friend's desire to " play politics," the request from Cobb rekindled the political flame in Benning's heart. His bosom was now filled with an unquenchable desire to be " in it." Cobb opened in Benning a void, which could not be filled from afar. With great zeal, Benning read the papers. He especially enjoyed reading the Northern papers such as the *New York Herald*, which provided Benning with the inside track concerning the Northern " Hunkers and Whiggers ". Benning grew weary of the old voice of the South, with its " dog-in-the-manger growl of the *Charleston Mercury*. He has been so long showing his teeth that we have come to believe that is all they are made for." 26 Henry was eager to pick up where men like Calhoun had left off and become the new voice of the South- disunion. As soon as the political opportunity presented itself, Benning thrust himself into the arena.

In 1849, Van Leonard won a seat on the State Senate and Benning's old mentor; George W. Towns was vying for re-election as Governor of the State of Georgia. For Henry Benning, these were exciting times, as abolitionists in the North were becoming more fervent in their quest to destroy the institution of slavery. Benning spent a great deal of time analyzing their actions and strategy, and he was convinced that the South would have to take drastic action to counter the abolitionist movement and the Northern Legislators. Furthermore, Benning was appalled at the weak nature of his former Georgia alumni, now in positions in Congress, to champion the South and stand firm against northern political aggression. Benning's desire to enter the political fray increased and with a well-defined dark premonition of the future, Benning wrote his most stern remarks in a very lengthy letter to his old friend, Howell Cobb. On July 1, 1849, Benning recorded:

> It is apparent, horribly apparent, that the slavery question rides insolently over every other everywhere - in fact, that is the only question which in the least affects the result of elections. It is not less manifest that the whole North is becoming ultra anti-slavery and the whole South ultra pro-slavery... It can be but a little time, whether so soon as next Congress or not, before, owing to the causes now at work, the North and the South must stand face to face in hostile attitude.

Benning then expresses his desire to see Cobb stand firm and " take at once a position, however extreme, which you know you must." Benning then outlines a bold, detailed, strategic plan for Cobb to follow in legislative action. Benning continues his letter with an explanation of his personal stance on the topic of slavery with:

> I think then first, that the only safety of the South from abolition universal is to be found in an early dissolution of the Union... I think that as a remedy for the South, dissolution is not enough, and a southern Confederacy not enough...The only thing that will do when tried every way is a consolidated Republic formed of the Southern States. That will put slavery under the control of those most interested in it, and nothing else will; and until that is done, nothing is done. You see therefore that I am very extreme in my opinions and that you must weigh them as you weigh what I recommend to you. During the last six   months, I have given much attention to this problem of problems to the South, and have made up my own mind in my own way. I am no Calhoun man. He in fact is off the stage; the coming battle is for other leadership than his, a leadership that is of this generation, not of the past.

Benning concludes his dissertation with:

I must beg you to realize the current emergency. Let your eye take in the whole case at one view- see nothing but the facts as they are, and then decide in the light of the evidence and that only. If you do, I am sure for the reason that I confide in is the conviction that the Northern Democracy is no longer trustworthy. That being so, it dictates our course just the same, let the defection proceed from one cause or another. We must act upon what is, not upon what produced it. 27

With these words, Henry Benning had crossed an imaginary line that Howell Cobb could not. Howell Cobb was a proud son of the old South too, and a slave owning planter on a grand scale, however, he was not prepared to sever the Union. While the majority of Georgia Democrats were not pro-Union, neither were they " ready to follow Calhoun into a sectional party, and they could not forget their local differences with the Whigs." 28 Thus, Benning's fervent and emotional plea for secession was met with little support. Surpassing even John Calhoun's theory of disunion, in 1849, Benning may have been the first Southerner to formally propose a plan of secession and the formation of a new republic, even if it resulted in a civil war. Benning's fellow alumni, Howell Cobb, Alexander Stephens and Robert Toombs were still very conservative pro-Union men. Yet, politically, this chasm was reflected throughout the Southern States, as both pro-Union and States' Rights Democrats grew increasingly further apart. Benning had chosen a very radical position from which he would never withdraw. For Henry Benning, Calhoun was " off the stage" and a new generation of leadership should strive for secession - the only logical course to resolve the question of states' rights and the issue of slavery.

Chapter 5

States' Rights

It is interesting to note that a decade wrought with division began
with an act of compromise. The Compromise of 1850 provided a much-
needed reprieve from the ever-increasing tensions between North and
South. Signed into law by President Millard Fillmore, an omnibus bill with
diametric provisions ensured that California would be admitted as a free
state and the territories of New Mexico and Utah would have no
restrictions upon slavery. Additionally, the Fugitive Slave Act was passed,
which created a federal law that required the return of fugitive slaves to
their rightful owners. This final provision was rarely enforced, however, as
once a slave got to sympathetic northern soil, he became free. As law,
however, it did somewhat placate the desires of Southern slaveowners. The
actual plan was devised by the " Great Compromiser," Senator Henry Clay
of Kentucky, architect of the Missouri Compromise in 1820, and well
respected on either side of the debate. Nevertheless, the road to
compromise contained many obstacles. In spite of the provisions that
yielded to both sides of the argument, many Southerners disapproved of
the plan. The great Southern orator, John C. Calhoun was one of these
men, but he failed to see it through, as he died on March 31. Another
dissenter to the Compromise of 1850 was Henry Benning.

When Clay proposed his compromise, which included the admission
of California as a free State, the Southern states called for a convention to
debate the issue. Benning was elected as a delegate from Georgia to attend
the convention in Louisville, Kentucky. As a member of the Muscogee
Southern Rights Association, Benning spoke at local meetings and
defended a pro-secession platform. Another member elected from
Muscogee County was Martin J. Crawford, Benning's close political ally
and friend. Other Georgia delegates included former Senator Walter T.
Colquitt and former governor, Charles J. McDonald. 1 The convention
began on June 3, 1850 and it was attended by nine Southern states. Two
delegates from each state were selected to represent and report resolutions.

McDonald and Benning were selected to represent Georgia. 2 On June 5, Benning presented a package of twenty-three resolutions which reflected the Southern States right to secede, the right to own slaves, that the North should support the Fugitive Slave Act, and the enforcement of the line created in the " Missouri Compromise. " The latter provision created controversy as the delegation knew the North would not accept it. In effect, Benning was stating that the South would not yield the rights of slavery in the western territories. Several historians believe this is precisely why Benning proposed it. 3 Yet, as Benning argued, the law established by the Missouri Compromise stated that all the western territories were divided along the " Missouri line," latitude 36 degrees, 30 minutes. All territory north of the line would be free, and the land south of the line, would be slave territory. For Southerners, the Missouri line was the fulcrum in the fragile balance of compromise, and northern politicians simply refused to recognize its importance to the South.

After a week of debate, the final product of the convention was the adoption of twenty-eight resolutions, which reflected Benning's condemnation of northern politicians and the provisions, which hailed Southern rights. However, the proposal concerning the enforcement of the " Missouri line" was not approved. In the end, the final provisions provided a condemnation of the North and a rejection of the compromise plan proposed by Henry Clay. The final provision called for the convention to reconvene after Congress voted on the Clay compromise proposal. 4 The convention terminated on the twelfth day of June and the delegates returned to their respective states. Overall, the convention held in Nashville produced little more than spirited debate and a weak message aimed at the North. Yet, the delegates and the press kept the issue in the forefront throughout the summer.

In Muscogee County, as throughout the South, local politicians held public barbecues and rallies, which kept the political fervor alive. In Columbus, Georgia, Martin J. Crawford, Henry Benning and John Howard provided the voice of the states rights platform. Combined with " lots to eat and lots of excitement- food for both body and mind," all day gala events were held to win the hearts and minds of the locals. 5 In one of the numerous events held in Columbus, Benning gave a rousing pro-Missouri line speech. During the speech," there was a silence - a straining of eyes and ears - of the audience to catch every word, except when the speaker rose with eloquence upon the wrongs of his country, and then there would be an outburst of applause." 6 In Columbus, the states rights advocates reformed their party and entitled it the Southern Rights Association, which included Benning, Howard, Crawford and Colquitt. The party held weekly meetings to discuss the issues and keep their platform alive. 7 Fighting equally as hard and leading the opposition (pro-Union) in Columbus was Judge James Johnson, Benning's nemesis. Both parties diligently argued their views, but the voice of disunion in 1850 was immature. While many Southerners joined the Southern Rights Association, most Georgians still believed in retaining the Union.

As the issue came closer to a vote, Benning and the Southern Rights Association pushed their platform throughout Georgia. This effort called upon Georgians to embrace the idea of a " consolidated republic" as the only way to maintain the individual property rights of the Southern states. 8 The anti-thesis to Benning's argument was that even in a Southern Confederacy," there would come internal quarrels, a second disunion, and we should exhibit the melancholy aspect of a parcel of little pitiful republics." 9 Furthermore, in Washington, as the Clay compromise was debated, pro-Unionists such as Toombs and Stephens, argued that a " United States South" would not benefit the people of the South, and urged their constituents that the Union must be preserved. During the first few weeks of September, the omnibus bill was officially passed by the Legislature and upon President Millard Fillmore 's signature, all provisions of the Compromise of 1850 became law.

Immediately, Georgia Governor George W. Towns, a Democrat and advocate for Southern rights, ordered the members of the Nashville convention to reconvene, in November. The Governor issued a lengthy proclamation and telegraphed it to Washington, which stated " The destiny of the South is decided. She will not submit... The cotton states will all unite with Georgia, so will the rest of the slave-holding states." 10 As determined as Governor Towns could be, the fact remained that the representatives of Georgia had voted in favor of the Compromise of 1850. Northern Whig papers ridiculed the Governor's actions with," we do not tremble in our boots in view of this new crisis got up by Quattlebums of the South. " 11 The newspapers, North and South became choked with editorial volleys of disrespect, depending upon the personal slant of the editorial staff. The Columbus Times recorded that the issue would be " settled by sword and its blood... The country is this moment in a revolutionary crisis." While this remark was a premature observation, it was visionary in its eventual reality. 12

Meanwhile, the Georgia State Convention was held on December 10, 1850 and filled with spirited debate. At the state level, Howell Cobb was running for Governor under a newly formed party called the Constitutional Union Party. Returning to their home state to campaign, Cobb, Toombs and Stephens organized their new party on a platform of conservatism, compromise, and loyalty to the Union. The party filled a void that most Georgians were eager to join. Ultimately, the outcome of the State Convention reflected the division, which existed throughout the Southern states. It appeared, however, that slowly, the balance of support was shifting towards the philosophy of compromise. 13 Yet, there were still many Georgians supporting the voice of disunion, and the year 1851 saw a continuance of fierce political debate.

Benning continued his efforts on behalf of the Southern Rights party, also referred to as the " fire-eating party. " In July of 1851, Henry Benning was nominated for a seat in the Georgia Congress. 14 With great zeal, Benning campaigned against his old nemesis in Columbus, Judge James Johnson. With a strong supporting network of friends in high places and favorable local press coverage, Benning's prospects for success seemed assured. At the age of thirty-seven, Benning was passionately engaged in political affairs and his quest to see the South rebuilt as an independent nation. All this combined with an established career in law, a beautiful wife, and a loving family; Benning was achieving the life of his dreams. Adding to all the wonderful things happening in his life, his wife Mary was pregnant again. With both a child and an election due in October, Benning was poised to achieve even greater rewards.

As the election neared, anxiety and tensions concerning the future of the South reached a feverish pitch. Finally, at the polls, in October of 1851, the people of Georgia expressed their will. Across the political spectrum, the Constitutional Union Party carried the majority of the Georgia vote and Benning suffered another political defeat. Benning was crushed. Increasing Benning's pain and mortification, that same month, his wife gave birth to a baby boy, which died within a few short hours. 15 Wrought with anguish, Benning retreated from the political battlefield and returned to the profession of law. Benning's peers filled political posts throughout the state. His rival, Judge James Johnson assumed the congressional seat, which Benning so earnestly desired. Herschel V. Johnson, Robert Toombs and Alexander Stephens resumed their respective chairs in Congress, and Howell Cobb replaced George W. Towns as the Governor of Georgia.

While Benning had lost another political battle, his standing in the community was only enhanced. Many in Columbus still believed that secession was the only recourse in dealing with the North. Benning resumed his work at the firm of Jones, Benning and Jones. Consequently, with the legal practice flourishing, it provided capital for his agricultural endeavors on his plantation. Benning purchased additional lands, which throughout the 1850s tripled in size and scope. During the crisis of 1850 and the political campaign of 1851, Benning became very close with his friend and associate, Martin J. Crawford.

Martin Jenkins Crawford was six years younger than Benning and he was also a lawyer. Originally, from Jasper County, Georgia, his family moved to Harris County when he was young. He was the son of a wealthy planter and Georgia gentleman, Major Hardy Crawford, whose ancestry was originally from Virginia. Martin J. Crawford attended the Brownwood Institute in LaGrange, and culminated his education with a degree from Mercer University. Returning to Hamilton, Georgia, Crawford like Benning, was accepted at the bar at a very early age. Before moving to Columbus in 1849, Crawford also represented Harris County in the State Legislature. 16

Crawford owned extensive lands in Harris and Muscogee Counties, including a summerhouse and acreage adjacent to Benning's land on the east side of the Chattahoochee River and Standing Boy Creek . This land was highly desirable due to its proximity to Columbus, and its abundant natural resources. For Benning, it was an ideal situation to expand his plantation, and it came with a place to spend the long hot summers. Crawford sold the property to Benning, which became a source of enjoyment for the Benning family. 17 Crawford bought a home in Columbus, and joined with another gentleman formerly of Harris County, Porter Ingram in the practice of law. Together, they formed the successful law firm of Ingram and Crawford. Both Ingram and Crawford were well liked and regarded as gentlemen of integrity and strong virtues. Martin J. Crawford was a handsome man, tall and slender with locks of curly dark hair. While he loved to tell stories and jokes, he is also described as " polished, dignified, and courteous in manner." 18 Crawford and Benning were close friends and would support one another politically, professionally and personally, for many years to come.

While Benning returned to his interests in Columbus, Howell Cobb took the reins of the Georgia executive government. Cobb had won a very costly battle. The ill feelings between Cobb and Benning were great and only time would heal their wounds. Furthermore, while Cobb had won the ultimate position of authority in the office of Governor, many Georgians were bitter concerning his pro-Union stance. Politically, his home state had suffered numerous self-inflicted wounds. With division amidst the Democrat party, the South was weakened with internal strife. A meeting was planned to discuss a political compromise to be held in Atlanta on September 18, 1852. From the capital in Milledgeville, Cobb wrote to his wife," Politically things look well... nothing can now prevent our complete triumph but the rash counsel of imprudent men." Cobb feared getting into a " useless quarrel upon immaterial points and ruin everything." Cobb considered the issues, which caused the political chasm outdated and desired to achieve party reunification. Cobb finishes with," From this section of the State, Southern Rights and Union men all speak of going to the meeting in Atlanta with the greatest spirit and feeling. The future is bright and brightening." 19

Howell Cobb also wrote a letter to his old friend, Henry Benning expressing a desire to see him again at the upcoming meeting in Atlanta. Cobb also provided him with the same upbeat sentiment as reflected in the letter to his wife. Nearly a year had passed since the Constitutional Union party crushed the Southern Rights party in the election, and surely, the wounds had healed. Both parties were democrats and Cobb desired to see them rejoin, however, Benning responded to Cobb's appeal with:

> Dear Howell, I thoroughly reciprocate your sentiment of
> happiness at seeing that we are likely soon to be together again.
> You are much mistaken when you say there seems to be an
> unusual feeling in favor of conciliation so far as we in this
> region are concerned. The feeling is not precisely " universal"
> but it is very general. Union Democrats and Southern Rights
> Democrats are I believe acting together now as if nothing ever
> happened to make them cut apart, with the exception of some
> ten or dozen, mostly S. R. men. 20

Benning then explains that the Southern rights men will not support the Union Democrats, but they will not support any members of the Whig party either. He then provides a special political comment concerning James Johnson, whom Benning lost to in the election for Congress. Benning states that Johnson " avows himself to be a Whig," and therefore the Southern Rights men will not show support for him. 21 For Southern Democrats, Whigs," Whiggers," " Whiggery," and " Whiggerdom," were ugly words. Benning remained very bitterly opposed to Congressman James Johnson. Benning continues his letter with:

> I regret that it will not be in my power to be in Atlanta on the
> 18th, for I want much to have a full and free talk with you and
> such friends as I should probably meet there, in respect less to
> the present than the future.

You know well that it has been my conviction for the last two or three years that nothing we could do, short of general emancipation, would satisfy the North. Your idea was that the measures of the Compromise would substantially effect that object, and you went for them for that reason chiefly, I think. Should it turn out that I am right and you are wrong it will not be long before it must be known. And it is therefore now time for you to be making up your mind for the new " crisis." Suppose the Whig party shall be beaten, and especially at the North, will that not disband it and send the elements of which it has been composed into the union with this late Pittsburgh free-soil anti-slavery concern? Manifestly. What then? That concern takes the North. The Democratic Party there, in conjunction with pretty much the whole South, may be able to make one fight, say in 1856- a grand Union Rally- but then the thing will be out. Is it not so? You must have thought of all this. Have you made up your mind as to what is to be done? 22

With this chastising letter, Benning effectively severed communications with his old friend " Fatty," for some time to come. While Benning was simply being candid with his old friend, Cobb was the Governor and wielded the ultimate executive authority in the state. Cobb wrote similar appeals to other Southern Rights Democrats in an attempt to heal the wounds; however, most remarks were not favorable. One such answer to Cobb stated," We honestly differed and respectively pressed upon each other our opposing views, until unkind feelings were in many instances produced, nor can we now venture to rediscuss those questions without reviving angry feelings." 23 Eventually, the Southern Democratic party would find common ground and rebuild their party, but in 1852, the wounds had not yet healed.

For the next year, Henry Benning shunned the world of politics. He continued to focus on the law, his plantation, and his family. During this time, Benning's younger sister, Augusta Palmyra was married to Mr. Madison Lewis Patterson, on June 30, 1852. Patterson was a successful, local attorney and distant kinsman of Henry Lewis Benning. Back in their lineage of " Old Virginia," the Lewis family lines crossed, and provided both men with the source of their middle names. Patterson was described as a small man with blue eyes and sandy colored hair. Thus, by 1852, both of Henry Benning 's sisters were " well married" to friends of his, and they were both, fellow attorneys. On June 22, 1853, Mary Benning gave birth to another child. This one was a healthy baby girl and the Bennings named her Anna Caroline. Ironically, in the fall of that year, tragedy struck the Benning home again. The Benning's little girls, whom Anna Caroline had been named for, Caroline Matilda, age seven, and Anna Malinda, age six, succumbed to some unknown malady similar to the death of their sister Sarah, who died at the age of three, in 1846. They died in September of 1853, within five days of each other, Anna on the twelfth and Caroline on the seventeenth. **24**

Shortly after the deaths of his daughters, Henry Benning reconsidered his withdrawal from " the stage," and he set his sights on the Georgia Supreme Court. The Supreme Court seat that Benning desired was occupied by Judge Eugenius A. Nisbet, whose term was due to expire in December of 1853. Nisbet was well respected throughout Georgia, but he was a Whig by political affiliation, and Benning differed with many of his judicial opinions. **25** Benning weighed the circumstances, reconciled his situation, and again, thrust himself into the political arena. Eliciting the support of his fellow Democrats, Benning campaigned vigorously amongst the Georgia legislature.

In the fall of 1853, the political climate in Georgia had changed. In the Georgia Gubernatorial election of 1853, Benning's old classmate Herschel V. Johnson won the office of Governor. Robert Toombs returned to the Democratic Party and was elected as a Georgia Senator. Alexander Stephens continued his post in the Congress. On November 15, 1853, the Georgia General Assembly voted for a new Justice of the Supreme Court and Henry L. Benning defeated the incumbent Judge E. A. Nisbet by 10 votes. Nisbet immediately forwarded his resignation to Governor Johnson, and Benning took his seat on the bench for the first time " at the January term, 1854, in Savannah." **26** For the first time in several years, Howell Cobb was " off the stage," and he returned home to practice law. Although Henry Benning had not won a political office, he had nonetheless achieved a post of high esteem and worthy regard. As a judge, Benning had attained a position of which he was extremely well suited. At the age of thirty-nine, Benning was also the youngest Supreme Court Justice in Georgia history. For the next six years, Henry Benning seized the opportunity to make his mark.

Chapter 6

Supreme Court Justice

Just before Benning's ascension to the supreme bench of Georgia, the state published its first organized law digest. The *Digest of the Laws of Georgia* was lauded by Governor George W. Towns to be of great importance for not only lawyers and judges, it " would also have " great utility with every class of our citizens." 1 Compiled by Thomas Rootes Reade Cobb, the State court reporter and younger brother of Howell Cobb, the digest was created to " provide Georgia lawyers, judges, and untrained justices of the peace with a portable, well-organized, easily understood digest." 2 While Cobb's book had great utility, it would be seven more years before the state achieved the all encompassing product necessary to quick-reference court cases and legal precedence. Additionally, as prescribed in the Georgia Constitution, the court worked in the fashion of a circuit, which required frequent and lengthy travel, throughout the state. Years later, this practice was amended to provide the judges, attorneys, litigants, and the public, a permanent centrally located forum. Furthermore, in the 1850s, as the struggle concerning states' rights rose to the forefront, the relationship between Southern state courts and U. S. federal courts was severely strained and overshadowed with an impending civil war.

Thus, as Judge Henry Lewis Benning began to exercise his newly appointed authority, the first and most important responsibility was to define as best he could," what is the law?" While the matter of " judicial review " had been established with *Marbury v. Madison*, in 1803, and the question of " judicial power" in *Martin v. Hunter's Lessee*, in 1816, the Supreme Court of the United States was operating on a doctrine with which many people did not agree, especially states' rights advocates. Even today, this precedent of an " extra-Constitutional" power achieved by a liberal interpretation of the Constitution raises heated debate. One final note of legal significance is the fact that not all state cases automatically receive " judicial review" at the U. S. Supreme Court. Constitutional interpretation is a difficult task, but as you read Benning's legal opinions, keep these two important facts in mind:

1. For a case to move from a state supreme court to the U. S. Supreme Court, it must present a substantial Federal question, that is, an important question involving interpretation of a provision of the U. S. Constitution or a statute passed by Congress.

2. In all cases involving the interpretation of a state constitutional provision or a statute passed by the state legislature, *where no federal constitutional question is implicated, the decision of a state court is supreme and is not reviewable by the U. S. Supreme Court.* 3

Adding to this backdrop of potential difficulty was the ever-expanding nature of our nation and the many dilemmas associated with the issues of slavery and sovereignty. As the federal government grew, its exercise over state and territorial issues created passionate debate. While the federal government was experiencing growth pangs, so too were the individual states. All state governments are somewhat different, and Georgia's Supreme Court had only been in existence since 1845, so the supremacy of the court was reliant upon eight short years of established legal precedents. Benning's fellow judges of the Georgia Supreme Court were exemplary men and had established a strong record of respect and admiration. Benning's peers on the court were Judge Joseph Henry Lumpkin and Judge Ebenezer Starnes.

At age fifty-four, Lumpkin was a founding member of the court and considered one of the greatest legal giants in Georgia history. He also served as the President or Presiding Officer of the Court until the position title was later changed to Chief Justice. Benning had a lot in common with Lumpkin, both professionally and personally. In 1850, Lumpkin was an advocate for dissolution of the Union and while he sometimes differed with Benning concerning certain legal matters, he genuinely liked Benning. 4 Lumpkin's daughter Marion, was the wife of Thomas R. R. Cobb, Recorder of the Supreme Court. Lumpkin was also the founder of the Phi Kappa Society at Franklin College, of which Benning was also an alumnus. 5 Lumpkin was described as being " the most genial hearted man we have ever had in this state...He wore his hair long, which set off his gentle, handsome, intelligent face, and well proportioned figure." 6

When Benning assumed his seat on the bench, Judge Ebenezer Starnes was forty-three years of age. Starnes was also an alumnus of

Franklin College, and he had served as the Attorney General of the Middle Circuit. Starnes also served as the Superior Court Judge of the Middle Circuit from 1847 to 1853. Starnes is described as having " a grave and dignified demeanor; he was a lawyer of ripe learning and a man of kind heart." 7 History also records an insightful portrayal of Judge Starnes provided by Judge Eugenius Nisbet, with," He delivers himself most unpleasantly. His voice is bad and he hems and haws and drawls outrageously. But his judgments show clear discrimination and strength." 8

Just as the descriptions of these great men imply, they brought to the bench a wealth of knowledge combined with their own individual backgrounds and unique human characteristics. In addition to this, concerning their court opinions, one must consider them " in the light of the atmosphere which then pervaded the entire state." 9 Furthermore, due to the seething political caldron " however much we may deplore the influence which settled opinions on cardinal political principles may have upon a judge, it would be absurd to expect them to be immediately dissipated because he had assumed judicial office." 10 These words as expressed in a 1921 speech, delivered by Alexander R. Lawton, President of the Georgia Bar Association provide sound guidance when considering the court opinions of Judge Henry L. Benning. Lawton's address was entitled," Judicial Controversies on Federal Appellate Jurisdiction," and it provides an insightful analysis of Benning's opinion in the case of *Padelford, Fay & Company v. The Mayor and Aldermen of the City of Savannah*, 14 Ga., 438 (1854). 11

This case was one of Judge Benning 's first opportunities to express the opinion of the court, and the case was concerned with a matter dear to Benning's heart. Benning's eighty-two page opinion in the case presents a broad spectrum of technical legal issues, but the foundation of his argument is the constitutional clash between federal and state authority. Years later, Georgia Chief Justice Bleckley stated that Benning's " expression has never been overruled, but simply ignored... regarded now from a practical standpoint [it] seems visionary." 12 Benning's ultimate summation in this case consists of two parts. First, is the judgement against the plaintiffs, wherein Benning upholds the superior court ruling of Judge W. B. Fleming. Secondly, Judge Benning delivers a lengthy dictum regarding his interpretation of judicial powers expressed in Article III of the U. S. Constitution.

In legal terminology, Benning's opinion in this case is referred to as an *obiter dictum*, which means that his opinion addresses matters " not directly upon the question before him," and " by the way," he takes the opportunity to provide collateral information. 13 Most antebellum arguments concerning constitutional interpretation of states' rights and federal authority were ultimately settled with a bloody civil war. But in 1854, the only battles being waged were fought with words, interpretation, and opinions. In this case, in the supreme forum of the State of Georgia, Judge Benning delivered a forceful *obiter dictum* combined with a states' rights *coup de main* (sudden attack).

The case of *Padelford v. Savannah* concerns an ordinance established in 1842, by the City of Savannah, in which a tax was levied on commission merchants. The tax was for one-half of one percent on all sales of commodities within the corporate limits for commission or on joint account. This tax was applied to the sale of " Negroes, goods, wares and merchandise or other commodity, article or thing sold within the corporate limits." 14 The plaintiffs, Padelford, Fay and Company, imported goods from overseas, sold them in their original packaging and refused to pay the prescribed city tax, based upon a similar statute in Maryland, which was struck down in the case of *Brown v. Maryland.* In the *Brown v. Maryland* case, the U. S. Supreme Court ruled that the application of a tax upon imported goods was unconstitutional. The Justice of the Superior Court of Chatham County, Judge Fleming, ruled against the argument presented by the plaintiffs' attorney, and upheld the city's tax ordinance. Thus, the Padelford case continued on appeal to the Georgia Supreme Court, and the judgement of Henry L. Benning.

While Judge Benning was new to the bench, he spoke with the voice of authority. With a large towering frame, and a powerful voice, he commanded the respect of the court. In his own unique style, Benning's opinions were initiated with a statement, which clearly defined the question before the court. Speaking in " a low guttural tone and a syllabic precision, that heightened the idea of his manly force of character," Benning delivered his opinion in the case of *Padelford v. Savannah*:

> But a single question is presented for decision in this case; and that is whether the Ordinance of the City of Savannah violates the Constitution of the United States. The plaintiff's in error insist that it violates two of the provisions of the Constitution- that which declares that Congress shall have power " To regulate commerce with foreign nations and among the several States'; and that which declares that imposts or duties on imports or exports, except what may be absolutely necessary for executing its Inspection Laws."

The question is one of the utmost importance. The State has
passed many unconstitutional Tax Laws, if this be
unconstitutional. **16**

Benning then cites six detailed examples of taxes enacted by the State of
Georgia, 1804 through 1850, and he declares:

The same principal that will make the Ordinance of the City
Council unconstitutional, will equally make these acts so.
Indeed if the Ordinance violates the provision in the
Constitution, as to the regulation of commerce, it is not very
easy to see what is left to a State to tax. It can lay no tax that
will not more or less affect commerce; more or less prevent
consumption, and without consumption there can be no
commerce. The question then, deserves the most serious
consideration. The question, it is insisted by   counsel for
plaintiff, has been settled in their favor by the case of *Brown v.
Maryland*, (12 Wheat, 449.) That case, therefore, will be
noticed. **17**

Judge Benning then articulated a detailed review of the *Brown v.
Maryland* case. Benning pointed to specific instances in the case which
highlighted that the situation expressed therein was not applicable to the
case of *Padelford v. Savannah*. Specifically, Benning explained that "
Brown v. Maryland held to be unconstitutional only the *prohibition* of the
sale of the import by the importer without a license from the State, whereas
the ordinance of Savannah in no way obstructed the sale, but only laid a
tax on the proceeds of the sale of *all* commodities, including imports." **18**
    The learned judge provides further clarification concerning imported
goods, duties imposed upon imported goods, taxes imposed on sales of
goods (imported or otherwise), and the differences between them. He
summarizes these definitions examined in *Brown v. Maryland*, their impact
upon the *Padelford v. Savannah* case, and concludes with," According to
the principles, then, of Brown vs. Maryland, the State can, rather than
cannot, tax this something- this money-the proceeds of the sale of the
imports." **19**
    Finally, Judge Benning terminates the judgement phase of his opinion
by adding that all members of the court agree with this determination," but
speaking for myself, I am not willing to let the decision rest on this ground
alone." **20**
    Benning's *obiter dictum* provides an encompassing review of the
Constitution. In detail, he recites its history, its construction, the fierce

debates between the Federalists and anti-Federalists, and its difficult ratification. The most important feature of Benning's dissertation of the Constitution is the fact that " he denies the doctrine of implied power and supports the doctrine of narrow construction." **21** Benning devotes pages of analysis to his opinion concerning the dangers of liberal constitutional interpretation. He highlights the importance of the tenth and eleventh amendments, which provide for explicit regard for states' rights. Additionally, Benning provides court cases, which further highlight the importance of these two amendments. Then, with great alacrity, Judge Benning delivers his *coup de main* declaring the equality of the courts.

Judge Benning details the judicial powers as strictly defined in the Constitution. Specifically, Benning highlights that Article III of the U. S. Constitution draws a clear distinction between original and appellate jurisdiction. Additionally, Benning clarifies that " inferior" courts mentioned in the Constitution, are not state courts; they are those courts created by acts of Congress, such as federal military courts, federal district courts, federal tax courts, etc. The distinction between the courts that Benning focuses upon involves the inferior federal courts, and state court jurisdiction. Benning highlights " that the *appellate jurisdiction* delegated to the Supreme Court, applies only to the *Inferior Courts of the United States*, ordained and established by Congress, *with Judges for life*, and not to State Courts, which are not ordained and established by Congress, and which are presided over by Judges who do not hold their offices for life." **22** In many cases, the ultimate appellate authority is the State Supreme Court. Only when there is a constitutional question of legal interpretation does the case proceed to the U. S. Supreme Court. Otherwise, all cases would eventually terminate at the U S. Supreme Court level.

To highlight the constitutional division of powers, Benning repeats the words of Chief Justice Marshall, in the Supreme Court case of *McCullugh v. Maryland,* with," In America, the powers of sovereignty are divided between the Government of the Union, and those of the States. They are each sovereign, with respect to the objects committed to it, and neither sovereign, with respect to the objects committed to the other." **23** Summarizing the issue of constitutional powers, Benning states that:

> Now, if the General Government, by its judiciary, can come out
> of its sphere, into the sphere of a State government, and ravish a
> case thence out of the hands of the State Judiciary, the two
> Governments are not equally supreme within there respective

spheres. But they are by the admission of [Alexander] Hamilton
and [John] Marshall, equally supreme in their respective
spheres; therefore, the Government cannot do this, with respect
to the latter...none but a superior can give an order; none but an
inferior is bound to obey one.
The question, when tried by the rule of strict construction, does
not admit of a doubt. That rule is, that the General Government
has no powers, except such as have been *expressly* delegated to
it; and that the delegations of express power are to be strictly
construed. Now, jurisdiction over State Courts is not *expressly*
given to the General Government, or any department of it.
Therefore, according to this rule, such jurisdiction is not given
at all. **24**

Judge Benning summarizes the matter of jurisdiction with," Now it
must be manifest to any one, on a little reflection, that if the United States '
Courts have power over the State Courts, they have power over the State
Laws-power over the operation of those Laws, within the territory of the
States- power *to nullify every act of the States*. Was this the intention of the
makers of the Constitution - these very States?" **25** Concluding his
argument concerning powers and jurisdiction thereof, Benning declares
that:

The Supreme Court of Georgia is co-equal and co-ordinate with
the Supreme Court of the United States, and not inferior and
subordinate to that Court. That as to the reserved powers, the
State Court is supreme; that as to the delegated powers, the U. S.
Court is supreme; that as to the powers, both delegated and
reserved-*concurrent powers*-both Courts, in the language of
Hamilton," are equally supreme" ; and as a consequence, the
Supreme Court of the United States has no jurisdiction over the
Supreme Court of Georgia ; and cannot, therefore, give it an
order, or make it a *precedent*. **26**

Finally, Judge Benning points out that in reality, partisan politics play an
essential role in the matters of constitutional interpretation. Benning states
that:

There are now, and have been before now, in these United
Sates, but two parties, with a deeply marked line of separation
between them. The party which stands on the side of the
delegated powers, and that which stands on the side of the

reserved powers- the National party and the States' Rights party.
Now, the effect of the decisions of the Supreme Court, to which
I have referred, is to put up the National party and to put down
the States' Rights party. The decisions are, therefore, political.
27

    Judge Benning continues his argument that supports a strict
interpretation of the Constitution, based upon the human folly of
interpretation. He points to historical evidence that highlights the dangers
of a liberal interpretation of the Constitution, and that we should heed only
those powers that are " expressly enumerated." Specifically, Benning
argues that powers achieved through implication will be slanted based
upon the politics of those conducting the interpretation of their implied
powers. He then terminates his obiter dictum declaring that previous court
decisions should not be used to establish precedents because of the nature
of politics, social changes, and that " all decisions on Constitutional
questions, must be more or less partisan." **28**
    While Judge Benning 's opinions concerning constitutional
interpretation and the division of governmental powers were not directly
applicable to the case at hand, they were nonetheless important in
highlighting the growing struggle between federal and state powers.
Benning's *obiter dictum* provided a forum to address a serious problem,
which would eventually separate the nation. Furthermore, his opinion in
this case provides an insightful measure of the foundations of his political
beliefs. For his day, Benning's remarks concerning constitutional
interpretation were visionary. Many statements of today's legal authorities
express similar comments concerning the dangers of " loose" constitutional
interpretation. One states that," This approach to jurisprudence has led to
some remarkable and tragic conclusions," and another comments that,"
mistakes occur when the principles of specific constitutional provisions-
such as those contained in the Bill of Rights - are taken by some as
invitations to read into the Constitution values that contradict the clear
language of other provisions." **29**
    While Benning's opinion in the *Padelford v. Savannah* case raises
important issues, it received little notice in the press, and beyond the State
of Georgia, it was largely ignored. Ironically, in the North, a similar case
before the State Court of Ohio, as supporting evidence, Chief Justice
Bartley referred to Benning's opinion as " exposing and condemning in
strong and severe terms this unwarranted exercise of power by the

Supreme Court of the United States under the Twenty-fifth Section of the Judiciary Act." **30** It is noteworthy, that Benning's opinion articulated in this case, was also the foundation of his states' rights arguments expressed throughout his failed Congressional campaign. Furthermore, in days yet to come, Benning's argument against federal power would be refined and repeated throughout the South, and by most Southerners.

Judge Benning did not frequently get the chance to comment so freely. Most of the cases that the Georgia Supreme Court reviewed dealt primarily with the resolution of the case at hand. Most cases dealt with bankruptcies, wills, and criminal matters, and most of these did not provide the judges with opportunities to add political commentaries. Some however, do provide additional insight concerning Henry Benning 's philosophy and ideology of important issues. Benning was certainly concerned with politics, and while the ensuing conflicts between governmental powers and constitutional interpretation were surging, the singular topic that rode atop the crest of the flood tide, was slavery.

Chapter 7

Judge Benning and Slavery

" The desire to own menial servants, at least, is very general, and is restrained only by the price of Negroes...every citizen would own one or more if he had the ability to do so." 1 The previous statement appeared in a local Columbus newspaper and provides a common thought which permeated antebellum Georgia. Slavery was simply a societal norm. This norm and this society were the ones in which Judge Henry L. Benning was born and raised. It even became fashionable in Southern society to attach specific young slaves to individual family members. Seaborn Jones engaged in this practice and he bequeathed to each of his children and grandchildren specific slaves to become their personal servants. For example, Jones matched his granddaughters Mary and Sarah Benning with young female slaves whom they were growing up with," Anarchy" and " Peanut." 2 Thus, by 1854; Henry Benning was following the norms of his society, and emulating his father-in-law. While Benning engaged in the practice of slavery, he was also a man that had achieved the laurels of college valedictorian, accomplished lawyer, Attorney General, State Supreme Court Justice, and respectable family man. As educated and religious men, Benning and his peers wrestled with the concept of slavery. As Northerners challenged the practice of slavery, Southerners were forced to examine an institution they inherited from their forefathers.

Throughout this period, learned men, on both sides of the issue, intensely examined the " peculiar institution. " Benning's friend and Court Reporter, Thomas R. R. Cobb, wrote a multi-volume book on the subject. Entitled, *An Historical Sketch of Slavery, From the Earliest Periods*, Cobb probed history to explain in elaborate detail, its origins, occurrences, and norms. Cobb pointed to the great societies of ancient Rome, Greece, and Egypt, where slavery served as a social foundation that supported their economies. In the words of Thomas Cobb," In every organized community there must be a laboring class, to execute the plans devised by the wiser

heads, to till the ground, and to perform the menial offices necessarily connected with social life... the poorer and less intelligent applied to the more opulent and intelligent for employment. The return was food and raiment." 3 Thus, Cobb defined the institution of slavery. When adopted by his generation
as a patriarchal relationship between the protector and the protected, Cobb expressed that:

> The children of the planter and the children of his slaves hunted, fished, and played together. An almost perfect equality existed, in their sports, between the future master and his future slave. To dispense exact justice to all was the office of the planter. Obedience and respect from all was his reward. Such a state of society made slavery, in the Colonies, a *social institution*. It was upheld and maintained, not for gain solely, but because it had become, as it were, a part of the social system, a social necessity. 4

Thus the question arises- a " social necessity" for whom? Today of course, the predominant response would be the wealthy Southern planter. Yet, in the antebellum society of the South," within the organic community of a slave society, they argued, the master could not ignore the human obligation to care for his bondsman." 5 Furthermore, pro-slavers argued that the slave in Southern society was far better off than his Northern brother who was wallowing in poverty with low wages and free to starve. In Cobb's book, he also examined the conditions and status of free Negroes living in the North. Cobb recorded the observations and comments of northern governors and other prominent members of the northern states. Cobb highlighted supportive evidence that emancipation had not helped Negroes. Cobb published extracts concerning the status of Negroes in the northern states with comments such as:

> Pennsylvania: They exhibit all the characteristics of an inferior race, to whose personal comfort, happiness, and morality, the supervision, restraint, and coercion of a superior race seem absolutely necessary.

> Indiana: The majority of them are not doing well. We have sent off thirty or forty this year to Liberia, and hope to send off one hundred or more, next year, and finally to get rid of all we have in the State, and do not intend to have another Negro or mulatto come into the State.

Illinois: As a class, they are thriftless and idle. Their condition
far inferior to that of the whites.

Connecticut: They are, with us, as an inferior caste; and in
morality fall much below the whites.

New Jersey: Immoral; vicious animal propensities; drunkenness,
theft, and promiscuous sexual intercourse quite common. One-
fourth of the criminals in the State prison are colored persons;
while they constitute only one twenty-fifth of the population.

Cobb also pointed out that although Negroes were free in the North,
with the exception of Vermont, northern States still restricted Negroes
from voting, to be jurors, to hold elective office, and to marry whites.
Furthermore, Cobb highlighted that Negroes " are more healthy and long-
lived, in a state of slavery than of freedom." 6
   Provided with these examples of emancipation, Southerners found
support for the institution of slavery. The argument that Southern Negroes
were better off than those in the North, was simply a matter of perspective.
As expressed previously, in Columbus, Georgia, those slaves belonging to
Christian owners were fed, clothed and their religious needs well attended
to, however, freedom was their greatest desire. As expressed by a former
Columbus slave, Mary Gladdy," their great, soul-hungering desire was
freedom- not that they loved the Yankees or hated their masters, but merely
longed to be free." 7 Yet, the " masters" clung to the ethnocentric belief that
it was their responsibility to care for their ignorant black brethren, and
besides, freedom in the North had not improved the plight of the Negro.
Summed up by Clement Eaton in his masterful, *The Mind of the Old South*,
he states that:

The Southern mind, having reconciled the existence of slavery
within a Christian society, cherished a romantic delusion that
Southern civilization was superior to that in the North- in all that
constitutes the gentleman and a gallant people. Nevertheless,
there remained a deep sense of insecurity in the mind of the
Southerner as he looked into the future and realized that the
South was becoming more and more a minority section in the

nation. In these years, in a changing world, Southerners sought desperately to preserve the landmarks of the past. **8**

It must also be noted that some Southerners were influenced by the scientific study of Ethnology, a theory that espoused physical proof that Negroes were inferior to the Caucasian race. Numerous articles and several books were written in the mid-1850s, which highlighted Negro inferiority. " Scientific racists such as Dr. Samuel Cartwright and Dr. Josiah Nott," reported that Negroes heads were constructed like " the lower animals and monkey tribes," and therefore, their " smaller brains supposedly limited blacks' intellectual capacity." **9** Furthermore, it was reported that blacks had different characteristics in many parts of their anatomy which reflected their inferiority. Two popular period magazines, which Henry Benning read," *The Southern Quarterly Review* and *DeBow's Review* became avowed exponents and many of their articles reflect the same trend of opinion among their contributors." Finally, the title of a book written by one of the " scientific racists" best highlights the prevalent thesis of this group- *Negroes and Negro Slavery: The first an inferior race: The latter its normal condition.* **10**

While racial overtones were certainly prevalent throughout the South, most Southerners rejected the observations of the " scientific racists. " The scientists rejected the *Holy Bible*, thus most Southerners viewed these scientific theories as " more amusement than reliable information." Many people refuted the scientists and one wrote," if forced to choose between the Bible and ethnology, southerners had best stick to the Holy Writ." **11**

Above all else, religion provided the bond amongst all classes of Southern society. This fabric of shared religious heritage was inextricably woven throughout the ideology of the South. Its threads bonded rich and poor, black and white. When the Methodist Church split in 1845, Southerners isolated themselves from their northern brothers and sisters, and bound the South, ever stronger. From 1845 onward, this chasm between North and South was filled with doubt, suspicion, lies, and outright hatred. As the abolitionist movement in the North gained momentum, the northern churches embraced the idea, which further inflamed the South. Northern writers such as Henry David Thoreau and Ralph Waldo Emerson, fervent abolitionists, also called for society to embrace " free love," transcendentalism, socialism, and to reject organized religion. Harriet Beecher Stowe wrote *Uncle Tom's Cabin*, which portrayed an unfair depiction of slave owners as cruel and inhumane people. These events had a direct impact upon other religious denominations, which also divided along geographic boundaries, ever-widening the gap between the North and South. To the Southerner, the events in the north were viewed as a conspiracy to undermine the beliefs and institutions of the South. George Fitzhugh, a Southern economist of the 1850s, summed up these suspicions with:

> We warn the North that every one of the leading abolitionists is agitating the Negro slavery question merely as a means to obtain their ulterior ends... a surrender to Socialism and Communism- to no private property, no church, no law, to free love, free lands, free women, and free children. 12

Amidst these religious and intellectual overtones, politics of the 1850s also fueled the fire of discord between North and South. In 1854, Democratic Senator Stephen Douglas of Illinois introduced the Kansas - Nebraska bill. Enacted into law on May 26, the act struck down the Missouri Compromise, and provided that states in the western territories were free to choose if they became free or slave states. This event sparked a violent and bloody fight between pro-slavers and abolitionist. Men such as abolitionist outlaw, John Brown, led raids and murdered pro-slavery advocates in his quest to maintain Kansas as a free state. Throughout the latter 1850s, Brown plotted to invade the Southern states and create a race war.

In addition, in 1854, political opposition split the Whig party, which combined with " Free Soil" Democrats and formed the Republican Party. Staunchly opposed to slavery, the party grew rapidly throughout the North. One of the leading proponents of the Republican Party was a former Whig Congressman from Illinois, Abraham Lincoln. Southerners detested Lincoln. Not only did he call for the emancipation of slaves, he also rejected religion. 13
Throughout the nation, this political caldron filled with religious differences and bitter opposition slowly began to spin out of control. And once again, rising to the top of this spinning quagmire of divisive rhetoric, as Henry Benning had stated years earlier," It is apparent, horribly apparent, that the slavery question rides insolently over every other everywhere." 14
As a judge, Benning was now in a unique position to affect the issues at hand. As illustrated in the case of *Padelford v. Savannah*, Benning did not hesitate to make his mark on the issue of federal and state powers. The year 1854 also provided Benning the opportunity to adjudicate an issue concerning slaves. Specifically, what is the legal status of a slave? Can

slaves be people too? The case was *Roland Baker, plaintiff in error, vs. The State of Georgia. Zachariah Sheffield, plaintiff in error, vs. The Same, Georgia Reports, Vol. XV, No. 72, p. 498 (1855).* In this case, the plaintiffs were charged with a high misdemeanor in Marion Superior Court, and tried before Judge Crawford, in the March Term, 1854. On appeal, the cases were then combined and forwarded as one case to be tried before the Georgia Supreme Court. Meeting during the July term in Americus, Georgia, Judge Henry Benning provided the opinion of the court. 15

The case centered upon two men, Roland Baker and Zachariah Sheffield, whom were indicted for aiding a prisoner to escape. The fleeing prisoner, whom Sheffield and Baker provided assistance, was a Negro slave, known as Sam. Judge Benning provided the following background scenario:

> The Negro was in jail, upon a charge for an assault, with intent to commit a rape; on the evening of the escape, the Negro pushed through the door and over the jailer, and ran off, the jailer pursuing; about one hundred yards from the jail, the Negro fell and the jailer overtook him and got him, and hallooed for help. A man came up and ordered the jailer to let the Negro loose; he refused, and the man drew a pistol and placed it to the jailer's head, with a threat to fire if he did not release the Negro; the Negro was loosed and escaped. Other evidence was introduced, to show a concert of action between the Negro and this friend, and to identify the prisoners as the aiders.

> The defendants' counsel requested that the court should find the defendants, not guilty, because while the Georgia Penal code addresses aiding prisoners escape, it does not refer to aiding a Negro slave to escape from custody. Furthermore, the defense argued that the defendants were simply rescuing Sam, and therefore they could not be held liable for aiding and abetting the escape of a prisoner. The Superior Court, Judge Crawford had refused to allow the jury to apply this technical issue to the case in question, thereby forcing the issue- if a slave cannot be a citizen of the state, can he legally be a prisoner of the state? In his manly, commanding voice, Judge Benning states the following," May a Negro slave be a prisoner, lawfully committed or detained in jail, for any offense against this State- for the offense, say, of attempting to commit a rape on a free white female? This offense when committed by a slave, is a capital one." 16

Benning then explains in great detail that according to Cobb's *Digest of Law*, and the Act of 1811, that slaves will be remanded to jail when accused of crimes and placed under the control of the local authorities and " of course, when so committed, the slave becomes a prisoner for 'an offense against this State'." 17 Benning then continues to repeat the charge that Sam was a prisoner, and sent to jail charged with the crime of attempting to rape a free white female and," This being so, the aiding of him to escape from jail, is something that falls within the very *words* of the section aforesaid of the Code, on which the indictment is founded. Falling within the words, why does it not fall within the meaning? 18 Benning then repeats the arguments as expressed by the defense counsel:

First, because a slave is a chattel, and no chattel can be a prisoner.
Secondly, because the Code, except in the thirteenth division has white persons only, in contemplation, and therefore, as by the thirteenth division, a Negro cannot be a prisoner. When it speaks of prisoners, it must mean prisoners only, as happen to be white persons.

Judge Benning then states," It is true, that slaves are chattels, for most purposes. It is equally true, that they are not so for all; for many, they are persons." 19 He then points to the laws that support this argument. Specifically, numerous provisions listed in Cobb's *Digest of Law*, and the Legislative Acts of 1811, 1816, 1821 and 1833, which establishes the parameters of trials and punishments for slaves and free people of color. Benning then reads these measures of the Penal code in elaborate detail, arguing that the defense cannot use any of the aforementioned reasons to establish an adequate argument to support the actions of Sheffield and Baker. Summarizing the decision of the court, Benning emphasizes the folly expressed by the defense that aiding the prisoner to escape was really a rescue. He then ends the opinion of the court and upholds the decision of Judge Crawford and the Marion County courts. 20
While it seems difficult to fathom, the counsel for the defense did get their clients case all the way to the Georgia Supreme Court, where it forced the State of Georgia to address the question- are slaves people or property? The primary importance of this case however, lies in Henry Benning's personal belief that while slaves are chattels," for many they are persons."

This reflects Benning's personal experience with slaves. It must be recalled that Benning was nursed and raised by a black " Mammy", Queen. Benning always insisted that his children treat her with respect. He was born and raised amongst them. His religious beliefs supported that while they were slaves, they were people too. Thus, in spite of being a slaveholder, throughout Benning's life, and after his death, the blacks that knew him, highly respected him, and he regarded them as people.

It is interesting that several years later, the U.S. Supreme Court ruled in the case of *Dred Scott v. Sandford,* that slaves could not become U. S. citizens. In this case, viewed as a major victory for pro-slavery," Chief Justice Roger B. Taney read blacks out of the Constitution in order to invalidate Congress 's attempt to limit the spread of slavery." **21** During the 1830s, in the slave state of Missouri, a slave named Dred Scott was owned by a U.S. Army surgeon, Doctor John Emerson. When master and slave migrated from Missouri to Illinois and on to the Wisconsin territory in 1834, Dred Scott lived in free territory for four years. In 1838, Emerson and Scott returned to Missouri. Doctor Emerson died in 1843, and Dred Scott sued the surgeon's widow for his freedom. The local courts granted Scott his freedom, but the Missouri Supreme Court reversed the lower court ruling and the case continued on to the U.S. Supreme Court. Chief Justice Roger B. Taney tackled the debate as the nation anxiously anticipated the important verdict. The ruling of the court would also decide if laws such as the Missouri Compromise were legal. The ominous decision of the court declared that blacks were simply property and that Scott and other blacks could not sue in courts, because they were not U.S. citizens. Immediately, the court's decision made the Missouri Compromise unconstitutional, stating that the Constitution upheld the right of states and territories to be slave states if they so desired. After recovering from a state of shock, the abolitionist movement returned to the fight with even greater zeal and fortitude.

The constitutionality of slaveholding had been upheld by the highest authority in the nation, and in the South, the U.S. Supreme Court ruling was perceived as a great victory. It is ironic to note that Benning's Georgia Supreme Court ruling that blacks " are persons" too, stands in stark contrast to the ultimate federal decision that blacks had no rights as U.S. citizens.

Meanwhile, between the dozens of court cases, Mary and Henry Benning produced another child. Mary delivered their final child, another daughter, Sarah (Sallie) Jones Benning, on January 17, 1855. The Bennings now had one son and five daughters. In 1855, the Benning children consisted of: Seaborn Jones, age fifteen; Mary Howard, age fourteen; the twins, Augusta Jones and Louisa Vivian, age seven; Anna Caroline, age 2; and the infant, Sarah Jones. This was the composition of the Benning family at its zenith. While the Bennings had six living children, they had also lost four, one son and three girls. John and Mary Jones also added another child to their family on November 8, 1854, a daughter and she was named in honor of her mother, Mary Louisa Jones. The Jones family had been blessed with five children, of which four had survived. **22**

Throughout the 1850s, the Bennings continued to live in " El Dorado," but their plantation (summerhouse) became more important as a refuge during the long hot summers. It had become fashionable amongst the wealthy residents of Columbus to spend their summers away from the city. Most families went to neighboring country manors, along the river, and in the higher elevations of Pine Mountain, with its crystal springs. The Benning family was no exception, while Mary and the children enjoyed the cool banks of the Chattahoochee River, Henry focused on planting. Throughout the 1850s, Benning purchased additional lands surrounding his plantation, expanding it to its ultimate size of 3,265 acres. While the Benning plantation was large, in contrast, the Woolfolk plantation had expanded to 5,500 acres, and an annual production of 400 bales of cotton. Additionally, in spite of the increased acreage, Benning's cotton production actually declined to 32 bales annually, although he did reap thousands of tons of hay. **23**

In October of 1855, while Benning focused on his family, his plantation and the court, the world of politics marched along. Many of Benning's friends were very actively engaged in political affairs. Democrat Herschel V. Johnson continued his reign as the Governor of Georgia. In Columbus, Martin J. Crawford ran for Congress on the Democratic ticket, and won a resounding victory. **24** In that same election, another of Benning's old friends won re-election to his seat in the Congress, Howell Cobb. In addition, the following year, upon the presidential election of Democrat James Buchanan, much to the chagrin of Henry Benning, Buchanan appointed none other than " Fatty," Howell Cobb as his Secretary of the Treasury. **25** Since 1853, upon the decline of the Whig party and the emergence of the Republican Party as the new nemesis of the Democrats, nearly all Georgians rallied to the aid of the Democratic Party. In fact, politically, the South was predominantly Democrat and the North, Republican. Georgia was and would remain a staunchly pro-Democratic state.

While Henry Benning would have enjoyed this turn of events, as a Supreme Court Justice, he was effectively locked out of politics. The year

1855, did however, see a change of venue for the Supreme Court of Georgia. The legislature voted out Judge Starnes, and replaced him with the former Governor, Charles J. McDonald. 26 It was during McDonald's term as Governor, that Henry Benning won appointment and served as the Solicitor General of the Chattahoochee Circuit. The Georgia Supreme Court now consisted of Judges Lumpkin, Benning and McDonald. The Georgia supreme bench was certainly filled with a trio of esteemed and learned men. Adding to this situation, Benning was additionally pleased with the newly appointed Court Reporter, his brother-in-law, Mr. Benjamin Y. Martin.

For the next several years, Benning quietly focused upon his responsibilities as a Justice of the Supreme Court. Throughout his tenure on the bench, Judge Benning was lauded as being instrumental in the judicial validation of several state laws. Moreover, amongst his peers, his analytical prowess in legal issues were regarded as " distinguished." 27 Yet, Benning's pinnacle of judicial expression had already been achieved in the case of *Padelford v. Savannah*, but his greatest judicial challenge still loomed on the horizon. Years before, during the " Columbus Bank Cases," Benning had served as the defense attorney for several stockholders of insolvent banks. One of these stockholders was his father-in-law, Seaborn Jones. Another prominent Columbus family that Benning represented was the McDougalds. Benning had served General Daniel McDougald during the Creek War, and for years thereafter, the firm of *Jones, Benning, and Jones* was employed by the McDougalds as their legal counselors. As the banks dissolved, many of those suffering losses were very wealthy and influential men and women of the local community. Furthermore, the attorneys aligned on either side were prominent and powerful men as well. Some of these attorneys were Hines Holt, Robert Toombs, Walter T. Colquitt, and John Berrien. Judge McDonald was also personally involved in these intricate financial matters. 28

Most of the cases had been resolved, however, one attorney in particular, Mr. William Dougherty, continued to push the cases before the court. Former Judge Nisbet, whom Benning replaced on the bench, had also fought against Benning in these cases, and was aligned with Dougherty. Thus, while Benning sat on the bench, cases similar to those in which he had argued in the lower courts resurfaced in the Supreme Court. With legal enemies lining up against him, Henry Benning now faced a major dilemma.

Chapter 8

The Columbus Bank Cases

In the year 1857, the people of the State of Georgia elected a new Governor, Joseph E. Brown. Brown was viewed as a champion of the people for his powerful executive stance taken against the numerous and seemingly arrogant banks that operated throughout the state. During this era, throughout our nation," wildcat" banking was disorganized and decentralized, with the individual banks issuing specie of their own design. The U.S. treasury system and banking laws were very much in their infancy, and the individual states supervised banking practices within their respective states. The resulting method of banking was wrought with counterfeiters, fraud, schemers and criminal conspiracies. Many banks dissolved, leaving the clients and billholders with little recourse. In Georgia, the banks were required by law to conform to certain practices, and many of these banks defiantly disobeyed the law. Governor Brown applied his executive power against the banks, and Georgia historian, Isaac Avery records that:

> Gov. Brown was the direct cause of a wholesome and sweeping reform in our whole scheme of banking, a reform going to the very vitals of our prosperity, affecting commerce and agriculture. He so clearly and forcibly brought to light the evils of the then existing system, and he was so unyielding in pressing their reform, that a permanent change for the better was effected through his powerful instrumentality. 1

The many banks, which served the public and commercial development of Columbus, Georgia, were not known for their stability.

The Columbus banks consisted of the: Bank of Columbus; Chattahoochee Railroad and Banking Company; the Insurance Bank; Planters' and Mechanics' Bank; Bank of St. Mary's; Phoenix Bank, and the Bank of Chattahoochee. All of these banks served the Columbus community during the antebellum period and most of these banks suffered severe operational and financial woes. 2 In order to grow and serve the community, these individual banks required the investment capital of stockholders. And, due to the rapid growth of the city coupled with the potential wealth of investment, Columbus, Georgia was a lucrative market to bankers. Seaborn Jones and many of his influential friends were investors in these banking enterprises. Of course, the potential return was lucrative to these individual stockholders, however, when the banks became insolvent, the result was financially disastrous. In antebellum Georgia, banking laws were vague and banks were frequently wrought with weak legal charters and fraudulent financial foundations. Adding to this calamity, the only recourse the bill holders and clients had, in an effort to recoup lost capital, was to sue the stockholders.

While bank failures occurred throughout the antebellum South, Columbus, Georgia with its rapid expansion and numerous speculators, experienced a disproportionate number. As the banks failed, numerous lawsuits were filed, in which several of these cases during the 1840s filled the courts. In several of these cases, Henry L. Benning, of Jones, Benning and Jones legally counseled the stockholders. Another Columbus lawyer, Mr. William Dougherty served as the counsel for most of the plaintiffs, as they sued the stockholders of the insolvent banks. The defendant stockholders won in most of these cases, as the court held that they were not pecuniarily liable for the insolvent banks. The cases of: *Lane v. Morris; Hightower v. Thornton; Hightower v. Mustain; Carey v. Jones ; Robinson v. Carey; Lane v. Harris; Robinson v. Lane;* and *Beall v. Robinson,* are all bank cases which pertain directly to this matter. 3 For years, the cases were fought in court after court, with Dougherty leading the vanguard against the stockholders. Eventually, several of the bank case suits wound up back in the Supreme Court, whereupon in the case of *Robinson v. Lane,* Chief Lumpkin's opening remarks reflect his personal frustration with:

> I propose to write a brief opinion in this case, not because the points adjudicated are unimportant, but for the simple reason that a decision in these bank cases settles nothing. I am warranted in saying this from the experience of the past six years. With every change in the court, the same questions are reproduced for re-adjudication. And we are authorized to infer, that this practice, so subversive of the fundamental object for

which this tribunal was organized, is to continue so long as this litigation shall last. **4**

An informed observer referred to these seemingly militant cases with," The war involves many people of wealth and influence, and calls forth the strong men of the bar in that part of the state to protect and defend the stockholders against the suits on the defunct bank bills." **5** Henry Benning had served as one of those strong men in the " war," and now serving on the supreme bench of Georgia, was called upon to re-enter the fray.

Benning's nemesis in the bank cases was William Dougherty, whom an acquaintance, Herbert Fielder describes as:

> Genial in social life, stutters slightly and occasionally, though fluent in conversation, and is full of heart-stirring and mirth-provoking anecdote. He is powerful, logical, brief and bold in argument, and almost irresistible before the court or jury. He is withal an enemy, and the subject of enmity, because he has long been the hero of a financial warfare against the stockholders of certain banks that failed, with a large number of their bills in circulation in the hands of the people, to make them liable to the holders of those bills. He has a large personal interest as well as great stock of professional ambition and reputation in the issue.
> **6**

Yet, as a legal practitioner, Fielder states that Benning was regarded as the stronger of the two. **7** Thus, when the case of *Lane v. Harris* (16 Ga. 217), appeared before the supreme court, Dougherty moved that Benning should dismiss himself from the case because he had previously represented other stockholders of the same bank, including his father-in-law, Seaborn Jones. Benning refused on the grounds that " it was his stern duty imposed by law and his oath of office, which he cannot shirk or evade, to preside in all cases that come before the court, in which, by his election, qualification, and commission, he has had given to him power and authority to preside." **8** Dougherty's move to disqualify Benning from the case failed, however, the overall outcome of the case was a victory for his client. Benning dissented with a stern sixteen-page opinion, but the case was lost. While Dougherty had defeated Benning, this was just the beginning of Benning's problems.

As with any case involving wealthy litigants, the *Lane v. Harris* case received press coverage, as well as notice amongst the Georgia legislature. Many members agreed with Dougherty, and felt that Benning should have declined to preside in the case. 9 Dougherty followed through with similar requests for disqualification aimed at both Judges McDonald and Benning. During the summer term held in Macon, on July 1, 1858, the bank case issue reached a critical stage. The judges would not yield their authority, and this time Dougherty petitioned the General Assembly to consider the issue. Benning vehemently defended his position, and presided along with McDonald in the case of *Robinson v. Beall.* 10 According to Avery," A resolution was introduced in the Senate advising and requesting Judge Benning and McDonald to resign their offices. The matter drew a great deal of feeling, but the Senate voted to lay the resolution on the table for the balance of the session by a vote of 67 yeas and 45 nays." 11 While the legislature chose not to formally settle the matter, it spilled into the press where Dougherty and Benning continued their clash of wills.

The bank cases were both complex and potentially embarrassing for everyone involved, but especially for William Dougherty. As stated previously, Dougherty had a " great stock of professional ambition and reputation in the issue," as he had served as a legal counselor on all of these cases. 12 Moreover, as evidenced in the trials and subsequent disclosures, William Dougherty was also an investor in the insolvent banks. Thus, Dougherty had personal financial incentives to achieve victory for his clients. 13 Furthermore, Dougherty had purchased additional stocks from clientele at extremely reduced prices, therefore, if judgments were won against the stockholders, he would also receive a handsome profit. Specifically, William Dougherty and Edward Carey were the largest creditors in the Planters' and Merchants Bank, the Chattahoochee Railroad and Banking Company, both of which were insolvent. The two investors were also the largest creditors of the umbrella financial organization of both failed banks, the Bank of Columbus. For Dougherty and Carey, their financial interests in a legal victory numbered in the hundreds of thousands of dollars, while their actual investment costs were numbered only in hundreds of dollars.

Amidst the numerous allegations and financial disclosures, notable men such as Seaborn Jones, Thomas Hoxey, Hines Holt, and even Chief Justice Lumpkin were listed as stockholders in these failed banks. Dougherty highlighted that Benning and his defense of Seaborn Jones in a similar bank case corrupted the current judicial matter. Yet, Benning and Dougherty had previously faced off in other bitterly contested legal cases, which most likely caused Dougherty to pursue Benning. These cases also involved financial matters such as trusts and railroad stocks. Specifically, the cases involved the Hoxeys and McDougalds, which were pitted in court with lawsuits aimed directly against Dougherty and his friend Edward Carey. **14** Both families were very prominent citizens of Columbus , and Benning had won acclaim for his legal prowess. Thus, these cases may have provided Dougherty with the motivation to seek vindication. Throughout the next year, Dougherty's assaults grew into a cancerous innuendo aimed at the professional destruction of Judge Benning. Editorials appeared throughout the Georgia newspapers exclaiming that:

> We are disgusted at the attempts making throughout the State, to get up indignation against the Supreme Court, on account of the recent decision of that tribunal in the Bank cases...The position of Judge Benning was a peculiarly delicate one. But what we ask was he to do?... It is thought best that a judge should not preside in such cases as the one under consideration, let the law be so amended. **15**

In his quest to achieve victory, Dougherty carefully worded and legally alluded implications at both Judges Benning and McDonald. On November 2, 1859, Dougherty directly assailed Benning by circulating a pamphlet in the Georgia Legislature entitled," To the Creditors of the Broken Banks of Columbus," wherein Dougherty expressed that Benning should be rejected in his bid for re-election on the supreme court because of his judicial actions in the bank cases. Dougherty also released the pamphlet to the press, while never disclosing the fact that he was the primary creditor of the failed banks. **16**

In the spring of 1859, Judge McDonald resigned from his position on the supreme bench and died shortly thereafter. McDonald was replaced by Linton Stephens of Sparta, Georgia. **17** Linton was only thirty-six years old, thus superseding Benning's record for achieving the same post at age thirty-nine. Congressman Alexander Stephens was the elder brother of Linton. Attorney and author, B. A. Thornton, described Linton Stephens as having a " rather stout build, with dark hair and rather heavy eyebrows, giving the eye a deep-set appearance, and conveying the impression of inflexible determination." **18** Linton Stephens was just, admirable and worthy of his selection to the post. Meanwhile, at the bequest of William Dougherty, the Honorable Richard F. Lyon was being considered amongst the legislature as a possible candidate to oppose Judge Benning in his re-election bid for the bench. With his six year term nearly expired, Benning fought back diligently to maintain his post. To defend his honor, Benning published a pamphlet concerning the bank cases and provided narratives and letters, which answered Dougherty's allegations in detail. **19** Benning's supporters rallied to his aid with editorials such as:

> For Judge Benning, he and his friends have no fear. Truth is mighty and will prevail. The people of Georgia are honest and generous, and when they know the truth, will protect an upright man and an honest and fearless officer. **20**

In spite of Benning's support, William Dougherty had planted a seed of doubt in the Georgia Legislature, and in the fall of 1859, the Honorable Richard Lyon replaced Benning. Isaac Avery, the imminent historian of Georgia noted that," The incident did great injury to Judge Benning a long time, which he keenly felt." **21**
Ironically, Benning's legal prowess in the bank cases was instrumental in his achievement of a seat on the supreme bench, yet it was these same cases that caused his usurpation. Moreover, his removal from the bench was caused primarily through his interpretation of applicable laws. In the absence of a specific State law, Judges commonly relied upon similar English law, and in this case *(2 Kent Com. 307)*, commonly referred to as the law of extinguishment, Benning highlighted the need to fully codify the laws of Georgia. It was not until after the *Robinson v. Beall* case, that the Georgia code was amended by the Legislative Act of 1858 and State law specifically addressed stockholder liability and bank charters. While, it was also a common practice for antebellum judges to politely resign themselves from cases in which they had previously argued as an attorney, it was merely a practice, not a prescribed rule or law. Furthermore, while the bank case before Judge Benning was similar in nature, it was not the same case in which he had previously presided as counsel. **22**
In tribute to Judge Benning 's service on the Georgia Supreme Court, one of his peers summarized his contributions with," He was cool, deliberate, clear in statement, honest in his convictions of rights, sternly logical, always earnest and at times vehement and truly eloquent." **23** Yet, Benning's service was not conducted without personal sacrifice. The lengthy arduous travel associated with the duties of a circuit court placed a heavy burden on his wife, Mary, and his sister Caroline Matilda, the wife of Benjamin Y. Martin. While Martin was a lawyer and the reporter of the Supreme Court, his in-laws, the Bennings and Jones, were much more affluent. Financially, Benning's State salary as a Supreme Court Justice was $3,500, while Martin's salary was $1,000. In a more graphic comparison, Martin's net worth in 1860 was $13,500, while Benning's assets totaled $96,300. Benjamin and Caroline Martin were raising five young children, while also caring for Henry and Caroline's mother,

Malinda Benning, age 73. During the long hot summer of 1858, while Benning and Martin were heavily engaged with the court, Caroline died, August 24, 1858, at the age of 34. **24** Shortly thereafter, forty-four year old, Benjamin Y Martin followed his wife in death, leaving behind his five orphaned children: Jacob, age sixteen; Mary, age fourteen, Ella, age nine; Pleasant, age seven; and Charles, age two. Mary and Henry Benning took the Martin children in and raised them as their own. The aged Malinda Benning then moved into the home of her other daughter, Augusta. Augusta's husband, Madison Lewis Patterson, was a successful lawyer too. **25**

In addition, during the summer of 1858, Henry and Mary Benning sent their only son, Seaborn Jones Benning to college. At the age of eighteen, amidst a class of 129 cadets, with an annual tuition of $225.00, Seaborn entered the Georgia Military Institute in Marietta, Georgia. John and Mary Jones also sent their first-born son, Seaborn Leonard Jones to Marietta for a rigid education. **26** For Mary, the beautiful, yet " tiny little woman" who had borne ten children for her husband, would certainly miss her eldest son. Mary's parents were beginning to show their advanced ages, her children were maturing rapidly and Henry was seemingly always away, tending to the " affairs of the court. " While conducting these affairs in 1858, Henry wrote to Mary stating:

We are here for a month. I fear for more than a month. We shall have about ninety cases. We have heard fifteen and one month is gone... you see then that we have been going at the rate of three cases a day at which rate it will take us five weeks to get through. I hope the rate may improve, but fear it will not.

After breaking the ice with how hard he has been working, he then informs Mary that," You see that our lives will have to depend entirely on you. By the time I shall be able to get home, it will be too late for planting." He also tells Mary that he is having some things forwarded to Columbus," so you must keep an eye to the depot." **27**

In 1859, as the wife of a Supreme Court Justice, Mary was a very busy lady. Between the plantation and the daily household routine, her parents health declining, her own five daughters, ranging in ages from three to eighteen, Benjamin Martin's five children, and her eldest son and husband away, Mary's responsibilities were quite vast. While she had slaves to perform the menial tasks and physical labor, the slaves required supervision too, and the Benning's did not employ an overseer. Adding to these myriad preoccupations, Mary and her sister-in-law, Mrs. Mary

(Leonard) Jones, also served as managers of the female orphanage, which now cared for the lives of twenty-one young ladies. Mrs. Seaborn Jones served as the President, and Mrs. Lovick Pierce was the Vice President. Mr. Seaborn Jones was hired as an attorney and financial agent for the Ladies Education and Benevolent Society of the City of Columbus. The society ran its orphanage on donations, and Mr. Jones invested their surplus cash in railroad stocks, which dividends provided for a stable balance sheet. **28** With her parents deeply entwined in her life and her husband's frequent absences, Mary Benning clung to her faith and family for stability. In October of 1859, Reverend and Mrs. Lovick Pierce opened the doors of a new Methodist Church in Columbus, St. Paul. In a show of support for their pastor and dear friends, the Jones family, including their daughter, Mary Benning and her young family, all became charter members. **29**

The year 1859 also saw a radical change in the life of Mary Benning 's cousin, Augusta Jane Evans. Miss Evans had experienced some difficult times, but very dissimilar from her cousin Mary. As a youngster, Augusta's parents Matthew and Sarah experienced a bankruptcy and the mortgage on their mansion " Sherwood Hall " was assumed by Mary's father, Seaborn Jones, and the home was occupied by the Howard family. The Evans family first moved across the river into Alabama, then to San Antonio, Texas during the height of the war with Mexico. The Evans family experienced first-hand the difficulties of the frontier and an ever-observant Augusta recorded her feelings and observations. After the war, the Evans family returned to the east and settled in Summerville, a suburb of Mobile, Alabama. During this time, Augusta developed considerable skill as a young authoress and had even written a book entitled *Inez, A Tale of the Alamo*. In her book, Miss Evans, a devout Methodist, openly attacked Catholicism and challenged their reverence of saints. While the novel was not well received, the Benning-Jones family supported her efforts and encouraged her to write. In an age wherein women were generally discouraged from self-expression, the Southern families of wealth educated their young women in the classics. Both Mary Benning and Augusta Evans grew up amidst personal libraries filled with classic literature. For these women and their many antebellum sisters, independent thought could not be quelled indefinitely.

During the summer of 1859, Augusta submitted another manuscript to prospective publishing firms in New York. This story was a romantic novel entitled *Beulah,* and it was soon destined for fame. Miss Evans dedicated the novel to her Aunt Mary Jones, and her cousin John A. Jones accompanied her to New York to meet with prospective publishers. Upon their arrival, the publishing firm of Appleton promptly denied her proposal.

Undaunted, Augusta and John called upon J. C. Derby ; another respected New York publisher of the firm, Derby and Jackson. Derby later recorded in his memoirs that Augusta was a " young lady of pleasant address and marked intelligence," and he referred to her cousin, John as " a fiery young Southerner." **30** Mr. Derby was impressed with their honest and forthright manners and he agreed to have the novel read by members of his family. At their next meeting, Derby tortured the young couple with suspense concerning his decision. While John Jones appeared disinterested and looked around the room, examining books, he was really preparing to throw a book at Derby the instant he rejected his cousin's book. Mr. Derby continued to toy with Augusta's emotions until he happily informed her that his family had wholeheartedly agreed upon the merits of her novel and that it should be published immediately. Mr. Derby was very impressed with these bold, young Southerners and he also recorded in his memoirs that " Colonel Jones was a most estimable man, devotedly attached to his cousin." **31**

William Fidler, Augusta's biographer, noted that while in New York, she observed first-hand the zeal of the Abolitionists, and upon her return to Mobile, she began writing anonymous editorials in the local newspapers. Her articles were " counter-propaganda" aimed at northern anti-slavery rhetoric and her perception of an immoral people. Augusta returned to New York in the fall of 1859 with her uncle, Augustus Howard. While her visit was to examine galley proofs of her book and await its printing, Augusta began a relationship with the editor of the New York *World,* James Reed Spaulding. Spaulding was an idealistic northern writer, whom was captivated by the talents and charm of a talented young Southern writer. Spaulding courted Augusta tirelessly and even traveled to Mobile and asked her to marry him. Augusta delayed her answer as national events began to drive a wedge in their relationship. **32** Ultimately, their love would be shattered by ominous differences, including the anger of her cousin Mary's husband, Henry Benning, who viewed Augusta's relationship with a Northerner as a betrayal.

Yet, Benning had little time to dwell on the affairs of Augusta Jane Evans. During the latter days of his tenure as an Associate Supreme Court Justice, national events began to overshadow everything and Henry Benning was soon consumed with political passion. In November of 1859, when Benning surrendered his seat on the bench to Judge Richard Lyon, he immediately struck forth in yet another political quest. Elections were being held for delegates to the National Democratic Convention, which was scheduled to be held in the spring, in Charleston, South Carolina. The convention would nominate a candidate and determine the platform for the presidential election of 1860. Henry Benning won a position as a delegate, and gleefully dove back into the Georgia political arena. **33** Although the Columbus Bank Cases and William Dougherty had caused Benning great anguish, he was now free to politically be " in it."

Benning was again in politics, in a new decade with all its opportunities and possibilities. During the time that Benning served on the bench, 1853-1859, the political climate in the South had shifted. A flurry of national events such as the emergence of the pro-abolitionist Republican Party, a severe economic depression in the North, and bloody battles between pro-slavers and abolitionists in the western territories prompted many Southerners to reconsider the ideology of secession. In addition to these events, the Southern populace was outraged when the abolitionist outlaw, John Brown carried out his threat of a southern invasion. In October of 1859, Brown and his band of rebellious followers stormed the federal arsenal at Harper's Ferry, Virginia (now West Virginia), in order to obtain weapons. Brown's plan was to arm the Southern slaves and initiate a race war throughout the south. However, Brown and his rebels were crushed by federal soldiers led by U.S. Colonel Robert E. Lee, and Brown was hanged on December 2, 1859. Southern state militia companies saw an immediate resurgence of volunteers. Furthermore, the resulting paranoia of John Brown 's raid even spurred Southerners to form vigilance committees to screen Northern travelers for potential insurrectionists activities. **34**

Perhaps now, the Southern people would embrace Benning's political ideology of secession. As a Georgia Democratic Delegate, Benning would be " in it," and charged to nominate a candidate and formulate a platform for the next presidential election. While the selection of a Pro-Southern presidential nominee would take major consideration, Benning's theory for a party platform was well known. As he originally expressed in 1849:

> I think that as a remedy for the South, dissolution is not enough,
> and a southern Confederacy not enough...The only thing that
> will do when tried every way is a consolidated Republic formed
> of the Southern States. **35**

Chapter 9

Benning and Columbus, 1860

As the year 1860 began, the ideology of secession was not yet fully emblazoned in the hearts of the Southern people. In Columbus, Georgia, economically, times were good. The city had grown to be the third largest in the State with a total population of 9,621, of which 5,933 were white, 3,547 slaves, and 141 free blacks. Within Muscogee County, 40% of the 1,972 families owned slaves. 1 Henry Benning was a " master" of 96 slaves, while the largest slaveholder in Muscogee County, John Woolfolk owned 180 slaves. 2 Financially, Benning had also achieved the status he so earnestly desired. The 1860 census reflects that among the financially affluent citizens of Muscogee County, Henry Benning ranked eighteenth, with a total net worth of $96,300. In contrast, John Woolfolk ranked sixth, with assets totaling $196,307, while Benning's father-in-law, Seaborn Jones ranked seventh, with a net worth of $179,500. Topping the list of the wealthy Columbusites were two financial agents, J. Rhodes Brown, worth $410,000, and Paul Semmes an agent for the Bank of the State of Georgia and Brigadier General in the Georgia Militia, worth $314,000. The occupations of the twenty wealthiest citizens of Muscogee County, consisted of: five Planters; five Lawyers; four Industrialists/ Finance officers; four Merchants; one Editor; and one Auctioneer. 3 (see Table 1)

General Henry Lewis Benning

Table 1: 20 Wealthiest Citizens of Columbus, Georgia in 1860

	Name	Net Worth	Occupation
1	T. Rhodes Brown	$ 410,900	Bank/ Factory Agent
2	Paul Semmes	$ 314,500	Bank Agent
3	Robert Dixon	$ 300,000	Lawyer
4	John Mustian	$ 270,000	President, Muscogee R.R.
5	John McKee	$ 212,000	Manufacturer
6	John Woolfolk	$ 196,307	Planter
7	Seaborn Jones	$ 179,500	Lawyer
8	Louis Lovington	$ 162,150	Auctioneer
9	Mrs. P. H. Wildman	$ 140,000	Planter
10	Hines Holt	$ 137,200	Lawyer/ Editor
11	John Birch	$ 137,000	Merchant
12	Joel E. Hunt	$ 123,000	Planter
13	Peyton Colquitt	$ 111,000	Lawyer/ Editor
14	Thomas Wynn	$ 111,000	Merchant
15	William Heard	$ 108,398	Planter
16	Joseph H. Daniel	$ 105,200	Merchant
17	James Cook	$ 102,700	Planter
18	**Henry Benning**	**$ 96,300**	**Lawyer/ Judge**
19	Jasper W. Warren	$ 87,000	Editor
20	Joseph Kyle	$ 84,000	Merchant

Henry L. Benning had achieved both professional and personal success. Professionally, his reputation as a talented attorney and respectable jurist was unsurpassed. Equally adept on the farm and reflecting his ancestry of " Old Virginia," Benning was also renowned as a highly capable gentleman planter. While Benning had surpassed the achievements of his forefathers, and risen to the level of aristocratic respect and wealth, he never forsook his agrarian, hard-working familial roots. In personal relations, amongst rich and poor, black and white, Henry Benning was admired, respected, and highly regarded throughout southern society.

Begun in 1835, both Henry L. Benning and the city of Columbus had traversed a parallel course of continuing success and remarkable achievements. Filled with immense potential, both the man and the city had been provided with unique opportunities, and seizing them all, each had achieved success. Benning's personal and professional relations amongst the prominent citizenry of Columbus affected the futures of both the man and the city. In particular, Benning's familial ties with the early Columbus industrial entrepreneurs, Seaborn Jones and John Howard affected both Benning and the city of Columbus. It was Benning's father-in-law, Seaborn Jones, with his City Mills, who established the first industrial operation in Columbus. And John Howard, Mary Benning 's uncle, whose Howard Factory initiated large-scale textile manufacturing in Columbus. Jones had also provided the citizens of Columbus with its first water works, as well as one of its earliest and most trusted law firms.

Financially, the assets of the Jones and Howard families contributed to the growth of the local economy through investments in banking, railroads, planting and industrialization. Their wives served the church and community through their work with female orphans and the impoverished at-large. These selfless contributions to municipal growth, economic support, and the community spirit of Columbus were instrumental in the establishment of the city's foundations. Additionally, the influence and affluence of these two men also affected and contributed to the success of Henry Benning. In return, Benning proudly served the city and state with his able jurist abilities, while his wife, Mary eagerly volunteered her time within the community. Moreover, these entwined relations served to perpetuate the achievements of both Benning and the city of Columbus. Benning's prominent role in state affairs and the city's reputation as the " Lowell of the South " supported the prestige of both. While there were many other families that contributed to the growth of the city, Benning and his family were certainly instrumental in the successful establishment of its roots. As Benning noted upon his arrival in Columbus in 1835, that the " city" was " nearly deserving" of the title, he too, had struggled to achieve success. Thus, within a twenty-five year period, 1835 to 1860, both the city of Columbus, and the man, Henry L. Benning, had successfully transformed from obscurity into prominence.

The rapid growth and established prominence of the city of Columbus was phenomenal. As reflected in the statistics of 1860, Columbus, Georgia was a fully industrialized city. Since Benning's arrival in Columbus, the total population had nearly tripled, and the city had transformed from a frontier " trading town," into an industrial giant. Second only to the city of Richmond, Virginia, Columbus " fabricated more cotton and woolen goods than any Southern county or city." 4 Nestled in the heart of the Southern cotton belt, with major textile mills working the raw fiber into fabric for shipment via steamboat, road and rail, the city's destiny was fulfilled. Early in 1860, The Eagle Manufacturing Company purchased the Howard Factory, and the local newspaper reported," We understand that these factories run 10,000 cotton and 1,300 woolen spindles; that they have 282 looms weaving cotton and 1,000 pounds of wool per day, and employ 500 hands, at an expense of $240 per day for their labor." 5 On a smaller scale, one of the other textile mills ," the Grant Factory produced 480,000 yards of osnaburg, 80,000 yards of kerseys, 78,000 pounds of yarn, and 6,000 pounds of rope." 6 Despite the economic success of these factories, they also generated a social dilemma with which future generations would have to contend. A northern traveler noted while traveling through Columbus," The operatives in the cotton mills are said to be mainly 'Crackers girls' (poor whites), who earn, in good times, by piece work, from $8 to $12 a month." 7 The employees in the textile factories were chiefly female, and predominantly, very young, as the looms required nimble little hands to manipulate the threads and fabrics.

In manufacturing, Columbus had a total of four major textile mills , three large grist mills, a large cotton gin, a steam engine builder, three planing mills, two carriage dealers, an iron works, and a machinist firm. In professional services, the city had 43 Lawyers, 19 Doctors, 6 Dentists, 6 bank agents, 6 insurance agents, and a multitude of service providers. Downtown, Columbus was filled with several book stores, music stores, drug stores, dress makers, hat makers, shoe stores, restaurants, hotels, cigar shops, lumber yards, furniture stores, and a plethora of bars, with names such as " The Smile," and " The Pleasant Hour. " Supporting the financial needs of Columbus remained a challenge, however, and only one bank survived the flurry of insolvency- the Bank of Columbus. 8 The volatile banking industry was representative of the many obstacles presented to a growing city due to growth, diversity, and uncertainty. As an aspiring politician, attorney and jurist, Henry Benning had also faced many challenges and dilemmas. Yet, for Benning, and the city of Columbus, their greatest challenges lay before them.

Amidst this backdrop of growth and success, the events of 1860 unfolded rapidly. From December of 1859, through April of 1860, internal party squabbling and local debates concerning the protocol of the impending " Charleston Convention " resulted in several changes to the Georgia delegation. Benning's brother-in-law, John A. " Jack" Jones was added as a delegate, and Benning became the chairman of the Georgia delegates. Benning's old college chum, Benjamin C. Yancey, and his brother, William Lowndes Yancey, both legislators from Alabama, joined Benning in defining a pro-secessionist strategy. The Democratic Convention met in Charleston, South Carolina on the 23d of April through the 2d of May, but they were unable to reach a consensus on a platform and presidential nominee. Among the choices for president were Stephen Douglas, from Illinois, and Howell Cobb of Georgia, of which the former was the predominate choice. **9** Yet, the Democratic Party could not get beyond the issue of a platform, and as usual in 1860, when Northerners and Southerners engaged in debate, the topic of slavery always rose to the forefront. Present at the convention were delegates from the " majority" , which consisted of the southern slaveholding states, plus Oregon and California, (seventeen states), and the " minority," which consisted of sixteen non-slaveholding states.

Within the delegation, committees were chaired which formulated and presented several platform propositions. The various platforms presented consisted primarily of two schools of thought. First, the " majority" favored a platform that called for congressional protection of slaveholding rights in the south and in the territories. This platform was known as the Cincinnati platform, and naturally, this was the southern platform of choice. Secondly, the other platform consisted of several " minority" variations, which all failed to address slaveholding in the western territories. **10** When the delegates voted on the platform of choice, the minority " squatter sovereignty " platform of Stephen Douglas won. The convention erupted, and William L. Yancey of Alabama addressed the delegates from the northern states with an appeal to return to the north and let the people know," The fate of our country hangs upon the issue...Union or Disunion...Tell them they are pressing the South to the wall." **11** After his speech had ended, he and the majority of the southern delegates walked out, thus seceding from the convention. The Georgia delegation met briefly and split into two parts. Benning and the majority departed while a minority led by Mr. Solomon Cohen, of Savannah remained in hopes that a " better spirit might prevail. 12 With the convention in disarray, a final platform and candidate could not be determined. In the end, while a " better spirit prevailed," the shattered delegation could not attain a viable conclusion, and they voted to reconvene in Baltimore. Some leaders advocated a convention to be held in Richmond. Alexander Stephens supported Baltimore, while Howell Cobb chose Richmond, and Governor Joseph E. Brown suggested a delay. 13 It was all too apparent that people both in the North and South were plunging into an abyss of unrelenting division.

Henry Benning and John A. Jones returned to Columbus, whereupon Benning issued his report stating why the delegates chose to secede from the convention. In his report, based upon pure jurist logic, Benning explained that prior to the exit, the Georgia delegates which seceded carefully reviewed the circumstances facing the delegation and they carefully reviewed three questions: 1. Were the propositions contained in the resolutions true?; 2. Were the democracy of the South at liberty, in honor, to insist upon them?; 3. Were the propositions important to the South?

Benning explained that all of these questions were answered positively, and the other platforms were simply unacceptable. Therefore, based upon this criterion, they chose to leave. Furthermore, he recommended that the same delegation should also attend both the upcoming conventions in Baltimore and Richmond. 14 The minority Georgia delegation which remained in the convention also issued a statement regarding the situation, and agreed that the victorious platform in Charleston was unacceptable. Most southern cities cheered the seceding delegates with cannon fire. In Columbus, a round was fired for William L. Yancey and each of the seceding states. 15

Throughout Georgia, local rallies and speeches were conducted while disjointed efforts to formally organize additional state conventions were debated. Finally, a " Meeting of the Giants " was held in Milledgeville on June 4, 1860, where it was decided that the same Georgia delegation that withdrew in Charleston would attend the Richmond convention. Henry Benning, John Jones and the rest of the Georgia delegation made their way to Richmond, yet again, chaos intervened and the only thing decided in Richmond was to wait until after the Baltimore convention was held on the 21st of June. 16 When the Baltimore convention was held, division immediately occurred as many of the southern delegations which had seceded at Charleston were refused entry to the convention. Interestingly, the Georgia delegates were accepted, but Benning and the other Georgians withdrew after the other southern delegates had been rejected. During the course of the next few days, the convention worsened as Caleb Cushing, the convention chairman resigned. Amidst the piecemeal shattered remnants of a convention, Stephen Douglas was nominated as the candidate for the presidency, and Governor Fitzpatrick of Alabama was chosen as the candidate for Vice-President. Fitzpatrick declined and was replaced by Herschel V. Johnson. Meanwhile the seceding delegates with additional delegates from northern states, with Caleb Cushing as their chairman, hastily organized a National States Rights Convention and met in Richmond. This time, John C. Breckinridge of Kentucky was nominated for President, and Joseph Lane of Oregon was nominated as the Vice-President. Finally, with total chaos permeating the Democratic Party, the self-inflicted political wounds proved fatal. **17**

Meanwhile, the " Black Republicans," as the party was called, officially endorsed the abolitionist from Illinois, Abraham Lincoln. In Columbus, Georgia, the act was considered to be " a declaration of war against the rights of the South," and this would lead to " War." Meanwhile, the ever conservative, pro-Unionist, Alexander Stephens traveled through Columbus with Presidential nominee, Stephen Douglas, where they spoke to the citizens pleading for their votes. **18** In contrast, reflecting the secession spirit voiced ten years earlier, Henry Benning and Martin J. Crawford led rallies and presented pro-Breckinridge speeches aimed against the Black Republicans, and declaring that the South would not submit to the North. Most Georgians including Governor Brown endorsed the Democratic ticket of Breckinridge and Lane. On the eve of the election, Georgia Governor Joseph E. Brown issued a stern warning," Let us have no more *compromises*, and if the full measure of our rights is denied in the future, let us stand by our arms." **19**

The presidential election of 1860 consisted of the following nominees and their respective parties: Abraham Lincoln, Republican; Stephen Douglas, Democrat ; John C. Breckinridge, National Democrat, John Bell, Constitutional Union Party. On November 6, 1860, the votes were tabulated and Republican Abraham Lincoln was elected as the sixteenth President of the United States. The results of the election were (popular vote) Lincoln, 40%; Douglas 29%; Breckinridge, 18%; and Bell, 13%. The results of the electoral vote: Lincoln 180; Breckinridge, 72; Bell, 39; Douglas, 12. Lincoln carried all of the northern states, while Breckinridge took the southern states excepting Missouri (carried by Douglas), and Kentucky, Tennessee, and Virginia, carried by Bell. **20** These statistics are important because Lincoln did not achieve the majority of the popular vote. As evidenced, 60% of the people voted for someone other than Lincoln. Moreover, the electoral vote was obviously split between the North and South, and these circumstances as viewed by the southern populace provided support to refute the election.

After the election, the local southern state militias began preparing for war as " secession fever" spread throughout the south. In the capital city of Milledgeville, Georgia, the state legislature delved into session where it contended with the most critical issues and its gravest crisis in state history. The representatives were swamped with messages from other state representatives, local constituents, and even the Governor, whom advocated secession. Governor Brown dispatched a special message on November 7, 1860, calling on the legislature to prepare for the defense of Georgia, that in his opinion, the Southern states had the Constitutional right to secede, and he urged them to form a secession convention. While the message was lengthy, the Governor left little doubt as to what he viewed as the proper course of action. Governor Brown's remarks can be summed up in his words with," In my opinion, the time for bold, decided action has arrived... The argument is exhausted, and we now stand by our arms." 21

The state legislators also received resolutions from various counties addressed to their representatives. Muscogee County included the following resolutions in their message:

> *Resolved,* That the election of Abraham Lincoln and Hannibal Hamlin to the President and vice-presidency of the United States ought not to be, and will not be submitted to.

> *Resolved,* That we respectfully suggest to the Legislature to take immediate steps to organize and arm the forces of the State. 22

Muscogee County and most other Georgia counties also included a resolution urging a convention to " redress" the crisis. Actually, the Georgia legislature was already prepared to debate secession during its current session, and had invited Henry Benning, Thomas R. R. Cobb, Alexander Stephens, Robert Toombs, Herschel V. Johnson, Martin J. Crawford and other prominent Georgians to address the legislature during the week of November 12-18, 1860. On November 15, 1860, the legislature responded to the desires of the Governor and the people of Georgia by scheduling a formal convention to be held on the first Wednesday in January 1861. The same legislative committee addressed communications to prominent Georgians requesting their attendance at the convention and to provide their learned advice concerning what course of " resistance" Georgia should follow. Among this virtual " who's who" of Georgia, the following men were requested to attend: Joseph E. Brown ; Robert Toombs, Alexander Stephens ; Joseph Lumpkin ; Richard Lyon ; Linton Stephens ; Thomas R. R. Cobb ; Herschel V. Johnson ; Benjamin H. Hill ; John H. Howard ; Martin J. Crawford ; and Henry L. Benning. 23

Several of these men were already attending the current legislative session and were prepared for an historic showdown. With great forethought, the legislature was prepared to hear speeches, both pro and con concerning secession. In the Hall of the House of Representatives, Thomas R. R. Cobb led the debate with a presentation delivered on Monday, November 12, 1860. While his brother, Howell Cobb was still serving in Washington as President Buchanan's Secretary of Treasury; the younger Cobb had embraced the ideology of Henry Benning and was now a devout secessionist. Thomas Cobb poured his heart into a well prepared speech, which called for an end to party politics, to " bury the hatchet of controversy," and he called for " immediate unconditional secession." 24 Cobb also stated that he had studied and prayed about the dilemmas facing the South, and his conclusions had been reached through logic and divine guidance. Cobb very eloquently outlined his justification for secession highlighting that in his opinion: the recent election was unconstitutional; that a delayed decision would only strengthen the north; that soon Federal authorities would be in Georgia prosecuting slaveowners; and that he feared for the future of the South. As he neared the end of his speech, its tone turned from logical persuasion to a passionate cry, and he added," I think I see in the future a gory head rise above our horizon. Its name is Civil War. " Moreover, his conclusion reached a powerful crescendo and terminated with," put a tongue in every bleeding wound of Georgia's mangled honor which shall cry to Heaven for " Liberty or Death!" 25

Following Cobb's oration on November 13, 1860, was the speech of the effervescent Robert Toombs. Toombs had long been a favorite son of Georgia. Toombs was an accomplished attorney, a Congressman, Senator, successful planter, and he was ultimately, a consummate politician. Still serving as a U. S. Senator, after years of encouraging pro-Union rhetoric, Toombs was torn between loyalty to the Union and his love for Georgia. Yet, within the midst of crisis, the rising tide of disunion, and the obvious Southern rejection of Lincoln, Toombs was now leaning towards secession. Toombs had achieved one of those " fat places" that Benning so earnestly craved as a youth. Yet in Milledgeville, Toombs displayed a willingness to cast off his cloak of security and " to meet the conflict with the dignity and firmness of men worthy of freedom." 26 His speech reflected the uncertainty which Toombs was certainly experiencing, and he seemed to be searching within himself for justification to secede. Like Howell Cobb, with his wealth and position in Washington D. C., Toombs was simply behind the times and out of touch with the sentiment of most Georgians. The Toombs speech is laced with romantic notions such as " vindication of our manhood... defense of our rights, and, we need no declaration of independence." After a lengthy dissertation which supports secession, and that Southerners have simply claimed respect of their rights and justice, Toombs concludes his speech with " Emblazon it on your banner- fight for it, win it, or perish in the effort." 27 While his speech was not as effective as the passionate appeal of Thomas Cobbs, it indicated that Toombs was committed to secession, and his support carried a lot of weight with the men of Georgia. With Toombs aligned with the secessionists, any counter argument would require the skills of a remarkable politician.

On November 14, 1860, the Honorable Alexander Stephens addressed the legislature. Commonly known as " Little Aleck," Stephen's physical stature was small and frail, yet in many ways, he was a giant among his peers. Following his old friend in presentation order, the massive and manly character of Toombs stepped down as " Little Aleck," with his high-pitched voice took center stage. Toombs and Stephens were opposites in many ways, but they were also genuinely close friends, and their relationship complemented one another. While Toombs was brash and impetuous, Stephens was cool and restrained. Both Stephens and Toombs were experienced politicians and tactful orators, but Stephen's intellect and soft-spoken nature mesmerized audiences with his logic and humanistic appeal. With his usual quiet resolve, he delivered the anti-thesis to secession.

Despite the fact that he was a frail little man with a weak wispy voice, Stephen's mind was sharp and he focused his efforts on the task at hand. He knew that he faced a resistant audience. Throughout his years of public service, Stephens had always favored conservative restraint and served to bolster pro-Unionist thought. For years, he had worked to maintain open dialog with northern politicians and he felt confidant that the dilemma could be resolved as a nation. In Milledgeville, Stephens faced overwhelming odds. Yet, with an earnest display of his courage and convictions, he presented a valid argument against secession. Armed with intelligent dialog, Stephens made Toombs look like a buffoon. His argument was delivered in a clear and concise manner, which called for moderation and continued debate with the North.

Stephens began with," My object is not to stir up strife, but to allay it; not to appeal to your passions, but to your reason. Let us therefore reason together." **28** After establishing a tranquil mood, Stephens points out that the election of Lincoln is not in itself, adequate cause for secession. He argued that a Democratic majority in the House and Senate would restrict Lincoln's actions. Stephens highlighted several important components of the Toombs speech, and argued against them. Specifically, Stephens countered fears which Toombs had raised concerning topics such as the " evils" of the northern governments, submitting to " Black Republican rule," and the imposition of possible tariffs, which were met with applause from the audience, yet laced with frequent obnoxious comments from Toombs. Yet, Stephens simply used Toombs' comments to make additional counter-points. Stephens then argued at length that in spite of the rancor displayed in the North, historically, Georgia had prospered. He further suggested that Georgia should engage the north, and the other disgruntled Southern states with more dialog, and if it does not work," I should be willing as a last resort, to sever the ties of our Union with them." **29** Stephens concluded his speech with an appeal urging the audience to follow the state motto-Wisdom, Justice and Moderation. Ending his speech on a positive upbeat note, the audience applauded his remarks.

Stephens provided the legislature with an alternative to secession, and the next few speeches delivered by Benjamin H. Hill and Herschel V. Johnson, delivered on November 15 and 16, 1860, reflected the same sentiment. Yet, for most Georgians, this prudent course laced with continuing dialog seemed largely a waste of time. As Governor Brown stated earlier," the argument is exhausted." On November 19, 1860, the final speech was delivered before the Georgia legislature. The final oration was provided by Henry L. Benning, thus, the speeches ended where they had begun, with the voice of secession. After eleven long years of perfecting his argument, Henry Benning was now in a position to deliver the most powerful speech of his career. Blending well-hewn points of jurist logic with passionate appeals, Benning commenced his speech with," Fellow citizens: The points for our consideration are, what is the disease - the precise disease under which the South is laboring and what is the remedy? **30**

Benning then proposed that the " Black Republican" election of Lincoln would signal a definite termination of slavery. He pointed to history, and highlighted that the people supporting Lincoln were the same lot that refused to honor the Fugitive Slave Act. Benning also predicted that in the future, the North would rapidly dissolve and abolish slavery throughout the nation. Benning highlighted that the elected leadership and the entire Black Republican party " hates slavery; that is the word-hates slavery." **31** Benning then summarizes and repeats his first proposition that as soon as possible, the newly elected party will abolish slavery. Benning continued with:

> My second proposition is that the North will soon acquire that power, unless something is done to prevent it... The North has now eighteen States, and the South fifteen. The whole of the public territory of the United States may at this time be said to be Northern territory. This is painfully true, and it is conclusive evidence that we shall have no more slave States from the public territory. **32**

With great detail and deductive logic, Benning argues that all too soon, only within the eight cotton producing states will slavery exist. Benning then warns that once the slaveholding states have been reduced in numbers, the North, which is the Black Republican party, will simply amend the Constitution, and " It will then take the power to emancipate your slaves, and to hang you if you resist their emancipation. " **33** Benning then mentions that in his opinion, the north will not wait, that they will simply appeal to a " higher law" expressed by New York Senator William Seward, whom believed that in certain cases, moral law should circumvent constitutional law.

Benning then introduces his third proposition that abolition would be a horrible calamity in the South, and that it will create a race war. Then, the north will side with the Negroes, and defeat the Southern people, exploiting the land and fully conquering the southern states. Benning then examines possible methods of addressing abolition and to keep the north from imposing it upon the south. He supposes that even if a constitutional amendment were one supporting slavery, the north would simply ignore it. Benning then states that in the North slavery is considered to be sinful, criminal and in " a league with hell and covenant with death. " Benning then states that due to the feelings in the North, that this sentiment will keep them from abiding by pro-slavery covenants. Benning added that when dealing with northern politicians:

> Constitutions are of no efficacy, promises are of no avail, because she holds them to be void when they favor slavery. Even, then, if we could get such amendments as these to the Constitution, the remedy would be ineffective, insufficient.

Why? Because the North would not keep them, and that same
hatred to slavery would still exist. **34**

Benning then addresses solutions or " remedies to the disease " as
expressed by other gentlemen from the South. Benning highlighted the
plans expressed by Stephens and Hill as unrealistic, unattainable and filled
with delay. Delays that would inevitably provide the North time to
strengthen their anti-slavery position. Benning then provides a viable
solution to the " disease," stating that within the Union they will not find a
remedy. Benning declares that the only remedy available must be sought
from outside of the Union. Benning emphasized his stance declaring:

> Well, I say that a separation from the North would be a
> complete remedy for the disease -a complete remedy for both
> diseases, a remedy not merely to prevent abolition, but also to
> heal the fugitive slave ulcer. How would it do this? If you were
> to separate from the North, the *power* to abolish slavery by the
> North would be taken away. That is clear. The *will* to do so
> would also cease. **35**

Benning then states that disunion is the only logical choice. He then
questions why not separate and what arguments are there to the contrary?
Benning mentions that some people express fears that not enough states
will exit the Union, thus leaving those that do secede in jeopardy. Benning
declares that like brothers, the Southern states will rush to assist one
another. But Benning also adds that even if the other Southern states fail to
follow Georgia in secession, that the right thing is to go it alone if
necessary because:

> We should be able ourselves to maintain our cause.-(Loud
> cheers.) If they [other states] choose to keep their connection
> with the northern states let them do so. Men of Georgia! it is our
> business to save ourselves. (Continued applause.) And if
> nothing else will save us but going out of the Union, we must go
> out of the Union, however much we may deplore it. **36**

Benning then addresses the question of Southern preparedness for
war, and the fear expressed by some, that the Union would destroy the
South. Benning highlights that in his opinion the South is just as prepared

if not more so than the North. He points to the militias, the military schools throughout the south and " These schools will furnish our army with most accomplished officers, and when you have good officers, you will soon have good men." 37

Benning then focuses upon the strength of finances in the South, and the possibility that England may assist the south, as Europe depends upon the south for cotton. Furthermore, Benning adds that the northern states are dependent upon the south for marketing of their goods. Benning also predicts that secession may even force the north into bankruptcy. Benning then provides a very detailed and lengthy accounting of the manufacturing, capital, and debts, which support his theory of bankrupting the North, and bolsters his opinion that the South will become even more financially solvent upon the act of disunion.

The great jurist then delves back into the realm of the Constitution and the rights of men to seek self-preservation. He stresses that Lincoln and the Black Republicans seek to destroy the South and slavery, and then Benning appeals to the audience to adopt his remedy for the disease - secession. Then, in a forceful, passionate plea, Benning culminates his speech with:

Why hesitate? The question is between life and death. Well, if these things be so, let us do our duty; and what is our duty? I say, men of Georgia, let us lift up our voices and shout," Ho! for independence!" [Prolonged applause.] Let us follow the example of our ancestors, and prove ourselves worthy sons of worthy sires! 38

When the secession debate ended, the legislature took additional measures to bolster the states war footing by enacting into law an authorization for raising 10,000 troops, ordering rifles, carbines, coastal defense preparations, and an appropriation of one million dollars for military purposes. 39 On the 21st of November, 1860, the legislature also drafted an act authorizing and requiring the Governor to issue a proclamation for a state convention to be held on January 23, 1861, in Milledgeville, to determine a course of resistance for the State of Georgia. This act also called for each county to select two or three delegates, depending on the Act of apportionment (Muscogee County was authorized three). Immediately, Governor Brown issued his proclamation as directed by the legislature. 40

Returning home to Columbus, Benning was the man of the hour, as friends as well as former political foes rallied with Benning and embraced the desire to secede. A military organization was formed called the "

Southern Guard. " Paul Semmes, a long-time state and local militia leader provided leadership in organizing and preparing Columbus units for war. In Columbus, Martin J. Crawford, B. A. Thornton, Peyton Colquitt, and Alabama's William Yancey, all friends and allies of Benning joined him in stumping for secession. Benning traveled throughout the surrounding counties delivering his secession speech. After hearing Benning speak at one of the local rallies, Arthur Hood wrote to Howell Cobb," Benning made a glorious speech on Monday," and he pled with Cobb to join the secessionists. **41** A small remnant of pro-Unionist remained in Columbus, and ran against the pro-secessionist for the opportunity to represent Muscogee County at the upcoming convention. Among these men were attorneys Porter Ingram, Nicholas Howard, and Hines Holt ; however, they were duly defeated by Henry Benning, A. L. Rutherford, and James N. Ramsey. Even his old political nemesis, Judge James Johnson joined Henry Benning in the secessionist movement. Johnson, a future Governor of Georgia, was considered by many as the " Bell-weather of the Union party in this section of the State." **42**

While " secession fever" ran rampant throughout the South, most states proceeded along an orderly plan of debate.
In South Carolina, where many sectors of the state were predominantly black, fanatical emotionalism and rumors spread like wildfire. The state legislature had planned to conduct a convention to address the " crisis" in January, yet the fevered pitch of secession swept the state and the date was moved up. On December 20, 1860, the South Carolina State Convention met in Charleston and unanimously voted to secede from the Union. In Columbus, Georgia, the event was celebrated with great enthusiasm. " Bonfires blazed in the streets, fireworks sparkled and hissed, and altogether it was an extraordinary and most exciting and impressive spectacle." **43**

The people of the North simply failed to grasp how desperately the South clung to their beliefs, their institutions, and ultimately, their quest for self-preservation. The thought of forced abolition and emancipation was viewed by most Southerners, and especially Henry Benning, as a " disease. " Therefore, as Benning had expressed, secession was the only logical cure for the disease. Furthermore, this disease produced a genuine fear, and throughout the Southern states, the general belief was that:

> Emancipation would lead ultimately to the breakdown of all
> racial barriers and taboos and to the final degradation of
> amalgamation- a theme that was used widely in the campaign of

emotionalism, which preceded secession. These apprehensions over the future alarmed all classes of Southern society, non-slaveholders, as well as masters, and seemed to justify secession and in the last extremity a resort to war. **44**

Chapter 10

Secession and the Confederacy

Secession did not achieve mass approval until its ideology was viewed by the common Southerner as a valid struggle of rebellion against tyranny. Moreover, the theme of independence, which bonded the Union in 1776, resurfaced as a force of disunion in 1861. Throughout the South, newspapers re-published the Colonial era writings of men such as John Hancock and Thomas Jefferson. The articles were used in conjunction with editorials to highlight and draw parallels between the rebellion experiences of the founding fathers and the Southern dilemma of secession. Traces of this theme are interlaced within the secessionist speeches of Thomas R. R. Cobb and Henry Benning. 1

It must be remembered that the generation of Southerners debating a dissolution of the Union was the grandsons of those whom had fought to form it. For example, the grandfathers of Benning and Cobb, were veterans of the American Revolution, as were the forefathers of many Southerners. In Virginia, one of the most fervent secessionists was George Wythe Randolph, the grandson of Thomas Jefferson. These men were not acting impulsively. For Benning, he had been advocating the idea of secession since 1849. Ultimately, these men equated the tyrannical and oppressive ideology of Abraham Lincoln with that of King George III, which in their minds validated the cause of secession. While the ante-bellum era was dominated by the thoughts of men, Southern women also embraced the cause. The women's grandparents had also participated in the Revolution, and they too, equally despised the North. Quietly, behind the scenes, women caught " secession fever " and provided their husbands, fathers and sons with support. The ancient code of chivalry was very much alive in the South and with the support of their ladies, the pride and honor of Southern manhood was now at stake. In Benning's secession speech, he predicted in graphic detail the likely scenario if abolition was enacted and a war

defeated the South. He warned that," as for the women, they will call upon
the mountains to fall upon them." 2

One Southern lady recorded in her diary," We separated from the
North because of incompatibility of temper; we are divorced, North from
South, because we have hated each other so." 3 As the date of the Georgia
convention neared, Augusta Jane Evans, Mary Benning 's cousin
corresponded with Mary and Henry Benning, expressing her views. Miss
Evans, as a writer, had numerous acquaintances in the news media. A
female newspaper editor, Mrs. G. Virginia French, of the Atlanta
Crusader, had requested that Miss Evans join her in a pro-Unionist "
representative women of America" demonstration at the convention. Miss
Evans referred to this group as a " band of latter day Tories," and she felt
that the convention should be strictly " an occasion when women should
leave matters entirely to the wisdom of our statesmen." 4

Rumors had circulated throughout social circles in Milledgeville and
Columbus, that Miss Evans was planning to marry a Northern," Black
Republican" editor. Miss Evan's family, including the Bennings, was very
upset with her, and she promptly denied the affair. 5 Perhaps, through her
letter, she was seeking to regain Henry Benning 's good favor and at the
same time provide Benning with a woman's perspective of the situation.
Moreover, Miss Evans portrays her ability to write, and within a few years,
she became a best selling novelist. She also enclosed a letter she had
written to Mrs. French, which highlighted her feelings concerning the
North. The letter was very lengthy and liberal excerpts provide a uniquely
feminine perspective of the Southern state of mind on the verge of
secession. Miss Evans mentions that " if it were my privilege to address my
countrymen of Georgia on the 16th," she would state the following:

I am an earnest and most uncompromising Secessionist...For fifteen years, we of the South, have endured insult and aggression, have ironed down our just indignation, and suffered numberless encroachments because of our devotion to the Union... Presuming upon this devotion, northern fanaticism has grown on Southern endurance.... waves of Abolitionism, have rolled rapidly on till they threaten to pollute the sacred precincts of the " <u>White</u> <u>House</u>. " The Union has become a misnomer, and rather than witness the desecration of our glorious fame, we of the South will Sampson-like lay hold upon the pillars, and if need be, perish in its ruins... the law of self-preservation is imperative and as the thirteen States cut the chains of Great Britain to regain their birth right- Freedom; so we in the South sever the links that bind us to a people, who guided by the Demon of fanaticism; have insanely destroyed the ablest government, which the accumulated wisdom of centuries has ever erected... I regard it as an economy of blood, for the fifteen states to secede as promptly as possible... if necessary [we] will drain our veins rather than yield to the ignominious rule of Black Republicanism. As a native of the Empire State of the South, my heart clings to her soil, and I look forward to the meeting of her convention with a triumphant assurance that " knowing her rights, she dare maintain them;" and that in the calmest days of our coming Confederacy, I shall look back to the 16th of Jan., 1861, and exclaim exultantly," <u>I too am a Georgian</u>."... Delay is ruinous, suicidal- " <u>the time has come</u>." Such are my views regarding the vital issues of the day. 6

As the Georgia convention approached, the tension was compounded as Mississippi seceded on January 9; Florida on the 10th; Alabama, on the 11th; and finally it was Georgia's turn to formally consider the matter. Held in the antebellum capital of Milledgeville," The secession convention was the ablest body ever convened in Georgia." 7 There was little need for debate, however, as directed by proclamation of the Governor, Joseph E. Brown, the Convention of the people of Georgia began at 10:30 a.m. and it was initially chaired by Henry Lewis Benning of Columbus, Georgia. A roll call of the delegates was conducted, and Benning suggested that the convention should begin " with the blessings of God," and Reverend Williamson, a delegate from Telfair County, led an opening prayer. 8 The

President of the convention, the Honorable George W. Crawford, assumed the chair, and the historic convention was begun.

In a rapid sequence of events, rules were established, providing for organization and secrecy. By January 18, a vote established that Georgia would formally draft an Ordinance of Secession. Henry Benning was appointed by the President of the convention, the Honorable George W. Crawford, as one of seventeen authors of the Ordinance of Secession. A former opponent of the secessionist movement, the man whom Benning had defeated for his seat in the Supreme Court, Eugenius A. Nisbet chaired the committee and was given credit as the author of the ordnance. 9 Meanwhile, Governor Brown ordered that the federal garrison at Fort Pulaski, Georgia, be seized by Georgia troops. The convention voted a measure supporting the action of the Governor. On the same date, the convention was presented with a communications from the State of New York that stated clearly, that Georgia had joined South Carolina in committing treasonous acts in violation with the Constitution. The convention continued with the assembly of resolutions and voting on changes. On the 19th day of January 1861, at 2:00 p.m., the convention approved the final draft and affirmed that Georgia would secede from the Union. The vote tally was 208 yeas and 89 nays. On January 21, 1860 at 12:00 p.m., Governor Brown announced that the " hour had arrived." The Governor affixed his signature to the Ordinance of Secession, followed by the delegates of the convention, and then, with the seal of the State affixed to the document, the State of Georgia seceded from the Union.

Its final declarative paragraph states:

> The Union now subsisting between the State of Georgia and
> other States, under the name of the United States of America, is
> hereby dissolved, and that the State of Georgia is in the full
> possession and exercise of all those rights of sovereignty, which
> belong and appertain to a free and independent State. 10

Before termination of the convention, Robert Toombs was appointed
as the chair of the Foreign Relations committee, Henry Benning was
assigned to the Committee on the Relations with the slave holding states,
and Alexander Stephens and Thomas R. R. Cobb, were appointed to the
Committee to form a new Constitution of the State. 11 On January 24,
1861, representatives were selected to attend a proposed Southern
Convention to explore the formation of a congress of Confederate States,
to be held on February 4, 1861. This delegation included: Martin J.
Crawford ; Howell Cobb ; Thomas R. R. Cobb, Robert Toombs ;
Alexander Stephens ; Eugenius Nisbet and Benjamin H. Hill. 12 On
January 28, 1861, Toombs, as the chairman of the Committee on Foreign
Relations, appointed Henry Benning as the Commissioner to the State of
Virginia, with the assignment of providing that state with influence and
assistance concerning secession. Benning was also considered for a
position in the President's cabinet. 13 Meanwhile, Governor Brown
ordered the following facilities be taken into State custody: U.S. Federal
Arsenal in Augusta, Georgia on Jan. 24, 1861; The Oglethorpe Barracks
and Fort Jackson in Savannah, on Jan. 26, 1861, and they were all
promptly seized by troops of the Georgia militia. 14
Throughout these momentous occasions, Georgia was rocked with a
wave of hysteria. In Benning's hometown," the most brilliant display ever
witnessed in Columbus," filled the streets with military parades, ladies in
their best gowns, and torchlight processions. Above the streets, the air was
full of fireworks, patriotic banners, the clanging of church bells, cannon
fire, marching bands, shouts of cheer and enthusiastic speeches. 15
Volunteers joined the military companies, forcing the establishment of new
units. In addition to the ever-vigilant Columbus Guards, by February of
1861, Columbus also had the Southern Guard ; City Light Guards ;
Georgia Grays ; and the Muscogee Mounted Rangers. 16

Equipped with uniforms manufactured by the Eagle Mills, and outfitted with arms, these units formed the initial vanguard of the city's voluntary spirit. Under the watchful eye of Brigadier General Paul Semmes of the Georgia State Militia, these companies drilled and practiced in the city commons. 17 Recruitment was robust, as the entire community was filled with martial spirit and enthusiastic support. Additionally, the Columbus manufacturing firms and local entrepreneurs converted their production efforts to meet the needs of the military. Local entrepreneurial merchants and textile firms won contracts to supply military buttons embossed with the Georgia coat of arms, tubs, buckets, tents, shoes, and uniforms. 18

Meanwhile, the Southern Convention assembled in Montgomery, Alabama, on February 4, 1861, initiating a host of tasks necessary to the creation of a new country. The convention was in session for five weeks, and it included representatives from seven states: South Carolina, Mississippi, Florida, Alabama, Georgia, Louisiana and Texas. The other Southern states had not yet committed to secession, although non-seceded states were invited, their representation was negligible. The President of the Convention was Howell Cobb, having resigned from his office as the U.S. Secretary of Treasury, in the Buchanan administration. Among the numerous decisions achieved during the convention were: The formation of a provisional government of the " Confederate States of America ;" the former U. S. Secretary of War and Senator from Mississippi, Jefferson Davis, was elected as the President of the Confederacy ; the vice-presidency went to Alexander Stephens, of Georgia, whom interestingly had voted against secession. President Davis appointed Robert Toombs to the position of Secretary of State ; Hines Holt, was elected as the Third District Representative, Confederate Congress ; and Martin J. Crawford, of Georgia was selected to lead a peace commission to Washington D. C. On February 16, 1861, Howell Cobb administered the oath of office, and Jefferson Davis was inaugurated as the President of the Confederacy. The " Columbus Guards," led by their commander, Paul Semmes, was dispatched to Montgomery, and they provided President Davis with his first military escort and salute. 19

While the Congress of the Convention of the Confederate States of America took place in Montgomery, emissaries were dispatched from Georgia in accordance with the Ordinance of Secession. Henry Benning traveled to Richmond, where the Virginia Convention began on February 13, 1861. Benning delivered nearly the same secessionist speech he had delivered in Georgia, with several minor variations oriented specifically to the people of Virginia. Virginia was a very important state to the Confederacy, as it was very wealthy and bordered the capital of the United States. Benning highlighted the reasons why Georgia seceded, the strength of the Confederacy and the economic foundations established to support their newly formed nation. Benning also included an in-depth analysis of the overwhelming tide of pro-abolition in the North and their numerous violations of the Constitution. His arguments had been well honed during both the Georgia secession and the formation of the Confederacy. Benning's mission to Virginia was ominously important to the Confederacy. His task was no less than to convince the people of the State of Virginia to leave their country and join another one. Without Virginia, the Southern Confederacy would face strategic difficulties, yet the newly formed nation was already committed to their cause with or without Virginia. Inevitably, Benning and the other members of the Confederate cabinet knew that the dilemma the Virginians faced was the same one they too had faced, and it tore at their hearts. In Benning's closing phrases he appealed to the Virginians with," Above all, we have a cause- the cause of honor, and liberty, and property, and self-preservation." 20

Ultimately, Benning's mission was successful, yet Virginia proved to be a difficult state to sway into secession. Wise Virginians knew that due to their geographic position, danger was imminent. The majority of people in the western part of the state were ardently opposed to secession. While Benning was instrumental in urging the state to join the Confederacy, Virginia did not officially secede until after hostilities occurred at Fort Sumter, South Carolina. At that point, Lincoln requested troops and assistance from Virginia, forcing it to make a decision. Virginia officially endorsed secession on April 17, 1861, and " was no longer a member of the Federal Union, but in a new, heart to heart, defiant union with the Confederate States of the South." 21

During the meeting of the Confederate Congress, in Montgomery, Georgians, Alexander Stephens and Thomas R. R. Cobb, contributed greatly to the authorship and construction of the Constitution of the Confederate States of America. This document is very similar to the construction of the U. S. Constitution with the exception of several variations, which addressed specific Southern issues. For example, the preamble reflects the Southerners fervent religious beliefs, which invokes " the favor and guidance of Almighty God." Articles IV, V, and VI are devoted to states' rights, and Article I, Section nine, number four states," no law denying or impairing the right of property in Negro slaves shall be passed." On March 11, 1861, the government of the Confederate States of America adopted the Constitution. The document was official signed by the following men of Georgia: Martin J. Crawford ; Thomas R. R. Cobb ;

Francis S. Bartow and Benjamin H. Hill. **22** In Milledgeville, the ongoing Georgia convention continued its work on important matters of state, and ratified the Confederate Constitution. Henry Benning, having returned to his seat at the ongoing convention, voted in support of ratification of the Confederate Constitution. **23**

At the same time, Martin J. Crawford, of Georgia, John Forsythe of Alabama, and A B. Roman, of Louisiana, was in Washington D. C, performing their assigned duties as the Confederate Peace Commission to the United States government. Their duties were " for the purpose of negotiating friendly relations between that government and the Confederate States of America, and for the settlement of all questions of disagreement between the two governments upon principles of right, justice, equity, and good faith." **24** One of their primary duties was to negotiate the removal of federal troops from the garrisons of Fort Sumter, and Fort Pickens. Upon their arrival, they contacted Mr. Seward, the Secretary of State, whom coldly ignored their repeated efforts to conduct dialog. Seward established an intermediary, Supreme Court Justice Campbell, of Alabama. The commissioners were generally ignored, until they discovered that secretly the U. S. government was maneuvering troops and transports to reinforce the federal posts in the South. Finally on April 8, the commissioners demanded an honest response, whereupon, they were informed that the President had " determined to hold no intercourse with them whatever; to refuse even to listen to any proposals they had to make." **25**

The commissioners reported their news to President Davis, whereupon he remarked to the Confederate Congress," The crooked paths of diplomacy can scarcely furnish an example so wanting in courtesy, in candor, and directness, as was the course of the United States Government towards our commissioners in Washington. " **26** Martin Crawford and the other commissioners returned to the South. At the same time, a large federal fleet was sailing southward to reinforce Fort Sumter. Brigadier General P.G.T. Beuregard initiated the bombardment of Fort Sumter at 4:30 A.M., April 12, 1861. The next day, the garrison at Fort Sumter surrendered, effectively commencing a civil war. **27** Concurrently, a giant gasp, both North and South, was immediately followed by calls for War! War! War! While both sides pondered the impending fray, they prepared to man and equip their armies. On May 20, 1861, the Confederate capital was moved to Richmond, Virginia, where serious military and political organization began to take effect. With Virginia in the Confederacy, Arkansas, Tennessee and North Carolina soon followed, thus forming the eleven-state confederacy known as the Confederate States of America.

In Washington, Lincoln called for troops, and the Confederacy did likewise. In Columbus, Company D of the " Southern Guard" had already departed to become a part of the First Georgia Volunteer Infantry Regiment. Shortly thereafter, the Columbus Guards departed for their first assignment with the Second Infantry Regiment. General Paul Semmes resigned from his post in the Georgia Militia, accepted the rank of Colonel, and was assigned to command the Second Georgia Infantry Regiment, in Savannah. 28 A local merchant, F. W. Dillard was commissioned as a Captain in the Quartermaster Corps, and became a purchasing and contract agent for the Confederate military. He gained a promotion to Major and was placed in charge of the Columbus Depot, coordinating the efforts of local manufacturing firms with the needs of the Confederacy. His work in the supply of uniforms, tents, and knapsacks, greatly benefited Columbus and the Confederacy. 29 Columbus contributed to the Confederacy with immense contributions of men and material. Throughout the war, manufacturing firms provided a constant supply of material, and as the war progressed, Columbus increased production. Furthermore, as the war progressed, the city expanded its base of war produce with the manufacturing of rifles, pistols, swords, and several gunboats, as Dillard was promoted to the rank of Colonel, and Confederate purchasing agent for the Chattahoochee region. 30

Throughout the Confederacy, 1861 was a year in which Southerners poured their hearts into the war effort. In Columbus, Henry Benning and Seaborn Jones invested heavily in Confederate bonds. In March of 1861, Benning served as a local commissioner in securing the five million-dollar portion of Georgia's contribution to the Confederate loan program, organized to generate capital for the Confederacy. Additionally, in July, Benning joined a group of eighteen Columbus cotton growers in pledging 1,510 bales of cotton for the Confederate cause. Valued at $75,000, the gentlemen of Columbus set a worthy example for their fellow Southerners to emulate. 31

Seaborn Jones also made pledges to the Confederate cause. Opening his heart and his wallet, Seaborn Jones made public challenges to match his generosity to the cause. An article appearing in the local paper read," For our Country, who will unite with the undersigned, by putting in one hundred dollars each, to buy Bowie knives for the First Rifle Regiment. Seaborn Jones. " 32 With all the excitement of the impending crisis, the old code of chivalry leaned heavily on all Southern men. Henry Benning set forth to personally raise his own regiment and he encouraged the men of Columbus as well as the surrounding counties to volunteer for military service. Benning had thrust his heart and soul into the cause of secession, and with that victory achieved, he was prepared to bear its full cost. If necessary, Benning was ready to give his life for the continuation of a cause in which he so deeply believed. The chasm between North and South as he had predicted, so many years ago, would eventually culminate with war. Concerning the impending war, Benning remarked," War is upon us- a war which we did nothing to provoke and everything to avert." **33** Benning sincerely felt that the Southern states had constitutionally and peacefully withdrawn from the Union, and he was prepared to defend that right on the field of battle. Yet, Benning also realized the importance of preparation and training for war. He would wage battle as he had done in court, with courage, logic, diligence, and skill. His men would work hard, drill, and pursue their foe with an unwavering spirit. He warned his recruits, unless they possessed " more skills" and " more courage" than their enemy, the war would end in our " abject subjugation." **34**

Meanwhile, both Howell and his brother, Thomas R. R. Cobb were busy raising units in their hometown of Athens and Clarke County. Again," Fatty " bested Henry Benning, as Howell Cobb gained a commission as a colonel and took command of the Sixteenth Georgia Volunteer Infantry. **35** Henry Benning immediately followed suit and was commissioned as a colonel and given command of the Seventeenth Georgia Infantry Regiment. **36** On June 20, 1861, Henry's son, Seaborn Jones Benning graduated from the Georgia Military Institute, and he was appointed by his father to the position of regimental Sergeant Major. **37**

Numerous friends and acquaintances of Henry Benning volunteered for military service, and during the course of the war, most of them would serve under his command. Henry Benning 's brother-in-law, John A. " Jack" Jones formed his own company, which became Company I, of the 20th regiment. Captain Jones was a respected leader who had led men during the Creek and Mexican Wars. Jones appointed his brother-in-law, First Lieutenant Van Asbury Leonard, as his second in command. Captain Jones and Lieutenant Leonard gave their company the sobriquet," Southern Guards. " Jones's son, Seaborn Leonard Jones, an underclassman at the Georgia Military Institute in Marietta, left school, returned to Columbus and volunteered for service in his father's unit. Known by his family and friends as Leonard, he was named in honor of two highly respectable men, his grandfathers, Seaborn Jones and Van de Van Leonard II. Seaborn Leonard Jones was just sixteen years old, but he desperately wanted to serve the Confederacy. His father, Captain Jones applied to the Confederate authorities requesting a special waiver for his son who was technically too young for service. Seeking special consideration from President Jefferson Davis, Captain Jones asked that Leonard be assigned to his command as a " Cadet." Meanwhile, Leonard Jones was given the rank of Private, assigned to his father's company, and kept on the rolls as a Musician. **38**

In the Seventeenth regiment, companies C and F were organized in Columbus. Amongst the volunteers in these companies were Wesley C. Hodges, a long-time friend of Henry Benning. It was Wesley Hodge's father, Reverend Samuel K. Hodges that had married Henry and Mary Benning. Wesley Hodges was an experienced military man who had served during the Creek War and the Mexican War, and he would serve Colonel Benning admirably during the impending conflict. John Mott, a fellow classmate of Seaborn Benning and Leonard Jones at the Georgia Military Institute, also joined the Seventeenth and he would serve Colonel Benning as an Adjutant. In the Second Infantry Regiment, companies C and G also hailed from Columbus. These two companies were especially well organized, trained, equipped, and filled with veterans of the Creek and Mexican wars. Their companies were affectionately known as the " Semmes Guards," and the "Columbus Guards." In the Twentieth regiment, companies B, G, and I, all hailed from Columbus, and the First Regiment, Company B was from Muscogee County, and known as " Russell's Guards." **39**

These units were filled with friends of Henry Benning, and those whom Benning did not know, knew of him from his long and respectable service within Muscogee County and the state of Georgia. These men also brought with them, several of their hardiest slaves, to serve the officers as manservants and cooks. Amongst these slaves was "Old Billie," a devoted Southerner who served Benning as a cook. After the war, as a free man," Old Billie" would continue to serve his former masters, and fellow soldiers by honoring their memory and decorating their graves. **40**

The entire Chattahoochee Valley region was filled with patriotic fervor and across the Chattahoochee River, in Alabama, Benning's other brother-in-law, Madison Lewis Patterson was commissioned as a Lieutenant in the Fifth Alabama Infantry. From throughout the State of Georgia, the Confederate Army rapidly filled with Benning's peers. From Columbus, Benning's close friends and fellow regimental commanders included: Colonel James N. Ramsey, commander of the First Regiment Georgia Volunteer Infantry ; Colonel Paul Semmes, commander of the Second Georgia Volunteer Infantry ; and Colonel Martin J. Crawford, commander of the Third Georgia Cavalry Regiment. Incidentally, one of the company commanders in Crawford's regiment was John S. Pemberton of Columbus, whom after the war concocted the formula for Coca-Cola.

Four of Benning's fellow Columbus attorneys joined the ranks as officers: Peyton Colquitt ; Alfred Iverson Jr. ; Beverly A. Thornton and Raphael Moses. **41**

From other sections of Georgia, Benning's friends joined too. Fellow lawyers, politicians, and secessionists, whom Benning had worked with in the courts and delegations included: John B. Gordon ; Henry R. Jackson ; Ambrose Wright ; Henry McKay ; Lucius Gartrell ; Reuben Carswell ; Francis Bartow ; and Clement Evans. Benning's close friends from across the State that joined the Confederate ranks included, former Judge Linton Stephens, commissioned as a Colonel and commander of the Fifteenth Georgia Infantry regiment. Thomas R. R. Cobb entered the Confederacy as a Colonel, and raised a unique, combined arms unit known as Cobb's Legion. Henry Benning 's old classmate, Benjamin C. Yancey applied for a commission and was assigned as a cavalry major in "Cobb's Legion." **42** Robert Toombs resigned his post in the Confederate administration, and he too, joined the army. Toombs was commissioned as a Brigadier General and given the command of an Infantry brigade comprised solely of Georgia regiments. Toombs' chief officers included many old friends such as Paul Semmes, Linton Stephens, Raphael Moses, and Henry Benning. **43**

The Confederate army was filled with kith and kin, and they were eager to prove their mettle. While most of these warriors lacked military experience, they were a hardy breed and this Confederacy of Southern states relied upon their beliefs and formed an army to defend them. The depletion of Southern leadership from the halls of government to the ranks of the military left the Confederacy with a serious void. According to a Georgian who watched the events unfold," The war absorbed our old leaders, swallowed them up, as it were, in the leveling atmosphere of the bayonet." **44**

Henry Benning was one of the many Southern statesmen," swallowed up" in the impending fray. And, as he had predicted, years before," a consolidated Republic formed of the Southern States," would be required to defend Southern rights, and ultimately the issues which forged the Confederate States of America, would be "settled by sword and its blood." **45**

Chapter 11

Preparations for War

In 1861, throughout the South, the initial " atmosphere of the bayonet" permeated the Confederacy. Filled with patriotic devotion and a warrior spirit, citizens and soldiers alike rushed to the aid of their new nation. In the *Columbus Enquirer*, June 20, 1861, it was noted that the city of Columbus had provided ten companies of soldiers," enough to make a full regiment," and " our citizens have contributed $1200 for each company." **1** It was also noted that these figures did not include the private donations of food, clothing, and equipment necessary to outfit these units. Yet, concerning these numerous donations from the citizens of Columbus, it was also recorded that," Surely, she has done all that could be expected of her, unless the emergency was such a one as to require every citizen of the South to become a soldier." **2** During the course of the next four years, nearly everyone in Columbus would be required to provide some form of service to the Confederacy. While Southerners were prepared to fight, they were naive concerning the immense costs involved with war, which included both blood and money. Robert Toombs attempted to warn President Davis that war " was ninety per cent business and ten per cent fighting, and they must 'organize' victory." **3** Toombs message, however, fell on deaf ears, as Davis and he had never gotten along. Davis had served as the U. S. Secretary of War, when Toombs served in the U. S. Senate, and their differences would haunt the Confederacy.

Yet, for the common men and women of Columbus, Georgia, they gave freely in blood and money. Their voluntary spirit and contributions to " the cause " were unmatched throughout the South. Between May, 1861 and February of 1862, the city of Columbus contributed sixteen infantry and two artillery companies to the ranks of the Confederate Army. **4** Each company contained an average of ninety men and the approximate number of white males living in the city were 3,500. Thus, conservative estimates reveal that nearly one-half of the available population of Columbus carried a weapon into war. Adding to this number, a composite force of three hundred men were organized for home defense, and their ranks were filled with men solely between the ages of forty-five and seventy. 5 The young women of Columbus even formed an organization dubbed the " Ladies Home Guard," which sought to coerce into the army," men who have concluded to remain at home." 6 Yet, most of the ladies of Columbus frowned on this practice, and a group of church ladies, organized their own " Soldiers' Aid Society," whose mission was to provide benevolent care for the needs of the soldiers. This organization later changed its name to the " Ladies Soldiers' Friends Society," and after the war continued their work as the " Ladies Memorial Association. " 7

Mrs. Mary (Jones) Benning, Mrs. Mary (Howard) Jones, and Mrs. Mary (Leonard) Jones were members of the " Soldiers' Aid Society," also referred to as the " Ladies Soldiers' Friends Society," and worked throughout the war, providing care and assistance for soldiers. As the war progressed, Columbus became an important center for Confederate hospitals, and the ladies most important services rendered were as nurses. Mary Benning was very active in the hospitals, and " she visited the Hospital every day with flowers, delicacies and other edibles for the sick and wounded." 8 Mrs. Benning and her parents, also opened their home," El Dorado," as one of the many private residences for recuperating wounded soldiers. Henry Benning 's daughter, Miss Mary Howard Benning, was in her early twenties during the war, and she recalled that one particular soldier staying with them," did not seem to find his days of convalescence irksome." 9 The families of the Bennings and Jones were fortunate to be financially secure, however, for many women, the war completely destroyed their lives.

In Columbus, and throughout the South, life for the wives and families of common soldiers were filled with extreme hardships. Meager pay coupled with skyrocketing inflation forced many impoverished wives and daughters to seek employment in the textile mills . Working to fill the orders of Colonel F. W. Dillard, women and girls alike, spent long hard hours, earning little pay, and simply struggled to get by. Working to maintain their homes and feed their families, the lives of many women and children balanced precociously from day to day. Then, as the war progressed, the deaths of their fathers and husbands resulted in sudden and absolute poverty. Yet, in the early stages of the war, these events were unforeseen and unimaginable. In the early stages of the war, the proud ladies of the South energetically supported their men and fully supported them with optimistic patriotism. Most of these ladies did their part, preparing food for departing soldiers, conducting sewing circles, and rolling bandages, while anxiously pondering the future. 10

Mrs. Mary Jones and other ladies of the " Southern Guard " sewing circle, prepared and presented the company colors to her husband, Captain John A. Jones with:

> In presenting this flag to your gallant company, we desire to
> tender with it our kindest wishes for each one who may be called
> to defend its colors. May it prove a banner around which your
> brave men may rally in the hour of peril and ere long may its
> folds unfurl peacefully over the soil redeemed from the invader's
> tread. May each strong arm that dares brave the fearful storm
> return with palms of victory; and may the banner, untarnished by
> the vile touch of the enemy, wave, victoriously over the brave
> ones who periled their lives. For this we hope, for this we pray,
> that the " God of Battle," who ever defends a just and righteous
> cause, may protect and return you all victoriously to your homes.
> 11

While the tearful departures were wrought with anxiety, the general consensus in both the North and South was that the affair would end within thirty days. In the South, people exclaimed that the " Yankees will not fight," while the Northern press referred to the " rebels," as a " mere band of ragamuffins," and the " rebellion, as some people designate it, is an unborn tadpole." 12 Reflecting the sentiment of a short war, Union troops volunteering for the war, were sworn in for a period not to exceed ninety days. In the South, volunteers enlisted for various periods of service, however, most enlistments were for three years. The reality of war and its lengthy duration was soon realized. As Confederate forces were organized, they made their way to Manassas, Virginia, a strategic location, just southwest of the Union capital. Meanwhile, an ill-prepared Union army rapidly organized in Washington D. C., marched out to counter the gathering opposition.

With mounting pressure from the public, President Lincoln prematurely pressed his army into battle. On July 21, 1861, the Confederacy clashed with Union forces at the Battle of Bull Run, just outside Manassas, Virginia. Neither side was fully prepared; however, the Confederate army won a decisive victory. The Union troops were routed and they fled back to the capital in a humiliating defeat. Encouraged with victory, the men of the South were convinced they could defeat the North. They urgently organized and deployed their units to Virginia. Governor Brown urged Benning to get

his troops to Atlanta, by the Fifteenth of August, so they could be issued
arms. 13 Benning and his fellow Georgian warriors rushed to complete their
organization, and join their brothers in arms, lest they miss the war.

As for so many Southern warriors, Colonel Henry Benning and his son,
Sergeant Major Seaborn Benning, the war began with a heart-wrenching
farewell. While the men were full of confidence and excitement, exchanging
love for war is a difficult transaction. While Mrs. Benning was a strong
woman, yet her heart was saddened as she said good-bye to her brother,
nephew and numerous life-long friends. Realizing that her home and her life
would probably never be the same, Mrs. Mary Benning watched as the train
gradually pulled her dear husband and only son away from her and into a
future of uncertainty. Bound for Atlanta, Benning and his men would
encamp and muster into service. Over the course of three days, August 12-
15, 1861, unit organization was achieved, and the unit was supplied with
Enfield rifles, knapsacks, and blankets. Each regiment consisted of ten
companies. The Seventeenth regiment was formed by the following Georgia
counties and their respective companies: Webster (A); Muscogee (B);
Decatur (C); Mitchell (D); Muscogee (E); Dougherty (F); Harris (G);
Stewart (H). When the Seventeenth regiment Georgia volunteers was
organized, Henry L. Benning was elected Colonel; Wesley C. Hodges
Lieutenant-Colonel; Thomas Walker, Major; George H. King, Commissary,
and Reuben C. Shorter, Quartermaster. The company commanders were all
Captains, and their respective companies consisted of: D. B. Harrell (A);
Henry L. French (B); Foster S. Chapman (C); Charles G. Campbell (D);
John A. McGregor (E); D. B. Thompson (F); Augustus C. Jones (G);
Richard E. Kennon (H); Charles W. Matthews (I); John H. Pickett (K). 14

While the companies were actually raised and organized before their
arrival in Atlanta, formal elections were conducted and recorded as a tenet of
formal military necessity. In the early years of the war, Southern leadership
positions below the regimental level were conducted by popular vote. This
tradition followed the practice of the state militia, and it was very popular.
The men felt strongly that they should have the right to elect their leaders,
however, several of the high ranking Confederate leaders were former U. S.
Army officers and they frowned upon this method. This situation would
soon force Henry Benning, yet again, to rise in the defense of states' rights.
Ironically, in its infancy, the Confederacy was forced to rely on the
individual states for its strength in arms, men, and capital, yet, to maintain
power and authority, this union of confederate states still required a central
authoritative power, just like the one from which they had withdrawn. As the
war progressed, the practice of elected officials was abolished, and all
officer promotions and assignments were conducted through the office of the
Secretary of War. 15

Once the regiment was organized, Colonel Benning supervised his units as they loaded on trains and made their way north, through Tennessee, to Lynchburg, Virginia, and ultimately to the Confederate camps, located throughout the countryside of northwest Virginia. Reeling from their first clash of arms, both sides quickly initiated reorganization efforts. Elaborate defensive fortifications were being constructed around Washington, as the Confederacy focused on organizing their forces, and preparing for future operations. As the regiments arrived from their individual States, the Confederate army amalgamated them into brigades and corps. Benning's Seventeenth regiment was combined with the First, Second, Fifteenth, and Twentieth regiments into an Infantry brigade under the command of Brigadier General Robert Toombs, D. R. Jones Division, Army of the Potomac, C.S.A. 16 The First regiment was transferred out of the brigade in October, 1861, when the Army of the Potomac was restructured into the Army of Northern Virginia. The remaining regiments of " Toomb's Brigade " remained together throughout the war. Before this transfer, on September 4, 1861, Sergeant Major Seaborn Jones Benning had a number of friends in Company C, First regiment, and they lured him to join them. The younger Benning transferred, and the men of the company elected him to the rank of Lieutenant, on September 18, 1861. 17

Toomb's brigade was filled with many of Georgia's finest men. The regimental commanders were: Second regiment, Colonel Paul Semmes ; Fifteenth regiment, Colonel Thomas W. Thomas ; Seventeenth regiment, Colonel Henry Benning ; and the Twentieth regiment was commanded by Colonel William D. Smith. Within these regiments, also were many men of mark, and during the course of the war, they would be called upon to positions of higher responsibilities. Among these men were: Captain Dudley M. DuBose, the son-in-law of Robert Toombs ; Henry Benning 's son-in-law, John A. " Jack" Jones, whom was elected to the rank of Lieutenant Colonel and now served as the deputy commander of the Twentieth regiment; and Adjutant Lovick Pierce Jr. of the Fifteenth regiment, the son of Reverend Lovick Pierce, and Benning's pastor. The brigade was filled with many men who were all kith and kin, or fellow Georgians, and they all knew and revered their leaders. In addition to the Seventeenth regiment, the brigade was comprised of the following regimental organizations. The Georgia counties and their respective companies which formed the Second regiment:

Banks (A); Meriwether (B); Muscogee (C); Burke (D); Fannin (E); Cherokee (F); Muscogee (G); Whitfield (H); Marion (I); Stewart (K). The leadership of the Second regiment of Georgia volunteers was organized in May 1861, as follows: Col. Paul J. Semmes ; Lt. Col. Skidmore Harris ; Maj. Edgar M. Butt ; Adj. W. Redd; Captains. D. G. Candler (A); William T. Harris (B); William S. Shepherd (C); William R. Holmes (D); W. A. Campbell (E); Thomas E. Dickerson (F); Roswell Ellis (G); Jesse A. Glenn (H); Charles R. Wiggins (I); Jared I. Ball (K). The quartermaster was James Houston, and the commissary was S. G. W. Dillingham.

The following Georgia counties and their respective companies formed the Fifteenth regiment:

Wilkes (A); Franklin (B); Elbert (C); Taliaferro (D); Hancock (E); Elbert (F); Lincoln (G); Hart (H); Elbert (I); Hancock (K). The officers of the Fifteenth regiment Georgia volunteers were initially: Col. Thomas W. Thomas ; Lt. Col. William M. McIntosh ; Maj. T. J. Smith ; Commissary J. H. Willis ; Quartermaster H. V. Forbes ; Adj. B. H. Lofton ; Captains.

A. B. Cade (A); William T. Millican (B); L. H. O. Martin (C); S. J. Farmer (D); T. J. Smith (E); John E. Burch (F); Stephen Z. Hearnsberger (G), William R. Poole (H); William H. Mattox (I); J. L. Culver (K).

The following Georgia counties and their respective companies formed the Twentieth regiment:

Bibb (A); Muscogee (B); Jefferson (C); Polk (D); Harris (E); Fulton (F); Muscogee (G); Telfair (H); Muscogee (I). The organization of the Twentieth Georgia Volunteer Infantry regiment was as follows: William Duncan Smith, colonel; J. B. Cumming, lieutenant-colonel; John " Jack" Jones, major; James O. Waddell, adjutant. The Captains were: A. B. Ross (A); John A. Strother (B); Roger L. Gamble (C); James D. Waddell (D); R. D. Little (E); E. M. Seago (F); John R. Ivey (G); J. A. Coffee (H); Van A. Leonard (I); William Craig (K).

In October of 1861, the initial composition of four full regiments provided the brigade with nearly 4,000 men. The year 1861 was the peak year in terms of strength and composition, as the numbers continuously dwindled during the next four years. 18 During the war, this brigade earned the distinction of producing a general officer from each regiment. Paul Semmes, of the Second regiment ; Dudley DuBose of the Fifteenth regiment ; Henry Benning of the Seventeenth, and William Smith of the Twentieth regiment, all received promotions and served the Confederacy as generals, but only Benning and DuBose survived the war. The difficult life of a soldier forced most of the so-called " political officers" to resign. Many of the senior leaders had been prominent men in civilian society, however, for most of them, the military was distasteful, or they were simply not capable of leading men in battle. For example, the commander of the Fifteenth regiment, Colonel Thomas W. Thomas, a former judge resigned upon the realization that leading a courtroom was very different from leading troops in the field. His deputy commander, Lieutenant Colonel Linton Stephens, also a former judge, found the military was dominated by former " West Pointers," whom Stephens felt unworthy of his subservience. For Stephens, the matter was complicated with his brother serving as the Vice-President of the Confederacy, and he too, resigned on December 19, 1861. In the First Georgia regiment, Benning's old friend Colonel James N. Ramsey, also resigned in December. 19

Within the first few months of service, weak, ill, and elderly men faced the simple fact that they were not fit to perform the duties required of a soldier. By the close of 1861, the ranks of the brigade were thinned by the loss of 595 men, due to illness, desertions, and disabilities. (See Appendix B) **20** Adding to this dilemma, during November and December, the camps were wrought with illness. Due to poor sanitation, nasty, cramped, damp, and cold living conditions, coupled with the widespread potential for the spread of germs, the men of the brigade met their first enemy, disease. It proved to be their deadliest foe. Disease was prevalent and with inadequate health care, numerous men were evacuated to Typhoid hospitals in Richmond. Many never returned to their units. From 1861 to 1865, the brigade lost 1,002 men to illnesses; chiefly Pneumonia and Typhoid followed by Smallpox and Measles. **21**

In 1861, the leadership of the brigade was dominated by its two elders, Toombs, age fifty-one, and Benning, age forty-seven. Both men were strong willed, intelligent, devoted to their cause, and most importantly, they enjoyed good health. Toombs commanded the brigade from its formation in 1861, until his resignation in March of 1863. From then, until the unit surrendered in 1865, Benning commanded the brigade, thus producing the eventual name change to " Benning's brigade. " Dudley DuBose also commanded the brigade for a short time, while Benning was wounded. DuBose was a generation younger than the brigade's former commanders, and he served as the temporary commander for six months, May -October, 1864. DuBose excelled as a leader, and upon the return of Benning, DuBose was promoted to Brigadier General and given command of his own brigade. **22**

Before the war, Toombs and Benning shared a long history of public service with the state of Georgia, as well as their nation, providing them with valuable leadership skills. They had worked together, as well as against one another, and they knew each other quite well. While they were chiefly politicians, both men had some previous military experience, which was gained during the Creek uprising of 1836. Toombs had served as a Captain and company commander in the First Infantry Regiment, while Benning served as a Private in the 66th Infantry Regiment, and as an Aide on the General's Staff. While their experiences were short-lived, they both experienced the privations of a soldier, which provided them keen insights into the harsh world of a lower ranking soldier. **23** Benning and Toombs were deeply admired, respected, and their units eagerly followed their commands.

Perhaps, owing to their previous experiences in the army, Benning and Toombs led their troops from the front and willingly accepted the same deprivations as their men. Later in the war, following their example, DuBose led the brigade with the same leadership qualities of his mentors and gained deep respect from both his men and superiors. At the regimental level, the commanders were themselves, foot soldiers. As such, many paid the ultimate sacrifice. Each regiment lost several commanders in battle. It must be noted that snipers seek out the commanders, and focus their well-aimed fire upon them. Fortunately for the brigade, as commanders were lost, competent subordinates assumed their positions. Throughout the war, the brigade never suffered from a shortage of strong leadership.

All of the commanders of this unit displayed a deep affection for the individual foot soldiers of their commands. Many of the men were related or had known each other for years before the war. At the heart of any good army is the individual fighting man devoted to his cause. Forged into a fighting unit, this " band of rebels" whose forefathers had fought for their liberty from England, directly related their crisis to the epic struggle of the American Revolution. These men were prepared to give their lives to secure their rights. In their view, they were engaged in a quest for independence. This realization on behalf of the leaders undoubtedly led to success in battle. Toombs referring to his soldiers stated," Liberty in its last analysis is but the sweat of the poor and the blood of the brave." 24 During the war, Benning earned the affectionate sobriquet of " Old Rock," directly from his men, as they admired his steadfast courage in battle. Benning was shot twice and had at least three horses killed underneath him. All three commanders of the brigade, Toombs, Benning, and DuBose were wounded in battle, yet they continued to fight. 25

The brigade remained in several temporary camps throughout the fall of 1861, near Centreville and Manassas, drilling by day and performing picket duty at night. Drilling fields were prepared and a seemingly endless stream of training followed. A member of the Second regiment recorded that " The daily duties of the regiment are becoming harder and harder." 26 In January of 1862, the brigade completed their permanent winter quarters, constructed of heavy cloth, logs, lumber, mud and stone. Located on the outskirts of Manassas, this place was named Camp Georgia. In Company I, Twentieth regiment, First Lieutenant Van A. Leonard was promoted to the rank of Captain and given command of the company. A distant relative, Miss Dolly Whitaker sent him a headscarf to keep him warm. Captain Leonard wrote her a letter expressing his gratitude for the scarf, and told her about life in Camp Georgia. Leonard expressed that:

When I write, thoughts of home, of the past, all come welling up
and gayety for a while departs. It is sad to look on the spectacle,
which surrounds us here. Dirty tents, mud, ice and snow knee
deep, country desolated as by a poisonous breath and a whole
army cut loose from influences of home, of kindred, and women...
I have no doubt of victory, of a long and prosperous peace but
many of the young of our country will never survive the effects of
this campaign. **27**

Van Leonard was a respected man, a natural leader, and a member of a
proud family. In 1862, he was thirty-one years old, and his wife, Georgia
Flournoy, had provided him with four children. His father, Van de Van
Leonard II, was a business partner of Seaborn Jones and John Howard.
Moreover, Leonard was related to the Jones, Bennings, and Howards,
through marriage. His sister Mary Louisa, was the wife of his commander
and long-time friend, John A. Jones . Captain Van Leonard had a keen
insight concerning the future and he accurately predicted that many men
would perish in the war. Meanwhile, Captain Leonard and his men lived the
manly lifestyle of soldiers, as they proudly occupied their newly constructed
lodgings. Settling in for a long winter, the soldiers wrote letters to their
loved ones, carried out their duties, honed their new skills and contemplated
their future in the military. Although life seemed harsh to them, they at least
had good uniforms, shoes, pay and provisions. Colonel Millican, of the
Fifteenth Georgia, wrote in a letter to his wife," You spoke of sending more
clothing to me. I have more blankets than I can carry. I do not need any
overcoat nor any more white shirts!" **28** All too rapidly, these items would
become articles of luxury. In camp, Colonel Henry Benning, commander of
the Seventeenth Georgia Volunteer Infantry, settled in to the life of a soldier,
while his son, Lieutenant Seaborn Benning did likewise in a neighboring
camp with the First regiment, alongside his cousin S. Leonard Jones and
their commander Colonel James N. Ramsey. The Georgia regiments were
filled with kith and kin. The initial novelty of soldier life, excitement and
anticipation of war filled their camps and their hearts with an air of
invincibility.

Meanwhile, both the Union and Confederate armies concentrated on
improving the strength and composition of their forces. As the winter of
1861-62 ebbed, the approaching fair weather would support army maneuvers
and a renewed campaign. Strategy, contingencies and recruitment were the
orders of the day. In the north, General George McClellan replaced General
Scott, while in the south, President Jefferson Davis was officially elected to
a six-year term. In both capitals, the wartime footing created a tense
atmosphere of uncertainty complicated with a feverish pitch of organization

and planning for future events. In Toomb's brigade, the unit slowly took shape, honing their skills, memorizing drills, practicing battle formations, organizing commands and forming bonds necessary to establish an effective military organization.

As the officers in the higher ranks became disabled or resigned, the shifting realignment resulted in the ascension of several members of the brigade. In the Second regiment, Colonel Paul J. Semmes was promoted to General and given his own brigade. The same occurred in the Twentieth regiment, as Colonel William D. Smith was promoted to General and transferred to his own unit. This left a void that was filled by Colonel John Cumming and his new deputy commander, Lieutenant Colonel John A. Jones . In the Fifteenth regiment, Colonel William McIntosh ascended to the command upon the resignations of both Colonel Thomas W. Thomas and Linton Stephens. In the Seventeenth regiment, Colonel Henry Benning continued his command, thus forging a reputation as a fully committed officer and solid field commander. **29**

Meanwhile in camp, residing in the frigid fields of northern Virginia, the Infantrymen of " Toomb's Brigade " thought of home, gathered firewood and focused on staying warm. One observant soldier recorded:

Clear and cold this morning. All lying about in their tents, some sleeping and looking very lazy...The whole Army of the " Potomac" encamped around Centerville, the whole country filled with tents. I reckon there are 25,000 soldiers in 2 miles square. The hills are white with tents and looks like a city. It is a sight worth seeing. **30**

All too soon, the tranquillity of camp would be exchanged with the din of battle. For many soldiers, their lives would end with a violent death. The brigade was destined for the battlefields of: Garnett's Farm, Malvern Hill, Thoroughfare Gap, Manassas, Sharpsburg, Fredericksburg, Gettysburg, Chickamauga, Lookout Valley, Knoxville, Wilderness, Spotsylvania, Hanover Junction, Cold Harbor, New Market Heights, Fort Gilmer, Richmond, Petersburg, and Farmville. Ultimately, only the fortunate souls would survive the pestilence of disease, the pain of separation from home, the agony of nearly 6000 miles of travel, and the inexplicable horrors of war. Four long years of hardship lay ahead. When the brigade was formed, it consisted of approximately 4,300 officers and men; however, by April 9,

1865, the brigade would be comprised of only 812 men, present in the field.
31

Chapter 12

Command and Battle

By the spring of 1862, the Confederate leadership faced the reality that the Union forces greatly outnumbered them. This factor was further complicated by the mighty industrial capacity of the North to generate a seemingly endless flow of arms and material to supply their overwhelming forces. While the Confederates made excellent warriors, and had gained initial victories, as the strength of the Union army slowly increased, the Confederacy simultaneously declined. Throughout the winter, the Union had created a virtually impregnable fortress around their capital, and the Confederacy would never muster the strength to seriously threaten it. With 100,000 Union soldiers defending Washington D.C., General Joseph Johnston 's Confederates encamped around them, numbered 54, 000. Adding to this dilemma, President Lincoln dispatched General George McClellan with another twelve divisions of Union Infantry to the tidewater region of Virginia. Dominating control of the seas, the Union Navy maintained a toehold between the York and James rivers, at Fort Monroe and Hampton, Virginia. In a massive sealift of personnel and equipment, McClellan swung his Army of the Potomac (U.S.) down and around Virginia's eastern shore, and would threaten Richmond from the east. Pressing his Union forces northwest, up the peninsula towards Richmond, McClellan's army was a serious threat to the Confederacy. Known as the Peninsula campaign, the real war was now in full motion, and President Davis was forced to weigh his options.

His dilemma was easily resolved, as McClellan's bold maneuver had to be checked, or the Confederate capital would fall. Davis ordered Johnston's forces south, to bolster the defense of Richmond. On March 8, 1862, the brigade departed the comfort of their winter quarters, packed up their meager belongings, and began its first campaign, and the first of many lengthy journeys, under the " stars and bars" of the Confederacy. In a giant ribbon of men and wagons, eighteen miles long, the army moved slowly south through Virginia, by way of the Rappahannock River to Orange Court House. As the winter weather transitioned to spring, freezing sleet and snow increased the difficulty of traversing the muddied roads. In a repetitive cycle, at night, the mud would freeze, and slowly during the day, it returned to slush. On April 11, the brigade reached the railroad, where they loaded the trains and rode the rails to Richmond.

In the early stages of the war, Richmond was an exciting city. Serving as the hub of the Confederacy, her citizens were filled with patriotism and affection for their troops. As the units passed through the town, the city was full of cheer and gleefully watched as their heroes paraded down Main Street. As Toomb's brigade marched through, General Toombs turned the event into a spectacle. An officer noted that:

> He marched his troops down Main Street, past the crowds at
> Spottswood Hotel, with childlike delight. He put himself at the
> head of one regiment and moved it out of sight amid hurrahs,
> then galloping back he brought on another, ready himself for
> cheers, until the brigade was down the street. 1

On April 13, the brigade boarded the steamship *West Point*, and the troops were shuttled down the James River, to a landing six miles southwest of Yorktown, Virginia. The brigade then marched across a narrow section of the peninsula, passing Lebanon Church, and ultimately to their assigned sector of defensive earthworks, near Dam Number 1. The trenches were constructed to contain McClellan's advance to the lower portion of the peninsula, around Hampton. The Army of the Potomac (C.S.A.) under General Joseph Johnston , established a line of defense extending eight miles around Yorktown, as the massive Union Army laid siege upon it. The brigade was assigned to defend their sector from an impending assault. The brigade's sector was two miles below the city of Yorktown, and within several hundred yards of the Union front. The brigade was required to occupy these positions for a twenty-four hour period, every other day. The units were continuously rotated between the front and a safe location to the rear of the trenches. After several weeks of this duty, the brigade settled into a dreaded routine. Occasionally there were artillery duels and some sporadic sniper fire, as the earthworks slowly turned to mud, and the men despised their turn in them. General McClellen continuously increased the strength of his army and merely waited to launch his grand assault, with the ultimate goal being the capture of the seat of the Confederate government, Richmond. 2 Residing in the trenches, on April 20, 1862, a soldier in Toomb's brigade recorded:

Sun rose quite clear this morning. All were very hungry but our rations have not yet come. All are very hungry. We lie in the pit all day in the water and mud, but the sun shone part the day, in the evening it again rained, the firing of the pickets continued all day, we had none wounded. A few of our company had the chance to try their guns at the enemy; the balls would whiz occasionally over our heads. We lie in the pit all day, and at Eve our breakfast, dinner and supper came. We were very hungry. Each one drew his piece of bread and meat, though quite fat some still relished it well, and a few crackers to the man. It put me in mind of Negroes as all the meat and bread were cut up and put in a pan and brought to us, and so eager were we for it we crowded around the pan like Negroes. (War is a rough life but healthy to some.) **3**

As the Union forces grew in number, the Union commanders probed the Confederate line for points of weakness. Inevitably, in Toomb's brigade, as in all units, North and South, some unfortunate soul was destined to become the first battle casualty of his unit. After weeks of duty in the trenches, Private Jonathan B. Cone carelessly exposed his body above the earthen berm, and he caught the eye of a Union sharpshooter. Immediately, Private Cone was provided with a mortal wound. A well aimed, large caliber bullet ripped through his chest and demolished his left lung. In disbelief, his comrades watched as a pink frothy mix of blood and bubbles oozed from his chest. In pain, shock, and waves of nausea, Private Cone's distorted body gasped for air and expelled it with an irregular rapidity. The broken body of the young man combined with the nasty wheeze of a sucking chest wound horrified his friends. Ill prepared for casualty evacuation, his fellow soldiers hauled him out of the trenches, and placed him on a wagon, bound for the hospitals in Richmond. It was hoped with genuine sincerity that he would survive the fifty-mile journey and the surgeons could repair him. Cone was a young man and his body was strong, but nineteenth century medicine was too limited, and he slowly succumbed to an agonizingly painful death.

The next day, in the same sector of the line, the unit was exposed to its first experience with artillery, as a cannonball exploded just above their heads. Sprayed with shards of hot metal, the shrapnel from the exploding round tore through three men, horribly mangling their bodies. While these first casualties of war were shocking to Colonel Benning and his fellow Georgians, their future would soon be dominated by a lifestyle of misery and gore. With the total Confederate forces defending Yorktown at less than 20,000 men, and the burgeoning Union forces numbering 100,000, the Confederate leaders wisely began a retreat. As McClellan made final preparations to launch his assault, the Confederates withdrew, racing back up the peninsula towards Richmond, and a larger force to counter the Union offense. 4

The Union forces immediately occupied Yorktown, which served as a strategic port of embarkation. McClellan rapidly transported even more forces to join his army. South of Yorktown, the cities of Norfolk, Portsmouth and Suffolk were occupied by federal troops. Slowly, the Union forces began their move towards Richmond, setting the stage for the first major engagement of 1862. Having evacuated their portion of the defense works on May 3, the brigade marched up the Williamsburg Road toward Richmond. The Union forces pressed the retreating Confederates and fought them at Williamsburg, and again at West Point, Virginia. With thousands of Union bayonets reflecting in the sun, the flashing light effectively signaled a desire to lacerate the heart of the South. The spring rains muddied the roads, making the march extremely difficult. Coupled with constant pressure from overwhelming forces and fighting a rear-guard battle, the brigade finally reached the outskirts of Richmond on April 17, 1862. The unit changed positions several times, as the Confederate and Union armies maneuvered for battle. McClellan manipulated the Confederate army in an elaborate game of strategy, seeking the opportunity to strike and edging ever-closer to his prize of Richmond. 5

On May 25, 1862, the brigade observed what was then a technical marvel of science, the Union reconnaissance balloon of Professor Thaddeus Lowe. General Toombs shrugged off the Union display as silly, and boasted that the Yankees were afraid to show themselves. Full of bravado, Southern warriors, young and old had energetically joined the Confederacy. With a year of war already elapsed, the predicted duration of a thirty day war was defunct. Moreover, the harsh reality that soldiering was hard work and only suited for men possessing physical stamina prompted the Confederacy to take a closer look at the composition of their army. The forced march from Yorktown to Richmond resulted in death for scores of elderly soldiers. On May 30, the Confederate military commander, General Joseph Johnston had the eldest soldiers discharged from the army. General Toombs disagreed with many of General Johnston's decisions, and being a prominent politician, Toombs initiated a rapid and self-inflicted demise of his military career. Raphael Moses, the brigade commissary officer, was an old and trusted friend, remarked that

Toomb's " impulses were generous and noble, his faults were bluster, and a vivid imagination was not always hampered by facts!" 6 While Toombs brazenly defended his Georgia warriors, endearing the men to him, his impetuous actions were disrespectful and insubordinate toward his superiors. Filled with contempt for military regulation, and professional West Point officers, Toombs openly defied the rules established by General Johnston. All too frequently, he was known to openly scold his superior officers. Yet, despite his faults, General Johnston " said of him that, if not for his insubordinate spirit, he would have made a great commander." 7

Toombs also disliked and openly disagreed with President Davis. Filled with jealousy and contempt, Toombs remarked that " the utter incompetency of Mr. Davis and his West Point generals have brought us to the verge of ruin." 8 Ironically, Davis had considered Toombs for the position of Secretary of War, but Toombs remarked to his wife that he would not be " Mr. Davis' chief clerk" and " Mr. Davis will never give me a chance for personal distinction. He thinks I pant for it, poor fool." 9 Henry Benning respected Robert Toombs. Since college days, Benning had heard stories and observed first hand, that while Toombs was not balanced, his abilities were many and his devotion to Georgia, equal to his own. In all his reports, correspondence, and remarks related to Toombs, Benning always reflected a genuine respect, and he considered Toombs," a dear friend." 10 Their relationship on the battlefield created balance. In his temperament, Benning was just the opposite of Toombs, as he employed the fundamentals of logic, prudence and meticulous observation to his actions. Additionally, Benning learned from Toomb's mistakes as a soldier, blending his observations with a study of tactics and the art of warfare. Eventually, Benning surpassed Toombs as a battlefield commander. Henry Benning applied the same attention to the military as he did in all his endeavors. Always studious, Benning continuously hewed and focused his new martial skills throughout his tenure as a soldier. With an ever shrinking army, Benning would need all the skills and luck he could muster.

One of Colonel Benning 's first battles was fought with the pen rather than the sword. In the midst of the retreat from Yorktown to Richmond, Captain D. B. Thompson, company commander of company F, was one of the elderly, disabled officers, and he resigned on April 20, 1862. His next in command was First Lieutenant Henry McCauley, who assumed command of the company. Company F was from Columbus and Henry

Benning knew them both. McCauley had been a merchant of tombstones before the war, and Benning considered him an incompetent military leader. The company held an election for the vacancy left by Captain D. B. Thompson, and Second Lieutenant Phillip Gittinger won the position, however, Lieutenant McCauley refused to yield his position. Colonel Benning vehemently ordered him to step down. Popular elections were the proper method of ascension at that point in the Georgia units, yet McCauley knew that the Confederate leadership frowned on this method. 11 McCauley refused his commander's order, and Benning had him arrested. General Toombs supported Colonel Benning 's decision, the formal election process, and the confinement of the insubordinate young officer. While in confinement, but located near Richmond, McCauley wrote a damning letter to the Honorable G. W. Randolph, Secretary of War, demanding that he restore his " just powers." 12 Secretary Randolph, President Davis, and most of the former " West Pointers " had long expressed disagreement with promotion by popular election, and McCauley targeted them as an audience.

The Secretary of War ordered that Benning reinstate " Captain" McCauley to the position as the commander of Company F, Seventeenth Georgia. Benning continued to hold McCauley in custody and the young lieutenant sent yet another message to the Secretary of War. This one stated that, General Toombs or Colonel Benning had the Secretary's reply but," when I ask Col. B about it, he says that Gen. Toombs has got it, and I have called on Gen. Toombs, he says that Col. Benning has got it." 13 McCauley then demanded his immediate release and an investigation of his case," if I am to be kept in this way for their satisfaction or until they see fit to release me." 14 Shortly after this letter was sent, Colonel Benning released Lieutenant McCauley, but the young Lieutenant resigned his commission, and returned to Columbus, Georgia, and his tombstone business. At the same time McCauley was being mustered out of the service, Generals D. R. Jones and Robert E. Lee sent messages to Colonel Benning to obey the Secretary's orders and place McCauley in the position as stated, but McCauley was already gone.

The incident initiated a tremendous amount of friction between the State Governors, the War Department and President Davis. Governor Joseph E. Brown was an ardent believer in the right of units to elect their leaders and stood firmly behind Colonel Benning and several other commanders that became embroiled with this dilemma. Governor Brown remarked to President Davis that " I cannot consent to commit the State to a policy which is in my judgement subversive of her sovereignty and at war with all the principles for the support of which Georgia entered into this revolution." 15 In an angry letter expressing what he viewed as a clear usurpation of power from the states to the Executive of the Confederacy, Governor Brown expressed serious concerns regarding the battle between States' rights and the central authority in Richmond. While he pledged continued support to President Davis, Governor Brown warned that the people of Georgia " will watch with a jealous eye, even in the midst of revolution, every attempt to undermine their constitutional rights." 16

In an attempt to maintain the Union forces at a safe distance from the capital, the Confederates launched a surprise counter-offensive. This action accomplished very little and General Johnston was wounded. President Davis named General Robert E. Lee as the commander of the newly organized," Army of Northern Virginia. " Within this new organizational structure," Toombs Brigade " was designated as the First Brigade, First Division, of Magruder's Corps. The brigade's division commander was now, Brigadier General David R. Jones, and their corps commander was Major General John Magruder. Lieutenant Seaborn Benning was assigned to the same division, as the First Georgia (Regulars) were in the Third Brigade, commanded by Colonel George " Tige" Anderson, Benning's old friend," Fatty " Howell Cobb, who had been promoted to the rank of Brigadier General, commanded the Second Brigade. Colonel Paul Semmes, formerly commanding the Second regiment of" Toombs Brigade," was also promoted to the rank of Brigadier General, and assigned as the brigade commander of the First Brigade of McLaw's division, also a part of Magruder's Corps. 17

On June 1, the brigade was ordered to the vicinity of the Battle of Seven Pines, but arrived too late to take part in the action. Toomb's brigade was moved to a new location just below the Chickahominy River, and assigned to defend that sector from McClellan's forces located to the north and east. On June 9, the brigade assumed picket duty on a defensive line near a little farm and house owned by a local planter named James Garnett. Known as Garnett's Farm, the location would soon have added meaning to Colonel Henry Benning and the other members of Toomb's brigade.

Meanwhile, General Thomas J. " Stonewall" Jackson arrived from the Shenandoah Valley with his unit and greatly reinforced the Confederate Army. The Confederate Cavalry, led by J.E.B. Stuart, accomplished a daring reconnaissance, riding completely around McClellan's forces. This intimidating and bold maneuver provided Lee with valuable information and a much-needed boost to the troops morale. In order to end the threat to Richmond, Lee initiated the Seven Days' Campaign on June 25, 1862.

Colonel Benning 's son saw action during this campaign. Commanding a company in the First Georgia Regulars, assigned to George " Tige" Anderson's Brigade, Lieutenant Seaborn Benning successfully led his men in battle. **18** The Southern forces succeeded in breaking through the Union lines at Oak Grove and Gaine's Mill. Up until this point, the only battle Colonel Benning and his fellow Georgians had experienced was piecemeal, defensive maneuvers and retreat. On June 27," Toomb's Brigade" eagerly embraced the opportunity to give a hardy " rebel yell," and meet the face of battle, head on.

On June 27, 1862, General Magruder ordered his divisions to " move forward and feel the enemy." Toombs ordered his pickets forward of the brigade. Their duty was to make contact with the enemy, thus exposing their positions, which General Toombs would then exploit as he saw fit. Toombs placed his brigade in an offensive posture, and shortly after 7 P.M., the units on his right, commanded by Anderson and Cobb, engaged the enemy. General Toombs responded by ordering his units forward. Toombs directed Colonel Edgar M. Butt, with seven companies of the Second Georgia (about 250 men), to advance and take position in a ravine to his front and immediately in rear of the advanced pickets. As they advanced:

> A regiment of the enemy, stationed in line opposite us across the
> field, which I saw plainly, opened fire upon us. I ordered our
> men to lie down and fire deliberately at them, which order they
> obeyed handsomely. The fire then became general on the line
> opposite us and extended soon to our left and right, which
> placed us under an enfilade fire from two points. I occupied the
> position at the edge of the woods until nearly half of the men in
> the companies that I commanded were either killed or wounded.
> **19**

The enemy, attacked the Second regiment with three regiments, immediately pouring a heavy volume of fire into their ranks. For the next thirty minutes, these forces engaged in heavy fighting, until the Union lines were reinforced with another brigade, which sought to envelope and crush the Second regiment.

Toombs dispatched the Fifteenth Georgia, led by Colonel William J. McIntosh to support Colonel Butt in the ravine. " We crossed the field at double-quick under a most galling fire from the opposite side of a deep ravine, just beyond which our skirmishers were engaged; crossed the ravine by the right flank and formed line of battle and moved rapidly to the front. The engagement now became general and intensely fierce all along the line and raged till after dark, when the enemy retired and the firing ceased. Colonel McIntosh, who was at the front and on the most exposed part of the line, gallantly cheering the men on, fell mortally wounded early in the engagement and was borne from the field." 20 Simultaneously, Toombs deployed Colonel J. B. Cumming, of the Twentieth Georgia, to hold the right flank, while dispatching the Seventeenth Georgia, led by Colonel Henry L. Benning, to secure the left flank. Colonel Benning reported that the Union forces posted on both sides of the Labor-in-Vain ravine opened fire on his men and:

> The fire at once became warm along our whole line. The balls of the enemy came across the picket line engaged in the fight, and wounded a number of that part of the regiment it held in reserve near the fence at the Garnett spring. About fifteen minutes after the firing had commenced report was made to you that the enemy in considerable force was about to turn your left flank and cut off the pickets sent from my regiment. You then ordered me to take the reserve companies of the regiment to that flank and support those pickets and counteract any such movement of the enemy. I at once carried them there and formed them in line of battle. 21

For the next hour and a half, the Union forces attempted to extricate the Second and Fifteenth Georgia Volunteers from their positions in the ravine, as well as exploit weaknesses on either flank, but the determined Confederates held their ground. The Second regiment suffered casualties of fifty percent, while the Fifteenth regiment lost 71 men, including their commander, Colonel McIntosh. Captain Bunch and Lieutenant Tilley of the Fifteenth were also killed in action. The Seventeenth and Twentieth Regiments providing support received light casualties, which numbered, two killed, and seven wounded. 22

In the midst of darkness, and the men exhausted, the commanders posted pickets, and the bulk of the brigade slept on the field. The next day, the Confederates occupied the former Union positions, as the enemy had withdrawn from the field. The corps was ordered to pursue the enemy for the next day, occasionally encountering the Union rear guard. The following day, June 30, 1862, General Magruder ordered Jones's division to reinforce General James Longstreet's division, which had encountered the bulk of the Union forces. According to Colonel Cummings, commanding the Twentieth regiment, this action resulted in a " long march of about 20 miles through the hot sun. Several of my men were overcome by the heat and fatigue of the march." **23** Slogging through the marshy terrain as fast as they could, the hot summer sun made the journey a hellish event. Colonel Millican of the Fifteenth regiment added that," most of the water we drank was lapped from brackish mud holes filled with tadpoles and wiggle-tails, and on numerous instances, reddened with the blood and tainted dead and decaying carcasses of men and horses." **24** The brigade arrived around midnight, where they rested until four o'clock on the morning of the first day of July. That morning, General Lee organized his forces into a massive formation, which maneuvered and forced General McClellan's army into the heights of a large plateau. With the James River to McClellan's rear, Lee intended to trap and crush his foe. The high plateau was known as Malvern Hill and the scene of impending battle.

On orders from Brigadier General David R. " Neighbor" Jones, Toombs marched the brigade and formed it in line of battle on the New Market Road, facing the Union lines. Their enemy was massed and concealed within the woods, three-quarters of a mile beyond. Between these forces were the large plateau, and the battlefield of Malvern Hill. Generals Toombs, Anderson, and Cobb's brigades were ordered to assault the enemy in conjunction with several other brigades, in a deep, massive thrust aimed directly at massed batteries of Union artillery . Advancing across difficult terrain, interspersed with briars, deadfall, and ravines, the enemy batteries poured continuous fire into the ranks of the advancing Confederates. Amidst the noise and confusion, General Toombs lost control of the Second, Fifteenth, and Twentieth regiments, and their ranks were further interspersed and confused with retreating soldiers from units to their front. Colonel Benning described the ensuing melee as," a very heavy fire both of artillery and musketry, grape and shell, splinters and Minie balls flying thick about us and through us, and making gaps in our ranks at every step." **25**

Meanwhile, Colonel Benning 's Seventeenth regiment continued pressing forward, under the thick fire pouring down from the Union batteries. Toombs desperately attempted to rally his men and contain the retreating soldiers. " The stream of fugitives was pouring back over my line, frequently breaking it and carrying back with them many of the men." **26** Amidst the noise, chaos, and panic-stricken men, there was little Toombs could do to control them. With the rear elements pushing forward, and the front ranks turning back, the units in the middle were literally being crushed. At the front, the Confederates were being destroyed with continuous volleys of direct cannon fire, which incessantly poured into their ranks. Absorbing the bulk of the fire, the unfortunate frontal ranks desperately clambered to escape the fury of the cannon. Eviscerated by " grape shot," the men were torn into chunks of human flesh, hurled upon their comrades, and saturated the earth below them.

With darkness nearing, Toombs anticipated an impending assault from Union Infantry, and dispatched his Adjutant, Captain Dudley M. DuBose, to coordinate a maneuver with the neighboring troops of General Kershaw's brigade. Together, they launched what forces they could muster in an immediate assault into the Union batteries. Colonel Butt was at the front of these forces. As they lurched forward, Colonel Butt, commanding the Second Georgia regiment was wounded and permanently disabled. Lieutenant Colonel Holmes assumed command and attempted to rally his troops who were rapidly being decimated. Adding to the chaos, Union Infantry on their left flank, hidden in the dark forest began firing upon them as targets of opportunity. Something had to be done and Lieutenant Colonel Holmes decided to move forward. He reported that:

> Our regiment performed in good order under a most destructive fire of grape and canister, being under full range of the enemy's guns. After crossing a fence, our regiment was ordered to lie down and wait for support to come up. Soon one of the regiments of Kershaw 's brigade came up and moved forward and we ordered as a support; we followed close after them. They moved in order and made a most gallant charge, but were completely checked by the deadly fire from the enemy's battery. Their ranks being torn asunder, they had to fall back, which left our regiment in front without any support. Colonel Butt being wounded at that time, I had to assume command. I ordered our regiment to lie down until we could get a supporting regiment. We were under a most terrific fire of grape, but the men acted with the utmost coolness, not one exhibiting, that I could see the least fear. We lay under that fire for fully half an hour waiting for some regiment to come up that we might continue our charge to the battery, which was not more than 150 yards in front of us. 27

After this final attempt to perform as directed and with the loss of daylight, Toombs ordered his forces to retreat. The assault was a disaster and extracted a high toll in the loss of life. During the time the brigade occupied the open plateau in front of the enemy's batteries, its losses were severe, with 194 men, killed or wounded. In addition to losing a regimental commander, Colonel Butt, General Toombs also lost two of his adjutants. After the Battle of Malvern Hill, General Toombs recorded:

> I am happy to add that the disorders which did arise were due rather to the difficulties of the ground and the nature of the attack than from any other cause, and that as far as my observation went they extended to all troops engaged on the plateau in front of the enemy's guns... I consider the conduct of the officers and men highly praiseworthy and honorable to themselves and the army. **28**

Fortunately for General George McClellan, his forces dominated the James River. With numerous Union gunboats in support, McClellan surrendered the field and withdrew his army to the east, along the James River, to Harrison Landing. While the Confederacy suffered heavy casualties, Richmond was relieved from the threat of a Union siege. Lee's army suffered more than 5,000 casualties, most of them being torn asunder by the murderous fire of the point-blank artillery. Several thousand Union troops also littered the battlefield, and in the summer heat, Colonel Millican recorded that on the battlefield," The stench was awful. Thousands of soldiers heaving and gagging from the inhalation of the poisant atmosphere. Our horses even sickened from the effects of the noxious and pestilential odor." **29** The gruesome task of collecting the dead for burial was reserved for the lowly Privates and slaves. Men who were formerly husbands, fathers and sons, were now littered remains, visited by flies, and silently awaiting disposal. Eventually, the burial details covered the remains, but the lingering effects served as a reminder of the horror of war. The Peninsula campaign provided the first of many horrible battles that Benning and his fellow Georgians would endure. Yet, the experiences served to build confidence, and Colonel Benning emerged as a battle hardened veteran and competent field commander.

The next day was filled with many happy reunions as troops emerged from the surrounding woods, and rejoined their units. After the debacle, Benning recorded," The officers and men received the hot fire of the enemy, which they could not return, friends being in front, with great coolness and fortitude." **30** Colonel Benning had more than friends in front of his lines. His only son, Captain Seaborn Benning was commanding his own troops with the First Georgia Regulars. With his son wedged between the enemy and his own troops, Henry Benning could only pray that Seaborn would survive the carnage. The Bennings were among the blessed survivors of the horrible carnage of the battle on Malvern Hill, but many of their comrades were not. Some of the casualties were kith and kin of the Bennings, and one of the bleeding and lacerated bodies on the field belonged to Captain Van Leonard, commander of Company I, Twentieth regiment. The courageous leader fought with all of his heart, but as he had predicted months earlier, many young men would not survive the war. Lieutenant Colonel John A. " Jack" Jones ensured that his brother-in-law 's shattered young body was evacuated to the hospital. For the next several weeks Captain Leonard, wrought with horrible pain, agonizingly fought for his life. Finally, on July 17, 1862, in a Confederate hospital, in Richmond, he died. **31** Back at home, in Columbus, Jones's wife Mary learned that her brother was dead. Mary's father, Van Leonard II, had passed away just the year before on August 2, 1861. With her brother and father both dead, Mary would have to be strong, but at least she still had her dear husband, John and her sons, Leonard, Henry and Charles. The Jones, Benning and Leonard families mourned the loss of Van, and consoled Mary (Leonard) Jones as lovingly as they could. Meanwhile, Mary Benning was forced to ponder the reality of war. Would her brother John, her nephew Leonard, her son Seaborn, or even her own husband, Colonel Henry Benning, meet a similar fate?

Chapter 13

Colonel Benning

The fighting during the Peninsula Campaign bolstered the morale of the southern populace, and the Richmond defenses were strengthened enough to support an offensive campaign. General Lee was an excellent commander, and he reorganized his Army of Northern Virginia in preparation for the offensive. Lee promoted Longstreet to Major General and assigned him to command the First Corps, with three divisions commanded by Generals Lafayette McLaws, David R. Jones and John Bell Hood . Toombs and Anderson 's brigades remained in Jones's division. While the brigades of Generals Semmes and Cobb were reassigned to McLaws division. The other corps commander was Major General Thomas J. " Stonewall" Jackson. This reorganized structure would suit Lee well as he embarked on a campaign to threaten the North. Nevertheless, as usual, General Toombs was displeased with the arrangements. Several officers ascended in rank under Lee's reorganization, and Toombs felt that he deserved a promotion, and he continued his verbal attacks of President Davis and the other " West Pointers. "

Adding to his notoriety and impetuous reputation, Toombs became embroiled in an altercation with General Daniel Harvey Hill. Hill was one of the many West Point graduates that Toombs despised. However, General Hill was an accomplished military professional, abrasive and known for his caustic personality. General Hill had recently been promoted to the rank of Major General, and in his official report of the battle of Malvern Hill, he made observations, which did not reflect well upon the conduct of General Toombs. Hill's remarks cast doubt on Toombs leadership abilities. Specifically, Hill simply observed that in the disastrous charge at Malvern Hill Toombs " retreated in disorder." Toombs was infuriated, and demanded " personal satisfaction for the insult you have cast upon me," and " I prefer you to my friend Colonel Benning for all necessary arrangements." 1 Toombs open challenge to a duel was viewed as totally unprofessional and tolerated only because the Confederacy needed field commanders. Being a professional soldier, General Hill ignored Toomb's remarks and stated that " if the simple truth has been offensive, the interpretation of it has been your own." **2** Eventually, both Hill and Toombs would suffer from the ill effects of their unbridled remarks, but in August of 1862, their services were needed, as Lee launched an offensive campaign into Union territory.

General Jackson and his corps moved out first to secure the railhead at Gordonsville, Virginia and strike at General John Pope, whom Lincoln was depending on to guard the western mountains of Virginia. On August 9, 1862, at the Battle of Cedar Mountain, Jackson defeated a force twice the size of his own. With Pope's forces no longer a viable threat, Lee dispatched the other half of his army. Toombs brigade deployed via rail and arrived at Gordonsville on August 13. **3** The Army of Northern Virginia halted just south of the Rapidan River, where Toombs behavior clashed with the stern will of General James Longstreet. Longstreet personally ordered Toombs to post a guard at Raccoon Ford, a crossing on the Rapidan River. Toombs remarked that " his men were tired and worn out, and that he could guard the bridge with an old woman and a broomstick." **4** Worst of all, Toombs failed to carry out Longstreet's order. That evening, Toombs went off on a personal adventure, visiting with an " old congressional friend" who lived in the area. When Toombs returned to camp, he discovered that several of his regiments had been dispatched to guard the bridge. Infuriated, Toombs impulsively countermanded the order and the pickets were withdrawn. This was a tremendous mistake, as late that night, Union cavalry crossed the Rapidan at Raccoon Ford, which was not guarded. The ensuing raid by the federal cavalry on General J.E.B. Stuart 's Confederate cavalry, resulted in the capture of important documents and nearly General Stuart himself. Because of his impetuous and insubordinate behavior, Longstreet had Toombs arrested. The command of Toombs Brigade then devolved upon Colonel Henry L. Benning, commander of the Seventeenth Georgia. **5**

In a letter to the Vice President (and a close, long-term personal friend) Alexander H. Stephens, Toombs writes:

> I am here under arrest... he [Longstreet] ordered me under arrest for " usurpation of authority" a new crime to me and to the articles of war. This was the sole and only cause of my arrest, which of course was very unexpected to me.

In the same letter, Toombs relays the following premonition to his friend:

This army is now strong, stronger than it will ever be again. It will weaken each day, and you will find it difficult to keep it together next winter. All that is in it should be got out of it now, and I think a quick march into Maryland would cause Washington to be evacuated and close the war. 6

Meanwhile, the Army of Northern Virginia marched north, crossed the Rapidan River on August 18, and the Rappahannock River on the 26th. Longstreet's corps continued behind Jackson 's corps, turning right, to the east and entered Thoroughfare Gap. This natural passage in the Bull Run Mountains is located in the beautiful Blue Ridge region, west of Manassas, Virginia. After a very exhausting march, Thoroughfare Gap was reached by the brigade about 4 p.m. on the afternoon of August 28, 1862. The gap contained a rail line, a road and a creek, which wound its way, from west to east, providing an easy passage towards Manassas. Jackson's corps had passed through the gap and was again pressing Pope's army near Manassas. As Longstreet's corps passed through the gap, it was attacked by Federal troops assigned to General Rickett's Division, of General Pope 's Army of Virginia (U.S.). This unit was responsible for defending the area west of Manassas, and their mission was to halt his passage and separate the two Confederate corps. Just as " Benning's brigade " passed through the gap, following the Manassas rail line to the east, they were ambushed from both sides of the gap. 7

The brunt of the fire was coming from two Union batteries, which poured fire into the troops, along the railroad, from the south, with the Twentieth regiment in the lead, thus bearing the brunt of the lethal fire. General David R. Jones ordered Colonel Benning to assault the heights above them and hold it. These heights were Pond Mountain and Benning's task would be difficult. Seizing the importance of his task," Colonel Benning, who commanded the brigade, led the Second and Twentieth regiments in person up the side of the mountain to the right, and put them in position to repel any attack the enemy might make from that direction." 8 The heights were very steep, and scaling them was a difficult task, as the terrain was covered with dense undergrowth, consisting of stiff undergrowth, vines, bushes and ivy. Colonel Benning ordered the Twentieth, commanded by Major James D. Waddell, to scale the heights, and the Second regiment, commanded by Lieutenant Colonel Holmes, to follow behind them. Realizing that the Confederates were attempting to take the summit, the Union troops deployed their own Infantry in a race to the top. Disregarding the enemy's fire, from the Union batteries and Infantry rifle fire, Lieutenant Thomas, in a " rapid gait," led a group of skirmishers from the Twentieth regiment in a race to the top. The

Confederates emerged victorious, and the Union forces retreated down the mountain.

The Twentieth deployed a company of skirmishers emplaced along the face of the mountain as pickets. Meanwhile, the Union forces began to set up a battery on the opposite side of the gap. Major Waddell suggested that Colonel Benning should send the brigade's sharpshooters with their long-range guns to the top of the mountain. Benning adopted the idea and ordered thirty marksmen to concentrate on the Union batteries below. The Union artillery fire " was soon abandoned under our stinging fire," thus ruining the efforts of the Union forces. 9 Major Waddell added," My sharpshooters were seasonably directed to prevent the movement, which they did in admirable style and spirit in the space of less than five minutes, killing and wounding many men, among them a captain, and all the horses attached to their gun-carriages, which they succeeded in carrying off the field by hand." 10 Colonel Benning then deployed his brigade to perform a reconnaissance along the heights of the gap, which effectively cleared them from further enemy harassment.

Meanwhile, on the opposite heights of the gap, George " Tige" Anderson's brigade was engaged in similar combat. Lieutenant Seaborn Benning led his troops, clearing that side of the gap of Union troops. Sergeant William Andrews, of the First Georgia Regulars wrote that while in the heat of battle, Lieutenant Benning and Captain John Patton:

> walked our lines, stepping over the men and in 10 feet of the enemy's line of battle, and not receiving a scratch... why both of them were not killed, I have never been able to account for... it seems as though providence must have been watching over them." 11

With darkness approaching the Union forces retreated from the gap, and raced back to join the main force of Rickett's division. Longstreet's Corps passed on through the gap and encamped for the night, while General Jackson's corps met the enemy near Groveton, Virginia. With heavy fighting, Pope attempted to cut Jackson off, thinking that the Confederates were retreating towards the mountains in the west. Longstreet's men slipped into position on the field, to the right of Jackson's line. The next day, as Pope 's forces were committed to fighting Jackson's corps, Longstreet attacked the Union left flank. Having no coherent contingency plan for this situation, Pope finally sent forces to check

Longstreet's advance. This move saved his Army from a certain disaster, and it placed Colonel Benning at the forefront of the fight. **12**

On August 30, 1862, at about 4 p.m., with Jackson's corps pressing the Union from the north, Longstreet's forces swung into action pressing northeast, along Chinn Ridge with the ultimate goal of Henry Hill. General Lee now had the full complement of his army, and he wielded them on-line and in depth, commencing an assault into the Union lines of General Pope. On the right wing, General David R. Jones ordered his division forward. Colonel Benning arranged his line to the right of General Kemper's brigade, and to the left of General " Tige" Anderson 's brigade, which included his son, Lieutenant Seaborn Benning. The entire division headed northeast, on line, for nearly one and one-half miles, across the same open fields where the Confederacy had previously fought the First Battle of Manassas. Crossing the fields under Union artillery fire, Benning's brigade faced the Union left wing. The Union troops extended from north to south, and east, behind the Manassas -Sudley Road, with the main force located at the Henry Hill, just below the Warrenton Turnpike. However, before reaching Henry Hill, the brigade would first have to sweep Chinn ridge of Union forces that were waiting for the assault.

As Benning's line reached the Chinn house, the Twentieth Georgia Regiment veered around to the left of the house, while the other regiments (the Second Georgia, the Fifteenth Georgia, and the Seventeenth Georgia) pivoted around to its right. Colonel Benning went with the Twentieth regiment, as they focused on the Union forces, hidden below the house in a pine thicket. Benning led his forces into the dense forest, in a thundering charge. Benning's troops cleared the Union forces (two regiments) from the thicket and continued to press the fight. Emerging in a clearing beyond the woods, Benning could see that the Union troops were " running in complete rout-a huddled mass," and " They soon got out of sight by the speed they made under the fire in their rear." **13**

Also in this clearing, 400 yards ahead, was a Union battery, which immediately opened fire on his troops. Benning reported that:

> I reflected a moment on what was best to be done. It appeared to
> me that to stay where we were was certain destruction; to retreat
> would be exposing ourselves for a long distance to the enemy's
> shells and might have other worse effects. I thought that upon
> the whole it was better to try to take the battery, especially as I
> could not see any infantry supports near it. I determined to make
> the attempt, and accordingly gave the order to charge the
> battery. This order was obeyed with a shout, and on the
> regiment went at a run. **14**

When his troops had reached within 50 yards of the cannons, Benning realized that his men were in a defile, and he rested them, safely tucked in a natural depression. During their brief reprieve," a terrific storm of missiles was passing just over their heads." 15 Benning then ordered his men to take the battery, and they charged into the deadly fire, but in the interim, several guns were swung around to engage Benning's men on their flank. According to Colonel Waddell of the Twentieth regiment in a great " heroic example," Colonel Benning " conducted the charge in person and inspired the men with new zeal." 16 As Benning's troops charged the gun emplacements on Henry Hill, they were raked with fire from the front and flank, as well as advancing Union Infantry that was coming to the aid of the battery. Again, Benning quickly weighed his choices with:

> I thought it would be madness to let the regiment go on; that if they took the battery they would not be able to hold it, and therefore would after taking it either have to retreat or all be captured or exterminated. I preferred to fall back at once, although some of the men were almost up to the guns. I accordingly gave the order to fall back, and then the regiment in tolerable order fell back about 200 yards under a terrific fire from both of the batteries and from the infantry supports, when it came to the dry bed of the branch already mentioned. There I halted it and ordered the men to lie down in the bed of the branch, and thus get as much protection from enemy's fire as possible, and at the same time be in a position from which they could return that fire with some effect. This they did. 17

As Benning withdrew his men back to the defile and the pine thicket below, he realized that just beyond the thicket was two or three abandoned Union artillery pieces, and the Twentieth regiment captured them. Benning later reported the behavior of the Twentieth regiment during the Second Battle of Manassas as " brilliant," and " nearly one-third were bare-footed, without a piece of leather to their feet." 18

Meanwhile, Benning's other regiments, which had swung around the right of the Chinn house, pressed the Union battery from the flank of the Twentieth regiment. All three regiments engaged the battery and according to Captain McLewis of the Second regiment, the heavy Infantry, which came to the aid of the battery, was a brigade size force. Commanding the

Seventeenth regiment was Major Pickett, who was wounded early in the
fight. Captain Hiram French of the Seventeenth regiment reported that " a
brave officer and perfect gentleman," Captain A C. Lewis, took the
command, and as our ammunition was exhausted and the men nearly
famished for water (not having a drop during the engagement), he ordered
us to fall back to the edge of the wood...scarcely had he given this
command ere he was shot down by a ball passing through his temples.
Captain French took charge of the Seventeenth, and:

> At once we were ordered by our commander to open fire, and
> for over two hours fought desperately, the enemy contesting
> obstinately every inch of ground and terribly cutting our line by
> shell, grape, and musketry. Not a man of my regiment faltered,
> but all acted in the most praiseworthy manner. Our loss was, in
> proportion to the force engaged, extremely heavy. This could
> hardly have been otherwise, as the force we confronted were (as
> prisoners stated), first, Fitz John Porter's men, and next after
> these were beaten, Heintzelman's men-some of the best troops
> under the best officers in the whole Yankee army. [19]

Major James D. Waddell, of the Twentieth regiment summed the up the
action of the brigade stating:

> They drove the cannoneers from their guns, held the position,
> confronting seven hostile flags, supported by at least six times
> their own numbers, and only retired (in good order and under
> orders)."... Color-Bearer James Broderick was shot down at the
> instant of planting the colors in front of the belching cannons.
> Private Nunn seized the flag-staff ere it fell and bore it through
> the remainder of the conflict...It may not be improper to add that
> I carried into the fight over 100 men who were barefoot, many
> of whom left bloody foot-prints among the thorns and briars
> through which they rushed, with Spartan courage and really
> jubilant impetuosity, upon the serried ranks of the foe. [20]

Unbeknownst to Benning, during the battle for Henry Hill, his little
brigade was facing off against the three Pennsylvania batteries of Captain
Dunbar Ransom, and two brigades of Infantry, commanded by General
John Reynolds. Known as the " Pennsylvania Reserves," one of these
brigades was commanded by Brigadier General George Meade, who would
later command the Union, Army of the Potomac. In spite of the heavily
defended Union positions, the surprise and strength of the Confederate

forces overwhelmed them. With Jackson's corps successfully pushing the Confederate left wing, and Longstreet the right, (with Benning at the front), the entire Union army retreated toward Centreville that evening. At the engagement below Henry Hill, with General David R. Jones 's division assaulting in a half mile wide front, it was Benning's brigade that initially cracked the positions on Henry Hill, thus forcing the Union forces to retreat from that portion of the field.

One of Benning's Georgia warriors recorded that the battle was a " severe fight" and " none of the Richmond battles was half so severe as this one," yet," we whipped them out decently. The old 17th had a fair shake and did her work well." 21 In the rear of the formation and late in the evening, with the battle won, General Longstreet released General Toombs to return to his unit. " To our great satisfaction we unexpectedly met our gallant commander, Brigadier-General Toombs, who... was greeted with three hearty cheers, replying," Boys, I am proud of the report given me of you to General Jones. I could not be with you today, but this was owing to no fault of mine. Tomorrow I lead you." 22

The battle was a glorious Confederate victory, but not without great cost to the brigade. Benning's brigade lost 37 killed in action, and another 294 wounded. 23 Most of these casualties were a direct result of the brigade's efforts to dislodge the Union batteries around Henry Hill. At both Malvern Hill and the Second Battle of Manassas, the regiments of Toombs and Benning had faced horrific odds, as men rushed directly into artillery fire. Throughout the war, Infantrymen faced artillery in courageous, yet suicidal assaults, which resulted in horrific human carnage. The tactic of charging into the cannons was simply to overwhelm their crews, which sometimes worked, but always produced scores of casualties. When faced with massed infantry, the defending artillery crews fired " grape and canister" rounds. These gigantic " shotgun blasts," unleashed dozens of grape sized bullets and shards of metal, which ripped through the ranks of their opposition. One of the soldiers of Benning's Seventeenth regiment recorded that the artillery shell that wounded him, also struck two of his close friends, and killed one other. Yet, with an indomitable spirit, many of these men simply became " walking wounded," and continued to fight. In a letter to his sister, Lieutenant Robert Tondee recorded," I was struck with a piece of shell on the right hip joint, and it gives me some pain and troubles me in walking." 24

In spite of courageously leading his men from the front, Colonel Henry Benning, thus far, remained unscathed. The courage and discipline displayed by his men, reflected highly on the leadership of Benning and Toombs. General Longstreet noted the leadership ability of Benning at Thoroughfare Gap and again on the plains of Manassas. While Toombs had returned to his unit, Benning would continue to command the brigade for the remainder of the war, as Toombs was placed in temporary command of the division.

With the victory at Manassas, the Confederacy decided to continue their offensive, and invade northern soil. General Lee immediately dispatched General " Stonewall" Jackson with his forces to take the Union garrison at Harper's Ferry, while he led the remainder of his Army of Northern Virginia across the state line, into Maryland. The brigade, in line of march with the Army of Northern Virginia, crossed the Potomac River and entered Maryland on September 3, 1862. Passing through Frederick, Maryland, the brigade arrived in Hagerstown on September 11, displaying a serious threat to the State of Pennsylvania. The Southern army was doing well, gaining recognition, respect, and badly needed re-supply. Food was plentiful in the region, and the men triumphantly marched on Union soil. An invasion of the North was embarrassing for the Union, and Lincoln sent McClellan in pursuit of Lee. 25

McClellan's forces gave chase on a broad front, trailing closely behind and to the east of Longstreet's corps. Lee ordered Longstreet to block the Union movement at South Mountain, to gain time in retrieving Jackson's forces. Longstreet succeeded in delaying the Union forces, but he had to retreat from the field, under the cover of darkness, due to the massive opposition consisting of three corps. Lee ordered all of his forces to converge upon the heights, west of Antietam Creek , at Sharpsburg, Maryland. General Lee was a master at taking initiatives and shaping the battlefield. On September 15, 1862, Longstreet's forces were assigned to defend the Confederate right wing, on the outskirts of Sharpsburg, Maryland. Two of his divisions were still on the march, defending their supply trains from Union cavalry, and had not yet joined him at Sharpsburg. The terrain at Sharpsburg was advantageous for a defense, and Longstreet configured his positions wisely. In a broad front, the Confederates held the key terrain facing the approaching Union forces. On the extreme Confederate right, with two regiments (Fifteenth and Seventeenth) detailed miles to the rear, defending the army's supply trains from marauding Union cavalry, Benning emplaced his available forces in a defensive posture, overlooking the lower bridge of the Antietam Creek. On the morning of September 17, 1862, at 5:30 a.m., the battle of Sharpsburg (also referred to as the battle of Antietam) began.

The battle commenced on the Confederate left with a bloody assault from the Union I Corps. This action ended in a stalemate several hours

later with little tactical consequence, except for an incredible loss of life.
Around 07:30 a.m., the Union XII Corps attacked the Confederate left, and
the Union II Corps commenced their attack about 09:15 a.m., attacking the
center and pushing the Confederate lines back to the vicinity of the
Hagerstown Turnpike. The fighting was brutal, and the defending
Confederates in this fight included the brigades of General Paul Semmes
and Colonel George " Tige" Anderson. The First Georgia Regulars and
young Lieutenant Seaborn Benning were there too. Again, the fighting
ebbed after several hours of human carnage, which contributed to the war's
" bloodiest single day of fighting." **26** Meanwhile, on the Confederate right,
with his task of defending the lower bridge along the Antietam Creek,
Colonel Henry Benning listened to the ensuing fray while scanning his
front for the enemy. He did not have to wait long, as the entire Union IX
corps, led by General Ambrose Burnside appeared before the bridge.
Benning's tiny contingent of Georgia warriors courageously awaited his
commands.

Benning's position dominated the terrain above the bridge, and he
had emplaced the Second regiment, commanded by Lieutenant Colonel
Holmes, on the left and the Twentieth regiment, commanded by Colonel
John Cumming, and his deputy commander, Lieutenant Colonel John A.
Jones , on the right, overlooking the bridge. The men reinforced the steep
and wooded terrain with fence rails, deadfall and rocks, forming crude
barricades. Some hid behind trees, while others took up sniper positions
within the trees. They also placed themselves within natural depressions
for cover and concealment. Benning's men were natural woodsman and
skilled hunters, who excelled in imaginatively creating a formidable
position. Adding to their lethality, behind them on the ridge above, was a
Confederate battery of the Washington (Virginia) Artillery, aimed at the
approaches of the bridge. Colonel Benning also placed pickets and
skirmishers several hundred yards to the front of his position. As the Union
corps approached, the Confederate battery commanded by Captain Eubank
opened fire, which checked the Union advance for a short while. Benning
withdrew his pickets, just as Captain Eubank was recalled to bolster
another segment of the battle. Facing an entire corps of enemy, with just a
remnant of his brigade, and no artillery support, Benning was literally on
his own. According to Colonel Benning his troops:

Numbered not more than 350 men and officers, the Second
having only 97, and the Twentieth not more than 250. In their

front was Burnside's whole Corps of not fewer than 12,000 or
15,000 of the enemy's best men, with a numerous artillery. In
this forlorn condition were the two regiments at about nine
o'clock, when the fight opened in earnest. 27

With a combined arms thrust of troops and artillery, Burnside's
troops attempted to cross the bridge, but Benning's men successfully
repulsed them. With the Union troops attacking in five successive waves,
Benning's men continued to pour deadly enfilade fire into their enemy.
The pressure became heavier around noon, as even more Union troops
arrived, and artillery batteries were emplaced to focus enfilade artillery fire
on Benning's forces. Eventually, the Union troops discovered that the
creek was only knee-deep, and they began crossing it above and below the
bridge. As the Union troops began pouring across the creek and scaling the
heights, the Confederates frantically fought to deny the Union advance. "
Colonel Holmes who was one of the best of shots, took a musket, firing
some eight or nine times, called for a long range gun with which he shot
down the Color Bearer, remarking that he would not take five-hundred
dollars for that shot." 28 The Georgians were excellent marksmen, and they
did their best to contain the Union corps behind the bridge. With simply
too many targets, the tiny band could not possibly contain the
overwhelming waves of Union forces. Yet, Benning's troops did not yield
until they had no choice. In the ranks of the Second regiment," we held the
position until our last round of ammunition was exhausted." 29 Just as they
ran out of ammunition, Benning's friend and fellow commander of the
Second regiment, Lieutenant Colonel Holmes was killed. With the Second
regiment out of ammunition, and the Twentieth running low, Benning
wisely ordered a withdrawal. Leaving a small contingent led by Colonel
Cumming, Benning's main force ran up the hill to the rear, while
Cumming's men followed, providing what protection they could muster.
Colonel Benning stated that at the bridge:

> The Second Regiment lost in killed and wounded forty-two;
> nearly half of it's number. Among it's killed was Lieutenant
> Colonel Holmes, a good officer, and as gallant a man, I think, as
> my eyes ever beheld. The loss of the Twentieth in killed,
> wounded, and missing was sixty-eight, more than a fourth of it's
> number. No words of mine in praise of officers and men are
> needed. The simple story is eulogy enough. I must, however,
> bear witness to one fact: During that long and terrible fire, not a
> man, except a wounded one, fell out and went to the rear--not a
> man. The loss of the enemy was heavy. Near the bridge, they lay

in heaps. Their own estimate, as a paroled sergeant of ours taken
at the bridge told me, was at from 500 to 1,000 men killed. He
also told me that they informed him that at about 12 o'clock an
order came from General McClellan to take the bridge, cost
what it might, and that then the whole corps advanced to attack.
30

Just as the withdrawal from the bridge occurred, the Fifteenth and
Seventeenth regiments arrived on the heights from the opposite direction.
Released from their detail, they raced to join their unit on the field. Upon
their arrival, they were placed in a defensive posture, along the summit,
and above Antietam Creek. General Toombs arrived and placed Benning in
command of his reformed brigade and the Eleventh Georgia, commanded
by Major Little. Once his unit was reorganized, they repulsed several
companies of advancing Union skirmishers, until about four o'clock, as the
Union forces cautiously approached the Confederate lines. " Though the
bridge and upper ford were thus left open to the enemy, he moved with
such extreme caution and slowness that he lost nearly two hours in
crossing and getting into action on our side of the river, about which time
General A. P. Hill's division arrived from Harper's Ferry." **31** Toombs then
ordered Benning's brigade off the line for an ammunition resupply and
some badly needed rest, and they were replaced on the line, by General
Maxcy Gregg's brigade of South Carolinians. Benning re-armed his men
along Harper's Ferry Road, then headed towards Sharpsburg.

While they were on their way to take a much-deserved break, a
courier ordered them to double-quick along the road to Sharpsburg.
Unbeknownst to Benning, as the Union troops crossed the bridge and
scaled the heights, they had drifted around to the left of the Confederate
line, with no one to check them. Burnside's IX corps was in a position to
sever the Confederate lines and take the town of Sharpsburg. Benning
could not see his enemy as the field was obscured with tall corn. Benning's
troops double-quicked for nearly a half-mile up Harper's Ferry Road.
Along the road, tall stalks of corn prevented Benning from viewing the
fields below, but somewhere below them were Union troops. Just as the
rows of tall corn gave way to a fallow field, Benning suddenly observed
that " a brigade of them was standing composedly in line of battle not 200
yards from the road" **32** The lead enemy formation consisted of Colonel
Edward Harland's Connecticut Infantry, and they were dangerously close
to Sharpsburg. Benning's lead element was Major Little's troops, followed

by the Seventeenth, commanded by Captain McGregor, the Fifteenth, under Colonel Millican, and most of the Twentieth commanded by Colonel Cumming. Immediately seizing the opportunity, Benning ordered his men to attack the Union brigade. Captain McGregor, commanding the Seventeenth regiment observed upon reaching the enemy, that the enemy's long lines were " in position in grand style. I took my position and ordered my men to open fire upon them, at the same time, to be cool and aim well, which they did. After a short but desperate struggle, the enemy gave way, and we went forward." 33 Denying the Union commander little time to react, Colonel Benning leading his troops from the front, ordered his men to commence fire and attack. Benning recorded that:

> I carried the head of the line opposite to the right of the enemy, and ordered it to commence firing on the enemy without waiting for the rest of the line to come up. It did so with promptness and spirit. The rest of the line as it came up joined in the fire. The fire soon became general. It was hot and rapid. The enemy returned it with vigor, and showed a determination to hold their position stubbornly. In about ten or fifteen minutes a cannon or two opened on them, and their line, which had already showed signs of wavering, broke, and fled down the hill and was soon out of sight, concealed by the crest of the hill. General Toombs ordered pursuit, and our whole line rapidly advanced after them. 34

Within just a few minutes, Benning's brigade inflicted casualties in the Eighth Connecticut Infantry of nearly 200 men. Realizing that the Union force below the hill was unknown, but certainly larger than his own; General Toombs rode over to Benning's brigade and ordered a halt. Benning sent forward a small contingent of scouts armed with long range rifles. Most of the Union forces had retreated off the hill with the exception of a large group who took up a defensive position behind a fence. General Toombs personally led this assault, which succeeded in dislodging the enemy, but it carried a heavy toll. Captain Thomas Jackson of the Fifteenth regiment reported that," We charged the enemy a distance of half a mile, until we reached a rock fence, where we halted and continued firing until dark, at which point, the colonel was killed." 35 Jackson's colonel was William T. Millican, commander of the Fifteenth regiment.

On that fateful day of September 17, 1862, the fields around Sharpsburg, Maryland were saturated with the blood of approximately 22,000 men. Most of the casualties were young men, and for many of them, their lives ended on that single bloodiest day of the Civil War. While

Colonel Henry Benning was busy defending the lower bridge, over in the West Woods, near the Dunker Church, young Lieutenant Seaborn Benning was fighting for his life. Struggling to stem the flow of blood from his head, Seaborn's life was in jeopardy. Yet, in spite of the blinding pain, and the overwhelming odds against him, young Seaborn Benning managed to escape the swirling carnage, and he staggered to the rear. Eventually he was transported to the hospital in Virginia. Immediately upon notification that her only son was wounded, Mary Benning rushed to Virginia, retrieved her son, and returned him to Columbus to convalesce. As in all wars, those that survive their wounds, although transformed with some degree of disability, recommence their lives. Many of the less fortunate men lost limbs, but Seaborn was lucky. After several months of his mother's care, Seaborn would rejoin his father and his comrades upon the field of battle. Yet, for the remainder of his life, tasks would be more challenging than before, as Seaborn struggled with bouts of temporary blindness until the day he died. **36**

Continuing to fight despite overwhelming odds was the hallmark of the Confederacy. Benning's brigade, while dwindling in numbers, was gaining a spirit of dogged determination. In Benning's report of the battle, he humbly submitted that:

> The conduct of both officers and men was, as far as I could observe it, as good as it could be. To mention some names without mentioning all would therefore be unjust. The service they rendered...was, I think, hardly to be overestimated. If General Burnside 's corps had once got through the long gap in our line it would soon have been in the rear of our whole army, and that anybody can see would have been disastrous. **37**

Toombs official report of the battle concluded that," Colonel Benning stood by his brigade on the Antietam, guiding, directing, and animating his officers and men with distinguished coolness, courage, and skill; withdrew them from that perilous condition; again led them, with equal skill and courage, in the final conflict with the enemy. He deserves the special consideration of the Government." **38**

While the complement of General Toombs and " special consideration" from Richmond was important to Colonel Benning, he discovered that as a field commander, there were more important issues at hand. Colonel Benning knew that his band of warriors were confident in his leadership, and that in the heat of battle, he " stood by his brigade." In return for his steadfast courage and a hard earned genuine affection, Colonel Benning was bestowed, by his men, with the sobriquet " Old Rock. " 39 Benning's nickname was a reflection of both his personality and his actions. To his men, Benning was the epitome of strength and conviction. He had earned their respect before the war in the halls of justice, and in the forum of secession, but now his reputation rose to new heights. Prepared to give his life for " the cause," Benning expected no less from his men, and many opportunities lay ahead.

At nightfall on September 17, having suffered 160 casualties during the battle, General Toombs forces reoccupied the same positions, of which, they had held on the previous day. General Ambrose Burnside 's IX Corps was back on the eastern side of Antietam Creek, and had suffered more than 2,300 casualties. The Battle of Antietam had ended in a bloody stalemate, but it halted the Confederate offensive. With an even smaller army, and precariously extended, General Lee would have to retreat, lest he be surrounded in Union territory. Once again, the Union forces had gone into battle with superior strength, but armed with fortitude and dogged determination, the Confederate troops proved to be a worthy opponent. 40 Throughout the evening, the brigade scoured the field of the day's battle, collecting weapons and prisoners. With the exception of the moaning wounded, the night was warm and pleasant. Finally, with their duties for the day accomplished, they stretched out their weary bodies upon the blood soaked field, and in utter exhaustion, they slept. 41

The outcome of the Battle of Sharpsburg may have been quite different had the Confederate right wing secured by Benning's brigade, faltered. If Burnside's corps had achieved the heights, and the town of Sharpsburg, Lee's forces would have been flanked and easily " rolled up." Many historians have long credited General A.P. Hill for saving the day and driving the Union troops back down to the lower bridge. While Hill's assistance was certainly instrumental in supporting the right wing (after the Union assault was repulsed); it was General Toombs commanding the division and the Confederate right wing that held the Union at bay. Furthermore, it was Benning's brigade that held the bridge, then spearheaded the counter-attack upon the Union assault, and drove them back down to the Antietam Creek. The Georgians repeatedly repulsed General Ambrose Burnside 's IX Corps, which numbered 13,819 men. His attempts to cross Antietam Creek on the lower bridge were successfully delayed throughout the morning, with less than a brigade, (400 men, and a ratio of 34:1). The Union casualties suffered at the lower bridge, by a conservative tally, exceed 1,000 men. From that day forward, the lower bridge across Antietam Creek has been known as " Burnside's Bridge. "

Years later, after the war and concerned with correcting a distortion of the facts, Henry Benning recorded that:

> A.P. Hill 's troops came up before night, but none of them had
> much part in the fight; none of them had any part in first
> breaking the line. I give the above detail for the benefit of
> General Toombs, as I have understood that the credit of retaking
> Sharpsburg was perhaps claimed for General A.P. Hill. Toombs
> is the man, however. **42**

    The day after the " bloodiest battle of the war" found the two armies facing one another from nearly the same positions that were established on 17, September. As both sides pondered their next move, the next few days were spent in a quasi-truce, while reconsolidating their forces, evacuating their wounded, and burying the dead. General Toombs was hailed as " the toast of the army," in both the North and South for the gallant defense of his and Benning's brigade at the lower bridge. **43** On the evening of the 18th, Toombs and his staff were approaching Benning's camp, when a troop of cavalry approached them in the darkness. Toombs challenged the troopers, and they responded with " We are friends." Captain Troup, Toombs's Adjutant realized their scheme and fired into them. The troopers returned their fire, and General Toombs was badly wounded in the hand. Toombs and his staff continued on to Benning's camp, informed him of the affair, and to prepare his brigade to march, as General Lee had decided to retreat back into Virginia. **44**
    While certainly not defeated, the southern army had been significantly reduced in number, while the Union troops had been re-enforced. Luckily for the south, General McClellan over estimated his opponent's size and failed to strike again at the weakened Army of Northern Virginia. Lee's Army of Northern Virginia crossed the Potomac again and sought refuge within his home state of Virginia. The army then moved to Winchester on the 25th and concentrated their efforts on reorganization. On September 30, General Toombs and his son-in-law, Captain Dudley M. Dubose departed for Washington, Georgia on a leave of absence. Physically, Toomb's hand was shattered by a bullet, but his most painful injury was much deeper and filled with emotion.
    Toombs had performed admirably on the battlefield, but the man was a politician at heart. At Sharpsburg, he had commanded General David Jones ' division, proving that he could handle a higher command and rank,

but the Confederacy would not promote him above the rank of Brigadier
General. Toombs felt that he should have the promotion and the division.
General Jones was ill, and troubled with a weak heart. Adding to Jones's
burdens, his brother-in-law, Colonel H. W. Kingsley, commander of the
11th Connecticut Infantry, had been killed while charging Benning's
brigade at the lower bridge. Jones's health and his ability to command
rapidly failed, and he died the following year. While on leave, Toombs
would wait and see if the Confederacy would promote him. Awaiting the
decision, and healing from his wound, Toombs pondered whether to
continue his military career, while Colonel Benning continued in command
of the brigade. **45**

During the next few months, following the battle of Sharpsburg, there
were many changes made in Lee's Army of Northern Virginia. Benning's
brigade received a new division commander, General John Bell Hood, of
Texas. Replacing General David Jones, Hood had a reputation of being an
aggressive tactician and a highly professional soldier, and Benning's
Georgians worked well with the Texans. The division remained an integral
part of General James Longstreet 's Corps, although General Lee simply
numbered his corps, thus Longstreet's corps was thereafter known as the
First Corps, Army of Northern Virginia. Noted for his success as a
Commissary officer, Colonel Raphael Moses ascended to the same position
on Longstreet's corps. Several of Benning's other friends achieved
promotions and increased responsibilities, and among them were General
Howell and Colonel Thomas R. R. Cobb. Thomas was promoted to the
rank of Brigadier-General and given command of his own brigade in
McLaws division, while Howell Cobb was transferred to Georgia,
promoted to the rank of Major General and placed in command of the
military district of Georgia and Florida. Benning's son, Seaborn, healing
from his battle wound, remained at home on an extended furlough. **46**

Meanwhile, President Lincoln was infuriated with General
McClellan, who had consistently failed to exploit his advantages over Lee's
smaller forces. McClellan was replaced with General Burnside. The Union
forces restructured their Army of the Potomac into three " Grand Divisions
" , which consisted of well over 100,000 men. Slowly, the Union moved
their tremendous military machine south, again, towards Richmond. **47** On
the home front in Georgia, not only had many families lost their husbands,
fathers and sons, Lincoln had further insulted them with rumors of
emancipation for the Negroes. Recruitment of new troops swelled and they
were rapidly dispatched to the field. **48**

Chapter 14

Brigadier General Benning

In November of 1862, Burnside and his " Grand Divisions " of the
Army of the Potomac departed Warrenton, Virginia enroute to
Fredericksburg, where his army would cross the Rappahannock River.
With an army of 130,000 men, once across the river, the massive Union
army would continue traveling south, with their ultimate goal being
Richmond. Fortunately for the Confederacy, heavy rain had swollen the
river, thus creating a natural obstacle for the Union army. This movement
caught Lee off guard, but he swiftly put his army into motion, moved
parallel to Burnside, and then fish hooked in front of his adversary on the
opposite side of the river. Benning's brigade and their fellow members of
Longstreet's corps, arrived in Fredericksburg on November 22. Jackson's
corps swung east and was also emplaced at Fredericksburg. Lee had his
army construct lines of defensive trenches along the high ground
overlooking the town. With the establishment of an extremely formidable
barrier to Burnside and his grand plan, Lee efficiently blocked Burnside's
grand plan. Meanwhile, the Union forces waited for the arrival of their
pontoon bridges, which were urgently required to cross the Rappahannock
River. Waiting to repulse the Union advance, was Lee's Army of Northern
Virginia, although outnumbered, yet somewhat replenished and
restructured since the battle of Sharpsburg. By December of 1862, General
Lee 's army was now at strength more than 72,000 men, yet, as usual for
the Confederacy, the opposition forces were nearly twice their strength. 1
      On December 11, 1862, with winter rapidly approaching, Burnside
had to get his army across the river, and he decided to enforce a crossing at
Fredericksburg. In spite of the frigid weather, Union engineers worked
desperately to emplace bridging and pontoons across the Rappahannock
River. Meanwhile, Lee continued to strengthen his defenses, consisting of
a line extending seven miles, with General Longstreet on the left,

occupying the town and the heights, while Jackson's corps held lower
ground along the right. Militarily, the Confederates enjoyed the advantage.
In topography, the Union would have to traverse a large obstacle, the river,
then fight a steep uphill battle, against Longstreet's Corps entrenched in
the heights. If they attacked the Confederate right, Jackson's Corps had a
large open plain which would serve as a giant killing field if the enemy
approached in his sector. Lee also had three hundred pieces of artillery
aiming directly at Burnside's likely avenues of approach. Quietly waiting
for the inevitable hostilities to commence, Benning's brigade was safely
tucked within the earthworks near the Confederate center of the line.
Enjoying a unique opportunity to sit and wait for the battle to come to
them, the Confederates eagerly prepared the best positions that time and
their energies could construct. Benning recorded that," The brigade showed
the most commendable activity and energy in strengthening its position to
resist attack. In a single night, with eight spades, six or eight picks, and a
very few axes, it rendered its position impregnable to small arms." **2**

In spite of the cold weather, swift river currents, and Confederate
sharpshooters, Burnside's engineers achieved their mission, and the Union
army began their assault of Fredericksburg on December 13, 1862. The
Union assault was bolstered with an artillery duel. While the Confederate
artillerists focused on the Union main assault force, the Union artillery
countered the Confederate cannons and poured continuous fire into the
Confederate earthworks. Enduring the rain of artillery fire behind a
protective earthen berm, Colonel Benning stated that," Still, the brigade
was near enough to his batteries to suffer some casualties from the artillery
fire." **3** Throughout the day, as Burnside directed wave after wave of Union
troops into Fredericksburg, the Union artillery attempted to weaken the
Confederates, pouring their deadly fire into the Southern trench line.
Hugging the earth and enduring the horror of exploding shells, the
Confederate Infantrymen could only hope that the shells would miss them.
According to Benning, along the trench in his brigade," Shells were
bursting on its line, especially that part of the line occupied by the
Fifteenth and Twentieth Georgia, every few minutes during the whole
battle; and it is cause for thankfulness that the casualties were so few. The
men were quiet and firm under this long ordeal." **4** Testament to the
lethality and effects of indirect artillery fire, Benning's brigade lost two
men seriously maimed, and two men killed.

Yet, despite the artillery fire, Benning and his beleaguered brigade of
staunch Georgians were sparred the ensuing human carnage being waged
nearby. On the Confederate left, along the heights of Fredericksburg,
behind a stone wall at the base of Marye's Heights, Thomas R. R. Cobb
and his brigade bore the brunt of the Union assault. During a lull in the

assaults, Cobb was meeting with a several officers when a cannon round exploded nearby them. One of the officers was killed, and several were severely wounded. One of the wounded men was Thomas Cobb. Spurting blood from a severed artery, Cobb was evacuated to the rear where a surgeon desperately tried to repair the damage. In spite of the surgeon's efforts, Cobb continued losing blood and he slowly lapsed into a coma. Shortly thereafter, Benning's dear friend and fellow secessionist, was dead. In the profound words of his biographer," Thomas Cobb had given his life in defense of southern nationalism." 5

On that cold day in December, nearly 5,000 Confederate soldiers became casualties in defense of their country, but Burnside's Union army suffered more than 12,000 men. Yet again, Lee's Army of Northern Virginia had won a decisive victory against an overwhelming enemy. Burnside was determined to cross the river and continue his campaign, but he would not try again at Fredericksburg. In a driving, frigid rain, Burnside attempted to maneuver his army and threaten the Confederates elsewhere. Fortunately for the Confederacy, the weather turned the roads and surrounding area to mush. Burnside's giant military machine bogged down in an event known to his army as the " Mud March," which resulted in nothing but misery and an exercise in futility. Fraught with frustration, Burnsides was relieved and President Lincoln replaced him with General Joseph Hooker . 6

Just after the battle of Fredericksburg, Colonel Benning received a letter from General Toombs expressing his frustration with the military and he stated that," I am content to leave you as my executor," but also " I hope to join you next week." 7 It was clear that Toombs had decided to return, yet Toomb's future in the military, remained uncertain. Toombs also sent word that he had seen " Mrs. Benning, in Columbus, she was weak and sick, but improving." 8 Benning's frail little wife had been left to handle a tremendous load, and she was stricken ill that winter. Her husband had been gone for sixteen months and her only son was at home with a horrible wound. First, young Van Leonard had been killed, and now Thomas Cobb, was dead too. Mary had been to Virginia, where she saw, first hand, the horrors in the Confederate hospitals. So many of her friends and acquaintances had given their all for the Confederacy, and after a year of fighting, there was little to encourage her. Yet, resolved to support the Confederacy, Mary Benning could do little more than worry about her husband and continue to be strong for him and her family.

Meanwhile, on the field of battle, fate had been kind to Colonel Benning and his brigade. The Battle of Fredericksburg was the final tragic episode in the series of human slaughter during 1862. With Christmas just weeks away and the gray wintry skies overhead, both sides collected and buried their dead. After lying overnight in freezing temperatures, their stiff and distorted bodies had to be pried from their fixated positions and covered with clods of frozen dirt. Some were stacked in buildings and not buried until spring. Both armies then began preparing their quarters for another long winter season, camped in the field. 9 On December 28, 1862, the brigade settled into winter quarters near Guinea Station, Virginia. Although the Union forces were still located just on the other side of the Rappahannock River, the weather made another assault impractical. Again, the southern army concentrated on enduring the cold. Now, with winter well entrenched, the year 1863 made its silent debut.

The New Year saw General Toombs and Captain DuBose reunited with their brigade. On January 1, 1863, an election was held for the regimental command of the Fifteenth Georgia. DuBose won the election by an overwhelming majority. Private Thomas Ware of the Fifteenth Georgia recorded the victory of DuBose in his diary, and he also added that the year 1862 was over and that:

> Its shadows are stamped upon the heart of the nation. Its
> sorrows and sad bereavements are felt around every hearthstone.
> Many who greeted the last new year morn with bright hopes,
> and beaming prospects, now lie cold and still upon the
> battlefields, where midnight winds sing a requiem over their
> graves," Peace to their Ashes." The new year is upon us. May its
> sorrows be few; and ere its declining sun shall set, may the
> halcyon days again open and may we all meet around our
> firesides once more with our friends. So mote it be. 10

On January 19, 1863, Henry Benning was promoted to the rank of Brigadier General, and he was given a temporary assignment to Semmes brigade. 11 Shortly thereafter, amongst the troops, it was whispered that," Rumor is current in camps that General Toombs has resigned." 12 The rumors were true. Facing the realization that the Confederate hierarchy would not grant Toombs a promotion, he decided to relinquish his command and resign his commission. In an eloquent farewell, Toombs addressed his former brigade with:

> The separation from you is deeply painful to me. It is only
> necessary now for me to say that, under existing circumstances,

in my judgement, I could no longer hold my commission under President Davis with advantage to my country or to you, or with honor to myself. I cannot separate from you without the expression of my warmest attachment to you and admiration of your noble and heroic conduct from the beginning of this great struggle to the present time. You left your wives and children, kindred, friends, home, property, and pursuits at the very first call of your country, and entered her military service as soon as she was ready to accept you. From that day to this you have stood, with but few brief intervals, in sight of the public enemy or within hearing distance of his guns. Upon your arrival in Virginia, in the summer of 1861, you were incorporated into the Army of the Potomac. You have shared with that army all its toils, its sufferings, its hardships and perils, and contributed at least your share to its glorious career. You have been in the front, the post of danger and of honor, on all the great battlefields of Northern Virginia and Maryland, from Yorktown to Sharpsburg. Neither disheartened by the death of comrades or friends, nor by disease or toil, or privations or sufferings or neglect, nor intimidated by the greatly superior numbers of the enemy, whom you have been called upon to meet and vanquish, you have upon all occasions displayed that heroic courage which has shed undying luster upon yourselves, your State, your country, and her just and holy cause. Nearly one thousand of the brave men who originally composed your four regiments have fallen, killed or wounded in battle. Your dead have been buried on the battlefield, shed a manly tear over them, left " glory to keep eternal watch" over their graves, and pressed on to new fields of duty and danger. Though it may seem to be the language of extravagant eulogy, it is the truth, and fit, on this occasion, to be spoken. You have fairly won the right to inscribe on your battered war flags the proud boast of Napoleon's Old Guard: " This brigade knows how to die, but not to yield to the foe." Courage on the field is not your only claim to proud distinction. Since I took command over you I have not preferred a single charge against or arraigned one of you before a court - martial; your conduct never demanded such a duty. You can well appreciate the feelings with which I part from such a command. Nothing less potent than the requirements of a

soldier's honor could, with my consent, wrench us asunder while
a single banner of the enemy floated over one foot of our
country. Soldiers, comrades, friends, farewell! **13**

Upon the resignation of General Toombs, General Henry Benning
was transferred back to his former brigade, where he would assume
command. Benning would genuinely miss Robert Toombs. Together, the
pair had forged a reputation as excellent commanders, and their men were
bestowed with honor for their exploits on the field of battle. Yet, Henry
Benning, with his steadfast nature and determined sense of
accomplishment was better suited to the role of military commander than
his counterpart. Benning had well proven his abilities of command during
the previous campaigns and he earned the admiration of his superiors,
peers and subordinates alike. He was described as being a very physical
man, nearly six feet tall and of noble presence and bearing. His attributes
of courage, candor and high ethical values had been displayed throughout
his life. Now those attributes were hardened with military discipline and
Benning would prove to be one of the Confederacies most reliable and
dedicated Generals. **14**
The men of the brigade welcomed back " Old Rock," and while the
winter was brutally cold, the atmosphere in the brigade was warm and
filled with happiness. Food was bountiful, there was little threat of battle,
and the general mood was one of reflection and a longing for home. On
one of the long frigid evenings that winter, a soldier recorded that," The
band are playing some very good pieces, are playing at a late hour. I am up
reading at 10 p.m. the moon shines beautiful. Very cold." **15** General
Benning 's mind was occupied with thoughts of home, and a longing for
the love of his wife, Mary. Benning's brigade contained some excellent
musicians, and their band, composed primarily of members of the Second
regiment was enjoyed by all. According to First Sergeant William R.
Houghton of the " Columbus Guards:"

> Sometimes, the band would go to General Benning 's campfire
> and give him a serenade, for the brave old man was deservedly
> popular. He would smoke his pipe and look in the fire while
> they played beautiful airs, until they were about ready to depart,
> when he would say: " Now, give us *'The Gal I Left Behind Me,* '
> " and he would keep time with a vigorous patting of his foot
> whilst his favorite was being played, a distinction given no other
> air. **16**

As spring approached, the men unexpectedly received marching orders, and on February 16, 1863, General Benning informed his brigade to strike camp, and prepare to march at sunrise. General Lee took advantage of the lull in the war to move Longstreet's corps down into the tidewater region of Virginia. Their mission was to determine if the Confederacy could regain the city of Suffolk, Virginia. Upon moving out, the commanders were reminded why the armies remained stationary throughout the winter. As the corps marched, it began to snow. The snow quickly piled up to a depth of eight to ten inches. Upon halting that afternoon, the column of men had only marched eight miles. The next several days of marching were almost equally depressing, as the snow had turned to rain and the road was a slippery mess.

For the next five days, the corps trudged on, arriving at Richmond on February 21. They proudly marched down Main Street. The entire town warmly welcomed the heroes with the " fair ladies waving their handkerchiefs." That evening the corps camped on the outskirts of town near Manchester, but close enough for the young at heart to trudge back, for an evening on the town. The corps remained encamped just outside Richmond for the next five weeks. While there, the units were replenished and the men enjoyed some well-deserved rest and relaxation. 17

All too soon, with spring on the horizon, Longstreet's Corps assumed their line of march. They departed on March 29, 1863, enroute for Suffolk, Virginia, arriving there on April 16, 1863. **18** By sending Longstreet's corps to the vicinity of Suffolk, the Army of Northern Virginia was now defending Richmond from all possible threats. It was soon realized that assaulting the Union forces in Suffolk was not desirable, yet there was something to be gained in the region. Longstreet was authorized to obtain foodstuffs from the region, and the corps was dispersed throughout the area of southeast Virginia and the northern area of North Carolina. Benning's brigade was also tasked with foraging. For the next several weeks, they traveled throughout Chowan and Gates counties of North Carolina, obtaining supplies and forwarding the material via wagon details, back to headquarters.

With the weather turning warmer, and the threat of Union campaigns increased, Longstreet suddenly recalled his dispatched elements, urging the commanders to hurry. Benning rapidly marched his brigade towards Suffolk, Virginia, and in the middle of the night, Benning encountered the huge and menacing " Dismal Swamp. " Slogging their way through the swamp in search of a designated rendezvous point, Benning became misoriented. Private J. W. Lokey, of Company B, Twentieth regiment recorded that the march through the swamp was exhausting and " as dark as Egypt and we were as wet as drowned rats." **19** The swamp was so dark, the men could not see one another, and sound and touch became the only senses available. Trudging back and forth, throughout the night, the men became disgruntled and upset with their commander. Halting the unit to find his way, several choice remarks were uttered in the darkness, which were heard by General Benning. One of the bonds that endeared General Benning to his men, was that he was " very plain of speech, and would talk back in kind with compound interest to any of his men." **20** In reply to the complaints of his men, Benning simply stated," Don't curse your General boys, he is doing the best he can for you." **21** Eventually, the brigade made their way through the swamp, and his men laughed and joked about their experience in the swamp, for quite some time.

As Benning's brigade approached the environs of Suffolk, the soldiers could hear heavy cannon fire in the distance. On May 3, the brigade rejoined the corps, on line before the enemy at Suffolk, which were being threatened by enemy artillery shells bursting in the camps. Longstreet decided to try an assault on Suffolk. Benning's brigade was issued ammunition and moved toward the front of the action. Suddenly, they were halted and ordered to return to their original positions. General Benning was summoned to General Hood 's headquarters. When he returned, Benning relayed the plan to his brigade. **22**

Unbeknownst to the brigade, while they were away on foraging detail, General Hooker had launched his forces on another campaign into the south. Hooker was a much more aggressive commander, than Burnside was. With one corps of the Army of Northern Virginia away, Hooker was presently attempting to outflank and attack Lee. Longstreet's corps had been called upon to march immediately and rejoin the Army of Northern Virginia. Hooker 's Army of the Potomac now had over 135,000 men. Within their own ranks, were only 60,000 men. Immediately, all units were to quietly as possible retreat from the field. The men marched rapidly throughout the night, stopping in Franklin at 8 o'clock the next morning. They had marched a distance of 40 miles in 24 hours. **23** The corps ultimately arrived in Richmond on May 10. Meanwhile, in a brilliant victory, without Longstreet's Corps, Lee defeated Hooker at the battle of Chancellorsville. Lee forced the Union forces to retreat to the north side of the Rappahannock River, and ended yet another large Union assault that threatened Richmond. Tragically, during this battle, General " Stonewall" Jackson was accidentally shot by his own men, and died several days later, however, once again, the Confederacy was encouraged with a resounding victory against an even larger Union army.

Meanwhile, Longstreet's corps continued their march, arriving at Raccoon Ford on the Rapidan River on May 17. **24** Upon rejoining the Army of Northern Virginia, on May 27, having recuperated from their grueling forced march, the men of Hood's Division celebrated with a Division Review:

> At 10 a.m., all four brigades formed a line across a great field. " Texas " Brigade on the right," Laws" (Ala. Brig.) next " Bennings" and then " Anderson's" on the left, the position was hilly. Batteries of 24 pieces on the extreme right; line being formed. Officers to the front, General Hood and Staff rode up the lines and all the bands played, drums beat and flags dipped. Many local citizens from the country & Orange Court House came out to observe and cheer for the boys in gray." " So it was a gala day with Hoods Division. Everything passed off finely. Gen'l Hood was well pleased, the Div. numbering on review near 8,000; all was well pleased with the different maneuvers, and formed a greater liking to their brave chivalric leader; News encouraging from Vicksburg that we repulsed them 6 different times with small losses, their loss heavy." **25**

On June 6, 1863, Lee's Army of Northern Virginia was officially declared reformed and refit. Lee had his entire forces located around Culpeper Court House, in the heart of Virginia, and emerging from an astounding victory, they were well prepared for a new campaign. Lee reformed his army into three full corps and prepared to launch it northward, and the year 1863 seemed to hold great promise for the Confederacy. In Benning's brigade, although their ranks had dwindled, their spirits soared. Amidst rumors of an impending foray back into northern soil, Benning's brigade rested their weary feet, washed their dirty bodies and boiled the lice out of their clothing. For General Benning it was a glorious occasion as his son Seaborn had been appointed as a Captain and assigned to a position as his Adjutant. Benning's brother-in-law was promoted to a full Colonel, and he was placed in command of Benning's Twentieth regiment. When Jones assumed command as Colonel of the Twentieth regiment, one of his men wrote home that, Jones " intends to make every man toe the mark or suffer for a non-performance of duty... We have no doubts at all that he will be equally as diligent in guarding the rights and protecting the interests of his regiment." **26** With his son and son-in-law by his side, Brigadier-General Benning was surrounded by good men and he eagerly looked to the future and the conquest of battle.

On June 15, 1863, Benning's brigade was back in motion, heading northwest with the entire Army of Northern Virginia, on yet another campaign into enemy territory. On June 16, the brigade marched 17 miles to Marcum Station on the Manassas Railroad. Due to the heat, several men died of sunstroke. Lee marched them hard, but it was for a good reason. Once his troops reached the fertile Shenandoah Valley, they could march north, flanked on either side by high mountains. His cavalry and flanking forces protected these ridges. First, they had to beat the Yankees to the mountain passes. This resulted in a difficult forced march during the hot swelter of the summer sun. On June 17, due to the excessive heat and hard marching, over 100 men of Benning's brigade fell by the side of the lengthy column, unable to keep up. The men agreed that the march that day, was their most difficult to date.

Lee's army succeeded in its quest. Longstreet's corps entered the lush valley through Ashby's Gap on June 18. Once safe in the valley, Lee's cavalry could watch his flanks from the commanding ridges above, and march comfortably northward through a region filled with abundant resources to support his army. As the brigade passed through the fertile valley, the men crossed the Shenandoah River several times, as the river snaked its way through the valley. On June 20, the brigade crossed the Shenandoah for the third time and in spite of orders from the high command, the soldiers removed most of their clothing as they waded through the river. The river crossings were a splendid reprieve from the dusty trails and occasionally the men caught glimpses of young ladies. A soldier in Benning's brigade noted in his diary that, while passing through a tiny hamlet," a large crowd of girls came out to see us & waved their handkerchiefs, we passed them with music." 27 The army continued northward and crossed the Potomac River, at Williamsport, Maryland on the 26th of June. Filled with pride and stuffed with food, the Confederate soldiers were happy to back on Union soil.

On the 27th, the brigade marched through the town of Greencastle, Pennsylvania. The Georgians were not welcomed there at all. Sergeant Ware of the Fifteenth Georgia noted in his diary:

> People strong Unionist & looked mad & sullen at our
> appearance a great many closed doors; stores all closed the
> Streets & Hotels crowded with young men just out of service.
> Some nice looking girls dressed very fine, as every thing is
> cheap. Several Federal Flags were seen the girls had them on
> their bonnets. We marched through quick time with music. **28**

The regiment continued marching northward and along the route the southerners began collecting honey, poultry, horses and cattle from the local civilians. Twelve miles north of Greencastle, the Georgians passed through the large town of Chambersburg, Pennsylvania. Along the route, the Confederates obtained an abundance of butter, milk, chickens and beef, providing the troops with the best rations they had ever enjoyed. Yet, the army was getting further and further from Virginia. Thus far, this was the furthest north the southerners had been during the war. The people of Pennsylvania were very loyal and fervent members of the Union. Many of their men had been killed or permanently maimed by the Army of Northern Virginia and being invaded did not make them happy. The southerners were accustomed to marching through towns and receiving cheerful admiration from the ever-present ladies waving their handkerchiefs, but not here. Again, Ware recorded in his diary," Stores all closed & a great many people out to see us & looked frightened & mad." **29**

As the long ribbon of southern warriors pressed northward and deeper into enemy territory, the locals displayed an increasing disdain for the Confederates. The air of tension created a sullen mood amongst the invaders, and impending battle seemed a certainty. On June 28, the army was halted as Lee determined his next move. Meanwhile, General Hooker maintained his Union army on a northerly course, parallel to Lee's, but east of the Blue Ridge Mountains. The cavalry units of both armies maintained flank security for their respective forces, frequently skirmishing throughout the campaign trail. General Lee 's ultimate goal was to exploit the rich farmlands of Pennsylvania, gain international support from Europe, and all the while, achieving tactical victories against the consistently larger Union forces. Unfortunately for the south, this strategy was soon curtailed by two separate events. First, General Hooker was relieved of his command, and replaced by General George Meade. Benning's brigade had fought against Meade when he commanded a brigade at the battle of Second Manassas. Meade was a battle hardened veteran commander, a worthy opponent, a man of action, and an excellent tactician. Secondly, just as Lee's forward elements arrived within several miles of Harrisburg, the state capital of Pennsylvania and an excellent target, an incident of coincidence forced Lee to change his plans.

Lee's infantrymen were tough, and in the division Benning's men were assigned to, they were fondly referred to as " Hood's Foot Cavalry." Just like real horses, the " foot cavalry" needed their shoes replaced quite frequently too. Throughout the war, the Confederate soldiers rapidly wore out their shoes, and many marched miles and miles on their bare feet. Thus, the march to Gettysburg was extremely harsh on cheap leather shoes, as the cross-country trek through mountainous terrain was filled with briars and brambles. The lack of shoes forced even the toughest foot soldiers in the world to seek protection for their aching feet. According to Private William R. Houghton, of the Second regiment," On the march to Gettysburg I wore out three pairs in a month. The leather had been hurriedly tanned and the shoes came to pieces." **30** Strangely, this seemingly innocent necessity to clad their unprotected feet, provided the spark that initiated the worst battle the world had ever seen. On July 1, 1863, in search of shoes, two divisions of General A. P. Hill's corps ventured into the little town of Gettysburg, Pennsylvania. Unbeknownst to the Confederates, a Union cavalry division was already there, as well as, two corps of Union infantry. A heated battle ensued, and Lee was forced to send reinforcements into Gettysburg to drive them back, thus commencing the battle of Gettysburg, and the three bloodiest days of warfare in the history of the United States. **31** Simultaneously, to the south and east of Gettysburg, Meade rushed his army into position along the heights. Lee decided to meet him there.

Both the armies were strung out for miles, along parallel courses extending to the south. Generals Lee and Meade immediately ordered their armies forward, forcing rapid night marches in preparation for battle. The two opposing armies faced one another and prepared for hostilities. The Union forces were established in a four and one-half mile long defensive front, on the high ground extending from the east at Culps Hill and hooked around Cemetery Ridge and then south to two hills known as Big and Little Round Top. Meade strengthened the areas in the north facing the town of Gettysburg and to his western front, as these regions are where Lee concentrated his forces. Meade certainly had the advantage with a larger army and the occupation of the most prominent terrain features, in a defensive posture. Lee on the other hand would meet his adversary with the disadvantages of a smaller army attacking a larger one with fortified positions, across open fields with sparse opportunity for cover and concealment. Lee established his forces in attack formations, northward, around Gettysburg and in a line extending southwest, facing the enemy from the west and parallel to the Emmitsburg Road. General Lee felt confident in his men's ability to win the impending conflict; however, General Longstreet voiced disagreement. Longstreet's corps would initiate the battle by charging his forces into the Union lines located on and in front of the round tops. The other corps attacking to their respective fronts would then follow this action. Lee respected Longstreet's opinion, but declined to alter his plan. **32**

In Benning's brigade, the thought of a quiet night sheltered from a steady rain was destroyed as General Benning ordered his men to prepare to march. Their destination was the farmlands below Gettysburg. Seemingly, as if nature was preparing for their arrival, the night air and the cool misty rain peacefully cleansed the bountiful fields of grain. During the next few days, these fields would be forever tainted by human blood, as thousands of men waged war in the most violent and destructive battle the world had ever seen. Gettysburg was destined to be transformed from a sleepy little farming community into a stench-filled mass of bloated death. Men and women, North and South would reel from the events of July 2 and 3, 1863, and their lives would be changed forever. For Henry Benning and his family, the battle of Gettysburg would never be forgotten.

Chapter 15

The Battles of Gettysburg, Chickamauga and the " Riot at Raleigh "

Throughout the pre-dawn hours of July 2, 1863, General Henry Benning prodded his brigade at a hectic pace. Traveling eastward, as part of the trailing column of Longstreet's corps, orders indicated an impending battle. Benning's division commander, General Hood , stated " So imperative had been our orders to hasten forward with all possible speed, that on the march, my troops were allowed to halt and rest only about two hours during the night between the 1st to the 2d of July." **1** It was very uncharacteristic of General Lee to hastily prepare for battle, but according to General Longstreet, that was precisely the situation on July the second. The units were hurriedly maneuvered into their respective positions and by mid-afternoon, with the sun beating on the exhausted Confederates, Benning's brigade was ordered into assault position, facing east along the Emmitsburg Road. Major Wesley Hodges of Benning's Seventeenth regiment noted that," Notwithstanding the excessive heat of the day, and the circuitous route to reach said position, officers and men bore up cheerfully under the annoyances." **2** While Benning's men were exhausted and the heat oppressive, the ominous threat of battle heightened their anxiety. Realizing that sudden death may be but one breath away, adrenaline surged through their bodies, their pulses quickened, and then, the impending battle began.

Around 2:30 in the afternoon, as part of a massive corps assault, General Hood ordered his division forward. As planned, Benning maneuvered his brigade behind General Law's brigade to give depth to the attack. Following at a distance of four hundred yards, Benning maintained his brigade on-line as the corps advanced on axis towards the Union positions ahead. In the distance, concealed within the heights, were thousands of Union rifles aimed at the approaching Confederate lines. As soon as the gray lines were within range, the Union batteries began pouring artillery fire into the Confederates below them. The rolling, wooded terrain and the smoke filled air prevented the southern troops from a clear view of their adversaries, but the indirect cannon fire began to find its mark. Confederate casualties rapidly mounted, and the bodies of young men littered the fertile fields of Gettysburg. One soldier remarked," The roar was awful and the heavens surcharged with hissing, roaring balls screeching, screaming, bursting shells enveloped in sulfurous smoke that clouded the July sun. When the heavens are rolled together as a scroll in the last days I doubt whether it will present a more awe-inspiring spectacle than that historic field presented on that fatal day." 3

After advancing through the woods, a panoramic view provided General Benning with the ominous reality of the task at hand. Seven hundred yards to the front, General Benning could clearly make out several lines of enemy Infantry, as well as several batteries of artillery, all of which were located on the steep, rocky hills before them. The enemy's first line of defense consisted of three pieces of artillery, with three others just to their front. On either side of these pieces were full batteries on either side, providing complete enfilade coverage of the route ahead. On top of the hill, to their right, were five other cannons, with massed Union Infantry, on either side of the guns. Benning stated," What we had to encounter were thirteen guns, and two, if not more, lines of infantry pasted on mountain heights. The intervening spur over which we had to march to reach the first line was nearly all open." 4

As the formations advanced, Benning's brigade drifted into a position behind Robertson 's brigade, as Law's brigade drifted further to the right, and advanced up the largest obstacle, Big Round Top Mountain. Benning could see that there was no way the front line could defeat the enemy, so he led his brigade directly into the fray. In front of Benning, Robertson 's brigade split up as it assaulted a spur in front of Little Round Top Mountain. Known as Houck's Ridge, the steep heights are a natural mass of rough earth covered with massive boulders. Robertson 's First Texas regiment struggled to scale the heights directly forward, as the Fourth and Fifth Texas assaulted up the right side, and the Third Arkansas regiment ascended the left side. Law's brigade was further to the right, near the foot of Big Round Top Mountain, and entered the gorge between Houck's Ridge and Big Round Top Mountain. Initially, the Forty-fourth Alabama of Law's brigade bore the brunt of battle in the gorge known as the " Devil's Den," and as they were being cut to pieces, and " anxiously discussing the situation, Benning's brigade moving in splendid style, swept in ... one of us remarked: 'There is Benning; we are all right now.' " 5 Thus, as

Benning's brigade began the assault, his Fifteenth and Twentieth regiments melded with the troops of the First Texas regiment and scaled Houck's Ridge, as the Second and Seventeenth regiments poured into the Devil's Den, down below and to the right of the ridge. The entire area, above and below was strewn with boulders, ranging in size from a large cow to a small barn. Benning described the terrain with," The ground was difficult-rocks in many places presenting, by their precipitous sides, insurmountable obstacles, while the fire of the enemy was very heavy and very deadly." 6

The steep terrain, strewn with boulders was extremely difficult to surmount; yet the Confederates poured into and over them. Concealed within the rocks above, Union snipers fired down into the Confederates as they desperately tried to scale the heights and wrest the gorge from the enemy. Captain John A. McGregor commanding Company E, Seventeenth regiment, suffered the " plunging fire from above," as a bullet pierced his arm just below the shoulder and exited near his elbow, effectively destroying his left arm. 7 Several men died as bullets penetrated their brains," shot through the top of the head by the almost vertical fire," and in order to climb up through the giant boulders, Private William R. Houghton wrote," I had to throw my rifle forward and by aid of the rocks on either side pull up and repeat the operation." 8 On the heights above them, the Union Infantry was supported with three Union artillery pieces. Spewing their deadly grape and canister rounds into the advancing Confederates, Benning's task became a seemingly insurmountable objective. The wounded and dead, slid down between the huge crevices where one soldier recorded that:

> Buried in the recesses of the rocks, I could only hear... The incessant roar of small arms, the deadly hiss of minie balls, the shouts of the combatants, the booming of the cannon, the explosion of shells, and the crash of their fragments against the rocks, all blended in one dread chorus whose sublimity and terror no power of expression could compass. 9

Yet, despite the odds and their numerous casualties, Benning's brigade and part of Robertson 's brigade fought and clawed their way up the ridge, until they finally achieved their goal. The Union forces surrendered the ridge and retreated to the safety of Little Round Top. Meanwhile, below the heights, the Second and Seventeenth regiments fought through the gorge at the southern base of Houck's Ridge. Known as the Devil's Den, the narrow, boulder-strewn gorge forced the combatants to fight a violent, close quarter battle. Lieutenant Colonel Wesley Hodges of the Seventeenth regiment reported that:

The impetuosity of the charge of the Second Regiment and my own, and the nature of the ground, threw us beyond the first crest, from which we had driven the enemy, into a deep gorge separating the seized crest from the stronger one, upon which the enemy now displayed a heavy force; and, but partially sheltered by scattering rocks, under a plunging fire from above it, my command bravely held its position, and seven times broke columns of the enemy which were forming for a vigorous onset to dislodge us. **10**

General Benning had taken the Devil's Den and Houck's Ridge from Brigadier General John Hobart Ward's brigade, First Division, of the Third Corps. Ward's brigade consisted of the 124th Pennsylvania, the 99th Pennsylvania, the 20th Indiana, and the 4th Maine regiments. Benning's brigade took the guns as trophies for the Confederacy, perhaps winning the only Union artillery captured in northern territory. The cannons were 10-pounder Parrotts, and Benning's men also captured more than three hundred Union prisoners. Upon driving the Union forces from the Devil's Den, and Houck's Ridge, Benning paced along the line encouraging his men forward, yelling," Give them hell boys- give them hell!" **11** Benning's brigade and the remnants of Robertson 's brigade chased the retreating Union forces back towards Little Round Top Mountain. The Confederates surged forward into the Plum Run Valley, which winds its way between the Round Tops and the gorge of the Devil's Den, and the Union forces on Little Round Top rapidly turned the area below them into a death trap. Referred to after the battle as the " Valley of Death," and the " Slaughter Pen," Benning rapidly surmised that his forces would have to retreat or be slaughtered. The overwhelming obstacles and opposition before them were simply too much for his exhausted men to bear. " Old Rock " wisely applied logic and judgement to the situation, and ordered his regiments to halt their forward advance.

Company E, Twentieth regiment was Benning's most forward element, which had crossed Plum Run Valley, and attempting to climb Little Round Top. According to Lieutenant Pinkney G. Hatchett, commanding the company," the roar of artillery and rattle of the musketry was so terrific, he did not hear the command to halt... looking around, he saw the whole west side of the mountain literally lined with blue coats, and a second look showed that he was seventy-five or a hundred yards in front of the command." Suddenly a Union bullet pulverized Hatchett's ankle.

Realizing he had gone too far, and the rest of the brigade was retreating to Houck's ridge, he immediately began " retreating, crawling on his hands and knees over the same ground so proudly charged a short while before." 12 Meanwhile, the Seventeenth and Second regiment surging upward through the Plum Run Valley, retreated also. Despite the heavy volume of rifle and artillery fire, Benning's brigade withdrew into the safety of Houck's Ridge. Lieutenant Hatchett, crawling as fast as he could, survived the ordeal too. According to General Benning:

> The peak being thus taken and the enemy's first line driven
> behind his second, I made my dispositions to hold the ground
> gained, which was all that I could do, as I was then much in
> advance of every other part of our line of battle, and the second
> line of the enemy on the mountain itself was in a position which
> seemed to me almost impregnable to any merely front attack
> even with fresh men. Indeed, to hold the ground we had
> appeared a difficult task. The shells of the enemy from the
> adjacent mountain were incessantly bursting along the summit
> of the peak, and every head that showed itself was the target for
> a Minie ball. Several attempts by flank movements were made
> to dislodge us, but by the gallantry of the regiments on the right
> and left, they all failed. 13

With his brigade holding Houck's Ridge, Benning focused on reconsolidating his units, establishing a line of defense, evacuating Union prisoners, and treating his wounded men. Tripping over rocks and corpses, it would take days for General Benning to determine the precise number of casualties his brigade had suffered. Amongst the survivors of the assault," The men generally were almost worn down by hard marching, harder fighting, constant watching, loss of sleep, hunger, and almost intolerable heat." 14 The assault took a tremendous toll on a tiny, yet heavily burdened brigade. Their march the night before, combined with the difficult fight during the heat of the day, left the men utterly exhausted. As night fell, Benning could not rest on his laurels. There was too much work to do and no relief, at all. His toehold in Union territory left him vulnerable to attack, and the night was spent preparing for the next day's battle. Yet, Benning's beleaguered brigade had achieved the only solid Confederate victory along the entire Confederate line. The capture of Houck's Ridge and the Devil's Den was a great accomplishment and a proud testament of the Confederate warrior spirit, as Benning's men had little else. While his brigade had achieved a great victory, it proved to be Benning's costliest battle of the war, and it affected him, very personally.

The casualties included the commander of the Second regiment, Lieutenant Colonel William T. Harris, whom was killed after leading his men through the Devil's Den, and into the area later referred to as the " Slaughter Pen. " Upon winning control of the gorge, the Second regiment continued advancing along the Plum Run Creek, towards the Little Round Top. A Private in the Second regiment, John Malachi Bowden recalled that Harris raised his sword high in the air, yelling " Forward Men," and bravely leading them " about twenty yards in advance of his command, he fell, pierced by the enemy's bullets. He was my friend." Bowden also noted that just before the battle, Harris " called some of his friends around him and bade them good-bye, assuring them that he felt that he would be killed in this battle." 15 Lieutenant Colonel Harris died instantly, as several Union marksman drove well aimed bullets directly through his heart. Major William Shepherd immediately assumed command of the Second regiment. According to Shepherd, Harris had led the regiment " gallantly and coolly while advancing, and was in the act of cheering on his command when he received the fatal shot." 16

Benning lost another regimental commander in the assault on Houck's Ridge. As Colonel Jones led his Twentieth regiment into the Union artillery positioned atop the ridge, the cannons spewed their horrible carnage directly into the advancing Confederates. " Lawson McKelvey, one of the color guards of the Twentieth Georgia " suffered horribly as " a shrapnel had burst just at the flag destroying more than half of it, killing three or four of the guard and wounding McKelvey in twenty-two places, extending from his ear along his left shoulder and arm to the wrist." 17 Colonel John A. Jones was struck with shrapnel also, and as Private John W. Lokey, following some distance behind his commander, and weaving his way up through the rocks, was suddenly startled as," I passed Col. Jack Jones, of my regiment, lying on his back with about half his head shot off." 18 The effects of men charging into point-blank artillery fire was horrid. General Benning 's official report noted that after leading the Twentieth regiment in the victorious assault of the heights, Colonel John A. " Jack" Jones, his brother-in-law, was struck by a cannon shell. Benning stated that " a fragment of one of which, glancing from a rock, passed through his brain. He had behaved with great coolness and gallantry. He fell just as success came in sight. 19

In General Benning 's report, he also stated that," The captured guns were taken by the Twentieth Georgia, Colonel Jones." Later, the credit was given to the First Texas regiment who fought together with Benning's brigade in achieving victory, however, Benning also added that the guns, prisoners, and terrain could not have been taken, and certainly not held, if not for the contributions of all the men. In fact, on the far left of the Devil's Den, Colonel DuBose and his Fifteenth regiment suffered the highest casualties and fought against overwhelming odds while protecting the brigade's left flank. Benning stated that," Colonel DuBose not only drove back the enemy's line, but repulsed repeated attacks made to recover it, taking over 100 prisoners." **20** Benning also recorded that his son, Captain Seaborn J. Benning, although disabled, greatly assisted him as his Adjutant. He also noted that Lieutenants John R. Mott and Herman H. Perry assisted him later in the battle as Seaborn's disabilities prevented him from continuing the fight. With victory nearly achieved, a bullet shattered Captain Seaborn Jones 's left thigh. Again, Benning's only son was seriously wounded. General Benning had his son evacuated from the field, yet his broken body would never fully recover from his wounds. Still suffering from bouts of blindness, Seaborn would now have to cope with a mangled leg. Yet, Seaborn Benning was lucky, at least he survived. **21**

During the night of 2 July, the Confederate ambulances and surgeons were so busy that Benning's brigade received very little medical attention. The moaning of the wounded filled the night. For many men wrought with horrible pain and suffering, death was their only relief. Meanwhile, the Union forces reinforced their lines and strengthened their positions. Along the crests of the Round Top Mountains, Benning reported that:

> The enemy employed the whole night in throwing up two lines
> of breastworks, one above the other, on the mountainside. These
> works were formed from the loose stones which abounded on
> the surface of the mountain. The sound of the stones dropping
> into place could be distinctly heard from our line during the
> whole night. The morning light revealed the two long lines
> completed. The upper line was sufficiently above the lower for
> its fire to pass over the lower. The crest was still frowning, with
> its old line greatly strengthened since the day before. From this
> line, the fire of both artillery and infantry would pass over both
> of the lines below. **22**

As the sun rose on the morning of July 3, 1863, Benning could see the futility of a repeated assault. With both Union and Confederate lines well covered and concealed amongst the rocks, the Confederate right saw very little action, and neither side seriously threatened the other. For two full days, Lee's forces had repeatedly charged the Union left and right flanks. On several occasions, it appeared that Confederate forces would win their objectives, but the Union forces refused to surrender their ground. Longstreet's corps had come close to victory, and while Benning's brigade held key terrain, the Union still held the Round Tops, thus insuring the integrity of that flank. The Union right flank also remained solid. With the Union flanks secure, late in the afternoon of July 3, Lee ordered a final assault into the Union line. This time Lee focused his attack into the center of the Union line. The charge conducted by the pride of Virginia, and led by Major General George E. Pickett was gallant and determined, but ultimately, a staggering defeat.

There has been great speculation as to why General Lee uncharacteristically directed these desperate assaults. And it should be noted that early in the attack, had Longstreet's corps conducted a flank assault on an ill-prepared Union left, the battle might have had a different outcome. Furthermore, before the battle, General Hood pleaded with General Longstreet that by going around the high ground, he could trap the enemy in their exposed rear area. Longstreet refused his proposal, as he had tried to convince Lee earlier, but the plan was denied. 23 Had Benning followed Law's brigade in the assault onto Big Round Top Mountain, things may have changed too. Despite what may have been, in reality, the battle of Gettysburg nearly destroyed Lee's Army of Northern Virginia, and he was forced to withdraw his army. This offensive would be Lee's final excursion into northern territory.

Late that afternoon, General Lee withdrew his forces from the field, and a series of miscommunications resulted in a near disaster for Colonel DuBose and his Fifteenth Georgia regiment. On Benning's left, McLaws division withdrew without any warning, thus exposing Benning's troops to a vulnerable flank attack. Simultaneously, General Law sent conflicting messages concerning withdrawal routes for Benning's brigade, and the Fifteenth Georgia regiment was left to defend itself against a rapidly formed Union attack. Benning reported that Colonel DuBose:

Suddenly found himself in the immediate presence of two long lines of the enemy, one almost at right angles to the other, with his own line between the two, the head of it being not far from the angle they made with each other. They opened fire on him, which returned, so as to check their advance a little. He then fell back, and, availing himself of a stone fence fought his way out, not however, without a heavy loss in prisoners and some loss in

killed and wounded. He was fortunate to escape at all. His
escape is high evidence both of his skill and courage. **24**

Colonel DuBose and his Fifteenth regiment suffered the highest
casualties in the brigade. Among the wounded was the Fifteenth's Adjutant
and a good friend of General Benning, Lovick Pierce, Jr., who suffered a
gangrenous leg wound, but kept his leg. According to DuBose," My men
and officers fought bravely, but my loss was immense... In the battle of
July 2, I went in with 330 or 335 muskets, and lost 70 men killed,
wounded, and missing. In the battle of the 3d, I lost 101, making a total
loss of 171 men in the two days' fighting." **25** With the withdrawal of the
Fifteenth regiment complete, the Union forces regained the terrain they had
lost. Benning reformed his brigade along the Emmitsburg Road, and
around midnight on July 4, the Confederates began their long retreat back
to Virginia.

As Lee's Army of Northern Virginia slowly staggered back towards
the safety of Virginia, a violent summer storm swept over the field. The
Union pursuit was mercifully slow and Lee's crippled army would survive
to fight another day. Meanwhile, upon the fields of Gettysburg, it would
take weeks to clean up the carnage that remained. Masses of noxious,
distorted human remains and horseflesh were in dire need of disposal.
They lay where they had been violently tossed, in rotting heaps, and fully
exposed to the sweltering, summer sun. Most of them were eventually
dumped into massive trenches. Many, could not be identified and are
known but to God. **26** Many of Lee's important commanders and officers
were wounded or killed at Gettysburg. The Division commander, General
Hood , suffered the loss of an arm, and leading the assault in the
Wheatfield, Benning's old friend, General Paul Semmes was mortally
wounded. In Benning's brigade, two (half) of his regimental commanders
were dead, and his overall casualties numbered 308, in killed, wounded
and missing. Many of the missing became prisoners and were shipped off
to Fort Delaware, Delaware, and Point Lookout, Maryland. Some of these
men would later be exchanged for Union prisoners, and released, however,
dozens of these men died of their wounds, or disease.

The Battle of Gettysburg proved to be the " high tide" of the
Confederacy. In the three days of fighting at Gettysburg, the Army of
Northern Virginia lost 28,000 men of its 75,000-man army. The Union
Army of the Potomac suffered approximately 23,000 casualties. Before the
battle of Gettysburg, the peaceful little valley between the Round Top
Mountains and Houck's Ridge was known as Plum Run Valley, however,
since the battle it has been referred to as the Valley of Death. Benning's
losses drove his total strength down to 2,150 officers and men, present for

duty. Nearly all of Lee's Army of Northern Virginia was nearly at half strength, and would remain this way for the duration of the war. **27**

Following the pathetic slaughter at Gettysburg, the Confederates trudged southward and by the first day of August, the Confederates were safely encamped near Chancellorsville, Virginia. It was impossible to return the bodies of the dead with the retreating Confederate army and most of the dead remained lying where they were slain. Yet, Colonel John A. "Jack" Jones had been hastily buried on the battlefield, and his body would be retrieved years later, after the war. In Columbus, Georgia, the Benning and Jones families were in a state of grief, and Mrs. Mary (Leonard) Jones joined the burgeoning numbers of Confederate widows. Her in-laws, Seaborn and Mary Jones had lost their only son, and they embraced the responsibility of caring for their daughter-in-law. Mary was suddenly transformed into a distraught widow with four young children. Adding to the agony of her husband's death was the fact that Mary was pregnant with another child. For the Jones, Benning and Leonard families, the war was slowly destroying their world. Meanwhile, Mary Benning rushed to Virginia to retrieve her only son, Seaborn J. Benning. Yet again, Seaborn would return to Georgia to convalesce under the tender watch care of his mother, while General Henry Benning focused on refitting his brigade. **28**

Again, the Army of Northern Virginia was forced to rebuild their organization amidst an ever-shrinking base of resources. The battle of Gettysburg had proven to be a very costly endeavor. Slowly, General Lee was losing his most trusted and competent subordinate commanders. Replacements for the foot soldiers lost in battle were difficult to find. Desertions became more frequent. Many men had suffered the trials of battle for two long years, and most of them had never received a furlough. Army life was difficult at best, and the pain of separation from loved ones, for some men, became too intense. President Davis was forced to declare an amnesty before many would return to their units.

Meanwhile, the Union army was drafting men into compulsive military service. Their industrial might continued to fuel the northern military machine at a fervent pace. Additionally, the north continued choking the south with its maritime blockade. In spite of their gloomy predicament, the resilient Army of Northern Virginia was far from defeat. Benning's brigade, although maimed and reduced in size, was now hungry for retaliation. Their veteran chain of command would soon be intact again, and ready to meet the foe. The men would proudly follow General

Benning, and sooner than expected, they did. On September 7, 1863, Longstreet was deployed with Hood 's and McLaw's Divisions to the western theater to reinforce The Army of Tennessee. Most of these men were Georgians, and their own state was now in peril. The Army of the Cumberland, led by General William Rosecrans had pressured General Bragg 's forces to retreat below Chattanooga, Tennessee and into the state of Georgia. **29**

With a renewed fighting spirit, the Georgians packed up their gear and marched towards Petersburg, Virginia. Here, they boarded the trains for a long journey to Georgia. As they passed through Richmond, General Hood rejoined his Division. Still suffering from his wound received at Gettysburg, Hood proudly resumed his post and boarded the train. **30** Continuing southward, Benning's brigade stopped in Raleigh, North Carolina to change trains. The wait was several hours in duration, and Benning allowed some of his men to relax and unwind in town. During the Suffolk campaign, Benning's brigade had learned that North Carolina contained numerous Union sympathizers. Additionally, the state capital in Raleigh was the home of a pro-Unionist newspaper, *The North Carolina Standard*. Owned and operated by William Holden, whom later became Governor of North Carolina, the newspaper was despised by Confederate soldiers, and especially the Georgians. The stage was set for a conflict and the Governor of North Carolina would accuse General Benning with some very serious charges. Reported by the press as the " Riot at Raleigh," and " The Raleigh Mob," " Old Rock " Benning would have to withstand a different kind of foe, rumors. **31**

What exactly occurred, who knew what, and who did what, may never be known for certain, but what is certain, is the following. According to Mr. Holden, rumors had been circulating that as the Confederate soldiers went through Raleigh; they may call upon him, because of his pro-Unionist articles. Mr. Holden declared that he did not think that they would, however, on the evening of September 9, 1863, several unknown Confederate soldiers came to his house and stated that," A number of gentlemen desire to see the Editor of the *Standard* in his office." **32** Mr. Holden refused saying that it was too late, and the soldiers departed. Several minutes later, Mr. Holden noticed numerous soldiers with weapons appearing near his office, which was just around the corner. Mr. Holden had been entertaining some guests, and they immediately ran down the street to the Executive Mansion, informing Governor Zebulon B. Vance of the impending crisis. The Governor, a member of his staff, and the Mayor of Raleigh discovered that members of Benning's brigade were in town, and they set forth in search of General Benning. The Governor and his party were unable to locate the General, but they did locate Lieutenant Colonel Shepherd," at a hotel awaiting his supper." 33

Shepherd, commander of the Second regiment, accompanied the Governor to the office of the *Standard*. Upon their arrival, according to Mr. Holden, soldiers were " engaged, evidently under orders," busy (destroying his office), dismantling the press, and dumping the type into the street. 34 Colonel Shepherd ordered the men to cease and disperse, while Governor Vance chastised the mob. In the darkness, one of the soldiers stated," Governor we have done what we came to do, and will now retire." 35 The next day, Governor Vance sent a telegram to President Davis informing him that " A regiment of Benning's brigade entered this city last night at 10 o'clock, and destroyed the office of the *Standard* newspaper." 36 Governor Vance also requested that no more troops be allowed to disembark as they passed through the city. President Davis immediately ordered the city off limits and initiated an investigation into the " riot at Raleigh," however; this did not stop the Fourth Alabama regiment, and some unknown South Carolina troops from repeating the event several days later. Again, according to Mr. Holden, the Richmond *Enquirer*, the Raleigh *Register*, the *State Journal*, and the Charlotte *Bulletin*, all called for mob violence, and " urged the government, the people, and the soldiers to suppress the paper by force." 37

As the investigation proceeded, Benning's brigade continued on their rail journey to join the Army of Tennessee. In Raleigh and Richmond, rumors circulated that General Benning and his men had conspired to destroy the office, and that he had been overheard stating, prior to the riot, that he " should not be surprised if his men did tear down the *Standard* office." 38 With President Davis and Governor Vance calling for justice, it appeared that General Benning was damned for the affair, however, several facts soon came to light which vindicated General Benning. According to General Benning, when the brigade passed through the town of Weldon, a North Carolina Lieutenant detailed to arrest deserters requested that General Benning allow them to ride the train also. Benning approved the request, and after they continued the journey from Raleigh, these unknown North Carolina troops," freely avowed themselves as the authors of the deed, and claimed credit for it. They said they led some of my men into it with them, and I have no doubt they did, but I think not many, and these merely unorganized individuals, each acting for and by himself." 39 Benning also added that he counseled his men about the affair, and was going to speak with the North Carolinians as well, but they disembarked as the train passed through Charlotte. Furthermore, Benning denied any conspiracy on behalf of any of his officers, and during the mob affair, he was resting at the depot," with my head on a cross tie and slept till eleven o'clock, when the train to carry the troops forward came in from Goldsboro. " **40** Benning then loaded his men on the train, whereupon he learned of the situation concerning Mr. Holden. General Benning also stated at that point, there was nothing he could do about it as the troops had to continue moving, lest they hold up the line.

Mr. Holden printed rumors as facts concerning Benning. One unsubstantiated statement indicated that " a soldier reported the result of the mob to General Benning, at the depot, a few moments before the train left, and that, by his manner, he approved what had been done." **41** The press became choked with accusations and counter-accusations. Even Governor Vance made the dishonorable mistake of spreading rumors about General Benning. In a letter to President Davis and reprinted by Mr. Holden, Vance stated that:

> The soldiers who originated the mob, belonged to Benning's brigade, and were apparently led by officers, several of whom I saw in the crowd, but I heard none of their names, except a Major Shepherd. I also have reasons for believing it was done with the knowledge and consent of Gen. Benning, as he remarked to a gentleman an hour or two previous, that his men had threatened it." **42**

Apparently, Governor Vance forgot that it was Lieutenant Colonel Shepherd that assisted him in quelling the violence. Additionally, Shepherd wrote to the Governor reminding him that after the affair, the Governor " publicly thanked me for my timely interposition, and that many officers and men of the brigade were invited to share the hospitalities of the Executive mansion." **43** Shepherd also requested that Governor Vance write a letter on his behalf to the Secretary of War concerning this fact. Governor Vance did so and he discovered after checking into some of the " facts" provided by Mr. Holden, that some of them were not true. For example, Governor Vance reported that General Benning had discussed the impending mob violence with the depot officer, Colonel John D. Whitford. When questioned, Colonel Whitford denied ever discussing the affair with Benning and he had no knowledge of the situation as Mr. Holden had reported it. Governor Vance ended up writing Whitford a letter of apology stating," I repeat that I accept your denial and I take it for granted that I was mistaken." **44**

It must be noted that as Benning stated, members of his brigade were in fact present and probably did participate in the destruction of the *Standard* office, but exactly who is unknown. Additionally, the only known officers of Benning's brigade present at the event, assisted Governor Vance in the dispersal of the mob, and the Governor thanked them. Governor Vance was obviously confused and mistaken as to the " facts" he reported to President Davis, and his friend, Mr. William Holden was distraught, upset and he reported rumors. Thus, the actual course of events may never be known, and Henry Benning was simply a victim of an over zealous and desperate news reporter. Finally, in light of General Benning 's character and values, he probably did not know about the intentions of a few of his men to perform an illegal act. Over the course of the next few months, the subject was eventually dropped and General Benning continued to serve his country with pride and honor. Yet, it must also be noted that well after the attack on the *Standard*, Lieutenant Colonel Seago of the Twentieth regiment corresponded with Mr. Holden, stating:

> From what I learn, considerable injury has been done to your office. I hope this will be a warning to you and all others not to pursue a course calculated to encourage the enemy either by words or acts. The motives of this party were patriotic. They believe you to be opposed to our cause, and desire to betray us into the hands of the enemies of our peace, our property, and our independence. 45

Whether the " Riot at Raleigh " involved a conspiracy, which included Benning's officers remains uncertain; however, there is little doubt how both officers and men felt about William Holden's newspaper. Benning's brigade was willing to give their lives for " the cause," if required, and for many men, yet another opportunity was rapidly approaching. Although much preferred over marching, the men suffered through the next several days crammed within and on top of rail cars. Along the seemingly endless ride, the Georgians had plenty of time to contemplate the seriousness of future events. The 850-mile route entered their beloved state in Augusta, passed through Atlanta, where Benning managed to obtain shoes for some of his men. Yet, supply shortages were beginning to seriously hamper the effectiveness of the Confederate army and many men remained shoeless. Benning reported that he was " compelled to stop to ration and get shoes for barefooted men," yet, Private James A. Maddox, of Benning's

Twentieth regiment, despairingly wrote to his girlfriend stating that there were plenty of shoes for small men, but any man wearing a size ten or higher," seldom ever get shoes... I have never had the size of my foot bother me until I have been in the army." **46** With little time to spare, Benning herded his men back on the trains, and shortly thereafter, the riding terminated at Catoosa Station, four miles from Ringgold, Georgia. Thus ended the longest and most famous Confederate troop deployment via rail during the war. The anxious reinforcements of Longstreet's corps arrived on September 17, disembarked from the trains, immediately rushed to their positions, and the lines of impending battle were rapidly formed, just below Chickamauga, Georgia.

General Longstreet was hurriedly placed in command of the entire left wing of the Army of Tennessee, which consisted of Generals Buckner, Forrest and Hood 's (Longstreet's) Corps. The latter corps was comprised of the divisions commanded by Generals McLaws and Hood, with the latter division being commanded by General McIver Law. Law's (Hood's) Division consisted of the brigades commanded by Generals' Law, Robertson , and Benning. Benning's brigade remained in its original form, consisting of the 2nd, 15th, 17th and 20th Regiments, numbering a grand total of 1,200 officers and men. **47**

On September 19, 1863 at 3 o'clock p.m., General Benning was ordered to advance on the Union lines and assist General Robertson 's brigade, which was in contact with the enemy. The opposing Union forces were supported with a battery of artillery and defending a line along the western edge of the Chattanooga (La Fayette) Road at a tiny group of buildings known as Viniard's farm. With the battery on the southern tip of the field, the Union forces commanded the ground to the north and west, creating a virtual killing field, through which the Confederates were assaulting. With their blood curdling " Rebel Yell " and a swift assault, Benning's men crushed headlong into the Union line. Benning's men faced off against Colonel Hans Heg's brigade, which consisted of the 15th Wisconsin, 25th Illinois, 35th Illinois, and the 8th Kansas regiments. The battlefield was choked with smoke, and the men literally tripped and stumbled upon each other, shooting and hacking in a frenzy which mirrored the fight in the Devil's Den. The combatants were lacerated by swords, blasted with cannon fire, or shot at direct range. First Sergeant William R. Houghton wrote that he suddenly bumped into a large burly Union soldier, which caught them both by surprise. According to Houghton, while they both were shocked, he was quicker than the Yankee, and:

His astonishment caused him to open an otherwise large mouth very wide. I cannot say he uttered any sound, if he did I did not hear it. I was greatly astonished, remembering my absent bayonet, it seemed a hundred thoughts flashed over me in the brief instant of time I looked into the face of my foe, who was not over the length of a musket from me. In less time than it takes to tell it, I fired from my hip without raising my gun to my shoulders. I had frequently killed game that way, and struck the man in the waist. He threw up his hands and fell over. **48**

The ensuing fight was horrific, and Heg's brigade lost the fight to the Georgians. Colonel Heg was mortally wounded with a bullet in his bowels, and his men fled to the rear. Bennings forces pressed forward, crossing the road and taking what cover was available in a tiny ditch through which a small stream passed parallel to the road. Together, Robertson and Benning's brigades drove the Union forces westward, beyond the farm, onto a prominent ridge, behind the Viniard farm. As General Benning approached the ditch, his horse was shot out from under him, and he tumbled into the dirt. Scrambling for cover, General Benning's clothing was pierced by bullets, and he was slightly wounded. Benning also sought cover in the ditch, as he examined his wound. While his chest was bleeding, a bullet had barely grazed him across the breast, and he continued the fight. Both Generals Benning and Robertson anxiously awaited the arrival of reinforcements, which they firmly believed would arrive. Yet, Benning and Robertson were literally on their own, as the Confederate army was committed along the line, and there were no reinforcements available. While the Confederates were victorious in wrenching the Union line from Viniard's farm ; they suddenly found themselves trapped in their new position. With little cover and concealment, the Southern forces were being pummeled from enfilade artillery fire, which swept the ditch, up from the southeast and down from the northwest. The Confederates grudgingly held their positions in the ditch, which were rapidly transforming into a mass grave.

Again," Old Rock " characteristically applied his jurist wisdom and logic to the dilemma. Reflecting on the situation he faced, Benning noted in his official report of the battle that," finally toward sunset the enemy's fire from his battery and from his infantry, protected by the wood, became so heavy, and so many of our officers and men had fallen, that we had ourselves to retire a short distance." **49** No artillery had been attached to the Confederates for the assault, and there were no reinforcements, thus leaving General Benning with little recourse but to retreat. Benning ordered a withdrawal to the safety of woods on the opposite side of the La Fayette Road. Once a safe distance was achieved, Benning was able to discern just how costly the assault had been. His men had fought with a " dogged resolution," and Benning reported that " in the Twentieth Regiment, 17 officers out of 23 were killed or wounded." **50** The other regiments suffered nearly as many casualties in the officer ranks. The beleaguered brigade was nearly decimated; losing 133 men in killed and wounded. Captain James H. Martin of Benning's Seventeenth regiment, recorded that " every officer and man in my company was killed, wounded, or struck with a ball." **51** Benning's brigade remained in this position during the night with the Union troops occupying nearly the same line as they had held prior to the fight.

The next day, the fight resumed, and Benning's brigade was placed a little further north along the Chattanooga (La Fayette) Road, across from the Brotherton Farm. Again, around noon, Benning's brigade was ordered forward, across the road, this time in support of Law's brigade. Attacking to the west of the Chattanooga (La Fayette) Road, General Benning maintained his units several hundred yards behind Law's forces. After a short advance, in the woods near Poe's House, Benning detected that a federal column had maneuvered into a position to strike Law's brigade in a flank attack. Immediately, General Benning ordered a counter-assault against the rapidly approaching Union attack on Law's brigade. Benning reported that:

> After a sharp contest, they gave way and we pursued them. They
> made a stand at some artillery in the wood, but were driven
> again from this position and pursued several hundred yards
> beyond the guns, when they disappeared in the wood. In a short
> time they returned in heavy force and made a desperate effort to
> recover their ground. Here there was a very obstinate fight. At
> length I saw them turning my right to get into my rear. **52**

The flanking Union attack on Law's brigade, had suddenly turned directly into Benning's brigade, and this fight rapidly turned into a repeat of the violent clash on the previous day's battle. Again, face to face and hand to hand, the combatants fought for their lives amidst a cauldron of smoke, blood and gore. Captain James H. Martin of Benning's Seventeenth regiment, recorded that while struggling with a Yankee, his face was suddenly hammered and " I was shot through my lower jaw crushing it on both sides." **53** This tenacious fight pitted Benning's Georgia brigade against Colonel John Croxton's Kentucky and Indiana regiments. One of General Benning's Adjutants, Lieutenant Benjamin Abbott, recorded that a " hail of grape shot and bullets whizzed through our ranks," and several men dove for cover behind trees. General Benning lashed into them with," God damn you men, get from behind those trees and rocks and give 'em hell." Just as he finished yelling at his men, an exploding artillery shells killed both Abbott's and Benning's horses, throwing their riders onto the ground. Stunned, but unhurt, Benning jumped up and yelled at the men again, stating," God damn you men, stay behind those trees and give 'em hell." 54 General Benning followed his men as they rushed directly toward an artillery battery that was wrecking their brigade. Lieutenant Abbot recorded that the work of the cannons was " a volcano of fire," yet," it was Georgia we were fighting for and the question of fear did not enter into the consideration of the chances." Throughout Benning's brigade, the " old rebel yell broke from every throat, and a dash was made to the front that was never surpassed." 55 Charging directly ahead, the Confederates ripped through a hastily prepared Union breastwork protecting the cannoneers. Croxton's Kentuckians were tenacious warriors and fought nearly as well as the Georgians, but Benning's men defeated them, wounding Colonel Croxton and taking the highly prized Napoleon cannons, of the 8th Indiana battery. 56 General Benning reported that:

> We then fell back behind the cannon, facing so as to meet this new demonstration. The enemy followed a short distance, but not far enough to retake the artillery, and for some time kept up with us at long range a desultory fire. Finally they disappeared. The artillery taken consisted of seven or eight pieces. According to my count, there were eight-- four brass and four iron pieces. A flag was taken with the guns. The brigade, reduced as it was to a handful by the fight of the day before, again suffered heavily. 57

While Benning had won a small victory, the larger effect of the massive Confederate assault created a wedge in the Union line. General Longstreet took advantage of the opportunity and continued to plunge his forces directly ahead. General Benning mounted a Union artillery horse and rallied his men to press forward. Before the brigade moved forward, someone suggested that the General should throw a saddle on the horse, Benning excitedly blurted out," There is no time to saddle horses, we have

them going and must keep after them!" **58** Just in front of Benning,
Robertson 's brigade, near Dyer's field was being torn asunder. Greatly
concerned for his Texans, General Hood moved forward to observe the
situation. Shortly after reaching the front lines, a Union marksman
promptly shot General Hood him in the thigh. The wound was serious and
he was evacuated to the rear.

Amongst Benning's men, it was feared that Hood had been killed,
which ignited the passions of the Confederates and the pitch of battle
increased. Benning's men rushed to assist their sister unit and amidst the
chaotic charge, the noise, the smoke and the thick forest, Benning
temporarily lost control of his men. The tense and exhausting battle wore
General Benning down, and he uncharacteristically became stricken with
panic. Riding bareback and using a piece of rope as a riding whip, Benning
rode back and forth through the woods searching for his men. While at his
very worst, General Benning came across General Longstreet and his staff
reporting," Hood killed, my horse killed, my brigade torn to pieces, and I
haven't a man left." **59** General Longstreet calmly reassured Benning
stating," General look about you. You are not so badly hurt. I know you
will find at least one man, and with him on his feet report your brigade to
me, and you shall have a place in the fighting line." **60** Just as General
Longstreet finished talking, Benning's fellow soldiers broke through the
brush in a " cheerful, gallant march," and " Old Rock " immediately
regained his " usual, courageous, hopeful confidence." **61**

Longstreet's forces eventually broke the Union lines, and the defeated
foe literally ran for their lives, in droves, toward the safety of Chattanooga.
The retreating federal troops included the commander of the Army of the
Cumberland, General Rosecrans, whom President Lincoln immediately
relieved from command. With the Union army racing towards
Chattanooga, General Braxton Bragg, commander of the Confederate
Army of Tennessee, chose not to pursue them. Ultimately, the battle was a
stalemate, as the Union forces retreated to a stronghold in Chattanooga,
and the Confederate forces lacked the strength to move them. Meanwhile,
Benning tallied his losses of the two-day battle. Lieutenant-Colonel
Matthews, commander of the Seventeenth Georgia, and Lieutenant-
Colonel Seago, commanding the Twentieth Georgia were both mortally
wounded. Additionally, Colonel DuBose, commanding the Fifteenth
Georgia, and Lieutenant-Colonel Shepherd, commanding the Second
Georgia, were both seriously wounded as well. In the Second regiment,
Captain Abner Lewis, who took Seago 's position after he was wounded,
also fell with a serious wound. Colonel Benning had lost three horses shot
out from under him. His Adjutants, Herman H. Perry and Benjamin
Abbott, both had several horses killed. In his own words, Benning stated

that," Hardly a man or officer escaped without a touch of his person or clothes." **62**

General Benning 's official report indicates 133 casualties, however, just like himself, most of his men had spilled their blood on the fields of Chickamauga, and the actual number of wounded exceeded 400. After the battle, the Georgians walked amongst the wounded and dead, where they provided aid to whomever they could. For the mortally wounded, their final hours were spent in hopeless agony and the certainty of death. Some received a final sip of water, and a promise to notify their family. While soldiers on both sides felt some guilt about it, they freely " sacked the dead," scrounging shoes, clothing and accouterments. In harsh reality, dead soldiers have no needs. With the loss of their comrades, the survivors inherit additional burdens, including the continuing horrors of war. That evening, Lieutenant Benjamin Abbott wrote home stating," Tomorrow we leave the Chickamauga (the Indian 'River of Blood') to proceed against Chattanooga, where more blood will be shed fruitlessly." **63**

For General Benning, the seemingly fruitless loss of blood was taking a heavy toll on his unit. Captains now occupied the positions vacated by his regimental Colonels. Benning too, had nearly become a casualty, and his total brigade strength had dwindled to one-fourth of its original composition. Yet, Benning and his fellow Georgians had won a decisive victory, and maintained their native soil free from Union invaders. During the year 1863, Benning's brigade had performed heroically amidst battles whose murderous tempos reached terrific heights. Yet, despite their losses, and their horrific experiences, the hardships and battles forged a deep bond between Benning and his brigade. The genuine affection and respect for " Old Rock " solidified with each passing event, making the unit increasingly effective. Benning's veteran band of stalwart Confederates, ground and compressed over time, like their leader " Old Rock," simply became harder and harder.

While most Southerners remained committed to " the cause," several years of warfare eroded the previously blissful morale of the general populace. In hometowns throughout the South, shattered dreams, economic decay, and death on an unprecedented scale affected even the heartiest of souls. Doing her part for the Confederacy, Augusta Jane Evans worked at " Camp Beulah " as a nurse in a Confederate hospital. In the evenings, by candlelight, she wrote a novel dedicated to the " Brave Soldiers of the Southern Army." Entitled *Macaria* or *Altars of Sacrifice*, the novel was one of the most popular books published during the war, and except for the

Holy Bible, it was the most inspirational literature available. The book is filled with sentimentalism, pride and praise for a stalwart people. The book exalted loyal slaves, devoted families, Southern ideals, the Confederate leadership, and the soldiers in the field. The book was viewed in the North as pure propaganda and some Union authorities banned it. In the South, Miss Evans was praised for her efforts and devotion to " the cause." J. B. Lippincott in Philadelphia, and West and Johnson in Richmond simultaneously published the book. In the North, the book was not popular, and in the South, production was extremely limited due to a shortage of printing supplies. The 1863 edition produced in the South was bound with wallpaper, thus making the book extremely rare and highly valuable. **64** Perhaps Augusta's work redeemed her in the eyes of Henry Benning, but in reality, he had little time for anything but war.

Chapter 16

East Tennessee Campaign and the Battle of the Wilderness

General Bragg slowly moved his Army of Tennessee into defensive positions overlooking Chattanooga. His army stretched from the heights of Lookout Mountain, east across the Chattanooga Valley and then it hooked north, along the heights of Missionary Ridge. In this position, Bragg was content to lay siege upon the Union forces of Rosecrans, now encamped in and around Chattanooga. Bragg shelled him daily from the heights. General Longstreet, in concert with most of the army's high command was appalled, and verbally protested General Bragg 's tactics. Longstreet pleaded with President Davis to send General Lee to lead the army. President Davis and General Lee declined this suggestion. Soon thereafter, President Davis visited the Army of Tennessee, and discussed strategy with his field commanders. The conference resulted in a decision to continue the siege upon Rosecrans Union forces, and to detach Longstreet's Corps from General Bragg, sending them on a mission to repulse General Burnside 's forces. Burnside's Corps had been dispatched from Virginia to reinforce Rosecrans. Unbeknownst to the Army of Tennessee, Generals Hooker, Grant and Sherman were on the march to aid their comrade as well.

Shortly after General Hood was wounded at Chickamauga, General Micah Jenkins was appointed as his replacement. General Jenkins had amassed a fine reputation, and his abilities would soon be tested. Upon the arrival of Generals' Hooker and Grant, they immediately set forth on a plan to break through the siege by stealthily flanking the Confederate left, under cover of darkness and gain control of Lookout Valley. This task was soon accomplished, and on October 28, 1863, Hooker marched his men into Lookout Valley and he established a camp for his 5,000-man force. At Wauhatchie, about 3 miles up river near the rail depot, he stationed about

1500 men. 1 This area was the responsibility of General Longstreet, who immediately formulated a plan to attack the smaller force at Wauhatchie. Longstreet decided to dispatch the divisions of Jenkins and McLaws on the mission. Jenkins dispatched Law's brigade to keep the larger force from rescuing the smaller one, while Jenkins attacked it. Longstreet intended McLaws Division to assist Laws brigade, but General Bragg never relayed the order to General McLaws. Meanwhile, Jenkins commenced his mission, and attacked with a force of inadequate strength.

On the evening of October 28, 1863, General Benning 's brigade, as part of Jenkin's mission, participated in one of the few night assaults conducted during the Civil War. Benning provided a supporting role in the battle, which proved to be a futile attempt to halt the build-up of Union forces. The engagement at Wauhatchie was in actuality, the first hostile action to occur in the battles of Chattanooga. It is also important to note that General Jenkins had accomplished a well-executed night raid against a superior force. His men engaged a far greater force than planned (12,000 enemy). Additionally, they successfully returned to friendly lines, suffering approximately the same number of casualties that they had inflicted upon the enemy. The difficulties of a large raiding force operating in darkness is very difficult to coordinate, and General Benning employed his forces with leadership, while providing the security and support elements of a daring mission. General Longstreet undoubtedly had firm confidence in the abilities of the commanders and the men of Benning's brigade. Their ranks over the past several years of battle had diminished tremendously. Many of them were still suffering from their wounds received during the Battle of Chickamauga and despite their pain and suffering, the men of Benning's brigade displayed a stern devotion and ability to perform their duty. 2

On November 3, 1863, General Bragg ordered General Longstreet to move his two divisions and attack General Burnside 's Union forces, located near Knoxville, Tennessee. Longstreet was in favor of this move in the past, but Lincoln replaced Rosecrans with General Ulysses S. Grant, as commander of the Union army in the western theater. The strength of the entire Union army was increasing and so was the threat to Bragg's tattered forces. Grant had already taken control of Lookout Valley. In spite of Longstreet's disapproval, he was reinforced with four brigades of cavalry, and dispatched on his mission. 3 General Longstreet and his men were certainly happy to be relieved of General Bragg 's defensive positions; however, the cold fury of winter was rapidly approaching. While the departure of Longstreet's forces weakened the defense of Chattanooga, General Bragg was confident in his positions among the heights. In spite of the growing threat, Longstreet prepared his forces and set forth on a new campaign. On November 5, 1863, Benning's brigade and the rest of

Longstreet's corps began their journey into east Tennessee. Meanwhile, back at home in Columbus, Seaborn Benning continued to slowly heal from his wounds and on the 8th of November, 1863, Henry's sister-in-law, Mary (Leonard) Jones, delivered a healthy daughter, and named her Anna Vivian. Henry Benning yearned to visit his family, but General Longstreet needed " Old Rock " and refused his request for a furlough.

Benning and his fellow Confederates rode the rails to Sweetwater, Tennessee then disembarked and began a pursuit of Burnside's Union forces who attempted to halt Longstreet's northward thrust. Slowly, Longstreet forced Burnsides into a defensive posture, around Knoxville. Breastworks had been established on the west side of the town, and it was here that Longstreet decided to press battle. Before commencing the attack, however, Longstreet waited for several brigades being sent up as reinforcements, which proved to be a costly delay. Finally, just before dawn on November 29, in bitter cold weather, Longstreet assaulted Fort Sanders with massed Infantry. General McLaws was ordered to spearhead the attack by attacking a fortified position, which McLaws resisted. Finally, after a considerable delay, McLaws conducted an assault, but in a manner inconsistent with Longstreet's orders. McLaws and several other subordinates began a passive resistance to Longstreet's authority, and the attack ultimately failed. Longstreet was livid, and seeing the impracticality of pressing the fight, he withheld his forces from another assault. Benning's brigade was in line of battle in front of Fort Sanders, but committed to a minor supporting role and only suffered six casualties. Benning was however, officially honored by both Jenkins and Longstreet in their official reports for the brigade's service from Chickamauga to Knoxville. 4

That afternoon, a shocking telegram was delivered to General Longstreet. President Davis sent news that Bragg's army had been defeated at Chattanooga on November 25, and was retreating toward Dalton, Georgia. Longstreet was instructed to quit the siege of Knoxville and rejoin General Bragg. Then, another message arrived. This one stated that General Sherman was marching up to join forces with General Burnside. Effectively cut off from Bragg's army, Longstreet decided to evacuate the siege of Knoxville and move northeast towards Bristol, Tennessee. Longstreet planned to spend the winter in east Tennessee, and attempt to rejoin Bragg in the spring. On the 4th of December, Longstreet stealthily withdrew from his positions at Knoxville, and his corps of hardened, rebel veterans were effectively, on their own, in a region hostile to the

Confederacy. 5 Adding to this dilemma, the army ran out of food, and in Benning's brigade, once again, the men's shoes were literally falling off their feet. One soldier recorded that:

> On the East Tennessee campaign, we were cut off three months from railroads, mails and supplies. I saw hundreds of bare-footed men marching over frozen snow near Dandridge on the French Broad river, and saw the blood from their feet mark the snow. Sometimes an order would come for the barefooted to go to the butcher's pen. A man would put his foot on the hairy side of a fresh cowhide and a piece heart-shaped would be cut out. Then holes were cut near the edges, and it was sewed with thongs of the same material over his feet. They were better than nothing for a time, but when near the fire they shrank amazingly, and when wet by the rains, they became too large. Yet men clad in this fashion on empty stomachs drove the enemy, and after dark we felt among the shucks where the enemy had camped and picked and ate raw corn that had dropped from the horse's mouths. 6

With wrapped cloth and beef hides around their feet, the men continued the march. The weather was brutally cold with frequent rain and sleet. Out of necessity, they had to burn the fence rails of local citizens in order to survive the long, harsh nights. The Union forces pressed them hard with rear cavalry skirmishes, which resulted in the capture of many exhausted and freezing Confederates, who could not keep up with the main force. As the barefoot men marched along the frozen mud roads, the sharp, jagged terrain cut their feet, which resulted in the ease of Union forces tracking the Confederates bloodstained trail. 7

As the Confederates trudged through the snow, ice, and muddy slush, their stomachs terrorized the men with constant reminders of their hunger. Sergeant Houghton, of Benning's Second regiment wrote:

> I picked up in the road a piece of cabbage stalk, which constituted my entire sustenance for thirty-six hours. I was so hungry that I felt like I had reverted to the original type of savage man, and would have stolen bread from a baby, if there had been bread and a baby to be found. The country had been harried by both armies, and the secession element had been run off, leaving a population very forbidding in appearance, and all the boys used to say that all east Tennessee lacked of being hell was a roof over it. 8

Even General Benning became somewhat discouraged and upset with the situation, as he had applied for a furlough, which Longstreet denied. It had been more than two years since Benning had been home. His only solace was that his son, Seaborn was still at home on an extended furlough, and not suffering the deprivations of his beleaguered comrades. Sergeant Houghton noted that while traveling through Tennessee, the brigade passed a small stream and General Benning:

> Halted the brigade, knelt down and drank deeply of the stream. As he arose, I called his attention to a dead horse, which had fallen into and dammed up the little stream just above, the water making its way through the fragments. He looked over his glasses at the object, wiped his mouth with the braid sleeve of his coat, and said: " I don't care a d--n, it was as good a drink of water as I ever had in my life. Forward, march. " He was ever kind to his men, and on one occasion, took in person my application for furlough to General Longstreet, saying that one had been refused to him, but he would try for me, and he succeeded. **9**

After warding off frequent cavalry raids, on December 23, Longstreet's forces established winter quarters in various locations throughout upper northeast Tennessee. As winter's icy grip enveloped the region, Benning's brigade settled into an area near Morristown. **10** Sergeant Houghton recorded that:

> The winter of '63-4 at Morristown, Tenn., was peculiarly hard. We had no huts, rations were scant and poor, as were blankets, clothing and shoes. We did not get a mail for three months. Plug tobacco could not be had, and " stingy green" the unpressed leaf raised in the surrounding country, was all we had, and very scarce. We could hear of the men who would leave the fire and go behind a tree to take a chew, being fearful they would be asked to divide. **11**

Several minor skirmishes and cavalry clashes kept both forces occupied during the next few months, but Longstreet's troops were fairly secure, as the winter weather made open battle impracticable for both sides. During the lull in the action, General McLaws faced a court -martial for his insubordinate behavior displayed at Knoxville. Longstreet was a professional soldier and demanded respect, while many of his officers still believed in leadership by democracy. McLaws sought high-ranking friends to agree and support his actions concerning Longstreet's orders, and sides were soon formed. Benning had learned the importance of military discipline, and he maintained his distance from the unseemly affair. In a message from General Bragg to General McLaws, Benning was cited as an example worthy of emulation, for his professional behavior and " preferring his country to a faction." 12 Yet, the court martial resulted in a sixty day suspension of McLaws command, as the Confederacy could ill-afford a harsher sentence. 13

Meanwhile, urgent messages were dispatched requesting food, supplies, shoes and blankets for Longstreet's corps. In Columbus, Georgia, Mrs. Benning and the " Ladies Soldiers' Friends Society," organized a clothing drive and placed advertisements in the local newspaper requesting," Can another blanket be had?... Cannot every family in Columbus and its vicinity do something to relieve this want?... The Churches are requested to give from their carpeted floors, at least a portion for the use of the soldiers." 14 Colonel F. W. Dillard, Confederate Quartermaster in Columbus also rallied to help the troops. Appealing to the patriotism of Columbusites, Dillard pleaded with the people to contribute old shoes, cowhides, and beeves. " Shall it be said that our people at home disregard the cries of our defenders in the field?" 15 Longstreet's favorite commissary officer, Raphael Moses was promoted to Chief Commissary, and he succeeded in obtaining bulk quantities of meat to feed the soldiers. Despite the resistance of the east Tennesseans to help the Confederacy, Moses discovered the " secret places where the bacon was hid," and while," the sheep was very distasteful to the soldiers," the long winter became tolerable. 16 Shoes, blankets, and church carpets donated from the good people of Columbus were finally forwarded to the troops, and some of the wounded rejoined their units in the field. The blankets, clothing and shoes were rapidly donned, and the church carpets were put to good use too. " One ingenious fellow having worn out his clothes, made himself an entire suit including a peak shaped hat or cap out of a flaming red carpet, with figures on it so large that it took his whole body to display one rose." 17

With Christmas rapidly approaching, along with the supplies, the ladies of Columbus, forwarded the following letter of inspiration addressed to their " Soldiers of the Army of Tennessee:"

The ladies of Columbus, fully aware of the severe reverses which have befallen you in Tennessee, but appreciating the

matchless valor so often displayed by you, ever mindful of the
noble patriotism which has enabled you to undergo hardships
and privations of no ordinary character-cherishing the heroic
and chivalric bearing exhibited by you on every field, from
Shiloh to Franklin, bid you God speed in the proud task you
have assumed. The country may become demoralized, but the
women and the army will ever be undismayed and undaunted.
Human courage approaches perfection only when it can calmly
look into the face of danger. It has been your fortune to exhibit
this high type of manliness in a marked degree. Confronted by a
foe always numerically superior, you have disputed every inch
of territory with him and retired only when bravery availed
nothing. Thank God, the spirit that animated the martyred dead
who have fallen in this contest for freedom still lives within you.
We have no fears for the future. Our honor and welfare are in
the keeping of brave hearts and strong arms. Debarred from
sharing with you the dangers of the battlefield, our prayer shall
follow you, and history, in recording your virtues, will write in
letters of living light " THEY ENDURED AND
CONQUERED." **18**

The letter was signed by 126 ladies of Columbus, of which, most of
them had husbands in the field. It is not recorded who authored the
document, but the first two signatories were Mrs. Seaborn Jones and Mrs.
Mary Benning. Benning's brigade rebounded, and throughout Longstreet's
Corps, the Confederates survived the difficult winter in east Tennessee,
and their presence in supposed Union territory, twisted like a painful thorn
in Grant 's side. **19**
   Private James A. Maddox, of Benning's Twentieth regiment, happily
reported to his girlfriend, Jennie [sic] Smith that," The army has suffered
much for want of shoes and clothes, but they have been tolerable well
furnished recently, and are all or nearly so well shod and have very good
clothes, and I think we'll be able to carry on a spring campaign to some
purpose." **20** The loving and generous support from home kept the
Confederates going, yet, the men longed for home, and their families. The
long cruel winter was hard to bear, and the pain of separation seemed more
intense as the idle hours slowly passed. On Monday, January 24, 1864,
Henry Benning 's aged mother, Malinda Lewis (White) Benning passed
away at the age of seventy-five. **21** Malinda Benning had lived the last few

years of her life in the home of her daughter, Augusta Palmyra (Benning) Patterson. Augusta's husband Madison was serving in the Confederacy too, and together Augusta and Malinda kept one another company. Augusta and her siblings would miss their mother, but for Henry, who had not seen his mother in two years, his world seemed to be slipping away. Both of his parents were now resting eternally in Georgia soil, and that generation of Bennings became a memory of the past.

Nevertheless " Old Rock " had to be strong; too many men depended on his strength, wisdom, and leadership. Because of the operations that winter, Benning's brigade lost nearly 160 captured or deserted. The Confederate Administration was deeply moved by the tenacity displayed by General Longstreet 's men, in the face of such difficult challenges. They were so impressed, that they passed the following resolutions:

" No. 42. Joint Resolutions of Thanks to Lieutenant-General Longstreet and the officers and men of his command. "

Resolved by the Congress of the Confederate States of America, That the thanks of the Congress are due, and hereby cordially tendered, to Lieutenant- General James Longstreet and the officers and men of his command, for their patriotic services and brilliant achievements in the present war, sharing as they have in the arduous fatigues and privations of many campaigns in Virginia, Maryland, Pennsylvania, Georgia, and Tennessee, and participating in nearly every great battle fought in those States, the commanding general ever displaying great ability, skill, and prudence in command, and the officers and men the most heroic bravery, fortitude, and energy, in every duty they have been called upon to perform. " Resolved, That the President be requested to transmit a copy of the foregoing resolutions to Lieutenant- General Longstreet for publication to his command. " Approved February 17, 1864." 22

Special recognition in the Confederate States Army was seldom received, especially from the administration in Richmond. Everyone was expected to give 100% at all times, and if you showed aptitude, or special capabilities, perhaps you would be promoted and most likely tasked with additional duties. All of the Confederate forces were worthy of praise, but Longstreet's men had been tasked extensively. Throughout February and March of 1864, the Confederate hierarchy debated strategy concerning the future deployment of Longstreet's Corps. Finally, it was announced that Longstreet and his men would rejoin General Lee 's Army of Northern

Virginia. Longstreet's forces slowly made their way to Bristol, Tennessee, where they awaited trains to return them to the Army of Northern Virginia.

While awaiting the move to Virginia, Henry Benning received word that his father-in-law, Seaborn Jones was dead. The aged statesman had been ill throughout the winter, and spent a considerable amount of money on doctors and medications, but his body ultimately surrendered. Seaborn Jones, patriarch of the Benning-Jones clan passed away on his only daughter's birthday, Friday morning, March 18, 1864. Well known and loved throughout his native state of Georgia, the legacy of Seaborn Jones remains firmly seated in Southern history. While Jones possessed an " iron constitution," the tragic loss of his only son Colonel John A. Jones ," upon whom he doted with a more than parental fondness, crushed the hopefulness and vitality of his nature." **23** His family buried him in Linwood cemetery.

Gleefully, Longstreet's corps conducted their rail movement during mid-April, and reformed for the next leg of their journey, at Charlottesville, Virginia. Ironically, the Georgians were retracing the same route of their arrival, conducted in 1861. They even encamped on the same grounds where they had seen their first victims of the war. The corps marched from Charlottesville to the vicinity of Mechanicsville, Virginia, arriving there on April 22. Again, Benning's brigade was assigned to the Army of Northern Virginia, and they proudly rejoined their brothers-in-arms. Colonel DuBose had healed from his wounds in Georgia and was again the regimental commander of the 15th Georgia. General Charles Field was assigned as their new division commander. As always, General " Old Rock " Benning, commanded his brigade of stalwart Georgians. Additionally, several hundred companions who had survived their ordeals in Union prison camps reinforced the brigade. Exchanged as POW s from Camp Lookout, Maryland and Fort Delaware, Delaware prisons, they were supposed to return home as non-combatants, but they did not. Suffering from horrid conditions, disease and pestilence, thirty-three of their compatriots died in prison. Additionally, the brigade received nearly 100 young recruits. The brigade was now at an approximate strength of 2,000 officers and men. **24**

General Lee officially welcomed the return of Longstreet's forces with a " Grand Review". General Lee, mounted upon his horse, Traveler, embraced the return of his complete army, in an emotional ceremony. Again, with a rekindled spirit, the renowned Army of Northern Virginia was eager to face their foe. Lee's army had shared incredible victories, against overwhelming forces, but they had also endured the hardships of loss and death. Additionally, every man present realized that there were ominous challenges ahead. General Grant had been placed at the head of the entire Union Army, and Lincoln sent him to Virginia. Grant would direct personal supervision over General Meade 's forces, and soon launch headstrong into a new campaign. On the first day of May 1864, the armies of Grant and Lee faced one another from opposite sides of the Rapidan River, near the Orange & Alexandria railroad . The Union forces mostly consisting of fresh troops numbered nearly 120,000 men, while Lee's Confederate troops could muster only 60,000 men. Yet, Lee's army was comprised of rock-hardened veterans and ready to prove their merit. Grant had superior forces, but the battleground was on southern soil.

The strategy Grant brought to the field was to constantly wage war on Lee, press him back against Richmond, and crush him with overwhelming, unending assaults. Grant launched his plan, in the pre-dawn morning, on May 4, 1864. Four Union corps crossed the Rapidan River at Germanna Ford and Ely's Ford. His intent was to crush Lee's right wing. Lee's 2nd and 3rd Corps were immediately maneuvered into positions to offset the threat. Longstreet's 1st corps, which was stationed further south, marched up the Catharpin Road to establish Lee's right wing. This area was known as the Wilderness. Fighting had occurred, nearby at Chancellorsville, in 1863. The Wilderness region consisted of dense forest, with very thick underbrush, and the wooded battlefield was bisected with two east-west roads, consisting of the Orange-Fredericksburg Turnpike, in the northern region, and the Orange- Plank Road in the south. The resulting Battle of the Wilderness lasted for two days. The fighting in the northern region was a stalemate throughout the battle; however, the southern sector was Grant 's primary objective, attempting to flank Lee's right wing, with the prize of Richmond, behind it. 25

On the morning of the May 6, 1864, two Union corps, massed in depth, and led by Generals Hancock and Getty pressed an assault. The sector attacked was on the Confederate right wing, and defended by 3rd Corps of General A.P. Hill. The Union forces initially met with great success; however, Longstreet's 1st Corps came forward at 3 o'clock that morning, reinforcing Hill's Corps. Benning's brigade was last in the line of march, but was ordered to swing around the left of the enemy in concert with several other brigades. This resulted in the collapse of the Union lines. 26 The effect was later described by the Union corps commander, General Hancock as," rolled up like a wet blanket." 27

That afternoon, when everything was going so well for the Army of Northern Virginia, again, tragedy befell the Confederacy. In the midst of confusion within the dark forest, Confederate soldiers fired upon

approaching men on horseback. General Micah Jenkins fell mortally
wounded. Additionally, General Longstreet was shot through his throat.
His horse came to a halt, the soldiers realizing their grave mistake, helped
him off his mount and propped him against a tree. With a bloody froth
emanating from his mouth, General Longstreet managed to encourage his
men forward, saying," Tell General Field to take command, and move
forward with the whole force and gain the Brock Road. " Ironically, this
event occurred within the same area that General Stonewall Jackson had
been shot by his own men, in 1863. 28

Unfortunately, General Field was unable to follow through with
Longstreet's command. The assault slowed, as fire erupted within the dense
underbrush. Just as darkness fell upon the field. General Burnside 's Corps
re-enforced the Union front, preventing any further Confederate progress.
Throughout the night, the wounded screamed in agony, as a raging forest
fire helplessly consumed them. Casualties in Benning's brigade, as a result
of the battle numbered eighty-seven wounded, and forty men killed. 29
Statistically, the Battle of the Wilderness was the third most devastating
battle of the war for Benning's brigade. In addition to the loss of Generals
Longstreet and Jenkins, General Benning and his close friend, Colonel
Wesley Hodges, commander of the Seventeenth regiment were both
seriously wounded too. A bullet shattered General Benning 's left shoulder
joint, and he was evacuated from the field. 30 Colonel Dudley M. DuBose,
of the Fifteenth regiment took Benning's place, and continued the fight.

On the morning of the seventh, Grant left some of his men on the
front, as he slipped the majority of his forces around to the southeast,
towards Spotsylvania. Lee, in anticipation of Grant 's plan, dispatched
General Richard Anderson, now commanding General Longstreet 's forces,
on a 16 hour, forced march to Spotsylvania. Immediately, in order to halt
the enemy's advance, the exhausted Confederates constructed breastworks
and hasty defensive fighting positions. Benning's brigade, led by DuBose,
was assigned the right center brigade on the front line of Field's Division,
facing north, 1.5 miles northwest of Spotsylvania Courthouse. Breastworks
had been established to their front, as they rested and awaited the inevitable
assault from Grant 's forces. The other two Confederate corps soon joined
them. By May 10, Lee's forces were fully entrenched within a north
pointing " V" , defensive posture. On the afternoon of May 10, General
Warren 's Union V Corps assaulted Anderson's (Longstreet's) Corp's
section of the Confederate line. The men of Benning's brigade, in concert

with their southern brothers, repulsed the Yankee's charge. The Union casualties were nearly 3,000 men.

Several hours later, the Union forces consolidated their efforts on the apex of the " V" , referred to the troops, as the " Mule Shoe ". Here, the Union Army made great headway, but they were unable to maintain their advance, and withdrew. On May 11, both sides reconsolidated their forces, as a heavy rain soaked the field. On May 12, 1864 at 4:30 a.m., Grant launched an assault wave of 20,000 men into the " Mule Shoe". Lee reinforced this section of the line. The battle raged for several hours, which resulted in approximately 15,000 casualties. Since that fateful day, the " Mule Shoe" was referred to as the " Bloody Angle. " Smaller attacks and skirmishes continued throughout the next week. Slowly, on May 20, Grant slid around Lee's left wing, continuing the march towards Richmond.

Fortunately, for the men of Benning's brigade, their casualties were light. Again, on May 22, Lee sent troops to intercept Grant 's forces. This time at Hanover Junction, on the North Anna River, again, Benning's brigade and the rest of the Army of Northern Virginia established defensive lines. They held the line until May 27, and departed at 11 a.m. for Cold Harbor, once again, anticipating Grant 's move. Lee began establishing defensive lines at Cold Harbor on the 30th of May, as the gigantic, Union machine, lumbered further southward, on towards Richmond. Grant 's forces were now dangerously close to their ultimate goal, the Confederate capital. Lee bolstered his defense with additional troops from the Richmond and Petersburg perimeter lines. Grant decided to make an assault, and prepared his massive army for the task. For the first three days of June 1864, Grant sent wave upon wave of Union forces to their death. During three days of battle, the Union forces lost approximately 12,000 men. In a month since Grant had begun his trek towards Richmond, his losses reached a total of 50,000 men. In comparison, within the Confederate defenses, their losses during the battle of Cold Harbor did not exceed 1,500 men. Benning's brigade was entrenched on the Confederate left. The Union assaults focused primarily on the Confederate right; however, the unit still suffered several casualties at the Battle of Cold Harbor.

General Grant decided that he could not take Richmond with a frontal assault. He changed his strategy, moved further south, and concentrated his forces on Lee's vulnerable underbelly, and lines of communications, located at Petersburg, Virginia. The southern lines were being stretched exceedingly thin. Resources of nearly everything were dangerously low. Lee and his forces now braced for the realities of a siege, and a war of attrition. Even General Longstreet, miraculously healing from a dangerous wound, pondered the unthinkable southern thought. How much longer could the Confederacy continue to repel Grant 's superior forces and unending aggression? **31** In desperation, Virginia sent old men and boys into the trenches as members of the Local Defense Forces (LDF). The local citizens began to question the uncertainty of their future. General Grant, with an army of superior forces and abundant materials of war, answered their questions with a siege. The troops of Benning's brigade settled into a routine within the trenches along the defensive perimeter, guarding Richmond and Petersburg.

Meanwhile, General Benning asked his Quartermaster officer, Major Edgeworth Bird to notify his wife about his condition. Always legal minded, Benning directed Bird to send the message as precisely defined by the surgeons. Major Bird sent the following information concerning General Benning 's condition, via telegraph to Mrs. Benning, in Columbus:

> Severely but not dangerously wounded. He is shot through the left shoulder, bones of course fractured. He is sent to Orange Court House. **32**

Benning was transferred to the General Hospital in Danville, Virginia, and again, Benning's brave little Mary, rushed to Virginia, this time to aid her beloved husband. After two and one-half years, Mary and Henry Benning were reunited. Mary gingerly assisted Henry as he was furloughed for sixty days of recuperation. For the first time in several years, Benning was going home. A local newspaper posted several articles relaying that the " fearless, intrepid General Benning," along with Captain Mott and Colonel Hodges were inbound to Columbus. **33** Upon their arrival in Columbus, Henry Benning was officially assigned to a bed in a local Confederate hospital. Like most of his fellow soldiers, Benning was listed as a patient suffering from " Vulnus Sclop " , or in modern layman's terminology, a gunshot wound. **34** Benning's wound required cleansing and drainage to prevent death from gangrene and infection, which Mary was thoroughly experienced in treating. Mary Benning had been serving as a voluntary matron in the hospitals since the beginning of the war, and she welcomed the opportunity to care for her beloved husband. General Benning 's wound required a total of six months to heal, and he certainly deserved every minute of it.

During Benning's absence, Columbus had become an important refuge for recuperating soldiers. With General Sherman exerting pressure on Atlanta, Columbus became an important Confederate center, further south and far

from harm's way. Numerous buildings had been converted to hospital
facilities to establish ten separate hospitals in Columbus. Saloons, stores,
and virtually whatever was available, was converted into hospital facilities
to house wounded soldiers. Upon Benning's arrival," more than 1,350
patients were being attended to in Columbus. Doctor Francis Orray
Ticknor was the Chief Surgeon." 35 Doctor Ticknor was a local physician,
who lived southeast of Columbus on " Torch Hill," close to Raphael Moses
's plantation," Esquiline. " Ticknor was a respected member of Columbus,
a noted poet, and he and his wife were friends of the Bennings and Moses.
While General Benning quietly recuperated from his shoulder wound,
received at the battle of the Wilderness, Lee's Army of Northern Virginia
was incessantly pummeled by General Grant 's seemingly endless supply
of fresh troops. In Benning's absence, several personnel changed positions.
Colonel Dudley DuBose served as the acting brigadier. Colonel James D.
Waddell, suffering from disabilities, was transferred to Richmond, where
he served on the Court of Slave Claims through the remainder of the war.
Benning's Adjutant and Brigade Inspector, Captain Herman H. Perry wrote
Benning a letter, which was actually an informal status report. Perry
remarked that everyone was happy to hear that he was not " finished," and
they all sincerely missed him. Since Benning was evacuated, the brigade
had participated in several battles, including the battles of Spotsylvania and
Cold Harbor. As Grant pushed against Lee's army, the Confederates were
forced to defend a massive network of interconnected forts and trenches to
protect the cities of Richmond and Petersburg from a Union assault. Within
the trenches, deadly sniper fire returned to the lives of both armies. Perry
explained that:

> The duties here are simply to occupy the trenches from day to
> day, being relieved for two days, every six days, that a brigade
> remains on. The enemies lines vary from 200 to 300 yards in our
> front and having approaches by rifle pits in some places. The
> sharpshooting is severe. I cannot say that the brigade is getting
> on well. There is much dissatisfaction among the men and
> officers. Seaborn [Benning's son and Adjutant] is in good
> health. The health of the men is not good for want of vegetables.
> Hoping this finds you in much improved health. 36

Benning's health was slowly improving, although his left arm would
never fully recover and he regained only partial use of his arm. Yet,
Benning was lucky compared to so many soldiers whose lives were ruined
by their wounds. Benning's close friend, Colonel Wesley C. Hodges was
one of the less fortunate. Before the war, Henry Benning and Wesley

Hodges were friends. The Hodges family ran a large dry goods business
and warehouse, where Benning and other plantation owners stored many of
their valuable perishable goods, such as sugar. As members of the same
church and social circles, the Hodges and Bennings forged a bond that
complemented both their families. Furthermore, Hodges had served
diligently under Benning's command at both the regimental and brigade
levels. Together since the inception of the Seventeenth regiment, Hodges
had provided " Old Rock " with continuous and faithful service. Hodge's
wounds were severe, and his body was wrought with permanent
disabilities. 37 Wesley Hodges joined the ranks of the war's casualties; a
list that contained many men whom were close to Henry Benning. Among
the dead were Thomas R. R. Cobb, Paul Semmes, John A. Jones , Van
Leonard, numerous members of his command, and fellow Columbusites.
His own son, although permanently disabled was still at the front, and
Benning knew few men who had not been grievously affected by the war.

For Henry Benning, his convalescence provided him with time for
reflection and observation. During Benning's absence, his family and his
hometown had changed. His wife, Mary had suffered greatly. With the
supervisory burdens of her large home, her father's businesses, care of the
plantation, care of her aged mother, raising her five daughters, assisting her
sister-in-law's family, as well as caring for the orphaned children of the
Martin family, Mary Benning led a tremendously stress-filled life. In 1864,
the Benning's five daughters ranged in age from twenty-three to nine, so
Mary did receive some help from the older girls with daily operations.
Mary Benning 's spare time was occupied with work in the Confederate
hospitals, the " Soldiers' Aid Society," the Girls' Asylum, and her church.
She had lost her father, her brother, numerous friends, and the life she
knew before the war had been effectively turned upside down. Upon the
death of her father, Mary was forced to act as the Administratrix of his
estate, which entailed numerous and complex financial affairs. Amidst
these complicated affairs, Mary had to manage the family finances with a
reduced income, inflated prices, shortages of goods, and a Union blockade
which devastated the economy. The Jones and Bennings owned numerous
rental and leased properties, which were heavily taxed, yet filled with
tenants who were unable to pay. Additionally, her father had invested all
their available reserves in Confederate bonds, which were rapidly declining
in value. 38

Benning's hometown of Columbus, Georgia was suffering too. Just
as it was before the war, Benning's livelihood was entwined with the city

of Columbus. As the city progressed, so did he, and as the Southern economy faltered, both Columbus and Henry Benning did too. While the war had spurred industrial growth, Columbus was working overtime merely to help maintain the pulse of Confederate livelihood. Gone were the days of prosperity and commercial enterprise beyond the borders of the Confederacy. In 1864, Columbus was a city whose burgeoning population was a direct result of the war. As a commercial hub and an important Confederate base, Columbus enjoyed a unique situation, relatively safe from Union threats. The ten Confederate hospitals, and their ever-expanding body of patients became increasingly important during the latter months of the war, and struggling to meet the material needs of the Confederacy, the mills operated night and day. The war industries required a robust labor force and people from the surrounding communities needed work. As the city swelled to accommodate the new citizens, other opportunities increased, and until late in the war, the city of Columbus fared quite well compared to other Southern cities. **39**

Throughout the Confederate states, with a Union blockade and the continuous expenditures of the war, the South's major cities slipped into an economic crisis from which they would never recover. With General Grant in command of the Union army, his scheme of maneuver was to simultaneously press the war in both the eastern and western theaters. The Union leadership knew that by squeezing the two key Confederate states, Georgia and Virginia, the South's limited resources would eventually force a victory. Grant's primary focus was the cities of Atlanta and Richmond, who served as the hubs of the Confederacy. With Grant personally controlling the operations around Richmond, General William T. Sherman was assigned to oversee the western theater. Sherman's focus was Atlanta, which in 1864 was very vulnerable. Since the Confederacy lost its hold on Tennessee, at the battle of Chattanooga, the Union army of General Sherman swept into Georgia from Tennessee. General Bragg had resigned after losing the battle of Chattanooga, and Confederate Generals Johnston and Hood fought a retreating battle towards Atlanta. Throughout the summer of 1864, Sherman pressured Atlanta with increasing tension, which prompted the Confederacy to relocate many of the wounded, southward, to Columbus.

But Columbus could not possibly absorb all of Atlanta's wounded, and some were sent to neighboring hospitals in Alabama. As conditions in Atlanta worsened, the sense of impending doom escalated, and in Columbus," the crisis of the war was upon them." **40** When Confederate soldiers died, their families were left to fend for themselves. In 1864, according to Muscogee County statistics, there were 1,321 impoverished widows and dependent children eligible for assistance. **41** While the

government provided some relief, it was simply inadequate due to the
inflationary costs of basic necessities. The local newspaper recorded that,"
There is now in this community much suffering among the poor on account
of the high prices of provisions, and unless something is done, there will be
more still." **42** The people of Columbus supported one another very
generously, and a local " Relief Association " was established, through
which donations were collected and distributed to the poor. In addition to
the voluntary contributions, local taxes were collected and the city
bestowed $5000.00 towards aiding the poverty-stricken residents of
Columbus. Additionally, with unprecedented generosity, the city also
dispersed another $5000.00 amongst the refugee families from Atlanta, and
appropriated $5000.00 for the care of the wounded soldiers transferred
from Atlanta to Columbus. Even with assistance, inflationary prices made
the purchase of many goods impossible and even the wealthy were forced
to change their lifestyles. In 1864, the price of sugar was $8.00 per pound;
bacon $4.00 per pound; and shoes sold for the premium price of $100.00
per pair. **43**

Inflationary prices, shortages of goods, exorbitant taxes, and a long
horrific war began to take its toll on the South. Compared to cities such as
Richmond and Mobile, which were already suffering from severe shortages
and the resulting ill effects of riotous mobs, Columbus had fared quite
well. A Columbus laborer noted in an article to the *Columbus Daily Sun*,
that while the citizens of Columbus had little to eat," their condition is
much better than the poor soldiers, who are fighting the rich man's fight,
for they suffer all of the privations and hardships incident to the life of a
soldier, with a perfect knowledge of the sufferings of their families at
home." **44**

Meanwhile, in the killing fields of Virginia, the soldiers of Benning's
brigade continued serving their country and thought of their families, at
home. As for their leader," Old Rock " Benning continued his
convalescence, and for the next few months, he anxiously awaited the mail
and the papers for news of his brigade.

PHOTOGRAPHS, MAPS, and ILLUSTRATIONS

Image	PHOTO/ ILLUSTRATION	SOURCE
1	**Mary Howard (Jones) Benning** (portrait)	Mr. Henry Benning Spencer
2	**Henry Lewis Benning** (portrait)	Mr. Henry Benning Spencer
3	**Augusta & Louisa Benning** (photograph)	Mrs. Mimi Pease Childs
4	**Louisa Vivian (Benning) Spencer** (photograph)	Columbus State University Archives
5	**Anna Caroline Benning** (photograph)	Confederated Memorial Association
6	**Augusta Jones (Benning) Crawford** (photograph)	Confederated Memorial Association
7	**Sallie (Benning) Hull** (photograph)	Mrs. Mimi Pease Childs
8	**Seaborn Jones** (portrait)	Georgia Department of Archives & History
9	**Mary (Howard) Jones** (photograph)	Columbus State University Archives
10	**Eliza Grantham, Mary Benning & John Jones** (portrait)	Mrs. Mimi Pease Childs
11	**"El Dorado"** (photograph)	Photo by Author
12	**John A. Jones** (portrait)	Mrs. Mimi Pease Childs
13	**Van (de Van) Leonard II** (portrait)	Mrs. Mimi Pease Childs
14	**Frances R. (Darnell) Leonard** (photograph)	Mr. Leonard Garrard
15	**Mary Louisa (Leonard) Jones** (engraving)	Mr. Leonard Garrard
16	**Mary Louisa (Jones) Bruce** (photograph)	Mrs. Mimi Pease Childs

Photographs, Maps and Illustrations

Mary Howard (Jones) Benning (age 21)
Portrait by C.R. Parker, 1838
Image #1

Henry Lewis Benning (age 26)
Portrait by Edward Mooney, 1840
Image #2

Augusta & Louisa Benning
Twin daughters of Henry & Mary Benning (in their youth)
Image 3

Louisa Vivian (Benning) Spencer
Henry Benning's daughter and the wife of
Samuel Spencer.
Image 4

Anna Caroline Benning
Henry Benning's daughter (never married),
founder and leader of several patriotic
organizations.
Image 5

Augusta Jones (Benning) Crawford
Henry Benning's daughter. (Mrs. Reese
Crawford). Image 6

Sarah "Sallie" Benning Hull
Henry Benning's daughter. (Mrs. Herbert
Ladson Hull). Image 7

Seaborn Jones
US & Georgia Congressman, Colonel,
Georgia Militia, Attorney & Entrepreneur,
Henry Benning's father-in-law.
Image 8

Mary (Howard) Jones
Henry Benning's mother-in-law
Image 9

(L to R) **Eliza Grantham (Mary's cousin), Mary (Jones) Benning & her brother (in his youth) John A. Jones**
Image 10

"El Dorado," Antebellum Home of the Bennings & Jones
Image 11

John A. Jones
Son of Seaborn & Mary Jones, Attorney, Mexican War veteran, Commander of the
20th Georgia Infantry Regiment, CSA, and Henry Benning's brother-in-law.
Image 12

Van (de Van) Leonard II
Entrepreneur, business associate and close
friend of the Bennings & Jones.
Image 13

Frances R. (Darnell) Leonard
Wife of Van (de Van) Leonard II
Image 14

Mary (Leonard) Jones
Wife of John A. Jones & the daughter of
Van & Frances Leonard.
Image 15

Mary Louisa (Jones) Bruce
Henry Benning's niece & the daughter of
John & Mary Jones.
Image 16

Anna (Leonard) Garrard
Daughter of Van & Frances Leonard & the
wife of Louis F. Garrard.
Image 17

Louis F. Garrard
Husband of Anna Leonard Garrard, CSA
soldier, Attorney, State Representative, and
good friend of the Bennings & Jones.
Image 18

"Wildwood," Home of the Leonards & Garrards
Image 19

Anna (Leonard) Garrard & Seaborn Leonard Jones
Anna was Seaborn's aunt and he was the son of Mary Louisa (Leonard)
Jones & John A. Jones. CSA soldier and the nephew of Henry Benning.
Image 20

Augusta Palmyra (Benning) Patterson
Wife of Madison Lewis Patterson & sister
of Henry Benning.
Image 21

Augusta Jane (Evans) Wilson
Cousin of Mary Benning, noted nineteenth
century author & born at "Wildwood."
Image 22

Samuel Spencer
Henry Benning's son-in-law, CSA soldier
& President of the Southern Railway.
Image 23

Martin J. Crawford
Georgia Representative, Judge, CSA
soldier, & close friend of Henry Benning.
Image 24

Howell Cobb
Congressman, Senator, Governor, US
Secretary of Treasury, Major General
(CSA) & Henry Benning's distant cousin.
Image 25

Alexander H. Stephens
Congressman, Senator, Governor, Vice-
President, CSA, Political opposite of Henry
Benning, but a devoted friend.
Image 26

Reverend Lovick Pierce
Methodist Minister, Co-founder of Emory
University, Respected religious leader
throughout the South.
Image 27

William Shepherd
Commander of Benning's 2nd Infantry
Regiment, *Columbus Guards*, and a close
friend of Henry Benning.
Image 28

Robert Toombs
Attorney, Congressman and Senator from
Georgia, (CSA) Secretary of State,
Brigadier General.
Image 29

Linton Stephens
Attorney, Georgia Supreme Court Justice,
Commander of the 15th Georgia regiment,
Benning's brigade (CSA).
Image 30

Raphael Moses
Attorney, Georgia Congressman, Major,
CSA, served under Benning as Chief
Commissary Officer until promoted to the
same position under General Longstreet.
Image 31

Herschel V. Johnson
Attorney, U.S. Congressman, Supreme
Court Justice, Governor of Georgia, and
college classmate of Henry Benning.
Image 32

Joseph Lumpkin
Chief Justice of the Georgia Supreme Court
& Henry Benning's legal mentor
Image 33

James N. Ramsey (Colonel)
Commander of the 1st Georgia Infantry
regiment, CSA, a fellow secession delegate
and close friend of Benning
Image 34

General Paul J. Semmes
Columbus bank agent, long-time commander of the *Columbus Guards*, 2nd Georgia regiment (CSA), as well as his own brigade until he was killed at Gettysburg.
Image 35

General James Longstreet
Commander of the 1st Corps, Army of Northern Virginia (CSA), Know as Lee's "War Horse" (Benning's corps commander).

Image 36

General John B. Hood
Benning's division commander. Wounded at Gettysburg and Chickamauga, (1 leg amputated & 1 arm disabled). His tenacious Texas brigade fought beside Benning's brigade throughout the war.
Image 37

General Thomas R.R. Cobb
Attorney, Author, Georgia State Supreme Court Recorder, Brigade commander (Cobb's Legion, CSA). Younger brother of Howell Cobb, and a distant cousin of Henry Benning. Killed at Fredericksburg.
Image 38

General Henry Lewis Benning

This portrait originally graced the walls of the Spencer building in
Washington D.C., (early 20th century) while Samuel Spencer
(Benning's son-in-law) served as the President of the Southern Railway.
Image 39

Brigadier General Henry Lewis Benning

Portrait commissioned by Benning's grandsons, Henry Benning Spencer, Henry
Benning Crawford, and Benning Hull. The artist was Ms. Kate Edwards of Atlanta
and the completed work was presented to the U.S. Army Infantry School in June, 1940.
It is now a public treasure and an integral part of the National Infantry Museum,
Fort Benning, Georgia.

Image 40

General Henry L. Benning
Portrait engraving and a Benning's signature on file in the Georgia Archives
Image 41

1st Lieutenant Solomon Cottle
Co. B, 17th Regiment. One of the few of
Benning's regimental officers that survived
the war.

Image 42

Adjutant Lovick Pierce Jr.
15th Regiment. The son of Reverend
Lovick Pierce and Benning's spiritual camp
leader.

Image 43

Battle flag of the 15th Regiment
Image 44

Major Edgeworth Bird
Benning's Quartermaster Officer and a
prolific writer. His correspondence with
home during the war years is published in
The Granite Farm Letters.
Image 45

Colonel James Waddell
Commander of the 20th Georgia Infantry
Regiment and a close friend of General
Henry Benning and Major Edgeworth Bird.
Image 46

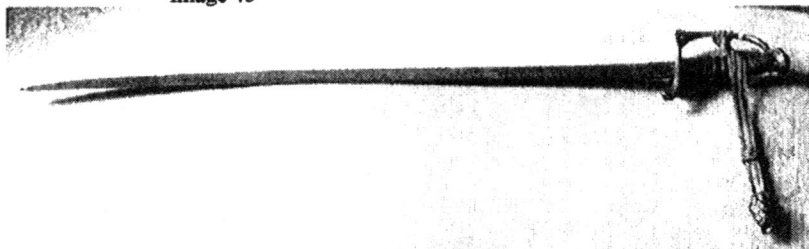

Sword wielded by General Robert Toombs during the Civil War
Image 47

Sergeant William R. Houghton
Co. G, 2nd Georgia. A member of the
Columbus Guards, he enlisted in 1861,
survived the war and recorded his
observations in great detail. As the co-
author of *Two Boys in the Civil War*, his
narrative is original, raw, and provides
valuable insight into the character of his
commander, General Henry Benning.
Image 48

Private Isaac Beckworth
Co. C, 17th Georgia. One of the few
soldiers from Columbus that enlisted under
Benning's command in 1861, served
throughout the duration of the war, and
returned with General Benning to
Columbus in 1865.
Image 49

Sergeant Thomas Langford
Co. H, 17th Georgia.
Image 50

Captain John A. McGregor

Co. E, 17th Georgia. A veteran of the Mexican War and a friend of Colonel John A. Jones, this company commander was one of Benning's finest officers. He successfully led his company through many battles, but while leading the charge into the "Devil's Den," he was wounded and permanently disabled.

Image 51

General Henry Lewis Benning: This Was a Man

Front row, L to R: **Major Roger L. Gamble, Captain Willis F. Denny**
Back row, L to R: **Lieutenants Nicholas Bostick and Bob Jordan**
This group of officers led Co. C, 20th Georgia Regiment, which was known as the "Jefferson County Guards." Jordan and Bostick died in battle, while Denny and Gamble survived, but suffered through their post-war years with permanent disabilities.
Image 52

Lieutenant Pinkney Hatchett

Co. E, 20th Georgia. While commanding his company during the Battle of
Gettysburg, he led his men through the Devil's Den and on into the
"Valley of Death." It was there that he was wounded, but at least he survived.

Image 53

Benning's CSA Appointment Order to Colonel
Image 54

Confederate States of America,

WAR DEPARTMENT,

Richmond, April 23rd 1863

Sir :

You are hereby informed that the President has appointed you

Brigadier General

In the Provisional Army in the service of the Confederate States: *to rank as such from the Seventeenth day of January one thousand eight hundred and sixty three. Should the Senate, at their next session, advise and consent thereto, you will be commissioned accordingly.*

Immediately on receipt hereof, please to communicate to this Department, through the Adjutant and Inspector General's Office, your acceptance or non-acceptance of said appointment; and with your letter of acceptance, return to the Adjutant and Inspector General the OATH, *herewith enclosed, properly filled up,* SUBSCRIBED *and* ATTESTED, *reporting at the same time your* AGE, RESIDENCE *when appointed, and the* STATE *in which you were* BORN.

Should you accept, you will report for duty to Genl R E Lee

Jams A Seddon
Secretary of War.

Brig: Genl: N L Benning
Pc Pc

Benning's CSA Promotion Order to Brigadier General
Image 55

Notes and Map of Gettysburg, by Henry L. Benning
Image 56

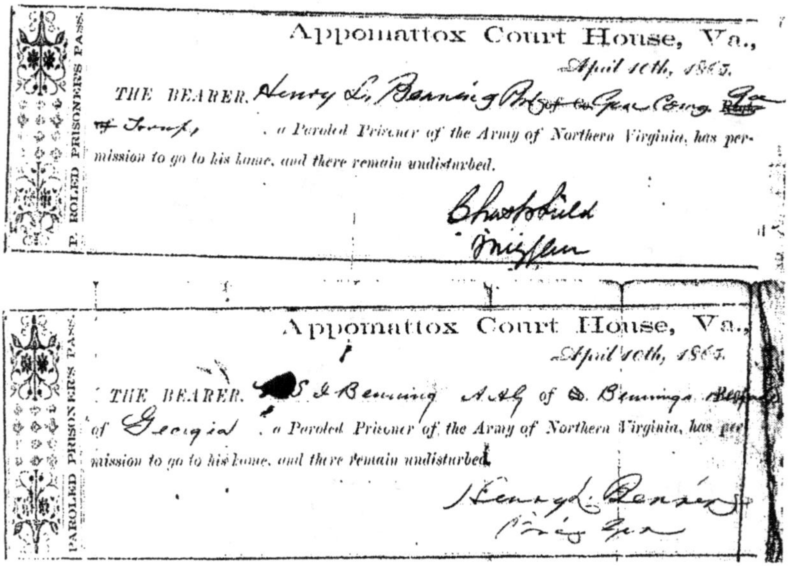

PAROLED PRISONER'S PASS.

Appomattox Court House, Va.,

April 10th, 1865.

THE BEARER, Henry L. Benning Brig. Gen. Comdg. [illegible] of Troops, a Paroled Prisoner of the Army of Northern Virginia, has permission to go to his home, and there remain undisturbed.

[illegible]

Griffin

PAROLED PRISONER'S PASS.

Appomattox Court House, Va.,

April 10th, 1865.

THE BEARER, [illegible] S. I. Benning A.A.G. of Benning's Brigade of Georgia, a Paroled Prisoner of the Army of Northern Virginia, has permission to go to his home, and there remain undisturbed.

Henry L. Benning

Brig. Gen.

Henry & Seaborn Bennings' Parole Passes
Image 57

UCV ribbons honoring Henry L. Benning
Image 58

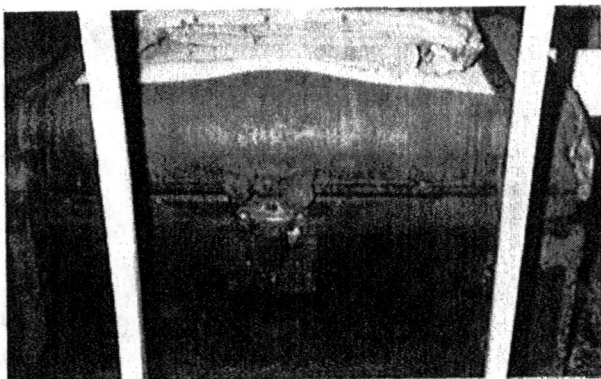

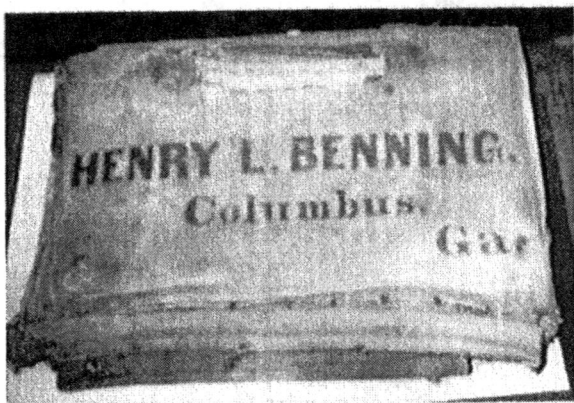

Personal Artifacts of Henry L. Benning
Image 59

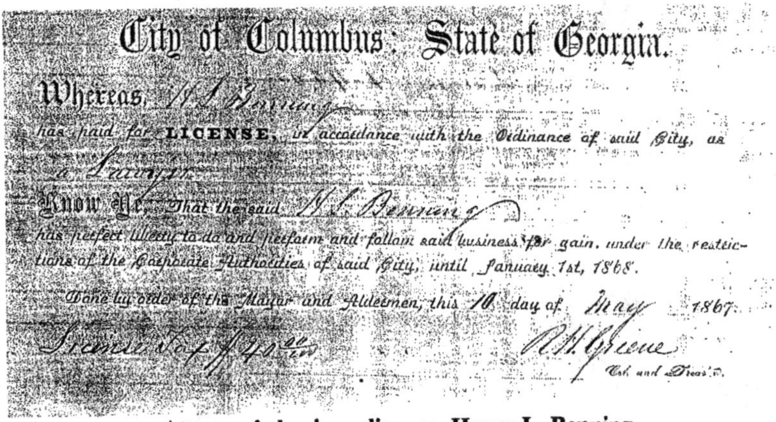

City of Columbus: State of Georgia.

Whereas, H. L. Benning
has paid for LICENSE, in accordance with the Ordinance of said City, as
a Lawyer

Know Ye, That the said H. L. Benning
has perfect liberty to do and perform and follow said business for gain, under the restrictions of the Corporate Authorities of said City, until January 1st, 1868.

Done by order of the Mayor and Aldermen, this 10 day of May 1867.

License Tax $40.00

R. H. Greene
Clk. and Treas'r.

Attorney's business license- Henry L. Benning

Image 60

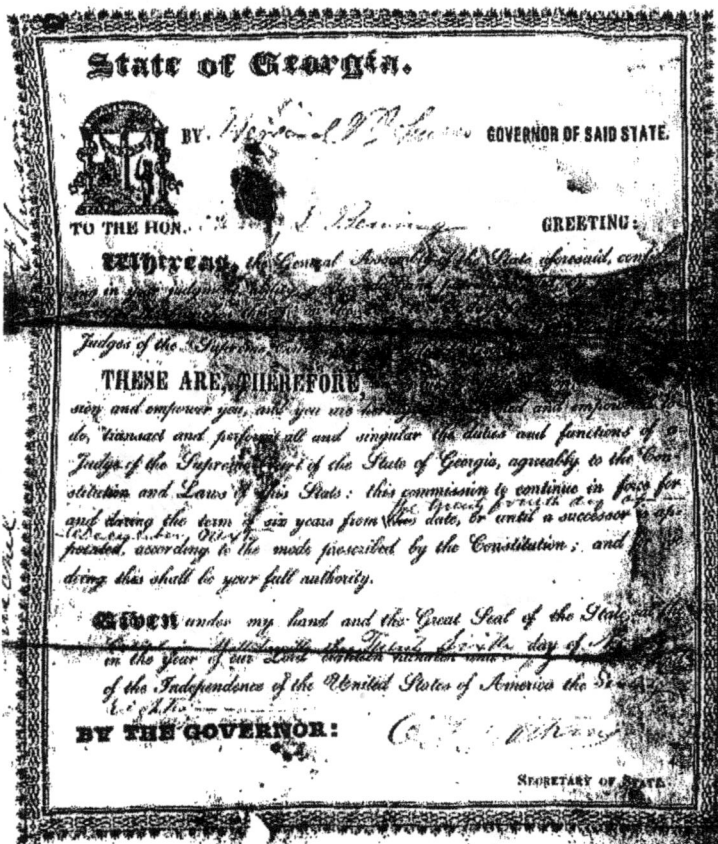

Supreme Court Appointment of Henry L. Benning
Image 61

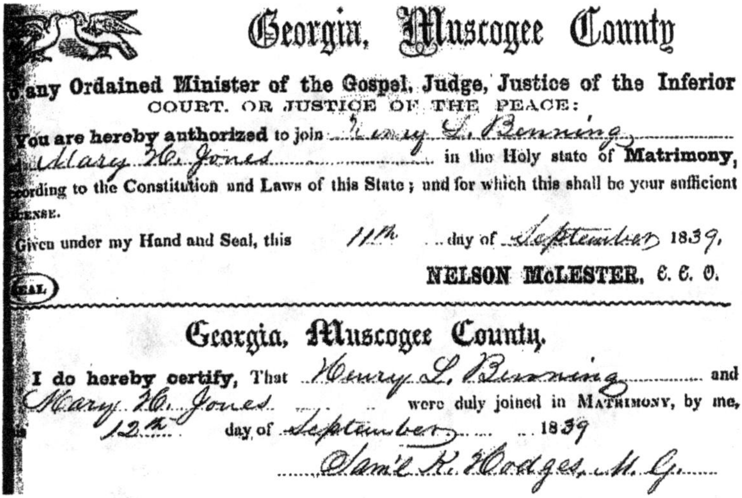

Georgia, Muscogee County

To any Ordained Minister of the Gospel, Judge, Justice of the Inferior
COURT. OR JUSTICE OF THE PEACE:

You are hereby authorized to join ....*Henry L. Benning*........
....*Mary H. Jones*........................... in the Holy state of **Matrimony**,
according to the Constitution and Laws of this State; and for which this shall be your sufficient
LICENSE.

Given under my Hand and Seal, this *11th* ....day of *September* 18*39*.

NELSON McLESTER, C. C. O.

(SEAL)

Georgia, Muscogee County.

I do hereby certify, That *Henry L. Benning* .... and
Mary H. Jones .... were duly joined in **MATRIMONY**, by me,
12th ... day of *September* 18*39*

.........*Saml K. Hodges, M. G.*......

Marriage License of Henry & Mary Benning
Image 62

Home of Henry L. Benning (Post-war residence)
1420 Broad Street (modern site of *Total Systems* corporate headquarters)
Image 63

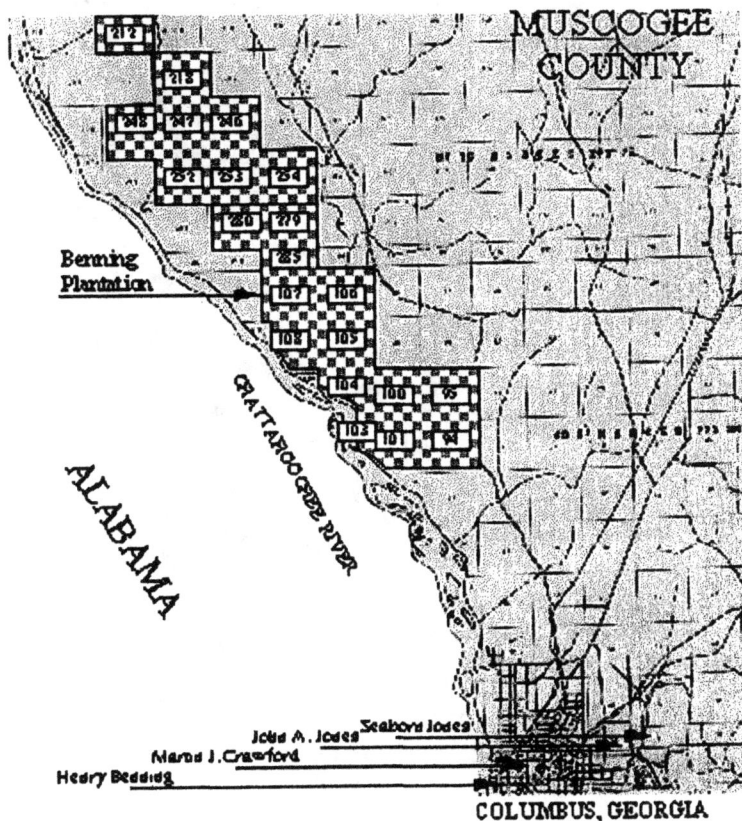

Map of Henry L. Benning Properties (1839-1875)
Image 64

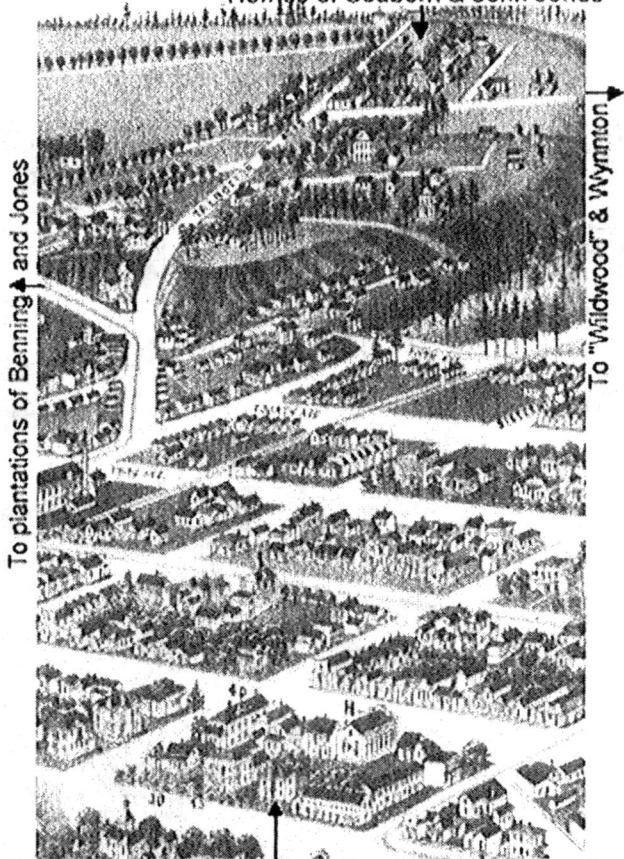

"El Dorado" & "Bonnie Doone"
Homes of Seaborn & John Jones

To plantations of Benning and Jones

To "Wildwood" & Wynnton

Post-war residence of Henry Benning (Broad Street)

Image 65

Henry Benning Family (1800-1880)

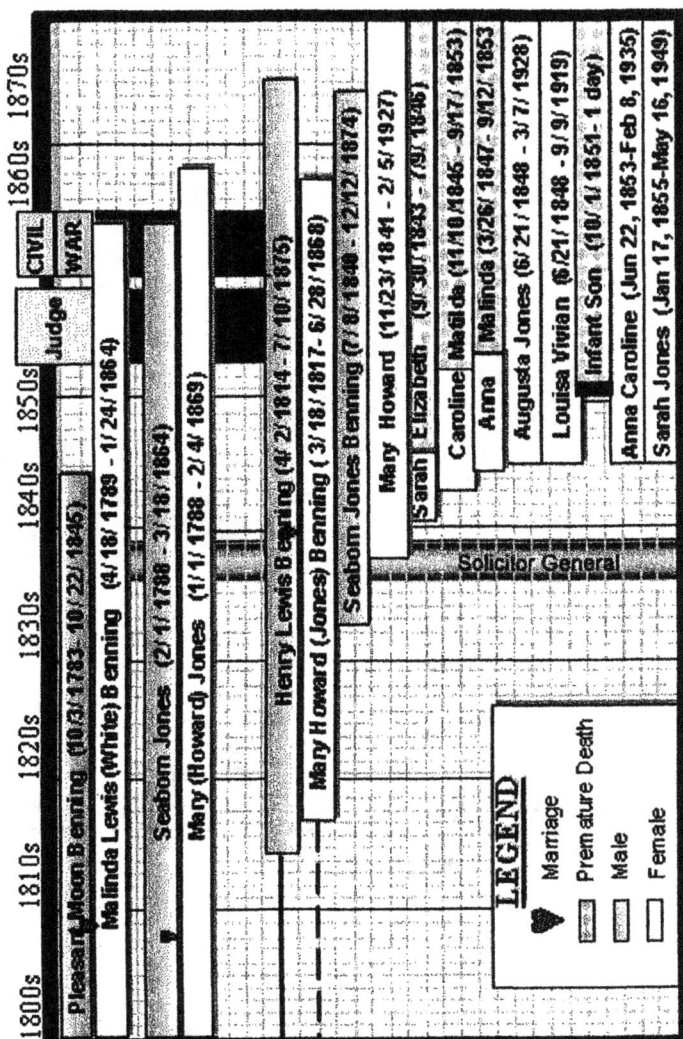

1800s 1810s 1820s 1830s 1840s 1850s 1860s 1870s

Judge

CIVIL WAR

Solicitor General

Pleasant Moon Benning (10/3/1783 - 10/22/1845)

Malinda Lewis (White) Benning (4/18/1789 - 1/24/1864)

Seaborn Jones (2/1/1788 - 3/18/1864)

Mary (Howard) Jones (1/1/1788 - 2/4/1869)

Henry Lewis Benning (4/2/1814 - 7/10/1875)

Mary Howard (Jones) Benning (3/18/1817 - 6/28/1868)

Seaborn Jones Benning (7/8/1840 - 12/12/1874)

Mary Howard (11/23/1841 - 2/5/1927)

Sarah Elizabeth (9/30/1843 - 7/9/1846)

Caroline Matilda (11/18/1845 - 9/17/1853)

Anna Malinda (3/26/1847 - 9/12/1853)

Augusta Jones (6/21/1848 - 3/7/1928)

Louisa Vivian (6/21/1846 - 9/9/1919)

Infant Son (10/1/1851- 1 day)

Anna Caroline (Jun 22, 1853-Feb 8, 1935)

Sarah Jones (Jan 17, 1855-May 16, 1949)

LEGEND

- ► Marriage
- Premature Death
- Male
- Female

Benning Family (1800-1880)-Chart 1

Image 66

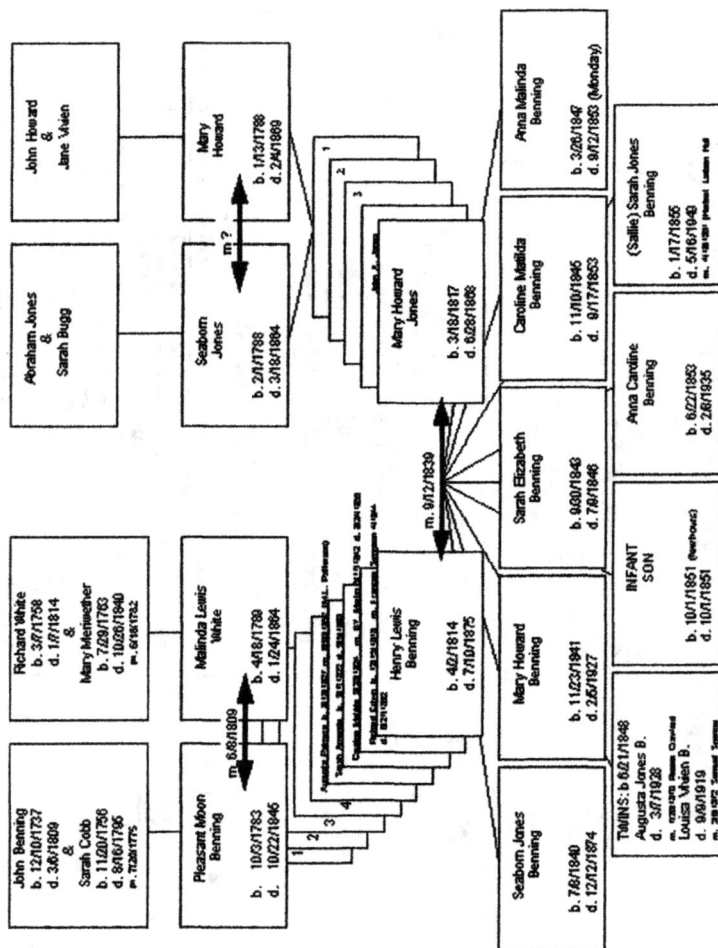

Family of Henry Benning-Chart 2
Image 67

Antebellum Print of Franklin College (now UGA)
Image 68

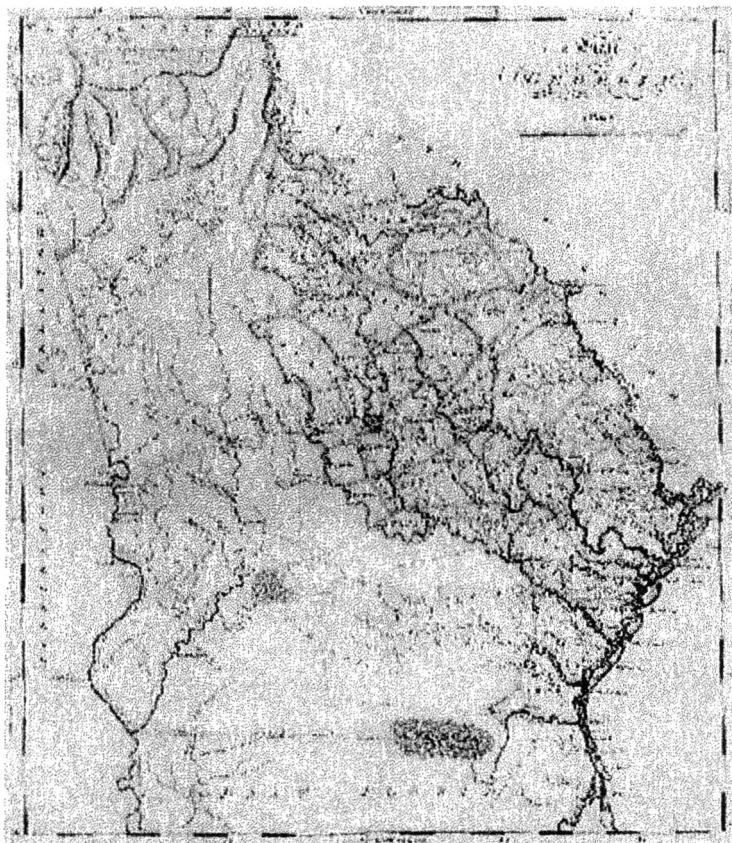

Map of the State of Georgia, 1814
Image 69

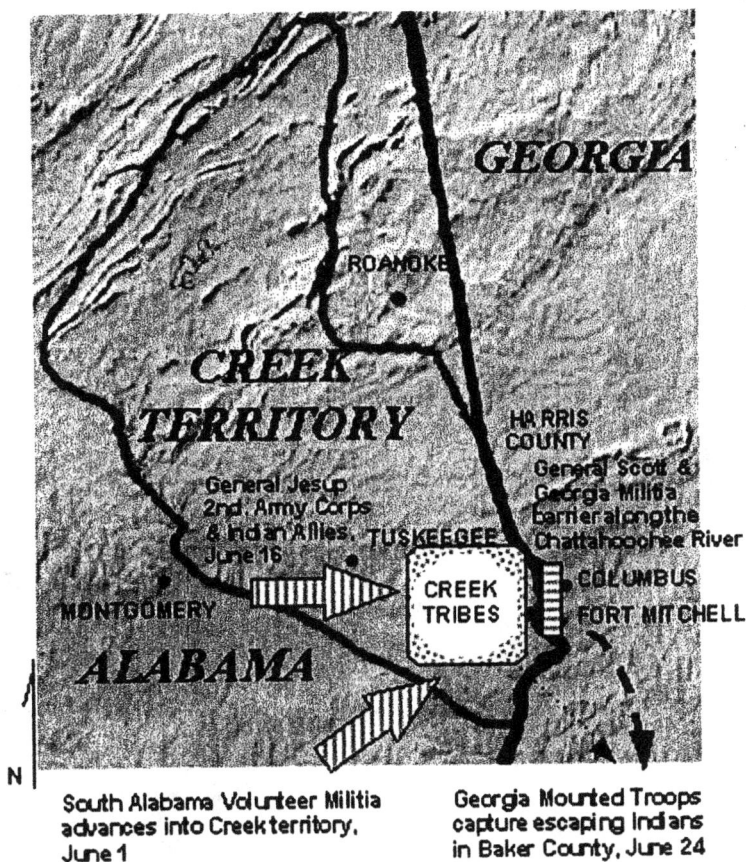

South Alabama Volunteer Militia advances into Creek territory, June 1

Georgia Mounted Troops capture escaping Indians in Baker County, June 24

Map of the Creek War, 1836
Image 70

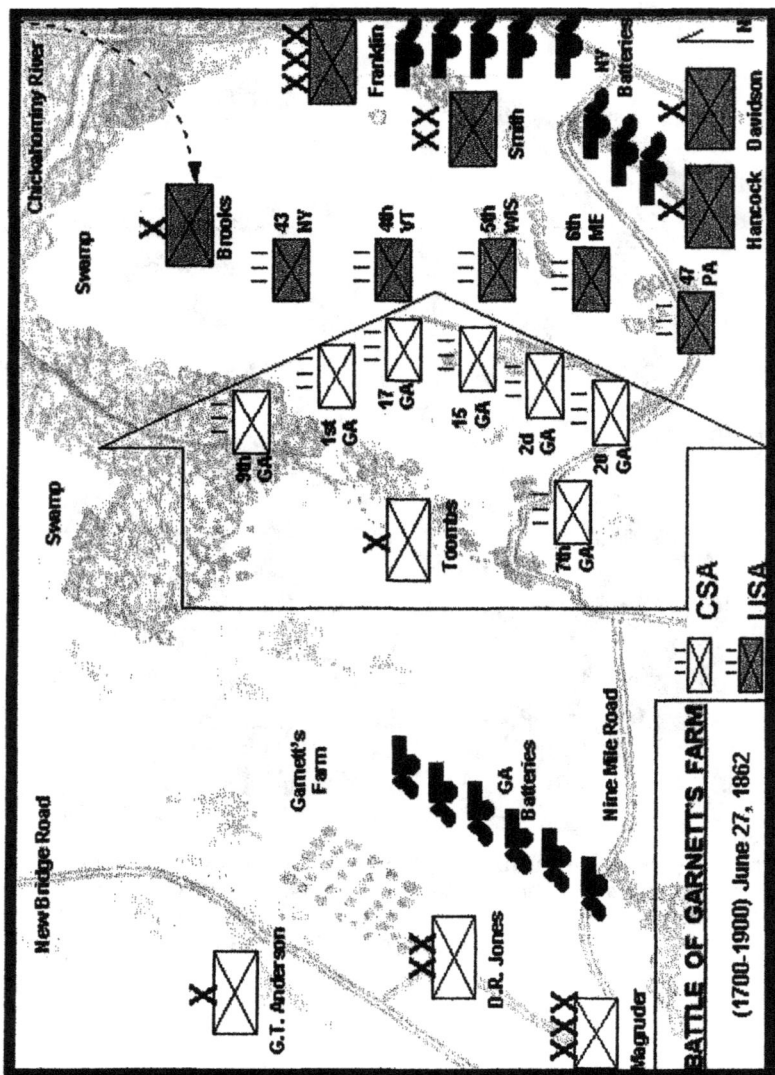

Map of the Battle of Garnett's Farm (June 27, 1862)
Image 71

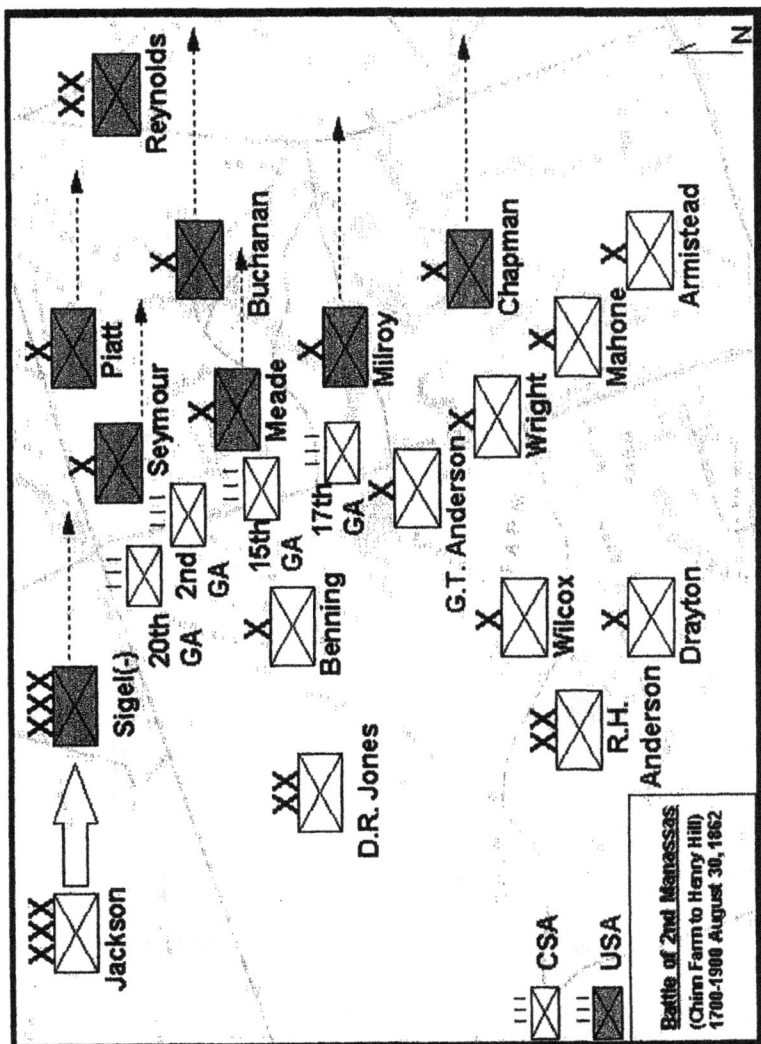

Map of the Battle of 2nd Manassas (August 30, 1862)
Image 72

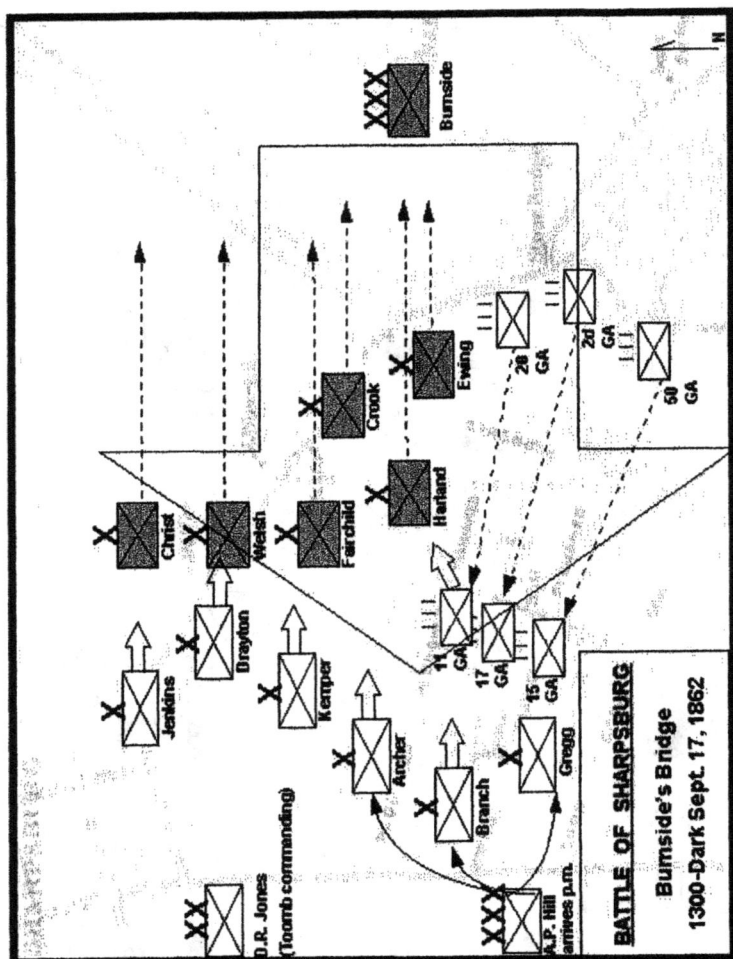

Map of the Battle of Sharpsburg (Sept. 17, 1862)
Image 73

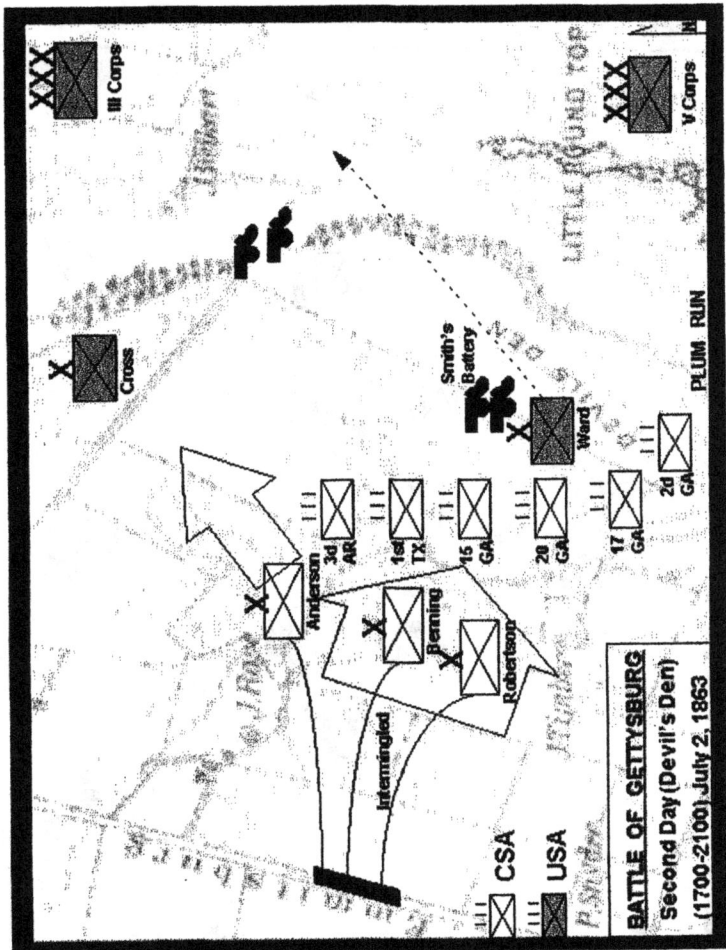

Map of the Battle of Gettysburg (July 2, 1863)
Image 74

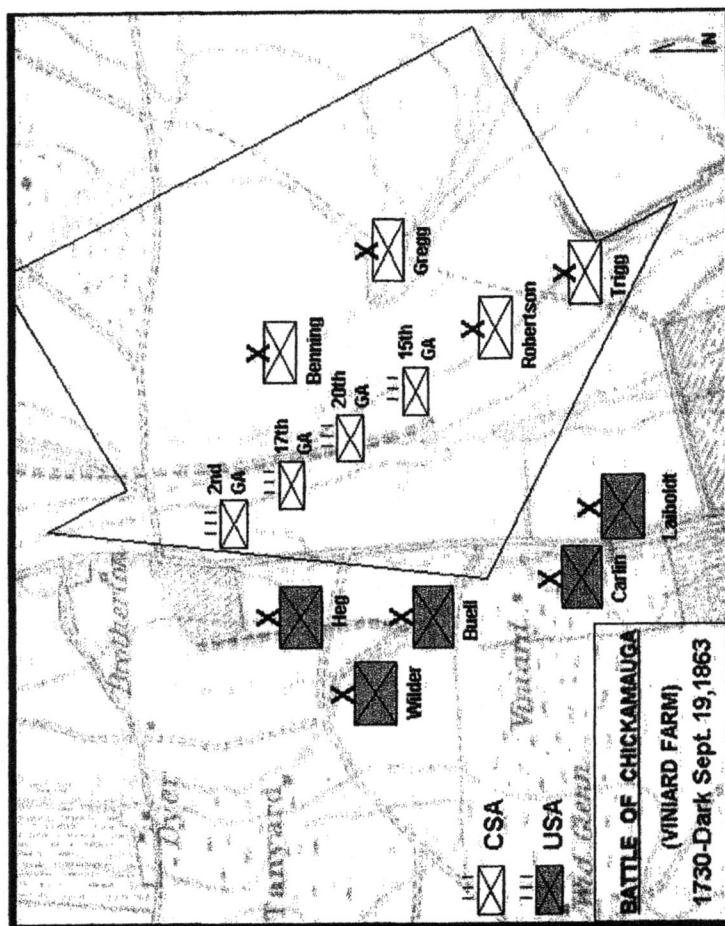

Map of the Battle of Chickamauga (Sept. 19, 1863)
Image 75

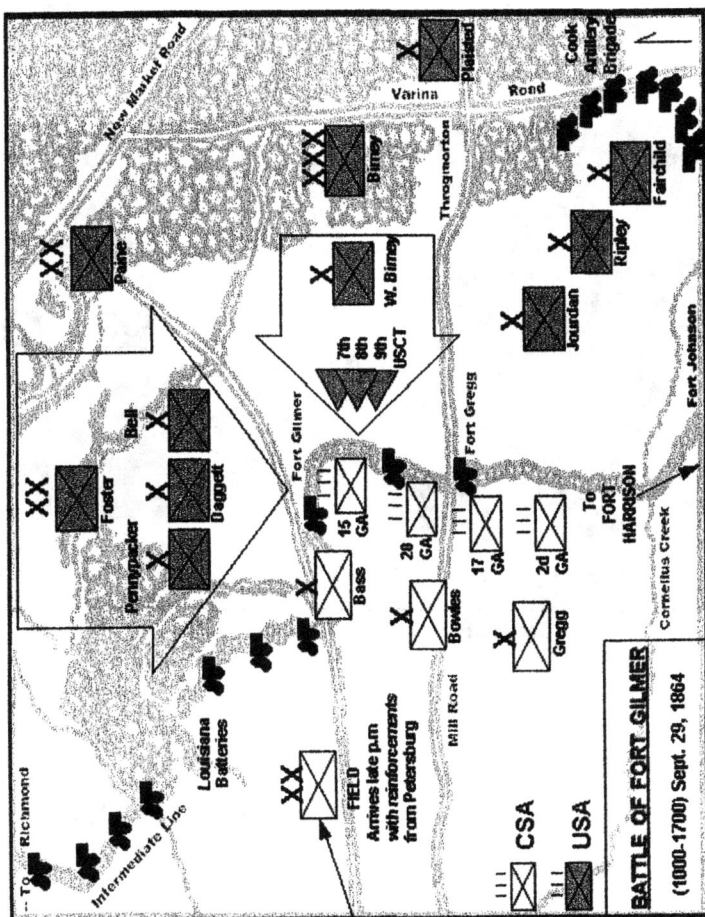

Map of the Battle of Fort Gilmer (Sept. 29, 1864)
Image 76

Battle of Sharpsburg, Burnside's Bridge
Image 77

Burnside's Bridge at Sharpsburg, Maryland
Image 78

Benning's Brigade at the Devil's Den
Image 79

Confederate dead at Battle of Gettysburg
Image 80

Richmond, Virginia Street Scene
Image 81

Richmond, Virginia Rail Depot
Image 82

Longstreet's Corps at Ringgold, Georgia
Image 83

Confederate Line of Battle at Chickamauga
Image 84

Battle of the Crater
Image 85

"With Fate Against Them" by Gilbert Gaul
Image 86

Surrender of Lee's Army of Northern Virginia
Image 87

Roll Call
Image 88

General Henry Lewis Benning: This Was a Man

Tomb of Henry L. Benning
Linwood Cemetery, Columbus, Georgia
Image 89

Photographs, Maps and Illustrations

Chapter 17

Confederate Apocalypse

As the summer of 1864 trudged by, the men of Benning's brigade, endured the heat, dug improved positions, and watched the Union lines across the demolished fields to their front. Since returning to the Army of Northern Virginia, despite numerous conflicts with the enemy, the unit had received fairly light casualties. Slowly, the troops' subsistence improved. The army was close to Richmond, and the troops on the line began to receive vegetables. Although the unit had achieved repeated success against Grant 's overwhelming Union forces, they could muster only half of their original numbers. As always, the brigade's reprieve was brief. General Grant, on June 12, 1864, stealthily maneuvered his four corps, down to the James River. Here, his entire army crossed the river, catching General Lee completely off guard. Responding to Grant 's move, on June 13, Lee marched his army south. Benning's brigade responded to his order and marched to a new position 13 miles south, near Malvern Hill. Quietly, the Confederates awaited Grant 's next assault, towards Richmond. For the next three days, the Army of Northern Virginia improved their trenches and continued to wait. Finally, early on the morning of the 16th, General Lee found out where Grant had gone. His entire army was making preparations to assault General Beauregard 's lightly defended entrenchments, east of Petersburg. Fortunately, the Union machine moved slowly. Immediately, Lee's forces rushed south, to assist in the defense of Petersburg. Benning's brigade and the rest of Longstreet's Corps took up positions about 13 miles north of the main defense lines in front of Petersburg, near Bermuda Hundred. On the 17th of June, Longstreet's corps drove back elements of General Butler's forces, gaining valuable territory. Meanwhile, Lee's other forces arrived to reinforce Beauregard 's defensive positions, and successfully spoiled Grant 's initiative to capture Petersburg. 1

Benning's brigade arrived at their position in the Petersburg line on June 18, and throughout the night, they dug their entrenchments. Up and down the Petersburg line, all of the Confederate forces worked diligently to improve their positions. On the 19th and 20th of June, weak Union assaults began to probe the line, but they were all successfully repelled. In the fighting on the 20th, Benning's brigade suffered several more casualties, killed in action. Thus, began the Siege of Petersburg. For the next several months, General Grant attempted several unsuccessful assaults at various positions, in and around the Richmond and Petersburg lines. 2

The siege added to the soldiers' misery. Soon, scurvy began to affect everyone. Due to the dwindling supply of fresh vegetables, the troops' gums became sore, and bled. A serious drought affected the region, and no rain fell for 47 days. This severe drought began on 3 June, and ended on 19 July. Body lice (affectionately referred to as "graybacks") added their very personal form of aggravation. Sanitation was primitive, and worst of all, it became a war of sudden death, from the handiwork of snipers. Anyone, exposing themselves to the enemy lines, for just a short moment, became a potential victim of human target practice. 3 On July 29, Benning's brigade was relieved from its position, near the center of the line, at Petersburg. Field's Division was reassigned to defend the area between Chaffin's Farm, in the south, up to the Darbytown Road, in the north, along the defensive perimeter, between Richmond and Petersburg. Meanwhile, General Grant had decided to expand his lines northward, towards Richmond. On August 13, Grant dispatched two Corps from City Point. They traveled north, up the James River and disembarked, under cover of darkness at Deep Bottom. Here, they formed their line of battle. At dawn, on the 14th, they attacked the Confederate defenses on a four mile front. Initially, with the element of surprise and overwhelming forces, the Union met with success. They punched a hole through the earthworks of General Law and General Anderson 's Brigades, but their progress was soon halted. 4

A news reporter from the Richmond Enquirer, witnessed the following scene: " Pausing in a ravine long enough to reform their lines, Colonel DuBose, being the only brigade commander then on the immediate field of conflict, assumed command of several detachments from other commands, and, acting in concert with Col. Howard and the Alabama regiments on the right and Col. Little on the left, with a yell that only rebels know how to make, charged and carried the works under a galling fire, and, Colonels DuBose and Little throwing their commands across the fortifications, swept the enemy pell-mell far beyond, inflicting heavy loss." The observant reporter added," Colonel DuBose, who has commanded Benning's brigade with unvarying success since the morning of the battle of the Wilderness, acted with conspicuous gallantry on this occasion, and no other officer of my acquaintance is more deserving of promotion." The fighting continued back and forth, throughout the next day, with frequent skirmishing and artillery duels. Again, the Union forces penetrated the Confederate lines, at the positions of the Alabama regiments. The reporter of the *Richmond Enquirer* continues his coverage with: " But, in the nick of time, Colonel Coward, of the 5th South Carolina regiment of Bratton's brigade, and Colonel DuBose, with the 15th, 17th and 20th Georgia regiments, reached the field, and though much exhausted by a rapid march, co-operating with each other, charged the heavy advancing columns in the center, and drove them back to the breastworks our men had vacated." " He [enemy] left in our hands on the Darbytown Road over 200 of his dead and many wounded, besides over 400 prisoners and 2,080 stands of arms and the colors of his " gallant Colored Troops. " The prisoners captured on this part of the field represent 54 regiments, which give some idea of the force with which he made the attack. " 5

The fighting near New Market heights ended with the Confederates maintaining their defensive lines intact; however, the Union forces would return, with a vengeance. With the battle ended, the soldiers went back to working in the trenches. The tasks of digging, strengthening and extending their lines, was never ending. Benning's brigade now assumed a semi-permanent position on the New Market line. This line was formed in the shape of a " U" , with the curve, facing the enemy. The curve also served as the center of the line, through which the New Market Road bisected. The New Market Road connected the New Market community with Richmond, which was 10 miles to the northwest. Immediately below the New Market heights was Deep Bottom, on the James River, where the Yankees had launched their assault on 14-16 August. Colonel DuBose, commanding Benning's brigade and Colonel Bass, commanding Gregg 's Texas Brigade, were the only veteran forces located between Richmond and another assault ; however, Lee determined that another assault at this location was not likely. He considered the most critical threat, to be directly in front of Petersburg. Tactically, in the big picture, he was correct; therefore, he concentrated his forces at Petersburg, and he maintained the remaining brigades of General Field 's Division, as a mobile reinforcement unit, which could be sent up, from Petersburg, if Grant attacked in the vicinity of New Market. 6

In the meantime, the soldiers of Benning's brigade, worked on their line, tried to stay healthy and read the newspapers with great anxiety. Back home, in Georgia, a dreadfully depressing and surrealistic nightmare was occurring. Union forces invading their home state were laying siege on Atlanta. Their old hero, General Hood attempted to repel General Sherman 's forces, but eventually, Atlanta fell, and the Yankees took the city on September 2, 1864. 7 Throughout the month of September, Union troops also continued their siege upon Petersburg. Suddenly, in a surprising assault, early before dawn on September 29, Grant renewed the offensive. He sent General Birney 's 10th Corps, marching all night, and he attempted to take the Confederate line at New Market heights. Almost simultaneously, he sent General Ord 's 18th Corps across the James River at Aiken's Landing. Ord 's forces concentrated their immediate efforts, northwest, up the Varina Road towards Fort Harrison. The Confederate forces standing between Richmond and the 24,000 men sent to threaten the capital city numbered approximately 6,000. 8 General Gregg, in command of the Confederate forces, headquartered at Chaffin's farm, sent the alarm of a massive attack, to General Lee. Field's mobile reserve unit, in Petersburg, was ordered to Gregg 's aid, but they did not arrive until too late that evening. Meanwhile, General Lee, himself, moved up towards Chaffin's farm to witness the battle. 9

On the battlefield, at the New Market line, the men of the Texas Brigade, commanded by Colonel Bass, Benning's brigade, still under the command of Colonel DuBose, and a mixed unit of dismounted Virginia cavalry, commanded by Colonel Gary, opened fire on General Birney 's " Colored Troops ", advancing in mass. The Union forces bravely charged the New Market heights, but they became entangled within the abatis. Unable to penetrate the obstacles, strategically emplaced on the sloping terrain, Birney 's troops were literally cut to pieces. A few brave men managed to reach the Confederate positions, only to be captured or, due to the hatred of Negro soldiers, simply murdered. The survivors staggered or crawled to the rear, in retreat. The lead brigade of the Union corps had been virtually eliminated. At Fort Harrison, the defenders went into action against General Ord 's rapidly advancing corps. Unfortunately, only four of the nine cannons within the fort were operational. Lieutenant Guerrant's " Goochland Artillery ", consisting of 35 men, made good use of the few operational cannons, unleashing their large caliber fury, directly through the human waves, rushing before them. There was a small detachment of militiamen stationed at the fort (LDF), but they were armed with old, smoothbore muskets, and only had 10 rounds each. Luckily, seven companies of the 17th Georgia had just arrived with a detail of convicts and Negroes, who were going to work on the entrenchments. Suddenly, the war had reappeared. They dispatched their detail to the rear, and joined the fray. **10**

According to Captain Judge Martin, Company G, 17th Georgia, the chaotic pace of events erupted as a courier " dashed up and said that the enemy were attacking the Texas Brigade, and I was ordered to go back and assist them." As the Seventeenth Georgia approached the Phillips House, just in front of the breastworks, they could see the heaps of Union bodies piled deeply on the battlefield in front of the Texans. The attack at the point of the line was over, but then Captain Martin states that:

Just as this attack had been repulsed a courier came down and ordered us to reinforce Battery Harrison. We then hurried as rapidly as possible along the line of breastworks ; and when we came in sight of Fort Harrison, it seemed that the whole world in front was full of bluecoats. When we reached the point in our line of breastworks where they turned into a right angle to Fort Harrison, four Federal flags had gone up on the fort and on the breastworks surrounding it." **11**

With the enemy now in command of Fort Harrison, and that portion of the exterior line, the Confederate troops withdrew towards Richmond. Benning's brigade and the rest of the forces in the vicinity of New Market heights, fell back to the exterior line of defenses, two miles behind the New Market line. The exterior line was a long trench, five miles in front of Richmond. The line was reinforced at various locations of tactical importance with fortifications. Fort Harrison, was the largest, and most heavily fortified. They all had been constructed with large ditches, in their front, which served as obstacles to an attacking force; however, General Ord 's Union forces, now occupied the premier property on the line.

Back on the New Market line, the Union colored troops continued to press their assault, as the Confederates retreated to their exterior line. Finally, Birney 's Corps had succeeded in taking the heights, but at an extremely high price. Upon seizing their valuable property, both Birney and Ord, reorganized their respective corps, surveyed their situation, and continued their assaults, on towards Richmond.

Meanwhile, General Gregg prepared his thinly stretched forces along the exterior line, and awaited the Union onslaught. The 2nd and 20th Georgia regiments, of Benning's brigade, made futile assaults to recapture Fort Harrison, but they were immediately repulsed. Colonel DuBose took charge of the situation along the exterior and intermediate lines. Retreating Confederate artillery pieces were employed within Forts Johnson, Field and Gregg. The 2nd, 15th and 17th Georgia regiments, and the Local

Defense Forces supported them. DuBose had the artillery fire upon the enemy within and around Fort Harrison. At the same time, the Texas Brigade and Gary's cavalry arrived on the line. At this point, General Gregg assumed command of the line. Behind them, extending west and north, General Ewell, commander of the Richmond interior lines, and militiamen, maintained their preparedness as a reserve force. Richmond was now in the direst straights of the war. Two Union corps were now just five miles from the Southern capital, but they had some angry Confederates between them and their prize.

Leading his men below Fort Harrison, General Ord was wounded and replaced by General Heckman. The new Union commander, slowly, with piecemeal, uncoordinated advances pressed alternating brigades against the Confederate defensive positions. Fortunately, for the Confederates, the terrain between their position at Fort Johnson and the Yankees at Fort Harrison, was a flat, open field. This situation enabled the artillery and riflemen, behind protective earthworks, to fire repeatedly and safely into the rushing Union mobs. Shortly after being replenished with ammunition, DuBose was attacked by several Union brigades. He surprised them by sending the 2nd and 17th regiments on a flanking maneuver, around their left. With their shrieking " rebel yell" , they tore into the unsuspecting Yanks, as the artillery opened on their front, firing canister shot at close range. The Georgians captured men of the Union XVIII Corps, which confirmed to Lee that he needed to send reinforcements, in larger quantity. Unfortunately, it would be several hours before they could reach the line. Although Benning's brigade and her sister units were at their smallest strength ever, they were being called upon to provide the largest service, yet rendered. As the Union lines slowly inched northward, throughout the day, Dubose stretched his thin line from Fort Johnson, in the south, to Fort Gregg, in the center, and Fort Gilmer in the north.

Fort Gilmer was the largest bastion on the line with the exception of Fort Harrison, with a deep 8-10 foot moat. The fort had two artillery pieces, fragments of Gary's men and the 15th regiment, commanded by Captain Madison Marcus. Finally, in the afternoon, General Birney reentered the battlefield, after securing the New Market heights, and re-organizing his exhausted Corps. He decided to concentrate his forces against Fort Gilmer. Birney attacked toward the Confederates front with piecemeal units of his New York and Pennsylvania regiments. They were easily repulsed with enfilade fire from the entire Confederate line, and retreated with 500 casualties. Next, Birney sent in a colored brigade consisting of the 7th, 8th, and 9th USCT regiments. These brave black men immediately began to experience the same deadly fire unleashed on the previous Yankee assault ; however, this time, the Georgians purposely allowed them to get closer, so as to send, up close, horrendous volleys of fire into the assaulting waves. Stumbling through the dense underbrush, and over the bodies of their dead and wounded comrades, with dogged determination, the colored troops managed to reach Fort Gilmer. They rushed directly down into the moat, where they could rest. The Georgians could not see directly over the parapet, and into the ditch below. The Union troops were unable to climb the vertical dirt walls, and tried heaving themselves on top, and over the wall. Three times, they tried to attack by lifting up their fellow soldiers, but with each assault that attained the height, the Georgians shot them back down. 12

Colonel DuBose wrote that: " Among the Negroes killed was a certain Corporal Dick who seemed to be a prominent man among his fellow soldiers, as soon as he fell, some of the buck Negroes cried out," Dare now, white folks done killed Corporal Dick, de best man in de regiment." 13 The news quickly ran along the line, that Negro troops were stuck in the moat. Many of the Georgians and Texans moved from their place in the line, over to Fort Gilmer, looking for a chance to kill the enemy. Shortly thereafter, the artillerymen lit fuses on several cannon shells and dropped them into the ditch. After the horrible carnage this caused, the colored troops surrendered. Some colored troops reached Fort Gregg, and even managed to steal the colors of the 20th Georgia. As evening fell, and the reinforcements, in great number arrived on the line, the colored brigade retreated, back to their lines. 13 General Gregg later reported to General Lee, that at the attack of Fort Gilmer, on September 29, 1864," the 15th Georgia captured 433 prisoners, and buried 119 enemy, up close to Fort Gilmer." Again, however, the battle was costly for the Georgians as well. Benning's brigade suffered a total of 86 casualties during the fray. 14

The Georgians of Benning's brigade welcomed the arrival of the remainder of Field's Division, four brigades of Hoke 's Division and General Lee, himself. Benning's brigade, along with the Texas Brigade, and Gary's forces, were relieved of their positions on the line. They fell back, behind the line, where they received some badly needed rest. Heroically, they had repulsed wave after wave of Union assaults, throughout the entire day, without rest. Although the Union forces could see their objective, in the distance, the tiny band of southern veterans denied the Yankees their prize. 15

General Grant, although robbed of what could have been a glorious victory, and the capture of Richmond, he had still gained a tactical achievement, with the capture of Fort Harrison. This situation caused

General Lee, grave concern. He wanted Fort Harrison back! On the
morning of September 30, 1864, with the Yankees threatening Richmond
at such a close distance, the citizens panicked. The local militia and reserve
forces, were called to duty. Businesses closed, people packed and left
town. The railroad from Petersburg to the Richmond defense lines became
congested with reinforcements. In the midst of confusion and chaos,
General Grant threatened the Petersburg line in the south. This prompted
Lee, to return some of his forces back to their original positions.
Fortunately, the two Union corps to his front were exhausted from their
actions on the previous day, and they had suffered nearly 3,000 casualties.
Lee decided to assault Fort Harrison with his 1st Corps, which was still led
by General Anderson. The Division of General Field, minus Benning's
brigade, the Texas Brigade and Gary's forces would lead the attack.

Around noon, the Confederate artillery began its preparatory barrages
on Fort Harrison. Field's Infantry Division crept forward, and at 1:45 began
their assault on Fort Harrison. These highly capable veterans tried their
best, with several assaults, but never got close to the fort. To assault the
fort, they were required to cross the same open field between Fort Johnson
and Fort Harrison, the same one that the Union troops were trapped in on
the previous day. The entire affair was a disaster. The Union forces cut the
troops in the open to pieces. That afternoon, Field's Division staggered
back to Fort Johnson in defeat as a heavy downpour of rain began
cleansing the field. The fields in front of the forts of the intermediate line
were littered with mangled corpses. Meanwhile, Union cavalry forces
extended their lines, due north, across the Darbytown Road, moving closer
and closer towards Richmond. On October 7, 1864, Generals Field and
Hoke moved north to repel the advancing Union cavalry units along the
Darbytown Road. The Confederates were unable to push the Union forces
back; however, they did achieve in the establishment of a north to south
defense line, with breastworks, across the Darbytown Road and behind
Cornelius Creek . It was a costly effort, and it resulted in the death of
General Gregg. **16**

On October 13, the Union cavalry attacked the new Confederate
defense line on the left (north) of the Darbytown Road. Benning's brigade
defended this position. The Georgians successfully repelled the enemy, but
Captain Madison Marcus of the 15th, rallying his men along the line was
killed. Minor skirmishes continued along the line until the end of October.
17 On October 19, General Longstreet having healed from his wound
received during the Battle of the Wilderness, returned to duty. In
November, General Benning also returned from his convalescence in
Columbus, Georgia, and resumed command of his brigade. While his
shoulder was not fully healed, the Confederacy was in decline and

desperately needed his services. Upon " Old Rock " Benning's return to the front lines, one of his peers and good friends known as " Old Reliable," Brigadier General John Bratton described the return of the " sturdy old patriot" as " real refreshing." General Bratton also stated that Benning had " recovered in a measure from his wound," and " there is a purity of character and fresh vigor in the old man." Additionally, while Bratton was certainly a capable and superior leader, he longed for the admiration and respect that Benning had won from his men. In a letter to his wife, Bratton wrote," If only I could make people love me, I might be a good officer." **18** While General Bratton desired the relationship General Benning had forged with his men, the circumstances and command relationships were very different. Benning had personally commanded his brigade for several years through numerous difficulties, whereas General Bratton had only commanded his unit for six months. Furthermore, Bratton inherited his brigade under severely strained conditions. The former brigade commander, General Micah Jenkins was very popular, and had met a tragic and untimely demise at the hands of his own men. During the same incident of fratricide at the Battle of the Wilderness, wherein General Longstreet was horribly wounded, Jenkins was shot through the brain and he died. General Jenkins 's men were deeply affected by the loss of their commander, which had a demoralizing effect upon them and created some animosity amongst the regimental commanders when Bratton was selected for command. **19**

Thus while both Generals Benning and Bratton were excellent leaders, their leadership styles differed greatly. Both of their brigades were assigned to Longstreet's corps, but Benning's brigade had experienced far greater losses than Bratton's brigade. Bratton's brigade frequently played supporting roles or arrived too late to participate in situations where Benning's brigade felt the full brunt of battle. The battles of Chickamauga and Fort Gilmer are two examples wherein this scenario occurred. Consequently, the heavy fighting, the resulting heavy losses, and shared experiences between Benning and his men forged a unique and mutually supportive relationship. While this bond between leader and the led was poignant, its price was extremely high. In statistical contrasts, Bratton's brigade enjoyed the distinction of having the highest number of survivors in Lee's Army of Northern Virginia, while the men of Benning's brigade suffered extremely high casualties. During General Benning 's six-month absence, from May to November 1864, his brigade suffered the loss of 341 casualties, thus bringing his total muster rolls down to a total of 703 officers and men. **20**. Yet, during the winter of 1864-1865, several dozen veterans of Benning's brigade, like their commander, mustered their strength and despite their wounds and demoralizing situation, they returned to the ranks of the Confederacy.

Representative of Benning's durable soldiers, who simply refused to quit the fight, was Sergeant Reuben W. Cleveland. Throughout the war, despite receiving horrible wounds, this battle hardened soldier returned to his brigade, again and again. Cleveland's first experience as a casualty was in 1862, at the Battle of Sharpsburg. His initial wound was a bullet, which perforated his left lung and according to him," my shoulder blade was shattered... the hole was kept open for seven months so the pus could drain out. Finally I got well." Cleveland received his second wound during the Battle of Gettysburg, where he was shot in the knee, and " the Yankee that shot me was within ten feet of me." A Negro servant helped him hobble to safety, then, according to Cleveland," I got well again and went back to my company." His third and final wound was received at the Battle of the Wilderness, where " a ball cut a groove along my skull... I was sent to Lynchburg, Va., to a hospital where I had a bad time, but being a man of tremendous constitution, I got well again." 21 Cleveland's resolve and commitment to the Southern cause was typical of his brothers-in-arms, whose devotion served as the life blood of the Confederacy. Most of Benning's men had been bloodied, and many of them had received multiple wounds, yet they continued the fight. Henry Benning and his son, Seaborn, had both suffered two wounds, and between them, the Benning's had suffered a pulverized shoulder, a shattered thigh, a damaged skull, and a bullet grazed chest.

In November, behind their trenches near Darbytown Road, Benning's brigade began construction of their winter quarters. Lee's entire army was devoted to the defense of Richmond and Petersburg with a massive network of interconnected forts, trench lines, and obstacles, designed to keep Grant 's Union horde at bay. According to several of Benning's soldiers who experienced it," the winter of '64-5 was very sad...the men grew gaunt and thin...clothing and blankets were tattered," and:

> At that time-November 1, 1864- and thereafter until April, 1865, 40,000 Confederates defended and held a line of entrenchments, forty miles in length, and stretching from Hatcher's Run, south of Petersburg, to the Chickahominy. To man its entire length, they must have stood in single rank, five feet apart. Of guns and ammunition only, of courage and determination alone, had they abundant supplies. Even fuel for the fires needed to warm their shivering bodies was doled out to them with sparing hand, for there was no forage for the skeleton teams that hauled it. The

quarter of a pound of bacon and the pound of meal that, under the rules of the War Department, were the daily assignment to each man were barely enough to maintain their strength. **22**

Heavy skirmishing continued around the south of Petersburg, but the lines in front of the Georgia troops remained quiet. As the Georgians prepared for the arrival of the wintry winds, a ruthless storm swept through their home state. General Sherman and his marauding Union forces, burned Atlanta and began their horrible " march to the sea." **23** The one thing that at all Georgian soldiers had in common with one another, from General to Private, was the fear and hatred of Sherman. His occupation of their home state was the topic of discussion and the foremost preoccupation of the entire brigade. **24**
The misery of siege life, boredom and constant concern for their homes dampened the spirits of the Georgia veterans. They had been fighting gallantly for so long, but there was nothing they could do about Sherman. For the common fighting man, this frustration was excruciatingly painful. Two members of Benning's staff, Major Edgeworth Bird, Brigade Quartermaster, and his clerk, Sergeant Samuel H. Wiley, were cousins and their homes were near Sparta, Georgia. Major Bird and Sergeant Wiley were kin to Colonel James D. Waddell of the Twentieth regiment, Colonel DuBose of the Fifteenth regiment, Major Benjamin C. Yancey of Cobb's Legion, and good friends of the Stephens, the Bennings and the Pierces. **25** It was surmised that Sherman's path would cut directly through their homes. Wiley and Bird maintained close communications with their families, and the severe anxiety of Sherman's impending arrival is very evident in their letters. Wrought with anxiety the collective despair experienced by all Georgian soldiers is highlighted in one of Wiley's letters. The letter is lengthy and repeats its theme of fear and frustration; yet, select excerpts capture the height of the soldiers' apprehension. In the letter written to his parents in November of 1864, Sergeant Wiley states:

> My dear Pa & Ma, how I wish I could step in to your room this morning, if you yet have a room-- if you yet have a home... Negroes stolen away-- stock & provisions all taken-- all your clothing destroyed-- your house burned and you all perhaps turned out without anything and even without a place to put your heads! All these reflections are caused by the knowledge that Sherman 's army is abroad in Middle Georgia... It is most

tantalizing--distressing-- Maddening... Every one here is
painfully anxious to hear. We conclude that our homes and
property are scathed and plundered, and--- well we imagine the
worst... Here I am in a safe place, behind an army of invincible
soldiers... how can I drive these thoughts away & find comfort
in the future. In the midst of all this state of things comes the
probability of the coming disaster: Sherman 's raiders among
you in your house--- stealing, plundering, & destroying
everything-- then burning your house... disported of everything,
turned out to seek the charity of a district equally impoverished.
My only hope is that Sherman 's peculiar situation obliged him
to be very hurried in his forays & therefore we are not clean
striped of everything... O how long must it continue! I am so
anxious to hear the fate of you all & our neighborhood. **26**

As General Sherman departed Atlanta, his orders directed his men to
" refrain from abusive or threatening language" directed at the local
citizens, however, he also ordered his men to " forage liberally on the
country," and if the soldiers were molested by the locals, then the
commanders should " enforce a devastation more or less relentless." **27**
Both the Union army and the opportunists which followed it, burned and
pillaged Georgia," liberally." In the wake of Sherman's massive army
sweeping through Georgia," bummers" committed most of the atrocities,
yet Sherman's front line soldiers were guilty of committing crimes too.
Sherman's famous declaration that," war is all hell," summed up the results
of his infamous journey through the south. Sherman's intent was to destroy
the will of the Confederacy, and he certainly put forth his best effort. While
" foraging " through Georgia, Sherman recorded that " We have lived
scruptiously- turkeys, chickens, and sweet potatoes all the way, but the
poor women and children will starve." **28** Sherman was surprised when he
realized that Southern pride ran deep. In Savannah, people approached him
and his men referring to them as " sneaking Yankee," and ruthless invader."
Upon completing his trek across Georgia, Sherman wrote to his wife on
Christmas Day stating that," I have come right through the heart of
Georgia, they talk as defiant as ever." **29** As Benning had declared in his
secession speech in 1860," Men of Georgia! It is our business to save
ourselves." After four years of war, and now Sherman's attack upon their
homes, they were literally fighting for life, as they knew it. For many of
the Georgians, Sherman had effectively destroyed their world, and loyalty
to the cause of Southern liberty faced its ultimate test. Some deserted their
posts, while those who remained fought with a renewed resolve and spirit.

On November 16, 1864, having proved his loyalty and abilities on many occasions, Colonel Dudley M. DuBose was promoted to the rank of Brigadier-General. He was then placed in command of Wofford 's old brigade, in Kershaw 's Division. While Benning and the men of his brigade were happy for DuBose, with the cold of winter, the scarcity of food, and Sherman 's devastation of Georgia, any cause for celebration, was effectively ruined. **30** Slowly the months of January and February of 1865 passed into history, as both armies guarded the lines, and tried to stay warm. Further south, however, General Sherman left Georgia, turned his forces north, and began cutting a path through South and North Carolina, towards Richmond. As Sherman swept through Georgia, communications were severed, and weeks passed before the men learned the fates of their families and homes. With great sadness, many of the soldiers from Georgia discovered that their worst fears had been realized, and Sherman had indeed ruined their lives. While the men were forced to set in the trenches and guard the capital, Sherman effectively struck a severe blow at the very soul of the Southern cause.

In a desperate attempt to counter the psychological impact of events at home, the ladies of Columbus rallied to the cause. During the month of March, Mrs. Benning, Mrs. Moses and the several key members of the " Soldiers' Aid Society " launched a campaign to bolster the morale of the soldiers. The ladies also worked closely with Major Raphael Moses who had been transferred home to serve as the Confederate Commissary for the State of Georgia. Together, they adopted new resolutions to support the Southern cause, and they pledged to " increase and encourage the troops." **31** Statistics derived from the rolls indicate that in 1865, fifty men of Benning's brigade deserted and according to one of Benning's men serving in the field," the loved ones at home, the helpless women and children, were starving. The fire in the rear caused many a good man to go home never to return." **32** For many men, the Georgia of their past had been vanquished forever, their lives were ruined, and they simply could not bear the strain.

For the staunch veterans that remained in the field, as winter subsided, Grant eagerly dispatched his army against them. On April 1, 1865, southwest of Petersburg, the Union army attacked Lee's right line of defense. The resulting combat was known as the Battle of Five Forks, where the Confederacy suffered a costly defeat. Grant 's assault was immediately followed on April 2 with a massive Union assault from the east, which resulted in a gradual collapse of the Confederate defensive lines. Grant 's superior Union forces had finally cracked the Confederate lines around Petersburg, and the defense of Richmond and Petersburg was doomed. As the Confederates retreated to secondary and supplemental lines of defense, General Lee realized that he would have to evacuate his army, or be annihilated. Late into the evening, Grant poured barrages of artillery fire into the Confederate earthworks. When the artillery fire ended, General Benning ran to the top of a hill to view the situation. In the distance, Benning could see that Fort Gregg, one of the last Southern bastions, had fallen. Benning could also see massive blue lines of infantry continuing their advance, and rapidly approaching his thin lines.

Facing the fact that he could not possibly halt the massive assault, Benning returned to his troops, ushered them further to the rear, and the hail of Union artillery resumed. As he withdrew, Benning anxiously observed the vast Union forces maneuvering into position to strike at his brigade. General Longstreet also observed the situation, and he successfully checked the Union assault with reinforcements. Rushing troops back to the line, Benning's tiny brigade was bolstered just in the nick of time. The reinforcements took up positions to the left and right of Benning's troops. Upon seeing the reinforced, entrenched line, the advancing Union forces halted. It was now late in the evening, and the Army of Northern Virginia had secured valuable time to complete their evacuation. Field's Division was selected to hold the line while the remainder of the Army of Northern Virginia began its retreat. Benning's brigade was chosen as the rear guard for the division as they, in turn, withdrew from the field, and joined the mass exodus to the west. With great pride and honor, Benning's brigade manned the trenches as the Confederate army began its withdrawal to the west. Around midnight, Benning's brigade stealthily slipped out of its entrenchments and joined the exodus from the field, last in the line of retreat. **33**

During the retreat, Field's Division took turns as the rear-guard (now the front line) as Grant relentlessly pursued Lee's army. The Confederate retreat proceeded rapidly, and Benning's brigade was able to disengage and joined the march. **34** Lee dispatched his forces on separate routes, forcing Grant to disperse his forces in pursuit. Lee's initial goal was Amelia Court House, where his army was to be replenished with rations. Nevertheless, the food never arrived, and Grant 's superior forces were closely pursuing Lee's army. Grant 's army sole mission was to cut through and secure the prizes of Richmond and Petersburg. Lee's ultimate goal was to link up with General Johnson's western forces, but this would never occur. For the next week, the Army of Northern Virginia marched incessantly westward. Lee followed a route parallel, along the railway, to Farmville. After fighting back Union forces at High Bridge, on the Appomattox River, Longstreet's

Corps was the first unit to reach Farmville. In Farmville, his beleaguered forces linked up with Confederate supply wagons, and food. Many of Lee's army failed to outmaneuver their pursuers, and on April 6, at Saylers Creek , Anderson's Corps fought bravely, but was defeated. His men were utterly exhausted and starving. Among the captives was General Dudley M. DuBose. The battle was a devastating loss for Lee's army, which was suddenly reduced by 8,000 men.

After Generals Lee and Longstreet evacuated Farmville, on April 7, they continued marching westward, with the intent of reaching Lynchburg. Grant deployed his cavalry forward of Lee's army, successfully denying Lee with an evasion route. Longstreet's troops established a line of defense, northeast of Cumberland Church, and a short distance outside of Farmville. Benning's brigade was assigned to the center of the line. In a " U" shaped formation, facing northeast, the remaining forces of Field's Division and the bulk of the Army of Northern Virginia awaited the Union's next move. That afternoon at 3 o'clock, the Union army lashed out at the Confederates with a corps of infantry led by General Miles. Several Union brigades pressed their assault against the Confederates that afternoon, yet they were all repulsed. **35** Late in the evening, the Union forces were reinforced, and Grant sent Lee a proposal. Grant 's note offered Lee an opportunity to surrender. Lee read the note and gave it to General Longstreet. Lee's old " War Horse," as he called him, immediately passed it back to Lee, urging," Not yet." **36** That night the Confederates slipped away from their positions and began a stealthy and rapid withdrawal toward the west. Again, the Union cavalry of Generals Sheridan and Custer rode forward to Appomattox Court House, where they effectively ceased Lee's escape. This move effectively placed Lee's army in desperate straits. As Lee's options dwindled, he was left with one of two choices; he could stand and fight against overwhelming odds, or surrender.

Meanwhile, the bulk of the Union pressed Lee's rear guard, and the Army of Northern Virginia was completely engulfed by Grant 's army. Benning's brigade, as an element of Fields Division, was emplaced south of the New Hope Church, along the Lynchburg Stage Road. Field's Division formed it's final line of battle facing the Union's entire 2nd and 6th Corps, which had a combined effective strength of 24,000 men. Exhausted and starving, Field's Division had dwindled to barely 4,000 veteran warriors. **37** Realizing the futility of continuing combat against incredible odds, General Lee decided to discuss terms of surrender. While the armies anxiously waited, Generals Grant and Lee conferred in the parlor of Wilber McLean's home, and terms of surrender were established. Generals Grant and Lee determined that each man would be required to pledge that they would " not take up arms against the government of the United States," and they would " be allowed to return to their homes, not to be molested by United States authorities, as long as they observe their parole and the laws in force where they reside." **38** Upon surrendering his army to the United States government, General Lee struggling not to weep, addressed his army. He somberly announced that terms of surrender were achieved, and he urged them to," Go to your homes and resume your occupations. Obey the laws and become as good citizens as you were soldiers." **39**

General Benning 's Adjutant, Captain Seaborn Benning affixed his signature to General U.S. Grant 's formal orders for procedures of surrender and delivered them to his father, General Henry Benning. In accordance with Grant 's directive, the men would " march by brigades and attachments to a designated point, stack their arms, deposit their flags, sabers, pistols, etc., and from thence march to their homes." **40** The proud yet beleaguered men of the Army of Northern Virginia wept. According to General Longstreet," The shock was most severe upon Field's division. Seasoned by four years of battle triumphant, the veterans in that body stood at Appomattox when the sun rose on the 9th day of April, 1865, as invincible of valor as on the morning of the 31st of August, 1862, after breaking up the Union lines of the second field of Manassas. " **41** In Benning's brigade, a member of his " Columbus Guards," recalled that " The last scene at Appomattox is imprinted on my memory. The tears, the oaths, the hysterical, insane laughter, the breaking of guns, swords, the prayer for death from men who had toiled and sweated, starved and bled for a cause they loved better than life." **42** According to Private John W. Lokey," When I heard it, I turned my face to the ground and cried." **43** No one had worked longer and harder in the struggle for states' rights and Southern liberty than General Henry Benning. While Benning was shocked, he reluctantly accepted the defeat, and as for surrender, it " broke his heart, and that in a minute, years were added to his age." **44** According to General Benning, his brigade was still perfectly organized and not at all demoralized. Upon hearing that General Lee had surrendered, the initial reaction of Benning's men was a desire to cut through the Union lines and escape. As always, the wise old jurist quickly surmised that continuing the fight would be futile. Yet, his men were eager to try, and Benning stated that," they only waited for the word from me; but I would not give it. On the contrary, I urged them to acquiesce." **45** Realizing that he had done all that he possibly could do for the Confederacy, Benning accepted their plight. As ordered, he surrendered his command, and he proudly rendered the final report of his brigade with," All present or accounted for." **46** While General Lee officially surrendered his army on April 9, 1865, the next few days were spent carrying out the required administrative actions directed by General Grant. On April 12, Lee's former army mustered for their final act as a unit and they surrendered their rifles, swords, ammunition, and flags (officers were allowed to retain their sidearms). The Union XXIV Corps had a transportable printing press and they provided a copy of General Orders, Number 43, which explained the terms of surrender established by General Grant, and individual parole passes for each man. Parole documents were then signed by the commanding officers and issued to each soldier. The copy of General Orders, Number 43 and their individual parole papers, were very important documents, which provided some security for safe passage for the men, as there were still Confederates fighting in the field. For General Benning and other officers, the documents also relieved them of possible legal persecution by the U.S. government. While General Grant was not very popular amongst the men of Lee's Army of Northern Virginia, he did provide them with liberal terms of surrender, saw to their needs, and did not offend their dignity. Union troops were ordered to refrain from celebration, or in any way show disrespect toward the former Confederates. Moreover, the Union forces went out of their way to care for the needs of their vanquished foes, and the defeated soldiers departed Appomattox Court House, on the 12th and 13th of April, 1865.

Paroled general officers were also granted the privilege of travel at U.S. government expense, however, General Benning chose to remain with his men. " Paroled, ragged, hungry and threadbare," private citizen Henry Lewis Benning urged his men to travel home as a group, and most of them remained with their former commander. Henry and Seaborn Benning, together with dozens of their friends and neighbors, embarked on the long journey back to Georgia. 47 During the journey, many of the men broke ranks and made their own way home. The exact number of men paroled at Appomattox may never be precisely defined. From 1861 to 1865, due to capture, disease, injury, disability, desertion, resignation or death, Benning's brigade slowly diminished to nearly 25% of its original strength. Conservative estimates and analysis of various reports and individual service records reflect that Benning surrendered 791 officers and men. **48**

Chapter 18

The Destruction and Reconstruction of Columbus

Benning's arduous years of combat coupled with eleven years of fighting for secession took its toll on " Old Rock. " Just a week before the surrender, and on the very day Grant cracked through the Confederate bastion at Petersburg, April 2, 1865, Henry Benning turned fifty-one years old. While there was little cause for celebration, Benning's optimism and professional bearing never waned. Moreover, his experience and proven command ability had marked Benning for professional advancement. During the latter days of his military career, Benning was placed in command of Field's division and he was selected for promotion to the rank of Major General. One of the last acts of the Secretary of War, John C. Breckinridge was to sign Benning's commission as a Major General. 1 Yet, fate did not allow Benning to rise to his full potential and his contributions to the Confederacy ended prematurely. As Benning and his party traveled home, unbeknownst to them, tragic events were unfolding throughout the nation, as the war was not yet ended. Although General Lee had surrendered his army, General Joe Johnston with his army, and pockets of other Confederate forces remained in the field. The Confederate government was still in existence too, although doomed and fleeing southward to avoid capture.

The month of April 1865, was a tumultuous time, in both the North and South. On the evening of April 14, 1865, John Wilkes Booth assassinated President Abraham Lincoln and Vice-President Andrew Johnson ascended to the presidency. In North Carolina, Confederate General Joseph Johnston discussed terms of surrender for his army with General William Sherman. In Georgia, Benning's old friend, Major General Howell Cobb, commanded home defense forces, and while Sherman had departed the state, new threats had emerged. General Cobb was busy organizing a defense plan for Columbus, Georgia, as Benning's hometown was being threatened from the west. Union General James H. Wilson's cavalry had cut a path of destruction through Alabama, and he set his sights on Columbus, Georgia. On April 16, Easter Sunday, General Wilson's veteran forces struck the Chattahoochee Valley, which was defended primarily by old men and young boys. Wilson maneuvered his forces into the most strategic launch sites, and under cover of darkness, Girard, Alabama , (now Phenix City) followed by Columbus, Georgia was attacked. The devastating assault of the Union forces crushed the defenders, and both towns on either side of the river, fell into Union hands.

General Wilson established his headquarters in downtown Columbus at the residence of Mr. Randolph Mott. Despite the fact that his son served in the Confederacy as an Adjutant for General Benning, the elder Mott was a pro-Union sympathizer. From his headquarters, Wilson dispatched patrols to perform " mop up" operations and he penned his official report of the battle. In Wilson's official report, he indicated that General Cobb and an estimated force of 600 Confederates escaped towards Macon. Wilson also reported that he captured 1,500 prisoners, 24 guns, one gunboat (*Jackson*), while his forces only suffered 25 casualties. 2 Another gunboat, the *Chattahoochee* was destroyed by the Confederates, twelve miles below Columbus, in order to prevent its capture.

Wilson's forces terrorized the countryside as his forces ransacked, burned and pillaged throughout the region surrounding Columbus. Wilson had been directed to destroy everything that the Confederacy could use to continue their operations. Railroads, trains, machine shops, and foundries were all destroyed. Wilson's forces also burned fields and crops, torched warehouses, mills and factories, took cows, horses and mules, and like Sherman's army, they too took advantage of the opportunities to plunder " liberally." General Edward F. Winslow's brigade remained in Columbus, while the main force of Wilson's raiders pursued the remnants of General Howell Cobb 's forces toward Macon, where he surrendered. Winslow finished the destruction of Columbus, by burning " fifteen locomotives, two-hundred and fifty cars, the railroad bridge and foot bridges, one hundred and fifteen thousand bales of cotton, four cotton factories, the navy yard, foundry, armory, sword and pistol factory, accouterment shops, three paper mills, over a hundred-thousand rounds of artillery ammunition, besides immense stores, of which no account could be taken." 3 According to General Winslow, the destruction of Columbus was also conducted by the local populace. Winslow's report states that:

Thousands of almost pauper citizens and Negroes, whose
rapacity under the circumstances of our occupation, and in
consequence of such destruction of property, was seemingly
insatiable. These citizens and Negroes formed one vast mob,
which seized upon and carried off almost everything movable
whether useful or not. 4

Before the arrival of the Union raiders, people hastily " concealed
jewelry and valuables, and buried their silver." Under cover of darkness,
several citizens visited the graves of their loved ones in Linwood Cemetery
where they hid their family treasures. Many people simply fled the area
with their few worldly possessions in tow. 5 Yet, throughout the
Chattahoochee Valley," there was much looting of personal property by the
invading hordes," and the " army left in its wake ravaged fields, burning
homes, and populace of women, children, and old men who were homeless
and penniless." 6 The occupation of Columbus lasted for just several days,
but the Union raiders vengefully brought the city to its knees. With the
surrounding countryside scorched, all industries ruined, the community's
stocks of baled cotton, and the facilities which housed them demolished;
the economic infrastructure of the city of Columbus was effectively
destroyed. Moreover, the citizens were famished, impoverished and
seemingly had nothing with which to rebuild. All the while, the war had
effectively ended prior to these atrocities being committed. Yet, in defense
of his actions, General Wilson insisted that before his entry into Georgia,
he was unaware of the surrender of Lee's army. Since Wilson's forces
were engaged in rapid offensive operations, and telegraphic lines were
down throughout the Southern cities, it is most likely true that he was
unaware of the fate of Lee's army. Additionally, before Wilson's raid, the
Columbus newspapers do not record the surrender of Lee's army, and
Wilson's men severed all lines of communications surrounding Columbus
on April 16, 1865. 7

On May 10, 1865, President Davis and his fugitive cabinet were
captured near Irwinville, Georgia, and the Confederate States of America
was officially terminated. While some renegade bands of Confederate
forces in the far western territories refused to surrender, the war was
effectively ended. Meanwhile, Henry Benning and his fellow compatriots
reached Columbus. Upon their arrival, the full realization of the losses, and
the depths of their shattered world became horribly self-evident. For Henry
Benning, his losses were immense. During his absence, Mary had done an
excellent job maintaining their finances, the home, the plantation, and their
family's well being. Yet, Mary was helpless in regards to the efforts of

General Wilson's raiders. As the Union army passed through the region, his forces or the trailing opportunistic civilians destroyed numerous properties. For the Bennings and Jones families, they lost crops, warehoused supplies, and their real estate properties downtown, including City Mills. Mary Benning was especially distraught concerning 170 sacks of corn, consumed in a warehouse fire. The corn was valued at $1,360, but more importantly, the corn was needed for subsistence. Unable to obtain the commodity locally, she tried desperately to obtain corn from a warehouse in Montgomery, Alabama, but Mary was notified that:

> Our country around [here] has been so desolated, so much corn
> has been burnt & taken by Yankees that there will I fear be little
> or none to sell. Indeed it looks as though we will all starve.
> Many families that were well off a few weeks since are now
> drawing rations from the Yankees, but if the corn could be
> bought, there is no way to get it to you. Our railroad is so
> completely destroyed that there is no hope of getting it in order
> for a long time. **8**

Additionally, they lost most of their horses, mules, and goats, as well as the bulk of their laborers. Most of the slaves ran away, or had already been impressed into service by the Confederacy. Yet, a number of loyal blacks remained with the Benning and Jones families and continued their loyal services well beyond the war years. According to Benning's daughter, Anna Caroline, their family was " impoverished by the war." **9** Yet, the Bennings and Jones families fared much better than most families in the region. Their home," El Dorado," remained unscathed, some of the loyal servants   remained, and they retained far more capital and resources than many families.

From his father-in-law's estate, Henry Benning inherited $4,390 in Confederate money, $1,700 in Confederate bonds, 168 yards of osnaburg (cloth), 400 pounds of sugar, eleven hogs, four gallons of wine, and two horses. The other heirs of Seaborn Jones were Mary Jones, his wife; and Seaborn Leonard Jones, the eldest son of John A. Jones , deceased. In addition to " El Dorado," the Benning and Jones families also owned five thousand acres of burnt land, and various rental properties, some burnt and others in disrepair. The rental properties included a blacksmith shop, several offices, nine tenant rooms and eight houses. **9** With the war ended, Henry Benning returned to his pre-war profession as a lawyer and farmer. Benning re-established his law firm, and it was entitled, *Benning and*

Benning. His son, Seaborn, although disabled by the war, studied law under his father's tutelage, and he took the responsibility as Executor of his grandfather's estate. **10**

As the Executor of the estate, Seaborn Benning maintained accurate records concerning the disposition of his grandfather's assets and properties. During the years 1865 through 1867, Seaborn spent a great deal of his energies attempting to settle unresolved debts, loans and arrangements made by the estate. Seaborn Jones had lent money to friends and invested in businesses that were now insolvent, totaling losses of nearly $10,000. Some people simply left town, and there was little hope of legal justification, as many people were bankrupted by the war. Seaborn's frustration in settling his grandfather's estate is recorded in his notes. After months of attempting collections, he states that," I have received nothing but promises to pay & in many instances not even that- many of the parties who gave the notes I have not succeeded in finding, some are dead, many insolvent, and some have run away. None pay any money." **11** Seaborn focused his efforts on rebuilding and making improvements to the properties. Few of the rental units had tenants and of those that did, the rent was paid " very irregularly and in many instances not at all- but even when the tenant did not pay, I sometimes allowed them to remain in the buildings." **12** Henry Benning became involved as a lawyer and he traveled to Brunswick and Dahlonega, Georgia to resolve several legal matters for the estate. Again, however, only a fraction of the debts was ever recovered. **13**

Despite their frustrations, at least the Bennings were free. Several of Henry's close friends were prisoners. At the war's end, vindictive federal authorities sought retributions from several key Confederates. Jefferson Davis, Alexander Stephens, Dudley DuBose (Toomb's son-in-law), and several others were imprisoned by government authorities for months after the war. Robert Toombs refused to surrender to authorities and from 1865 to 1867, he was a fugitive, traveling to Cuba and France. During his flight, Toombs relied on many of his old friends and along his escape route he stayed in Columbus with Martin J. Crawford, and in Mobile with Augusta Jane Evans. **14** In Washington, Georgia, the federal authorities suspected that Robert Toombs was being hidden in his home and they " turned Mrs. Toombs out in the most brutal manner." **15** The postwar authority in Washington, Georgia, Union General Edward Wild, personally conducted a search of the Toombs's household, confiscated their property, and only allowed Mrs. Toombs to take her clothing and a few personal affects from the home. Mrs. Toombs and her belongings were cast into the street by the vindictive Union authorities, hell bent on making an example of the Toombs family. General Wild publicly searched Mrs. Toombs and unrolled her nightgowns " to see if any 'contraband' was concealed in them." **16**

In response to this brutal treatment, Mrs. Toombs fled the country and eventually joined her fugitive husband in Paris. The couple remained abroad for several years after the war, and only upon the news of the death of their daughter, Julia, did they return to the United States. Toombs appealed to President Andrew Johnson to grant them official permission to remain at home, and his request was immediately granted. A general amnesty was eventually extended to all former Confederates and they were returned to their pre-war status as private citizens.

Throughout the South, the postwar years were tumultuous times, and Columbus, Georgia was no exception. The city had to be rebuilt. The factories were destroyed and with industry suspended, so were jobs. As indicated by the title of the era, Reconstruction, a return to normalcy would require Herculean efforts. The State of Georgia was placed under martial law, as was the city of Columbus. Northern commanders whom the Confederate soldiers fought during the war, were suddenly the ruling authorities throughout the South. General John Pope supervised the Third Military District, which included Georgia. General James Wilson, destroyer of Columbus, ruled the state of Georgia. In Columbus, General John Croxton, who Benning defeated at the Battle of Chickamauga, served as the commanding officer of the city. Amidst the poverty stricken population, blacks were suddenly thrust into a society that was ill prepared and resistant to their inclusion. From 1865 to 1872, the social upheaval and economic destitution created " a civil and moral chaos. The South was crushed and bleeding." **17**

Amidst these defeated people, the former slaves were loosed into their society with no direction. Suddenly a people who lived and died in bondage were granted unfettered freedom. Initially, savoring their freedom, the poor blacks wandered aimlessly and shifted leisurely about town. With no means of support, no roof over their heads and empty stomachs, many Negroes resorted to crime. Throughout Georgia, the whites appealed to the military provost officers for protection. The response of the military was swift and cruel. Blacks were warned that all idle Negroes would be arrested, placed on a ball and chain and put to work at the tip of a bayonet. The *Columbus Daily Sun* reported," Yesterday the soldiers were arresting all idle Negroes and putting them to work... This is right. Columbus is no place for idlers. Quite a number of freedmen were collected." **18** For months, the newspapers were filled with similar articles, which also reflected that poor whites were committing crimes too. People were simply desperate, and it would be quite some time before the situation was corrected.

On June 17, 1865, President Johnson appointed the Honorable James Johnson of Columbus as the Provisional Governor of Georgia. Johnson was Benning's old nemesis. In 1850, it was Johnson that defeated Benning for a seat in Congress. Incidentally, President Johnson also appointed William Holden, editor of the *North Carolina Standard* newspaper, as the Provisional Governor of North Carolina. Johnson publicly renounced the insurrectionist participation of Georgia in the war, he declared that slavery was extinct, and he announced that elections would be held in October for state offices. In a speech, given in Milledgeville, on July 15, 1865, Johnson declared that the war was a " stupendous folly of our own making," and his ill-chosen words were " not calculated to woo adhesion to his counsel." **19** The speech was made with General Wilson by his side, and a great insult was added to an injured people. Yet, the Georgian populace took the affair in stride, as there was little else a thoroughly defeated people could do. Voters from Columbus elected delegates for a State convention to elect their new legislature. Hines Holt, Porter Ingram and Absalom Chappel were elected to represent Muscogee County. **20**

Once a new legislature was established, Henry Benning energetically thrust himself into the political arena as a candidate for Supreme Court Justice. For Benning, it seemed as if " old times" had returned to Georgia, and reflecting those " old times," yet another political enemy resurfaced. William Dougherty, Benning's opponent in the " Columbus Bank Cases" used his influence and urged his old pro-Unionist friends to vote for Benning's opponent, Dawson Walker. Benning was defeated and the affair was viewed as a " strange victory, and keenly felt by General Benning." **21** Several of Benning's peers achieved victories, as Alexander Stephens and Herschel V. Johnson won Georgia's seats in the United States Senate. In October of 1865, the Georgia legislature also repealed secession, wrote a new State Constitution, and Charles Jenkins replaced James Johnson, as the Governor of Georgia.

Returning home, Benning focused his efforts on local affairs. Crime was still a major problem, and while a local civil administration was established in Columbus, the army still controlled law enforcement. Many of the locals wanted a police force, as burglary, street brawls, public drunkenness and fighting were common occurrences. The populace felt insecure, as the number of soldiers was inadequate to patrol both the town and the suburbs. Henry Benning and Martin J. Crawford appealed to the military authorities and won permission to raise several military companies of citizens. The local newspaper lauded their efforts and reported that," If we are all ready, there is no cause to apprehend danger. The surest method to avert evil is to be prepared for it." The unique bond which the former Confederate officers Benning and Crawford forged with their former Union enemies bears testament to their honor and genuine desire to reconcile their differences. A latter report warned criminals with," look sharp thieves," as the companies had been reinforced and they were actively patrolling the city. 22 Just as things began to look promising; the federal authorities complicated matters by assigning a company of U.S. Colored Troops to patrol Columbus. This situation confused a delicate partnership and would slowly enflame a populace whose collective emotions and temperament bore a fragile peace with their military rulers.

Meanwhile, the Benning and Jones families continued to rebuild their lives. While Henry Benning was distraught and frustrated with political affairs, he remained vigilant in his quest to rebuild his shattered world. As General Lee had requested, Benning was being a " good citizen as he was a soldier." Benning worked diligently to rebuild his career and to return his family to a semblance of normalcy. While their former slaves were free to leave the Benning household, many chose to remain with them as hired laborers. The Bennings had always treated them well and Mary had seen to their needs throughout the difficult war years. She kept them well fed and clothed, and in return, they worked hard for her too. This mutual care and respect had always served both parties well, and consequently the Bennings were able to continue a positive relationship with many of their former slaves. It is interesting to note that many of Benning's former slaves adopted his surname, which also resulted in several young Negroes named Henry Benning. 23 Founded upon the virtues of mutual respect and hard work, collectively the Bennings and their former slaves forged new relationships, planted crops, and worked together to rebuild their lives.

While Benning focused his efforts close to home, Howell Cobb inquired as to what had happened with his old friend, Henry Benning. Time and events had separated them, but in their hearts they would always be old friends. During the summer months and the early fall of 1865, Benning remained detached from the rest of the world and concentrated his energies upon his crops and rebuilding his farm. Cobb corresponded with Benning's close friend Martin J. Crawford and inquired about his old friend. Crawford provided Cobb with an update stating that, in Columbus," we are moving on here in a very quiet way, Benning is still out at his plantation," where he remained until October. 24 After four years of missed farming endeavors, Benning vainly attempted to regain control of his plantation. Yet, as most plantation owners were learning, without slave labor, farming on the scale they had previously enjoyed was generally an exercise in futility. New beginnings and restructured lifestyles were difficult for men such as Benning and Cobb who had worked so hard to achieve success. In those first months after the war, Howell Cobb was struggling to recoup his livelihood too. His plantation was much larger than Benning's and thus his dependency upon slave labor was greater too. Cobb quickly surrendered the idea of plantation operations and focused his efforts on his former profession in law. After the war, he relocated to Macon where he opened a private law firm. His wife remained near Athens until they could settle affairs and complete their move. Cobb's personal frustrations are obviously apparent in letters between he and his wife. In one of his letters, written during the Thanksgiving holiday of 1865, Howell states that," I am sticking close to my office and books, with the ardor of a new beginner. The " nibbles" continue and I have no fears that you will be driven to the necessity of opening a day school." **25**

Times were difficult for all Southerners, and particularly for those who were instrumental in secession and rebellion activities. The federal government faced a chaotic dilemma in returning citizenship to former Confederates. While some men like Henry Benning had surrendered and were officially pardoned by the government, many former Confederates remained unaccounted for. Some men had simply returned home, but pardons were required of all former belligerent participants. For common soldiers, this was simply a matter of reporting to federal authorities and they were officially granted their pardons. Yet, some men such as Robert Toombs refused to surrender, and he even boasted that he was proud to remain " unreconstructed," despite the fact that he was a fugitive and wanted by federal authorities. Other men, such as Benning's friend Martin J. Crawford, who had worked diligently with Benning for secession, and had served as a Confederate cavalry officer during the war, had never officially surrendered. With the war over, Crawford highly desired to rejoin the United States as a citizen, but since he had not been pardoned, he was not officially a U.S. citizen. Crawford's situation was further complicated by the requirement that all former Confederate officers with the rank of colonel and above must apply for and be granted a " special" amnesty. This application procedure involved bureaucratic backlogs, and took a considerable period of time to achieve. Crawford followed the governmental procedures to the letter, yet after months of waiting, his application yielded no positive results. As the year 1865 ended, Martin J. Crawford traveled to Washington D.C. seeking an audience with President Johnson.

Crawford desired to speak with President Johnson concerning two major issues. First for himself, Crawford desired a pardon so that he could get on with his life. Secondly, being a concerned former leader of civic and political life, Crawford wished to discuss reconstruction efforts and political matters with the president. The president granted Crawford an audience and freely discussed both topics that Crawford wished to address. Crawford was informed that his pardon would be granted, and concerning politics, Crawford learned a great deal of insight. Upon his return to Columbus, Crawford stated:

> Mr. Johnson talks very kindly and says that his greatest
> ambition is to restore the harmony & good feelings between the
> sections. That all efforts are directed to that end, indeed I was
> quite surprised to find him so amiable. He received me cordially
> and treated me with much consideration. He will have a hard
> time with the Republicans this winter, they come to Washington
> bent on mischief. **26**

Crawford also learned that the newly elected Southern representatives would not be received into the House and Senate," oath or no oath" until they agreed to let the Negroes vote. Crawford also stated that the tide of northern sentiment was flowing negatively in regard to the Southern states and politically, the future of the South looked bleak. Johnson, himself a Southerner serving in a predominantly Northern government faced difficult challenges to restoring a valid union of the United States. It was obvious that the wounds of war would take considerable time to heal. Furthermore, there were many Northerners hell bent on punishing the South. Yet, Crawford summed up his political discussion with President Johnson declaring," whatever is in store for us, we can't be hurt." **27**

As 1865 ended, the chasm between North and South remained vast and filled with contempt. So too was the gulf between blacks and whites. The absorption of an entire race of people suddenly thrust into a resistant society created tremendous social problems. Many Southerners desired a slower incorporation of the former slaves into society, yet northern politicians refused anything less than immediate and total equality for blacks. The victorious northern politicians forced unpopular laws on the defeated Southerners, which resulted in resistance, prejudice, animosities and outright hatred. As Martin J. Crawford predicted, the Republicans in Congress clashed with President Johnson concerning Southern reconstruction and national restoration. In December, 1865, the U.S. Congress formerly rejected the representatives of the former Confederate states, approved the Thirteenth Amendment to the Constitution, which officially abolished slavery, and they formed there own Joint Committee on Reconstruction. Yet, despite the efforts of abolition and reconstruction laws, they " could not immediately alter social and psychological traits in any people." **28**

The gulf between blacks and whites was evident, and would remain for generations. In its initial stages, racial bigotry was particularly ugly. In Columbus, Georgia, the local press heralded the approaching Christmas season with the headline, KEEP NEGROES FROM THE TOWN. The article exclaims:

> If there is one thing which ought to be done it is to keep idle
> Negroes out of Columbus during Christmas week. They will
> flock here in crowds, they will have no money and but little
> provisions. Many have been doing nothing for some time, eking
> out a precarious existence. Such people will throng our streets,
> they will find nothing to do if they had the inclination, and petty
> thieving and robbery will be the order of the day. **29**

In April, 1866, President Johnson declared that the Civil War was officially ended and peace restored to the United States ; however," the war waged none the less furiously against the South, not a war of blood, but a war of malice and proscription." **30** The federal government established the " Freedmen's' Bureau " to assist blacks with labor negotiations, education, and general social adjustment; however, it also created insolence and friction between whites and blacks. In Columbus, the Eagle Cotton Factory recommenced production and poor whites suddenly found themselves competing with blacks for employment. Federal educational aid was also extended to black children, while " the state let the white child abide in ignorance." **31** Opportunist from the North, known as " carpet-baggers" and local " scalawags" poisoned the Southern states by instigating confusion and conflict between the races. The ensuing hatred fanned the flames of the infamous Ku Klux Klan. Organized in President Johnson's home state of Tennessee, former Confederates and men whom opposed the societal progress of blacks, formed the secret society and wreaked terror throughout the south. Yet, during the Reconstruction Period, the " Klan" only existed in disorganized factions and according to Henry Benning, he was unaware of any " Klan" activities in Columbus. **32**

In June of 1866, Congress adopted the Fourteenth Amendment, which provided equal rights to all citizens, regardless of their race. Throughout the Reconstruction Period, Congressional committees investigated suspected violations of white hostilities committed against freedmen. Generals Steedman and Fullerton reported that in the Southern states," in general the relations of the white people and the Negroes toward each other were friendly; that it was a small minority, mostly of the non-slave-holding class, that hated the freedmen and caused disturbances." **33** In fact, former statesmen of Georgia testified that most Southerners conformed to the laws, and were eager to rebuild their lives. After the passage of the Thirteenth Amendment, Howell Cobb wrote to General Wilson stating," You will find that our people are fully prepared to conform to the new state of things; and as a general rule will be disposed to pursue towards the Negroes, a course dictated by humanity and kindness." **34** Henry Benning testified before a congressional committee that in Columbus," we are living very harmoniously, the citizens of Columbus voluntarily finance the Negro schools, and " there is no discrimination, so far as I know, between white and black." **35** Howell Cobb, Henry Benning, and most wise men realized the importance of Negro inclusion. They had fought for their beliefs and they lost. Subsequently, they accepted the need for societal transformation and they desired to move forward. The *Macon Telegraph* summed up the situation with," The faithful Negro must not be discarded- the South's duty is to its former slaves. " **36**

During the Spring of 1866, the ladies of Columbus also made strides toward healing the wounds of war by honoring the memories of their fallen dead. Among these ladies were Mrs. Seaborn Jones, Mrs. Henry Benning, Miss Mary Benning, Miss Anna Benning, Mrs. John A. Jones , Mrs. Francis O. Ticknor, Mrs. Raphael Moses, and many more of the same ladies that had provided the Confederate soldiers with tender care during their war. According to Miss Anna Caroline Benning," The Ladies Memorial Association like the Phoenix, rose from the Soldiers' Aid Society which was consumed in the fires that burnt the Confederacy. " **37** Since the inception of the city of Columbus, her citizens had always rallied to support worthy causes. The Ladies Memorial Association was well received and the whole city united " in a work of love." " The first Memorial address ever delivered in the United States in honor of the soldiers who fought in the war between the States, was delivered in Columbus, Ga., April 26, 1866." **38** The date, April 26, was significant, as this was the day General Joseph Johnston surrendered his army, and effectively ending organized warfare. Miss Lizzie Rutherford suggested the date, as it was also the peak of spring flower blossoms in Columbus, and the ladies agreed that it was an appropriate date for the memorial ceremony.

Henry Benning 's long-time friend Colonel James N. Ramsey delivered the memorial address at St. Luke M.E. Church, where prayers and songs complemented the solemn occasion. Afterwards, the entire city joined in decorating the graves in Linwood Cemetery. The observance was designed not to glorify the war, but simply to honor the memories of the dead. The Ladies Memorial Association resolved that they would perpetually observe Memorial Day," as long as flowers grow and the memory of brave deeds last." They also added, where war was concerned," to study its lessons is prudence, to profit by its teachings is wisdom, and to let its animosities actuate is madness." **39** The ladies' observance spread northward, and Memorial Day is now held nationwide, although it is observed in May.

As the year 1866 progressed, the Bennings continued efforts to rebuild their lives. That summer, they harvested an excellent cotton crop, and they realized a profit of $8500. The Bennings advanced $5,275 to Seaborn Leonard Jones, who desired to purchase a home in Texas, and to retrieve his father's body from the battlefield in Gettysburg. **40** Jones was only 21 years old, and with a deposit totaling $1,000, he committed himself to the purchase of a home in Texas. If he failed to secure the deal, he stood to forfeit his deposit. Reluctantly, the Bennings and his grandmother, Mrs. Seaborn Jones, yielded to young Master S. Leonard Jones desires. The family loaned him the money to accomplish both tasks. Jones embarked on his adventure, via the rails to Gettysburg, Pennsylvania. He succeeded in locating and retrieving his father's body, and he continued with his father's remains to the port of Baltimore. In Baltimore, Jones secured transportation for himself and his father's remains via the steamship, *King Fisher*. To Mr. Jones's horror, while enroute to Georgia, the ship wrecked and the passengers and crew abandoned the ship. The King Fisher sunk, along with the remains of John A. Jones , and young " Mr. Jones lost everything." **41** Mr. Jones was rescued from the sea by another vessel and delivered to Savannah. While Jones survived the ordeal, he lost his money, the remains of his father, and he had to borrow money to return home. Realizing that the young man had experienced a horrible ordeal, the family forgave his debt, and Leonard Jones moved on to Texas where he established a large ranch in Wharton County.

Throughout the years of 1866 and 1867, the Bennings continued to rebuild their lives. Seaborn Benning focused on improving and managing their properties, while Henry practiced law and raised crops. Gradually, as the economy improved, Henry Benning received more clientele and as before the war, his practice flourished. At home, Benning's daughters began courting and romance bloomed. The year 1867 was particularly exciting for the girls as their Aunt Augusta Jane Evans wrote her most successful novel," St. Elmo. " The book is a classic Southern romance, filled with emotions, sentimentalism and set amidst a mansion modeled after " El Dorado. " In 1867, the Bennings' youngest daughter, Sarah Jones, known as " Sallie," was then just twelve years old, but their other daughters were receiving gentleman callers and romance was " in the air." Mary was the eldest, and twenty-seven years old, followed by Anna Caroline, age twenty, and the twins, Augusta and Louisa, were both nineteen years old. Mary and Caroline Benning became very involved in the Ladies Memorial Association, many other societal organizations, and their church. Again, on April 26, 1867, they were instrumental in arranging the Memorial Day service, and Dr. E. F. Colzey provided the address at Temperance Hall. For decades to follow, their efforts helped form the foundations of the United Daughters of the Confederacy. **42**

Local events of note were few during these years; however, a local " scalawag," George W. Ashburn began stirring up trouble amongst the blacks. Before the war, Ashburn had lived in Macon and Upson County, where he was an overseer on several large plantations. Ashburn gained notoriety for being brutal with slaves, and he had difficulty maintaining employment. Yet, after the war, he capitalized on his familiarity with Negroes and he encouraged them to seek retribution from their former masters. Ashburn engaged in various scalawag schemes, which focused on taking advantage of blacks. He was an influential voice in the local offices of the Freedmen's' Bureau and the Negro Loyal League. Ashburn was married, yet he lived in a brothel with a black prostitute. He was referred to by most people as " obnoxious," yet he appealed to a few gullible blacks as their " especial friend." **43** According to Henry Benning, Ashburn " incited the Negroes in various ways, and embittered their feelings against the whites; insisted that they were entitled, according to the phrase then used, to 'forty acres and a mule, ' and that they should have it." **44** Ashburn and his affairs would soon bring embarrassment to all the citizens of Columbus

In Columbus, the city continued to rebuild. The mills were rebuilt and employment improved. Cotton prices soared as supplies were short and demand brought the return of " King Cotton. " With slave labor eliminated, black and white farmers alike rushed to meet the demand. Throughout the South, one of the few economic and employment opportunities afforded to

blacks was share and tenement farming. In 1869, the President of the
Georgia State Agricultural Convention held in Atlanta, Benning's old
friend Benjamin C. Yancey encouraged farmers to engage in the practice
of share cropping with blacks. Yancey stated that concerning the former
slaves, Georgia farm owners are " their best, their only friends," and within
a few short years," 338,769 acres of land in Georgia" was owned and
farmed by blacks. **45** The elimination of slave labor slowly forced the
division of large plantation lands. Henry Benning 's plantation was no
exception, and several hundred acres became the property of blacks. **46** In
Columbus as blacks gained economic independence, whites slowly
incorporated them into society and the former slaves were no longer kept "
away from town." While racial bias would be a continuing problem for
many years, during this same time, Columbus fared better than many other
Southern cities. Race riots in Memphis, Tennessee and New Orleans,
Louisiana resulted in the deaths of 80 Negroes. In Columbus, during the
years 1866 and 1867, only one racially motivated murder is recorded, and
the killer was not from Columbus.

The killing occurred in February of 1866, and the perpetrator was a
U.S. soldier. Amongst the U.S. Colored Troops sent to enforce law and
order in Columbus, was a certain soldier that mistreated the locals.
According to Henry Benning, the soldier " was very defiant and obstinate
on the street. He would walk straight forward and strike anybody that was
in front of him; would shove ladies off the sidewalk." **47** The soldier
performed this abuse of his position for quite some time, and he was
known to be a public menace. One day, the soldier bumped into a young
white man on the street. The civilian reeled, pulled out a pistol, and he shot
the soldier in the arm. The soldier ran to his barracks, where he and his
fellow soldiers began indiscriminately firing into crowds on the street. A
man by the name of Major Warner walked to the scene of the shooting to
see what was happening. Benning described the concerned gentleman as an
innocent," estimable citizen, and a quiet man." **48** The soldiers shot and
killed Warner, and upon the realization that they had killed an innocent
man, they ceased their frantic shooting spree. The citizens of Columbus
were outraged, and Mayor F. G. Wilkins," urged again and again upon the
officers to have an investigation, but none was had." **49**

In 1867, outrage was the sentiment throughout the South, as the U.S.
Congress rejected President Johnson 's reconstruction methods as being
too lenient. President Johnson dismissed his Secretary of War, who was a
radical Republican and resisted Johnson's policies. Johnson vetoed many
bills, which he deemed as unconstitutional, resulting in many Republican
congressmen accusing the president of being a southern sympathizer.
Congress also refused to allow the former Confederate states admission to

the Union unless they ratified the Fourteenth Amendment. Ultimately, a series of Congressional Reconstruction Acts abolished the state governments organized by President Johnson and they denied former Confederates the right to hold political offices. In Georgia, Governor Charles Jenkins was expelled and replaced by a military leader, General Thomas Ruger. In Columbus, Albert Lamar, Solicitor General of the Chattahoochee Circuit, and a close friend of Henry Benning, was dismissed.

General Ulysses S. Grant was placed in command of all the former Confederate states, and the U. S. Army administered affairs therein. General George Meade, commander of Military District 3 (Georgia, Florida, and Alabama) assigned direct appointments of important political offices in Georgia. The notorious scalawag, George W. Ashburn became a member of the delegation to write a new Constitution for the State of Georgia. Ashburn would travel to Atlanta, and represent Muscogee County as a member of the Constitutional Convention of 1867-1868. Throughout Georgia, scalawags and carpetbaggers suddenly dominated the government. The ranks of the Ku Klux Klan swelled, as former Confederate generals Nathan Bedford Forrest and John B. Gordon provided leadership " to preserve order and protect society." Military rule was tightened, the citizens were outraged, and the people of Columbus were " in a more insufferable condition than ever before." **50**

Throughout Georgia, people were highly concerned and worried about their future. On August 31, 1867, Henry Benning and Howell Cobb met and discussed the predicaments Georgia was facing. With the Republican insistence concerning ratification of the Fourteenth Amendment and the friction between Congress and the President, race riots, the Ku Klux Klan, and the military crack-down, Benning and Cobb feared an impending race war. Benning had predicted in his secessionist speech what seemed to be materializing in 1867. Howell Cobb recorded a synopsis of their meeting with:

> Benning and myself sat up all night talking over the present, past and future, that is we went to bed at half past three and were waked up at five in the morning. I found that our minds had been running very much in the same channel about the future prospects of the country, our final conclusion was that the next three months were pregnant with great events that would decide the ultimate destiny of the whole country.

The firmness of the President in adhering to his late policy, and the fall elections at the North, are the events in the early future, which would solve the problem of our fate in the South. If these should be favorable, we may yet have a happy and prosperous country. If otherwise we cannot see how the South can possibly remain inhabitable by white people. Let us then wait and pray....
51

Amidst these foreboding circumstances, the year 1868 made its debut.

Chapter 19

Final Years

The year 1868 was filled with the best and the worst of times for Henry Benning and the City of Columbus, Georgia. The year began with the meeting in Atlanta, of the infamous Constitutional Convention, which was cited by Benjamin H. Hill as a " mock mimicry" of democracy. **1** The conventioneers, primarily Republicans, ran up a huge tab and tapped the State Treasury for their expenses. The *Columbus Enquirer* reported that the convention was dominated by carpetbaggers, scalawags, people of ill-repute, and they all " had a gay time on peanuts and persimmon beer." **2** Politics were soon in a state of turmoil, hatreds enflamed, and an increase in crime and violence followed. In March, the Ku Klux Klan made its presence known throughout Georgia. Mysterious placards appeared throughout towns and communities conveying warnings, allusions of impending doom and blatant threats with the intent to create terror. In Columbus, the message included," Let the guilty beware!... Everywhere our brotherhood appears. Traitors beware!" **3** In Washington, President Johnson was facing impeachment from Congress. In Georgia, former Governor James E. Brown reemerged in political affairs, throwing his support behind the Constitutional Convention. Georgians were livid. According to Georgia historians, Brown's unpopular behavior seemed to reflect a philosophy wherein, the sooner Georgia accepted the victors edicts, the sooner Georgia would have " freedom" and " political rehabilitation." **4** Regardless of his beliefs, Georgians generally despised him, and the results of the convention were not well-received. Seemingly, everything was changing in Georgia, and even the capital would be moved from Milledgeville to Atlanta. Many Georgians were also concerned about the upcoming election for Governor. Rufus B. Bullock, formerly of New York was the front-runner, and many Georgians considered him as a carpetbagger and under the control of northern politicians.

If elected, Bullock would be arranging cabinet positions and making other key political appointments. Benning studied the situation intently. While he loved Georgia, he was torn between entering the current dysfunctional political scene or remaining silent. Concerned with affairs in his home state, Henry Benning corresponded with his old friend Howell Cobb. Once again they discussed politics, and Henry sought Howell's advice. Benning relayed to Cobb that " all judicious persons here think that good men may & should accept office from Bullock, but always with the purpose not to be Bullock men, but with the purposes being to serve the public good." 5 Despite the desires of men to do public good and get Columbus back on the right track, prospects of a return to tranquillity were suddenly shattered. In Columbus, George W. Ashburn was murdered. The murder looked very much like an assassination, and it was committed by a mob wearing masks. While the citizens of Columbus, Georgia, were shocked, more importantly, suspicious Republican brows were raised in Washington.

George W. Ashburn had returned to Columbus from the convention in Atlanta " full of self-importance" and he had announced intentions to become a U.S. Senator. 6 On the evening of March 30, 1868, Ashburn was spending the night downtown, in a local brothel. The building was a single story, three-room dwelling with doors connecting each room. Ashburn was staying with two prostitutes, Hannah Flournoy and Amanda Patterson. It must be noted that Ashburn had many enemies in Columbus, including blacks that he had crossed. Even some members of his own political party, the Freedmen's' Bureau and the Loyal League detested him. Regardless of whoever disliked the man, between midnight and 1 o'clock A.M., a group of men, wearing masks, broke into the brothel. Busting through the door in the front room, they passed through the first two rooms and confronted Ashburn in the back room. Ashburn had risen quickly and grabbed a pistol. When the men entered his room, shots were fired and Ashburn lay dead in the floor, with a bullet in his brain. The perpetrators fled the scene and a crowd formed in the streets. The police were summoned, and the following day, an investigation was commenced. 7

City Attorney John Peabody led the overall investigation, while the forensics evidence was compiled and analyzed by a panel of coroners. Witnesses were questioned, Ashburn's body and the murder scene were examined, and Mayor F. G. Wilkins promptly ordered a reward for the arrest of those responsible. State authorities added additional rewards and soon everyone began to " spy on everybody else." 8 The forensics examination revealed that Ashburn had been shot three times, but only the bullet through his forehead was lethal enough to cause death. There were a total of fourteen rounds of ammunition fired in the room, and apparently,

Ashburn had fired at least one round in self-defense. One of the intruders left a black mask at the scene and it was entered as evidence. Adding to the confusion, on that same evening, an upscale masquerade party was held nearby. Mr. Dudley Chipley's home on upper Broad Street was the scene of a grand party, and many of the city's prominent members were in attendance, and wearing black masks. Soon, many people were turning in suspected persons, whom they had seen wearing black masks. The investigation also revealed that the prostitutes had seen several of the intruder's faces, yet they were unable to positively identify them. Meanwhile, Generals Meade and Grant became involved, members of Congress heard of the murder, and they sent their own investigative team to Columbus. The military and civil police patrols were increased in Columbus and a military tribunal was ordered to convene. Captain Mills, the local garrison commander " began the wholesale arrest of local citizens." 9 A total of twenty-seven men were arrested, including three black Democrats.

The men were arrested without a warrant, locked in jail, allowed no contact with anyone, nor were they provided with legal counsel. One of the men arrested was a U.S. soldier, Sergeant Charles Marshall, suspected because he had uttered pro-Democratic statements, and because he had once threatened to kill Ashburn himself. Realizing the apparent folly of their wholesale arrests, some of the prisoners were released after friends posted outrageous bail bonds. Some of the men were taken to Fort Pulaski, on the Georgia coast where they were placed in sweatboxes and mistreated. One of these men was Mr. Dudley Chipley, host of the masquerade party, but he had also served as the district chairman of the local Democratic Party, which made him a suspect. " Inhuman means were used to extract confessions," and Mr. Chipley never recovered from the effects of his torture. 10 The people of Columbus held mass meetings against the cruel treatment inflicted by the military, but the authorities simply cracked down harder. Bribes for false affidavits against the accused prisoners and other citizens forced the citizens to hate their military overseers. The soldiers arrested many people for " suspicious activities" and in Columbus, there was " a reign of terror for weeks after the murder of Ashburn. " 11 Mr. Lambert Spencer, Vice-President of the " Young Mens' Democratic Club," was warned to curtail his activities, lest he be arrested too. The Spencers and other members of this organization, including the Kings and Garrards were prominent citizens and the resulting crackdown began to backfire on the Republicans. The outrageous behavior of the military authorities prompted many blacks and whites to align their political affiliations with the Democratic Party. Throughout the month of April, investigations, implications and accusations circulated amidst the community as the local citizens tried to maintain a semblance of normalcy and remain non-belligerent.

On April 26, 1868, the Ladies' Memorial Association conducted their annual pilgrimage to Linwood Cemetery. Earlier that month, Doctor W. J. Fogle, a prominent Columbus physician had traveled to Gettysburg to retrieve the body of General Paul Semmes. In a journey similar to young Seaborn Leonard Jones, Dr. Fogle succeeded in the retrieval of Semmes remains, and a re-interment in Linwood Cemetery was arranged as the focal point of the memorial ceremony for 1868. The body lay in state for three days at the local Presbyterian Church, and an honor guard of the " Columbus Guards " guarded his remains. At 3:30 P.M., on Saturday evening, April 25, Semmes funeral service was held at the church. His casket was draped with a silken flag, which bore the Coat of Arms of Georgia, and a picture of the general, in uniform was placed nearby. His casket was surrounded with wreaths and flowers. A military procession numbering one hundred and fifty men escorted General Semmes to his grave in Linwood Cemetery. A band led the procession," then came the surviving members of the Columbus Guards and the City Light Guards, marching in column by platoons, following came the hearse and pall-bearers, the ladies of the Memorial Association, General Benning and staff, Col. Martin J. Crawford, R. Thompson, and other Confederate officers ; Mayor Wilkins and the City Council, followed by a long line of carriages, making the entire line fully half a mile." 12

U.S. soldiers were deployed throughout the town as sentinels during the procession, and they carefully observed the entire affair with a watchful eye. Apparently, the funeral smacked of insolence and possible rebellion against the federal authorities. Parading the body of a Confederate General through the streets, especially during the on-going criminal investigation was a potential source of friction. At the burial site, one of the federal soldiers," fearing the Memorial Association had gone too far in their great desire to honor the dead, cautiously folded the draperies over the picture of General Semmes wearing the Confederate uniform." 13 One of the ladies immediately drew back the curtains and declared to the soldiers," Let no one dare touch the work of the Memorial Association." 14 Afterwards, one of the federal officers relating the affair, stated that the ladies of Columbus " were worse than a bunch of hyenas; that they dared to parade the body of a Confederate General through the streets of Columbus and give him a military funeral, and we dared not molest them." 15 On that day, the Ladies Memorial Association also erected a wooden cenotaph, as a monument to honor the fallen Confederate soldiers of Columbus. The ladies decided that this monument was not adequate and they pledged to build a larger and permanent marker in downtown Columbus. **16**

The following day, the ladies led the City of Columbus in laying wreaths and flowers throughout the cemetery, and Major Raphael Moses delivered the oratory for the occasion at the " Cenotaph. " **17** Raphael Moses also stepped forward and offered his services as an attorney for the defense of the accused in the Ashburn murder case. Equally perturbed with the unfair treatment, maligned investigation, abuse of power and outright criminal treatment of the prisoners, other prominent attorneys offered their services as well. Henry Benning, Martin J. Crawford, James N. Ramsey, James Milton Smith, Raphael J. Moses, Lucius J. Gartrell, and Alexander H. Stephens combined their efforts forming an unprecedented legal " dream team." **18** Stephens took the lead as the Chief Counselor for the defense, while the other attorneys handled administrative matters, technical assistance and performed the legal " leg work." Stephens was a brilliant courtroom attorney, blessed with charming manners, eloquent speech, and sharp, strategic delivery. While Stephens's stature was small and unassuming, he was prepared to stealthily destroy the efforts of the prosecution.

Generals Grant and Meade determined that the trial should proceed in a military court, and the accused men were transferred to McPherson Barracks, in Atlanta. A military commission of seven judges appointed by General Meade would determine the prisoner's fate. " Aligned against the defense were two military prosecutors, the Assistant Judge Advocate General of the Army, General William Dunn and Major William Smythe. Assisting the prosecution team was a civilian attorney, the former Governor of Georgia, Joseph E. Brown. Brown accepted the fee of $5000 stating that he did not wish to see a " radical" in the position as lead prosecutor. " For this he bore the hatred of the people of this section, who could not understand the action and considered him a traitor to their party." **19** For the rest of his life, Joseph E. Brown paid a heavy price for his actions, although his behavior was generally misunderstood. Throughout Georgia, he was vilified, despised, and many Georgians felt that his name " should not be mentioned in decent company." **20** It must be noted that in Isaac W. Avery's epic history of Georgia politics, he cites credible information which supports Brown's actions; however, in 1868, the " public obloquy of Georgians" was openly thrust upon Joseph E. Brown. **21** Fueled with hatred and despair, this period in Georgia history is amongst her darkest days. Joseph E. Brown and the Ashburn affair was one of the " darkest episodes of that dark day." 22

Amidst these trials and tribulations, Henry Benning decided to relocate his family. " El Dorado " was a beautiful old house, but it was difficult to maintain and far from his daily excursions into town. Additionally, Benning was becoming increasingly alarmed with crime in his community. The soldiers and police simply could not keep pace with the rapidly expanding city, and the corresponding increase in suburban larcenies. Benning needed a house closer to town and near his work. The law office of *Benning and Benning* was located in the uptown (northern) section of the business district, between Franklin Street and the upper bridge. 23 Nearby, Benning had noticed a two-story white frame house, which he decided would make an excellent home for his large family. The house was located at 1420 Broad Street, which was one block form his work, six blocks from the courthouse, four blocks from their church and many of their close friends lived nearby too. Just around the corner, on Troup Street, was the home of Benning's best friend, Martin J. Crawford. 24 While Mary Benning must have been upset concerning the impending relocation, for her family, times were seemingly returning to normalcy. Spring was well underway, long warm days had returned to the Chattahoochee Valley and the gay affairs of summer weddings and social activities were highly anticipated. Yet, unbeknownst to the Benning family, great sorrow loomed on the horizon.

On May 20, 1868, a marriage marked the final happy occasion the Bennings would experience in their old neighborhood as Van and Frances Leonard's youngest daughter, the " lovely" nineteen year-old beauty, Anna Foster Leonard was married to Louis F. Garrard. Known as " Annie," Miss Leonard was well educated and a refined Southern belle. Her husband was a lawyer and the son of William W. and Frances Isabel Gartery Urquhart Garrard. At the age of sixteen, Louis Garrard had left his studies as a cadet in the Military School at Tuscaloosa, Alabama, and volunteered for service in the Confederacy. Garrard served as a Private in " Nelson's Rangers," an independent cavalry company which served with distinction under their commanders, Generals E. Kirby Smith, Nathan Bedford Forrest and Stephen D. Lee. Their heroic deeds and battles won them great acclaim, especially at the battles of Franklin and Nashville. In these battles, Louis Garrard was noted for his gallantry and offered a commission, but the war ended before his commission was secured. After the war, Louis Garrard attended the University of Kentucky and studied law at Harvard University. Upon his graduation, Louis Garrard returned to Columbus and won a position at the bar. Several of Garrard's fellow soldiers and close boyhood friends also achieved success after the war. In particular, G.

Gunby Jordan (business tycoon) and Samuel Spencer (railroad magnate) became prominent sons of Columbus and won acclaim for their accomplishments.

The newlyweds, Louis and " Annie" had known one another since they were very young and their union was a beautiful occasion, which bonded two prominent Columbus families. The Garrard family lived in a large, handsome estate, known as " Hilton. " The Reverend and Mrs. Lovick Pierce previously owned their home, and it was located in the suburban heights of Columbus in a fashionable district known as Wynnton. Yet," Hilton," " Wildwood " and " El Dorado " were close enough to encourage close relations among the inhabitants, and love bloomed between the lovely young " Annie" Leonard and her dashing young attorney and beau, Louis F. Garrard.

The wedding of Louis Garrard and Anna Leonard was a grand affair, which included a visit from their friend and Mary Benning 's cousin, Augusta Jane Evans. 25 Miss Evans' parents had lived at " Wildwood," and it was there, in the dining room, where she was born. By 1868, Miss Evans was a best-selling author and a renowned celebrity. *St. Elmo* brought her fame, wealth, and most importantly for Augusta, acclaim as a gifted writer. The attendance of Miss Evans combined with the reunion of prominent friends and family made the Garrard-Leonard wedding the hallmark social occasion of that year. After the gala event, everyone went back to their normal routine and on June 9, 1868, Henry Benning purchased his Broad Street home from Columbus banker, John King, for $4000. 26 Mary Benning began preparing her large family for the impending move, while her husband continued his work with the Ashburn case.

Meanwhile, the military authorities realized that they did not have substantial evidence to warrant many of the accusations and the number of suspects in the Ashburn case was reduced to thirteen. Mr. Chipley had also managed to get a letter to Congressman Beck of Kentucky, whom read the letter to both legislative bodies in Washington. In his letter, Chipley appealed that he and his fellow prisoners should be accorded their rights in accordance with the Constitution. Chipley's appeal for due process resulted in their transfer to McPherson Barracks, a U.S. army post in Atlanta. Raphael Moses accompanied the prisoners to Atlanta where for the first time, they were formally charged for the murder of George Ashburn, on June 27. Their trial was set to begin on Monday, June 29. 27 The other members of the legal defense team made their way to Atlanta, and Henry

Benning hurriedly finalized his family's relocation preparations, as well as his trip to Atlanta.

Suddenly, on Sunday evening, June 28, 1868, Henry Benning's world was forever changed by an event from which he never fully recovered. While organizing and packing away a lifetime of treasures and memories, Mary Benning died. Leaving her home and a lifetime of memories must have grieved her horribly. Henry Benning had not only courted, and married her there, but she had given birth to ten children in " El Dorado. " She had struggled with all her heart to maintain her home despite the war, its tribulations and the deaths of several children, her brother and her father. She had lived nearly all her life in " El Dorado." Leaving the old mansion crushed her, and in a moment, she too was but a memory of a glorious age. Mary was only fifty-one years old, but according to her daughter Anna Caroline, her mother " was a woman of small stature, and her work and anxiety brought on death. " **28** While she was small and frail her constitution was strong and she died as she had lived- working. She had given an abundance of love and devotion to both her family and community. Both were equally shocked and bereaved. Henry Benning was devastated. Mary was the foundation of " Old Rock 's" life, and without her, his spirit crumbled and he would never be the same. Benning's close friend, James D. Waddell remarked that in " El Dorado," the " sunshine of her presence" was " glorious to behold," and Mary's influence upon Henry softened " into tenderness the austerity which the outside world thought he wore." **29**

Raphael Moses rushed back to Columbus to be with Henry and the Benning family in their time of loss. Mary was buried in the Benning plots of Linwood Cemetery, not far from her departed father, Seaborn Jones. She was laid to rest directly beside her four young children who preceded her in death, and a simple, elegant marker bears her name. The citizens of Columbus felt her death as she had unselfishly spread her love and generosity throughout the community. Mary's eulogy was filled with sincere praise, for her " zealous and conspicuous promotion of Christianity, for the alleviation of human suffering, and support of the common cause of our people." She was also revered as an " ornament and blessing to the community... many a poor soldier of the Southern army owed to her a debt of gratitude for her assistance in their hour of need." **30** Years later, Peggy (Margaret) Mitchell wrote an article in the *Atlanta Constitution* about Henry Benning. After researching Benning's life, she included comments about Mary Benning, which reflect characteristics of the fictional heroines in her famous Southern classic, *Gone with the Wind.* It is interesting to note that her news article was written years before she authored her famous book, which catapulted her career to the heights of a world famous author.

In the newspaper article about Benning, Mitchell wrote that, Mary's life was entwined with her husband's and therefore it should be mentioned that:

> She was a tiny woman, frail and slight, but possessed of unusual endurance and a lion's heart. The battles she fought at home were those of nearly every Southern woman, but her burdens were heavier than most. Left in complete charge of a large plantation, this little woman, who was the mother of ten children, was as brave a soldier at home as ever her husband was on the Virginia battlefields. She saw to it that the crops were gathered, the children fed and clothed, and the Negroes cared for. To her fell the work of superintending the weaving and spinning of enough cloth, not only to clothe her own children and servants, but also Confederate soldiers. While her husband was away she buried her aged father, whose end was hastened by the war. **31**

Mitchell continued her praise of Mary focusing on the fact that she bravely endured and overcame the burdens of life during the most trying times in Southern history. Many of the characteristics and virtues which Mary Benning displayed as well as her experiences, come to life in Margaret Mitchell's novel. After writing the Benning article, Margaret Mitchell began writing *Gone with the Wind*, and clearly, she was inspired by the life of Mary Benning. As Henry stated before he married her," she is the most perfect combination and condensation of mind, body and soul, beauty and truth," and for Henry Benning, the loss of Mary was ominous. **32**

Despite his tremendous loss, characteristic of the old soldier, Henry mustered his strength and on July 3, he and his old friend, Raphael Moses traveled to Atlanta to join the proceedings. **33** Upon their arrival, the trial was already in progress, and while Benning participated in defense strategy, his role on the team was uncharacteristically minor. Alexander Stephens, however, carried the day as his cross-examination of key witnesses and the resulting destruction of their testimonies is legendary. Stephens and the defense counselors effectively destroyed each of the arguments presented by Brown and the military authorities. Consequently, throughout Georgia, the public openly ridiculed the prosecution team. As the trial trudged through the heat of the summer, the prosecution continued

to endure the blistering cross-examinations of the defense team. The
military authorities squirmed under the pressure and they were soon
searching for a way out of the proceedings. Consequently, the brunt of the
blame fell squarely on Joseph E. Brown, and with the end of July rapidly
approaching, the military sought official relief in political affairs brewing
in Atlanta. The new Georgia General Assembly convened in Atlanta and
they quickly made history on July 21, 1868, as they ratified the Fourteenth
Amendment. Passage of this political hurdle cleared the way for Georgia's
return to the United States. Simultaneously, important events unfolded as
the military authorities issued a cessation of the Ashburn trial, the prisoners
were sent back to Columbus, and Rufus B. Bullock was elected Governor
of the State of Georgia. While the prisoners won their freedom, they were
never convicted or acquitted of the charges against them, as the affair
simply ended. **34**

The same week the new Georgia General Assembly convened was
the same week in which the Democratic Convention was held also. Many
of the leading men of Georgia were present in Atlanta for the famous "
Bush Arbor Convention," as speeches, rallies and festivities were held
throughout July 22-25, 1868. Among the orators delivering fiery speeches
against the tyranny of Congressional Reconstruction were, Robert Toombs,
Howell Cobb, Raphael Moses, James N. Ramsey, and Benjamin H. Hill.
Henry Benning was not his usual self and while he normally would have
fully exploited the opportunities of political revival, instead he shrank from
the public forum. Benning's peers, Toombs, Cobb, Hill, Moses and
Ramsey, however, rose to the occasion and delivered speeches of
legendary proportions. Even the junior orator of this group, James Ramsey
delivered a speech which resulted in " wild, upheaving applause that shook
the hall as he uttered thoughts that breathed and words that burned." **35** The
" Bush Arbor Convention" was " the largest political mass meeting ever
held in Georgia, and nearly every leading man was there except Joseph E.
Brown. " **36** Amongst the district electors sent to cast votes in the
upcoming presidential election were several old friends of Henry Benning,
James D. Waddell, Dudley M. DuBose, John B. Gordon and Raphael
Moses. **37** These men were also destined for future political offices and
three of them had served under Benning's command in the army. For
Henry Benning, the prospects of a political future seemed dim, and
coupled with the loss of his wife, his life had sunk to a new low. The flame
of political fire in Benning's heart had been effectively snuffed out.

Yet, the passions that embraced Georgia during the Secession
Convention of 1861 were rekindled in 1868, as the Democratic South was
once again pitted against the Republican North. The Democratic nominee
for President was Horatio Seymour of New York. While Seymour was a

Northerner, his Democratic platform contained attractive provisions for Southerners, which included an amnesty for all former Confederates; elimination of the Freedmen's Bureau ; and individual state resolution of the question of black suffrage. His opponent was Ulysses S. Grant, who supported the Republican theme of " Let us have peace." Grant and the Republican Party also displayed a genuine desire to eliminate military rule in the South. **38** In the presidential election, Grant soundly defeated Seymour, and in Georgia, Governor Bullock and the Republican Party dominated as well. Bullock, known as an infamous carpetbagger and perhaps the worst governor in Georgia history reigned for the next three years. In Columbus, James Johnson, Benning's old nemesis and Georgia's provisional Reconstruction governor, won the bench of the Superior Court in the Chattahoochee circuit. In disgust, Henry Benning and his fellow Georgia Democrats resolved themselves to a continuation of Reconstruction politics dominated by northern politicians and radical puppeteers.

Throughout the South, during the years 1868 through 1876, many Southern blacks achieved governmental positions. Whites generally despised the blacks for their affiliation with the carpetbaggers and the radical elements whom took advantage of the both the blacks and the politically powerless Democrats. This animosity created a rise in Ku Klux Klan activities to suppress the rights of blacks to vote. Consequently, in 1869, the new Republican administration proposed the Fifteenth Amendment, which guaranteed to all citizens, regardless of their race, the right to vote. Congress also passed a Ku Klux Klan Act, which targeted their efforts to discourage black voters. The law carried stiff penalties for denying blacks their rights, and important men such as Nathan Bedford Forrest stepped down from his position in the Klan, and he encouraged others to disband the organization. In the South, however, Klan activities increased despite rules imposed against them.

Meanwhile, Henry Benning moved into his new home at 1420 Broad Street, and he continued the practice of law with his son, Seaborn. Howell Cobb traveled to New York on a business trip, and while he was engaged in a casual conversation with his wife and friends, Benning's old friend suffered a fatal stroke. Cobb died on October 9, 1868 and his " Bush Arbor " speech delivered in Atlanta, three months before his death, served as his final contribution to his beloved State of Georgia. **39** Benning mourned the loss of his old friend, and Benning experienced several losses within the next year. On February 4, 1869, Benning's aged mother-in-law, Mrs. Mary

Jones died at the Benning residence. Mrs. Jones had reached the age of eighty-one, and she was buried alongside her husband, Seaborn, in Linwood Cemetery. 40 That same year, Benning's close friend, James N. Ramsey also died. On November 10, 1869, Ramsey succumbed to what was listed as " congestion," and the local paper cited Ramsey as the " Patrick Henry of the South." 41 Benning deeply mourned the loss of all his kith and kin, yet he continued to bear life's many burdens. One of his burdens was the support of his large and extended family. While several members of the Benning household had died, Henry Benning remained the patriarch and breadwinner supporting Mrs. John A. Jones , with two female children still at home, several of the his sister's female children, the Martins, as well as his own five daughters. Filled with a house full of a predominantly female persuasion, Henry's life was filled with perplexing problems as he struggled being both father and mother. Henry's daughter Anna Caroline, recorded that while her father was wrestling with a delicate feminine situation, he once stated," I feel as if I had the weight of the world on my shoulders." 42 Henry had but one goal where his daughters were concerned, and that was to see them well married. On July 20, 1870, one of Benning's twin daughters, Augusta Jones Benning was wed to Reese Crawford, the son of Martin J. Crawford. Reese was a successful young lawyer with an excellent reputation and a bright future. Thus Benning's first daughter to " leave the nest" was very well married and the families of Benning and Crawford were joined through the bonds of marriage. 43

In addition to his own family, Henry Benning also provided a home for two former slave families. Free to pursue the lives of their choice, Erin Smith, Wellborn Thornton and eight members of the Hartwell Robertson family continued to serve the Benning household, as domestic servants and laborers. Thus in 1870, Benning's own family consisted of eight people, and he also had 10 Negroes living in his home. Throughout the South, the records of the post-bellum era reflect several situations wherein former slaves continued to live within the homes of their former masters. Yet, it is interesting to note that in Columbus, Henry Benning maintained the largest arrangement of this unique situation. This is especially poignant when one considers the tremendous financial woes that the Benning household experienced after the war. With the loss of his slaves and reduced property values, Benning's net worth depreciated greatly. In 1860, Benning's net worth of $96,300 had been reduced to $19,000 by 1870. 44

While the Bennings continued to enjoy a comfortable lifestyle, according to Henry's daughter Anna Caroline, the family was " impoverished by the war." For the daughters of an affluent Southern family, the financial upheaval experienced by the Benning family was probably not as bad as they perceived it to be. Statistical analysis reflects that in terms of financial reality, between 1860 and 1870, Henry Benning's rank in net worth slipped from 18th amongst the " Top 20" wealthiest families to 89th. Yet, most families in Columbus were poorer than the Bennings, and throughout the South, the entire economic infrastructure had collapsed beneath them. Plantation owners were severely affected, as they could not possibly achieve the antebellum production and profit levels they enjoyed before the war. Thus the entire Southern economy was forced to adapt their manufacturing and agricultural industries in order to repair the economic infrastructure of the Southern states.

Fortunately, for the citizens of Columbus , this adaptation was quite natural due primarily to the preexistence of a successful transition to industrialization before the war. Still the economy of 1860 when compared with the same situation in 1870 was very different. Immediately after the war, with Negroes thrust into the labor market, an entire race of people suddenly competed with poor whites for employment. For the working class, the resulting situation created competition for low wage jobs and a struggle for mere survival. Yet, by 1870 the economy of Columbus provided a vast job market for anyone willing to work. With a plethora of manufacturing firms and competitive cotton farming, laborers enjoyed numerous employment opportunities. While the wages were low, there was plenty of work, and Columbus grew rapidly. The owners and directors of manufacturing firms achieved rapid success, and several local industrialists achieved prominence during this era.

In 1870, the wealthiest man in Columbus was Mr. Randolph Mott. Mott owned a flourmill, he was a bank director, and he was a co-founder of the Columbus Gas and Light Company. Several Northern families moved to Columbus after the war and capitalized on the potential industrial opportunities in Columbus. Among these families were the Woodruffs from Connecticut, and the Clapps of Massachusetts. George P. Swift and William H. Young also established themselves as captains of the textile industry during this era. Swift's legacy of prowess in the textile industry continues today and Young led the Eagle and Phenix Mills to fame and fortune. While textile manufacturing led an economic resurgence in Columbus, it would not have been possible without an abundant supply of cheap, raw materials. Several old, local farming families managed to generate wealth by providing the textile mills with the bulk of local cotton production. Among these were the Biggers, Woolfolks, Starks, Flewellens, and the Shepherds. Their large cotton farms supplied a great deal of the raw material, which fed the looms of the burgeoning mills. Yet, smaller cotton farms contributed as well, and many small-scale farmers earned a good living producing cotton.

The transition from an agricultural economy to an industrialized society spurred many changes and reversals of fortunes. Events of the years between 1860 and 1870 affected permanent changes in the South, and the citizens of Columbus adapted rapidly. These changes destroyed the financial integrity of many of the old Columbus families, but these transitions also brought opportunities to those with entrepreneurial spirits. By 1870, all of the wealthiest citizens of Columbus were somehow connected with industrialization, and the bulk of common citizens worked for these industrial giants. Yet, it is also noteworthy that amongst the " Top 20" wealthiest men of Columbus in 1860, only one managed to remain on this elite list into the 1870s. Mr. James Cook, a gentleman planter, who resided on his Rose Hill estate," Beallwood," owned vast tracts of land throughout the northern outskirts of Columbus. While Cook suffered a net worth reduction from $102,000 in 1860, to $58,000 in 1870, he still managed do quite well. Despite depreciated land values, his holdings were so immense that his family enjoyed financial security for many years. **45**

Meanwhile, Henry Benning continued his work as a prominent attorney and kept a watchful eye on Georgia political affairs. On the national level, in July 1870, the State of Georgia officially ratified the Fifteenth Amendment, and won the distinction as the final former Confederate State to return to the Union. This act provided that Georgia's representatives would again be allowed to participate in national politics. At the state level, the government of Georgia was wrought with corruption, scandals, and illegal financial scams. Just as the public learned that the state executive office was involved and implicated in illegal bond issues, Governor Rufus Bullock suddenly fled from Georgia. The void created some turmoil and political maneuvering, however, the former President of the Georgia Senate, Benjamin Conley assumed the office of governor, and the government trudged along. Benning's old friends, James D. Waddell became the Clerk of the Georgia House, while James M. Smith ascended to the position of House Speaker. As Governor, Conley righted the wrongs of Governor Bullock and he launched an investigation into the bond issue. In Georgia political affairs and opportunities for Democrats improved. **46**

In light of the developments in Georgia governmental affairs, Henry Benning 's political desires were energized. Amidst the tumultuous political affairs, throughout the South, the years 1870-1871 presented a continual rise in Ku Klux Klan activities. In April of 1871, the U.S. Congress passed a second Ku Klux Klan Act, which empowered the government to treat Klan activities as rebellious terrorist organization and suspend the writ of habeas corpus in enforcing the Fifteenth Amendment.

Shortly thereafter, Congress launched a series of investigations into suspected Klan activities in the former Confederate States. The 41st Congress formed a " Joint Select Committee to Inquire into the Condition of Affairs in the Late Insurrectionary States and witnesses from throughout the Southern states were called before the committee to provide testimony. One of the men selected from the State of Georgia was Henry Lewis Benning. Appearing before the committee on July 18, 1871, Benning provided an honest appraisal of conditions in southwest Georgia, as U.S. Representatives Blair, Beck, Poland, Coburn and Pool questioned him. 47 The congressional committee focused on activities of the Ku Klux Klan in Georgia, and as Benning reported during the years 1866-1871, Klan activity in Georgia was minimal compared to other States.

The committee prompted Benning with questions concerning the Ashburn murder case, the killing of Major Warner by the " colored soldiers," and one other murder of a black Democrat, in Columbus. The questioning revealed that Benning knew of no killings committed by " disguised men" with the exception of the Ashburn case, which was never solved. Most all of the testimonies presented by Georgia residents revealed little data concerning Klan activity and the only valid point made concerned the corruption of the Bullock administration, the disgust which Georgians felt for him, and his reign as an " iniquity of civilization." 48 In regards to the actions of the Ku Klux Klan in Georgia, most people including Henry Benning upheld the laws of the land, and viewed the Klan as an outrage. The *Savannah News* summed up the sentiment of the common man concerning Klan affairs in Georgia. The paper recorded that while Klan activities were undoubtedly occurring in the Southern States, people did not generally condone their crimes. " In the absence of the voice of protest, it has been assumed that these secret organizations possessed the approbation and sympathy of society. That silence has been misconstrued." 49 Most Georgians knew that hiding behind a mask and committing crimes would not resolve their problems, and therefore as the article went on to state, citizens where Klan activities occur should:

> speak out and call on those secret champions of society to
> unmask. It is time their faces should be scrutinized, their
> credentials should be examined. They assume to act in the
> interests of the community. The community should be entitled
> to know their representatives. It is time the community should in
> public meetings and through the public press declare its true

sentiments. There has been too long a reprehensible silence on this subject. **50**

Men like Henry Benning knew that Georgia would have to cast off its cloak of silence concerning politics, and he reentered the political stage to voice his opinions. Benning ran for and was elected as a delegate to the Democratic convention. The duty of the delegation was to nominate candidates for the upcoming Georgia gubernatorial race. Meeting in Atlanta on December 6, 1871, two of Benning's close friends ascended to prominent positions during the fall and winter of 1871. First during the fall elections for House and Senate seats, the former commander of the Fifteenth Georgia regiment, Dudley M. DuBose had been elected as a U.S. Congressman from Georgia. Secondly, Benning's close friend from Columbus and a fellow defense attorney in the Ashburn murder case; James M. Smith won the race for Governor. Governor Smith was inaugurated on January 12, 1872, and he would be the first effective Georgia Governor since 1865. **51**

Benning's spirit was uplifted and he was encouraged to engage in Georgia politics. In 1872, the State government wrestled with the dilemma left by former Governor Bullock concerning the bond issue. Bullock had left the citizens of Georgia with millions of dollars in worthless railroad and currency bonds. Henry Benning was asked for his advice concerning the issue. According to Benning, the question at the root of the problem was " whether the State's credit was affected injuriously." **52** Benning concluded that the State's credit was not injured, but he proposed that Georgia should cease from borrowing any more credit through bond issues. On this matter, Benning disagreed with his old friend Robert Toombs, but Benning was back on " the stage" politically. The bond debate continued for some time, while Benning focused on more important political and personal affairs.

In Columbus, on February 6, 1872, Benning's other twin daughter, Louisa (Lou) Vivian Benning was wed to Samuel Spencer, the son of a prominent businessman and old friend of the Bennings, Lambert Spencer. Sam Spencer was a hard working and well-educated civil engineer. His devotion to work even precluded the young couple from going on a honeymoon, but Sam's earnest desire for achievement would later provide him with great wealth and fame. **53** Meanwhile, in May of 1872, the U.S. Congress passed an Amnesty Act, which provided the opportunity for former Confederate officials to hold public office, at all levels. Henry Benning eagerly ran for and won the local election as a member of the delegation for the Democratic Convention. Held in Atlanta on June 26, 1872, besides Benning, several of his old friends and peers including

Robert Toombs, Benjamin H. Hill, Alfred H. Colquitt, I. W. Avery, John B. Gordon, A. R. Wright and Linton Stephens, seemingly brought the return of " old-time" politics to Georgia. As the names of the conventioneers were read aloud, Toombs exclaimed " Packed-By God!" 54

The majority of delegates and most Georgia citizens supported nominee Horace Greeley as the candidate for the Democratic ticket. Henry's son, Seaborn stated that in Columbus," all the older citizens are for him and but few of the young ones are against him." 55 Henry Benning fully supported Greeley, but Toombs, and the Stephens brothers openly opposed Greeley's presidential nomination. Politically, Benning's disagreement with these important delegates would cost him greatly in the near future. Benning was selected as a Georgia elector for the presidential race. In the presidential race of 1872, Horace Greeley won the bid for the Democratic Party, and he would face off against Ulysses S. Grant, the incumbent Republican President. It was an exciting race and filled with great debate. Benning was an avid Greeley supporter, yet many Georgians disagreed with Benning. Greeley was a newspaper editor and he had scalded the South prior to the Civil War concerning slavery and States' rights, yet Benning preferred Greeley and he continued his support, rather than face another four years of Grant 's Radical reconstruction efforts. Greeley's wife was terminally ill, and with the additional strain of losing the election, he became so upset and distraught, he went insane and within a few weeks, he died.

In January, 1873, Georgia's new Governor, James Milton Smith was inaugurated, as the Georgia legislature went into its first session of the new year. A seat had opened for Georgia's representative in the U. S. Senate, and Henry Benning joined the race. Benning faced extremely stiff competition, as Alexander Stephens, John B. Gordon, and Benjamin H. Hill were amongst the candidates for the senatorial seat. Initially, Benning embraced the opportunity with active political prowess. His relationship with the new Governor was strong and he escorted Smith to the inauguration. Among the senatorial candidates, Benning's speech was the first to be given in Representatives Hall and nothing less than his political future was at stake. This singular speech could either make or break his political career. Benning delivered a two-hour speech, which delved into the past, present and future of the Democratic Party. He explained the differences between the Republican and Democratic parties, and he delved into a lengthy dissertation that dwelled in the past. It was on this point that Benning probably lost his opportunity for a future in Georgia politics.

The Democratic Party needed " new blood" and the Georgia delegates sought an energetic infusion, someone and something, which Benning failed to provide. His speech dwelled on the past, including a lengthy historical overview of the Democratic Party, its glorious history and its eventual clash with Northern politicians. Reflecting on the past, his speech highlighted the clash of wills during the Civil War, and he included the statement," We will not give up the idea of sovereignty of states." 56 His speech transitioned into the present and he chastised the Republican party, as an evil opportunistic entity which preyed upon causes to vilify Southerners. Carrying his speech into the present, Benning referred to the basis of differences between the parties as simply the application of differences in constitutional interpretation. Concerning the Constitution, Benning stated that," Strict constructions for sixty years has made it a success, while a loose construction from 1860 up to this time has accomplished nothing." 57 Benning repeated many of the key points expressed in his obiter dictum in the Supreme Court case of *Padelford v. Savannah*, and then he progressed his speech into the future. Benning summed up his speech by rolling the political problems of the past and present as being problems of constitutional interpretation. Then he boldly predicted that," The contest in the future will be between a strict construction and latitudinarian construction of the constitution." 58

While Benning's speech was well received, it reflected the era of antebellum Southern thought, a disillusioned point of view that was considered to be old and tired as the idea of secession. The delegates did not share Benning's political philosophy, as the battle for his ideology had been fought, and lost. As a politician, Benning's chances for success waned, while the other candidates A. T. Ackerman, Herbert Fielder, Benjamin H. Hill, John B. Gordon, and Alexander Stephens moved ahead. While the newspapers recorded Benning's entire speech, it appeared under headlines such as," Old Rock Heard From," as if he had entered the stage from some mysterious ancient gallery. In effect, Benning did suddenly reappear on Georgia's political stage, and his ideology was found to be far removed from the political currents of 1873. Benning failed to receive a nomination, his name was not placed on the ballot, and politically speaking, Benning was dead. John B. Gordon won the election, although his speech was short and even reported to be simple and " sophomoric." Yet, Gordon appealed to the delegates with a fresh innovative spirit, as his speech was highlighted with brevity and sincerity. Gordon served Georgia well as a Senator, and from 1886 to 1890, he served as the Governor of Georgia. 59

Governor James M. Smith offered Henry Benning a seat on the Georgia Supreme Bench, but Benning declined, citing the reluctance of the

Georgia legislature to support him. **60** Thus, Henry Benning returned to his home in Columbus, and never again would he ascend to " the stage" of Georgia political affairs. While Benning was nearly sixty years old, with the exception of his disabled arm, his health remained good. Again Benning resumed the practice of law and he joined endeavors with Edmond H. Worrill, another former judge of the Chattahoochee circuit. The law firm flourished and Benning retired from farming. His life henceforth focused on matters close to home. Seaborn's episodic blindness continued to cause him trouble. Writing to his sister Louisa Vivian (Benning) Spencer in 1872, Seaborn wrote," My eyes have been affected in such a manner that I could scarcely see a sheet of paper for some days... In fact now, I am scarcely able to read a newspaper - A large sign on Broad Street when I would be standing sixty yards from it, the width of the street, it had a jumbled up vague appearance & had I not known the firms that occupied the different stores, I should have been very reluctant in piloting any stranger to any house... but by the blessing of God, my eyes, not altogether restored, are much better now." **61**

Seaborn was the eldest Benning child, and he had an abiding and sincere affection for his five younger sisters. Despite the afflictions caused by his war wounds, he joked liberally, discussed parties and exchanged gossip of " love" in the " ville," with his sisters. While Seaborn never achieved the acclaim of a lawyer like his father, he did assist Henry Benning and act as an administrative agent for routine legal matters in the local court. Seaborn's favorite hobby was fishing in the Chattahoochee River and he considered himself an accomplished angler. S. Leonard Jones, Seaborn's younger cousin, who tragically lost his father's corpse in a shipwreck, frequently accompanied Seaborn on his river excursions. Seaborn related to his sister Louisa a particular adventure they experienced in April of 1872. Leonard begged him to go hunting, so Seaborn " consulted Genl. [sic] Henry L. on the subject, as I am his Adjutant, who shrugged his shoulders, grunted & said 'Wild Goose Chase', but go on now, go ahead- you are your own man, you know best." **62** Their hunting adventure turned into a exercise in survival, as a tremendous storm ruined the trip. In short, the result was a disastrous and comical affair in which Leonard and Seaborn navigated along 150 miles of the Chattahoochee River, where they got wet, cold, and spent most of their time paddling and " cussing the luck." **63** Seaborn's health slowly declined and on December 12, 1874, at the age of thirty-four, he died. While his death was reportedly due to " consumption," his sister Anna Caroline wrote that her brother died

as a result of his war wounds. **64** Apparently, the shrapnel that blinded
Seaborn also disfigured his face. After the war, Seaborn never married, he
referred to himself as " ugly," and his tombstone reads," He bears the scars
of battle." **65**

Shortly after the loss of his son, Seaborn, Henry Benning also lost his
sister-in-law, Mary Louisa (Leonard) Jones. Joining her husband, Colonel
John A. Jones , Mary suddenly passed away in the Benning's home on
Broad Street, on April 15, 1875. Ever true to her husband, she died a
widow, at the age of fifty. Between her and the generosity of the Bennings,
her children had grown to adulthood, surrounded by love in a comfortable
home. **66** Bereft and somewhat embittered, Henry Benning sought peace
by delving deeply into the law. While Benning practiced primarily in
Supreme Court defense matters, he also practiced in the local Superior
Court. The Chattahoochee circuit was presided over by the Honorable
James Johnson, Benning's old nemesis, which certainly kept Benning on
his guard. Just like Benning, in 1875, Columbus too was back on the road
to success. The city was blessed with industrialization and rapid growth.
Under the leadership of the wealthy industrialist, William H. Young, the
Eagle Mills, was aptly renamed the Eagle and Phenix Mills. The mills were
modernized, and throughout the city, like the legendary Phoenix, it literally
rose from its ashes. Gone were the days of an agrarian based society, as the
nation fully embraced the Age of Industrialization, and Columbus served
as a leader in modernization. As before the war, economic growth and
modernization brought a steady stream of clientele to the attorneys of
Columbus, and Henry Benning 's life was seemingly back on track.

Henry Benning found solace as his time was fully engaged with legal
matters, and he logged many miles between his law office, his home and
the local Courthouse. He and his partner, Edmond H. Worrill, worked
intently as the courts went into session during the summer of 1875.
Benning's legal plate was filled with work and he even filed a personal suit
against the Mayor and Council of the City of Columbus. **67** Benning
balanced several cases and worked late into the evening hours, studying
legal precedence, case backgrounds and preparing his briefs. On July 8,
Benning was ill and weak, suffering with severe diarrhea, yet he continued
to work. Benning had a penchant for canned oysters, and perhaps he
consumed a tainted product. Benning was reported as suffering " intensely"
from " choleretic diarrhoea," which may have been caused by eating tainted
oysters. After he went home that evening, he worked late into the night
preparing for court on the following morning. A close friend, James D.
Waddell commented that Benning " never allowed the morrow's sun to rise
on unfinished work, if it were in his power to complete it today." **68**

On the morning of the July 9, 1875, although he was still ill and probably dehydrated, Benning began his normal routine trotting through town enroute to the Courthouse. Benning made a short cut on Broad Street, darting through Brooks Drug Store. While passing through the store, he suddenly staggered against a barrel, and collapsed, falling to the floor. Mr. John W. Brooks, druggist and proprietor of the store, as well as a gathering crowd of concerned citizens, immediately went to his aid. At first, struggling with a severe chill, pain, and confusion, Benning urged his friends to send word to the court that he " would be there after a little." However, he got worse. Benning was placed in a carriage and brought to his home, just down the street on Broad, the main avenue in downtown Columbus. Doctors Francis Stanford and Eugene J. Colzey, both prominent local physicians, examined Benning and gave what little aid nineteenth century medicine could muster. Facing the realization that " Old Rock " suffered from acute apoplexy, the doctors knew that Benning's condition and prognosis was poor. Referred to today as a massive stroke, Benning's daughters, Mary, Anna Caroline, and Sallie, all looked on in hopeless disbelief. Meanwhile, the aged General, as stalwart as always, fought the ultimate battle of his life. **69**

In spite of Benning's physical and moral strengths, the stress of work, his age, his many burdens and numerous sorrows, combined to erode his health. Benning slipped into unconsciousness. " His appointed time had come. In the midst of family and friends, and in the shadows and stillness of the midnight hour, and without pain and without struggle, he quietly and peacefully passed away." **70** The life of Henry Lewis Benning ended at 3 o'clock A.M., on July 10, 1875. He was sixty-one years old. On that morning, the citizens learned of Benning's fate.

When Benning's former servant," Old Billie " was told that " his General" was dead, he fainted. Perhaps the cause was a combination of old age and the blistering muggy heat of the summer, but the heart wrenching news of Benning's death was certainly a contributing factor. " Old Billie" had served Benning as a slave and cook throughout the war, and afterwards as a free man, he continued his devotion to Benning. One must question why a former servant would be so moved. Yet, Old Billie's motivation is not so surprising when you consider that the man he honored was defined as " a towering figure," " of absolutely crystal truth," and " a braver more chivalrous spirit never breathed." **71**

" Old Billie " was representative of the town, as the citizens of Columbus were all shocked by the sudden loss. The Columbus Bar

Association reported that," the sad news like an electric current, was conveyed from mouth to mouth throughout the city and surrounding countryside that General Benning was dead." Just the morning before, he had been seen in his usual stride walking briskly from his home to the Courthouse " with his books and brief in hand." 72 Throughout Georgia, the shock of Benning's death brought reflections concerning his life's work. The *Atlanta Herald* recorded that:

> General Benning 's life was no ordinary life; his death is no ordinary loss. It is a public calamity; for he was a full grown man, who walked conspicuously in the public eye and filled a large space in the public heart. Georgia has given to the century no man who commanded in a greater measure the confidence, respect and esteem of the people, or to whom those who knew him best in the relations of personal friendship were more devotedly attached. 73

Those who knew and loved him best were his daughters. Five loving daughters, Mary, Anna, Sarah, and the twins, Augusta and Louisa survived Benning. These refined ladies ranged in age from 34 to 20. The love and affection Henry's girls had for their father was deep and abiding. Henry's home reflected their femininity and charm. It was adorned with white Damask linens and drapes, marble topped mahogany furnishings, gilded china, and fine silverware. These items were cherished heirlooms and the few remnants salvaged from the war. Yet, on the beautiful Sabbath morning of July 11, 1875, their home was filled with melancholy, draped in black, and " Old Rock," lying peacefully in his coffin. 74 The *Columbus Sunday Enquirer* informed the citizens of the details concerning the funeral procession:

> The funeral of General Benning will take place this morning at nine o'clock from the late residence on upper Broad Street. Reverend W. C. Hunter, at the house, will read the Episcopal ceremony, when the column will be formed and marched to the cemetery. It is hoped that every Confederate soldier in the city will be in the line. The following is the order of the procession.
> 1. Military companies.
> 2. Confederate soldiers without regard to rank who are willing to honor the dead hero.
> 3. Fire Company No. 5.
> 4. Officiating clergymen.
> 5. The hearse with the remains.

6. The General's horse with military trappings, led by Old
   Billie.
7. The family of the deceased.
8. Pall bearers in carriages.
9. The Judge, members of the Bar and officers of the court.
10. Citizens generally.

As the procession lined up on the street, the summer sun gently rose behind the two-story white frame home of Henry Benning, bathing the town of Columbus in an early morning glow of genuine serenity. Inside, Benning's daughters, donned in their mourning gowns, gazed upon the face of their father one final time. This lion of a man, his face outlined with distinguished white hair and beard," seemed to be sleeping sweetly, and his face was very natural." In tribute to his military service, draped across the foot of the coffin lay a bullet riddled battle flag of the Confederacy. W. C. Hunter, the rector of Trinity Episcopal Church, delivered Benning's eulogy. As the weeping family departed the home and entered their place in the procession, the fantastic display of respect could not be overlooked. A multitude of people had assembled to pay their genuine respects and escort Benning to his final place of rest. 75

At the lead of the funeral procession was Colonel William Shepherd. During the war, Shepherd served under Benning as the respected and heroic commander of the " Columbus Guards," Second Georgia Infantry Regiment. Behind their commander, sharply formed for the march, stood the proud military columns of the " Light Guards " and the " Columbus Guards," many of them veterans of the war and " Benning's Brigade." Behind the military companies, in " caps and belts," stood the 32 members of Fire Company Number 5. Behind them, hundreds of former Confederate soldiers formed in a column of fours. Following the soldiers were the carriages of the clergymen, and the attending physicians. Next, the two-horse hearse in which Benning's coffin was carried was covered in flowers. Directly behind " Old Rock " stood the ever-faithful," Old Billie. " " Old Billie" wearing his Confederate gray coat, led Benning's horse, which was well groomed and prepared completely with sword and military trappings. Next were the pall-bearers (all distinguished gentlemen): Mr. John Peabody ; Judge Porter Ingram ; Mr. G. DeLaunay, Judge Martin J. Crawford ; Colonel W.A. Barden ; Captain Thomas Chaffin ; Colonel M. H. Bland ; and Major Raphael J. Moses. Next, came the carriages of the Benning family, followed by the Mayor, City Council, the Columbus Bar

Association, dozens of carriages filled with friends, and finally hundreds and hundreds of people on foot. And, the local newspaper noted that," The colored people were out in force." The editor of the *Columbus Enquirer* eloquently summed up the funeral procession with:

> Columbus, in all its history, has never witnessed such a
> numerous multitude of sorrowing citizens in the funeral train of
> any of its dead. The grief was universal. The high and the low,
> the rich and the poor, black and white, all denominations and
> associations, religious, social, and military-all with heartfelt
> sorrow joined the solemn train as it moved towards the final
> resting place of their friend.

> The funeral train slowly traversed the eight-block route, winding
> gently up hill, to its ultimate destination, Linwood Cemetery.
> The muffled military drums accompanied the solemn
> procession, finally reaching the Benning section, near the center
> of the cemetery. With the sun now glowing with full intensity, a
> graveside service was read, and the Columbus Guards rendered
> the final military salute for General Henry Lewis Benning.
> Henry was laid to rest beside his dear wife, Mary. The town of
> Columbus rendered their final respects, and returned to their
> lives with " a void no one can fill." **76**

A prominent Georgia Judge, Logan E. Bleckley was so moved by Benning's death, he honored him with this poem:

ON GENERAL HENRY L. BENNING

Poor Southern eyes, already red
With weeping for your noble dead,
If tears are left you yet to shed,
Give some to soothe this latest woe-
For gallant Benning let them flow.

Ah, death that spared him in the fight,
Has struck, in peace, a Georgia knight-
As knightly as the proudest lord
That ever lifted lance or sword;
No truer, braver chief than he
Adorned the ancient chivalry.

For firmness in the battle shock,
His comrades said he was a *rock*;
Old Rock, they said, and his command
(Whoever fled) were sure to stand;
And never was that hope betrayed
By Rock himself, or his brigade.

The tricks of war he did not learn;
In stubborn valor, grim and stern,
He trusted as the pious priest
Reposeth in the blood of Christ;
To him it seemed no fight could fail
If not a single heart would quail.

When vainer warriors would assume
The wreath, the star, the sash, and plume,
He moved among his soldiers gray,
As plain and unadorned as they;
Nor cared to shine, or to excel,
Except in doing duty well.

Additionally, in a touching tribute published by the Supreme Court of
Georgia, the question was asked," what manner of a monument should be
erected for Benning?" The esteemed gentlemen recorded that:

Brass is not durable enough; marble is not white enough! Let the
sterling traits of his character, as stamped upon the memory of
his countrymen, stand as his monument. Truth, integrity,
courage, moral and physical, unimpeachable veracity, honor and
honesty untarnished, all these were eminently his, and these will
endure forever; and let them stand as an imperishable monument
to the memory of an honest man. 77

A monument was never erected for Benning. As the judges declared,
his reputation will " endure forever." Yet, today, while many people
connect his name with the military post, Fort Benning, located just outside
Columbus, his reputation, his life, has faded from the modern world. Even
in his hometown, the historical marker that once pointed to the location of
his home and briefly described the man, is gone. The modern world of

progress has replaced the entire block where he lived and died. Benning's daughters placed a remarkably descriptive tombstone on his grave. Its simplistic form and brief remarks provide us with a graphic reminder of a genuinely honorable and well-loved man.

The headstone directly reflects the character of Benning. It commandingly faces the eastern sky. It is simple, yet stately. It is tall and prominent, but not obnoxious. It is solid and thick, yet clean edged, smoothly polished, and geometrically proportionate. It is a single monolith of Confederate gray granite, which rises above all others in its immediate vicinity. In the center is etched his name, his military rank and his sobriquet," Old Rock. " Below, a slab covers the tomb, which states, his name, his parents, dates of his birth and death, and finally the statement," This Was a Man." Certainly, Benning was a man among men. He is justly included in Northern's *Men of Mark in Georgia*. Fort Benning, which houses the U.S. Army Infantry School, is named for the man. As General Benning, commander of one of the finest Confederate brigades in Lee's Army of Northern Virginia, he earned the affectionate sobriquet," Old Rock." The name was bestowed upon him as a tribute, from his own men, who proudly followed him into the mortal hell of war. His military accomplishments at the Devil's Den, Burnside's Bridge, Chickamauga and other cauldrons of gore, are testaments of his spirit and courage. Before the war, as a Georgia Supreme Court Justice, Benning earned an enviable reputation as a champion of truth and justice. His jurisprudence, intellect and honesty are legendary in the annals of Georgia law, and his opinions concerning constitutional interpretation continue today. As a devoted husband, loving father, generous friend, accomplished lawyer, successful planter, and respected resident of Columbus, Georgia," no man in our city is loved like he." **78**

In our nineteenth century society, referring to someone as being " a man," was a great complement and reserved solely for men who rose well above their peers. Throughout the life of Henry Lewis Benning, his letters, speeches, opinions and deeds, reflect one singular undeniable fact... " This was a man." **79**

Chapter 20

Epilogue

Henry Lewis Benning was survived by his five daughters: Miss Mary Howard Benning; Miss Anna Caroline Benning; Mrs. Augusta Jones (Benning) Crawford; Mrs. Louisa Vivian (Benning) Spencer; and Miss Sarah " Sallie" Jones Benning. Mary, Anna and Sarah still lived at home, while the twins, Louisa and Augusta were married and living in their own homes. At the age of 34, Mary was the eldest and she served as the Administratix for her father's estate. Just like most of Henry Benning 's male kinsmen, he died intestate. Therefore, by law, Mary was required to create an " inventory and appraisement" of all of her father's possessions, conduct a " sheriff's sale" or auction of his properties, maintain an audited list of the estate's debits and credits, and record the affairs of the estate with the Muscogee County Court. 1 Mary Benning was kept very busy during the next several years as she untangled the many financial transactions, legal affairs, and property holdings of her deceased father. Adding to her burdens was the unresolved estate of her grandfather, Seaborn Jones, whose estate affairs had been passed through the responsibilities of her mother, her brother, her father, and ultimately to her.

The property listings of Seaborn Jones were vast and many remain a mystery. Jones maintained receipts and unrecorded deeds for thousands of acres of land, of which, many were located in the former Creek lands of Alabama. Some of the land was apparently purchased through barters, and the family eventually surrendered any claim to them, listing them in the estate inventory as " wild and abandoned." 2 When Mary accepted her Administratrix responsibilities, the estate of Seaborn Jones was nearly complete, with the exception of the sale of the City Mills property. For years, the Benning and Jones family leased the property, and it was finally sold in 1882, to the Eagle and Phenix Manufacturing Company for, $25,000. 3 The old family mansion," El Dorado " remained virtually abandoned and uninhabited from 1868 until 1878, gradually falling into a sad state of disrepair. Finally, in July of 1878, Captain James J. and Lelia B. Slade purchased the former mansion for $1500, from Louis F. Garrard. The old mansion was repaired, converted into a private school for girls, and its name was changed from " El Dorado" to " St. Elmo," in honor of Augusta Jane Evans novel, *St. Elmo.* 4 Today, the home is a private residence, and it remains a beautiful gem in the midst of the many architectural treasures of Columbus. It is interesting to note that another home owned by the Bennings and used as a rental property was known as the " Savannah House." Located in the historic district of downtown Columbus, it too is a unique and beautiful antebellum home.

It was in the realm of real estate that Mary faced her most daunting challenges, which took her thirteen years to complete. Ultimately, by 1882, she sold her father and grandfather's properties, which included, 3,438 acres, comprising 53 pieces of property, and totaling $76,725. 5 The value of these properties today would be measured in millions of dollars. An affluent suburban residential area known as Green Island Hills currently occupies the land that was the old Benning plantation . Other Benning properties were scattered throughout downtown Columbus and again, their value today would be astonishing. At the mandatory estate auction, Henry Benning 's law library sold for $900, and the bulk of his worldly belongings passed into the hands of his fellow citizens. His children were financially cared for, as Henry Benning also had a life insurance policy of $10,000 and each child received $1,000 cash through the estate. 6 To place the above values in their proper context, in 1875, an adequate home could be purchased for $1,000, and farm land sold for $3.50 to $5.00 per acre.

In the conduct of her duties as the Administratrix of the estate, Miss Mary Benning received a great deal of professional advice and support from her father's friends. Henry Benning 's former law partner, Edmond H. Worrill assisted her, as did Attorneys Louis F. Garrard, Raphael Moses, and Martin J. Crawford. For example, when the Benning home on Broad Street was entered in the requisite estate auction on December 7, 1875, Louis F. Garrard won the high bid and obtained the home for $2000. 7 On January 4, 1876, Garrard sold the house back to the three unwed Benning sisters, Mary, Anna and Sarah, for $666 each. 8 Garrard assisted the Benning's generously, and purchased several properties simply to help the girls maintain a semblance of their family's legacy. In postwar Columbus, while the cotton mills made a rapid return to prosperity, the average citizens experienced severe economic difficulties as consumer prices and taxes remained high, while simultaneously, the value of private land and homes depreciated. Except for close friends of the family, the Benning girls were literally " on their own." Their champions were men like Louis

F. Garrard who purchased Benning properties at auction, although his
underlying motivation was to keep the properties for the Benning girls.
Garrard's actions were chivalrous, yet, with high taxes, and a difficult
economy, he was soon forced to sell them at a loss. For example, in
January 2, 1877, Louis Garrard purchased the former Benning and Jones
mansion," El Dorado," and its accompanying 175-acre tract of land for
$2,708. Then, in July 23, 1878, Garrard sold the same property for $1500.
9 All of these transactions were perfectly legal, they are simply listed to
highlight the respect and assistance Louis F. Garrard and several others
extended to the daughters of their old friend, Henry Benning.

Mary, Anna, and " Sallie" lived comfortably at the Benning home on
Broad Street, where they attended Trinity Episcopal Church and engaged
in numerous social organizations and functions. Mary and Anna
energetically pursued interests in genealogy and historical research, while
their younger sister, Sallie was preoccupied with a young man, Herbert
Ladson Hull, and on April 18, 1881, they were married. Shortly thereafter,
the Hulls moved to Fort Worth, Texas, where they remained for the
duration of their lives. 10 Anna and Mary never married, and they spent
their entire lives living on Broad Street, in Columbus. Filled with a passion
for Genealogy and History, Anna and Mary remained committed to their
father, and they spent their adulthood honoring the memory of he, his
comrades, and their cause. Both Anna and Mary participated heavily in the
local Lizzie Rutherford Chapter of the United Daughters of the
Confederacy, the Colonial Dames, and the Daughters of the American
Revolution . Mary Howard Benning even worked professionally as a
Genealogist, and assisted other ladies who desired to document the lives of
their ancestors. 11 It was she, the eldest, who was the first of Henry
Benning's daughters, to die. Mary had lived her entire life in Columbus,
Georgia and she was ever faithful in decorating the graves and honoring
the memories of the Confederate dead. She succumbed to pneumonia at the
age of eighty-five, and died on February 5, 1927. She was buried beside
her parents in the Benning section of Linwood Cemetery. 12

Meanwhile, the other Benning sisters, Mrs. Reese Crawford (Augusta
Jones Benning) and Mrs. Samuel Spencer (Louisa Vivian Benning) busily
tended to family affairs and raised their children. Augusta remained in
Columbus where her husband Reese was a prominent attorney. One of
their children, Henry Benning Crawford, became a highly respected civil
engineer and he served two terms as the city manager of Columbus,
Georgia (1922 and 1926-1933). 13 Augusta Jones (Benning) Crawford

died on March 7, 1928, and she was buried in the Crawford family section of Linwood Cemetery.

Louisa Vivian Benning was the wife of Samuel Spencer. Spencer was the only son of Lambert and Verona Spencer, prominent members of Columbus, Georgia and friends of the Bennings and Jones families. As a young man, during the Civil War, Spencer served in the cavalry alongside Louis F. Garrard and G. Gunby Jordan, all under the command of Nathan Bedford Forrest. After the war, Spencer graduated with top honors from both the University of Georgia and the University of Virginia, and secured a reputation as an excellent civil engineer. Returning to Columbus, Georgia, Spencer worked for a short while for the Columbus Waterworks. Samuel Spencer and Louisa Vivian Benning had known each other for a long time; they fell in love, and were married on February 6, 1872. Due to his heavy work schedule and his drive to achieve, the couple delayed their honeymoon and Sam went to work on the railroad. For the next several years, he ascended the ranks of the railroad industry, piloted the Southern Railway to its heights and " at the time of his death, he was president of six railway corporations, and a member of the board of directors of nineteen others." 14 Spencer was truly a " captain of industry " in the railroads. He was honored for his rigid work ethics and his integrity. Additionally, his employees were totally committed to Spencer as he never forgot the importance of his employees, and was genuinely endeared to them. In 1906, Samuel Spencer died in a train accident on Thanksgiving Day. In addition to his wife Louisa, he left behind three children, Henry Benning Spencer, Vernona Mitchell Spencer, and Vivian Spencer. 15

Louisa Vivian (Benning) Spencer was an equally remarkable person as was her husband, Samuel. As a young lady, Louisa was well educated and joined her mother and sisters in the support of the Confederacy during the Civil War. After the war, she was a charter member of the Ladies' Memorial Association and the Lizzie Rutherford Chapter of the United Daughters of the Confederacy. She bore frequent moves and lengthy separations as her husband climbed the difficult ladder of success in the railroad industry. Eventually, after her husband achieved success and wealth, they settled in Washington D.C, where they lived on fashionable Massachusetts Avenue. Louisa was of durable Southern stock, yet elegant and a lady of high prominence in Washington and New York social circles. She was a member of numerous social organizations, a friend of the arts, a collector of paintings, books, and Chinese porcelains. " In church, civic, and charitable work, Mrs. Spencer was always lending her support and efforts, both financially and otherwise." 16 Mrs. Spencer died on September 9, 1919 and she was buried in Oak Hill Cemetery, in Washington D.C. 17

Of all Henry Benning 's daughters, one stands out for her devotion to the memory of her father and the South that she loved so dearly. Remaining in her home town of Columbus, for her entire life, Anna Caroline Benning was referred to as the " Mother of Patriotic Organizations," but her friends called her " Miss Tiny." **18** Anna inherited not only her mother's small frame, but also her iron will and hard work ethics. Anna Caroline never married and she spent her life as a " leader in every patriotic and cultural movement in Columbus." **19** Miss Benning founded the Columbus chapter of the *Colonial Dames of America*, the Oglethorpe Chapter of the Daughters of the American Revolution, and she served at the post of Regent for twelve years. Anna also held important posts in the D.A.R., at the national and state levels as well. " Inspired by her devotion to her father's memory and her own loyalty to the Southern Confederacy," she organized the Lizzie Rutherford Chapter, United Daughters of the Confederacy, in her home, serving as its President from its inception in 1895, until her death in 1935. In 1888, she joined with 35 other ladies and founded the *Woman's Reading Club of Columbus, Georgia* . Their charter states," With a desire to investigate for ourselves the leading questions of the day, and to attain and to enjoy a higher intellectual, social and moral culture, we, whose names are hereto appended, do form ourselves into a Society. **20** The ladies established very strict by-laws and they wrote a Constitution which spelled out exacting rules by which their organization operated. As Miss Benning's father had declared to the public while serving as a member of the *Columbus Literary Committee* in 1837," women are great readers, and they will converse what they read." Henry Benning encouraged all of his children to read, and Anna excelled in the arts and literature.

Miss Benning also served two terms as the Georgia U.D.C. Vice-President, and from 1917 till her death, she was the Honorary President of the Georgia Division of the U.D.C. Miss Benning was instrumental in recording the history of the Ladies' Memorial Association, the Soldiers' Aid Society and in 1898, the first work of her U.D.C. Chapter was the publication of the *History of the Origin of Memorial Day*. In its preface, Miss Benning wrote:

> The mission of the UDC is to record the deeds of the true and
> the brave who bore the star-gemmed cross of Dixie. It is
> therefore meet that the first work of the Chapter be a gift to the
> world of the story of the woman who originated that Sabbath of

the South, Memorial Day, which the nation has found so appropriate that it has incorporated it with holidays under the name Decoration Day . **21**

Anna Benning worked diligently to record the deeds of Lizzie Rutherford, her mother, and all the women of Columbus who toiled through the difficult years of the Civil War. Miss Benning also wrote the biography of her father for Northern's impressive work, *Men of Mark in Georgia*. **22** Miss Benning was also instrumental in the establishment of a permanent marker honoring the Confederate dead. In Columbus, on April 2, 1879, the Memorial Association met on lower Broad Street, in a designated park to honor the Confederacy. The foundation of the monument was laid on this occasion, and Anna watched as her sisters and nephew, each laid bricks in honor of her mother, father and grandmother. Mrs. Reese Crawford placed a brick " in memory of her grandmother, Mrs. Seaborn Jones. " Miss Mary H. Benning placed a brick " in memory of her mother, Mrs. Henry L. Benning," and Master Henry Benning Crawford laid a brick " in memory of his grandfather, General Henry L. Benning. " **23** In 1918, when Camp Benning was first organized and named in honor of General Henry L. Benning, Miss Anna Caroline Benning hoisted the first flag flown over the newly designated U.S. Army installation known today as Fort Benning. **24** Miss Benning's UDC scrapbooks, medals, and memorabilia are archived in the Simon Schwob Library, Manuscript collections 22 and 28, Columbus State University. Miss Anna Caroline Benning died of pneumonia on February 8, 1935. She was buried beside her sisters, her parents and her brother, in Linwood Cemetery, and her obituary in the local newspaper recorded that Anna Benning was " one of the most picturesque and beloved women of the state." **25**

At the age of ninety-four, the last surviving daughter of Henry L. Benning, Sarah (Sallie) Jones (Benning) Hull, died on May 16, 1949. Her obituary noted that her only surviving relatives in Columbus was her nephew, Henry Benning Crawford and her cousin, Mrs. Anna Vivian (Jones) Pease. Mrs. Pease was the wife of J. Norman Pease, the last child born at " El Dorado," and the youngest daughter of Colonel John A. Jones and Mary Louisa (Leonard) Jones. Sallie (Benning) Hull was returned to her hometown of Columbus and buried beside her parents in Linwood Cemetery. **26**

In addition to his five daughters, when Henry Benning died, his brother Richard Edwin Benning and his sister, Augusta Palmyra (Benning) Patterson also survived him. Richard Edwin Benning remained in Harris County, Georgia, where he farmed for his entire life. He and his wife, Frances " Fanny" Simpson, had a large farm located southwest of Shiloh,

Georgia where they grew primarily, cotton and corn. They also raised several children and the entire family is buried in a small, isolated, and private cemetery on their old farm. Richard Edwin Benning died on June 21, 1892. **27** After the Civil War, Benning's sister Augusta Palmyra, moved with her husband Madison L. Patterson to a plantation, just across the Chattahoochee River, near Cottonton, Alabama. Their home was known as " Wexford," located at Oswichee, Russell County, Alabama, where they raised five children. Augusta died on November 17, 1902, and she was buried beside her husband in the Patterson section of Linwood Cemetery. **28**

Another woman of note that survived Henry Benning was his wife's talented cousin, Augusta Jane Evans. Shortly after attending the Garrard-Leonard wedding in Columbus, Augusta was married too. On December 2, 1868, Augusta was wed to an old friend and neighbor, Madison Lorenzo Wilson. Mr. Wilson was considerably older than Augusta (27 years), but he was a gentleman, a wealthy Mobile business man, and they spent many happy years together in their mansion," Ashland." Augusta continued to write novels, but none of her latter novels achieved the success of *St. Elmo*. Augusta also wrote *Vashti* (1869), *Infelice* (1875), *At the Mercy of Tiberius* (1887), *A Speckled Bird* (1902), and *Devota* (1907). Mr. Wilson died in 1891, and Augusta Jane (Evans) Wilson followed her husband in death, the day after her seventy-fourth birthday, May 9, 1909. She is buried in Magnolia Cemetery, Mobile, Alabama. **29**

Following the death of Henry L. Benning, many of his friends continued their efforts in Georgia law and political affairs. Louis F. Garrard went on to become not only a renowned Columbus attorney, but he also served as a county commissioner of Muscogee County from 1872 until 1907. Garrard was also elected to the Georgia House of Representatives, and he served as the Speaker of the House in 1882 and 1883. In the state legislature, Garrard served on the finance committee, where he authored the " Baby Bond Bill," a law that reduced the state debt. In 1892 and 1900, Garrard was elected as a delegate to the Democratic convention, where he authored several party planks at the national level. In 1894, Louis Garrard ran for a seat in the U.S. Senate, but he was defeated. In personal matters, Garrard led an honorable life as a husband and father, and he also helped the surviving members of the Benning family. He freely provided Benning's daughters, especially Mary, Anna and " Sallie," with sound financial and legal assistance for many years after the death of their father. Louis Garrard lived his entire adult life in the former Leonard mansion known as " Wildwood," and a large portion of his well-manicured estate is now the grounds of the Country Club of Columbus. Both the Garrards and Leonards were horse lovers, and they maintained a large stable on the estate as well as a pond for fishing and a pool for swimming. In front of the home are a circle of large trees, and Garrard equally divided the property into lots for his children, and his descendants currently occupy several of these lots. Louis F. Garrard 's wife," Annie," Anna Foster (Leonard) Garrard, died on May 9, 1908, and he followed her in death, shortly thereafter on August 1, 1908. Louis and Anna Garrard were both buried in Linwood Cemetery, alongside their parents, and other members of the Leonard and Garrard families. The Leonard and Garrard plots are located directly adjacent to the Jones and Benning family section. **30**

While the physical structure of " Wildwood " is but a memory, evidence of the old mansion can still be found. Remnants of its architectural framework lie strewn upon the grounds, and restoration plans are currently underway. A grandson of Louis F. Garrard, Leonard Garrard fondly recalls the glory of the old mansion and he provided the author with an informative tour of the old neighborhood. Garrard fondly recalls the days of swimming in the pond and riding horses on the grounds of the old homestead. While the days of Leonard Garrard 's youth are but a sweet memory, the flora of " Wildwood" continues its perennial display of vibrant beauty. Originally bred years ago, and handsomely placed along the grounds, are hybrid Camellias and Azaleas. Wildwood Circle is lined with grand, stately hardwoods and ancient palms. These towering trees surround the drive, providing a refuge for a multitude of birds, and they gently diffuse sunlight throughout the grounds. The same drive that brought carriages filled with hoop-skirted ladies and their gentlemen escorts to " Wildwood" still meanders along the same quiet, sandy, unpaved path that cars travel today. Nearby, Leonard's Spring continues to pulse forth a cool clean stream, which slowly ambles its way down through the city below. Today, the Historic District from Wynnton to Rose Hill is a residential area resplendent with reminders of its glorious past and continuing contribution to the beauty of Columbus.

Henry Benning 's closest friends were his fellow residents of Columbus and in addition to Louis F. Garrard, Benning's closest confidants were Raphael J. Moses and Martin J. Crawford. Moses served several terms in the Georgia legislature, where he represented his district with distinction. On October 13, 1893, while visiting his daughter in Brussels, Belgium, Raphael J. Moses died. Moses had arranged in his will to be as economically prudent as possible concerning his funeral. Moses even specified that his coffin should be a plain pine box, and his funeral, simple and private. Per his request, the money saved was thus donated to a

Jewish Orphanage in Atlanta, as he was proud of his Jewish ancestry. Moses was buried as he requested, in his family's private cemetery on the grounds of his plantation," Esquiline. " Years later, the U.S. Government purchased the entire lands that once comprised the vast Moses plantation. In 1918, the U.S. Army established Camp Benning, and the Moses properties were included in the incorporation of the sprawling military complex. While World War I was waging, Stanford E. Moses, USN, Commander of the U.S.S. Cincinnati, and a descendant of Raphael Moses, learned that the old family homestead had been appropriated and condemned. The family was informed by the U.S. Army that," We expect to give absolute value of this place, outside of the 'sentimental value' as you realize the rifle range has no sentimental value to the government- that is when it comes to buying the property." 31 Today, the government ensures the sanctity of dozens of private cemeteries which were incorporated into Fort Benning when the post was formed. In recent years, Fort Benning has reduced its land mass, and the former Moses property is now privately owned.

Martin J. Crawford was Benning's closest friend. Benning's daughter Augusta married Crawford's son Reese, and they named their son Henry Benning Crawford in the honor of his grandfather. Shortly after Henry Benning died, Martin J. Crawford replaced his old nemesis, James Johnson on the bench of the Superior Court of the Chattahoochee circuit, and Benning would have enjoyed that situation. For years after Benning's death, Crawford provided assistance and advice to Benning's family, as if they were his own. For the next five years, Crawford served an honorable term as Judge of the Chattahoochee, and in 1880, Governor Alfred H. Colquitt appointed Crawford to the Supreme Court. Martin J. Crawford resided on the bench until July 22, 1883, when he succumbed to a lengthy illness and died. Crawford was buried amongst his friends and family in Linwood Cemetery, Columbus, Georgia. 32

While Henry Benning had numerous influential acquaintances, most of his close friends lived in Columbus. He also had several important friends beyond the city with which he maintained warm relations. One of these men was Alexander H. Stephens. While he and Benning differed somewhat in political ideology, their mutual respect and admiration for one another was deep. Stephens maintained a life-long service to the State of Georgia, and he served as Georgia's Governor from 1882-1883. Stephens died while in office, on March 4, 1883. Another close friend of Benning's, Robert Toombs, served in several congressional conventions and continued

to provide colorful speeches and words of wisdom, until he died on
September 30, 1885. Toombs's son-in-law, and Benning's Fifteenth
Georgia regimental commander, Dudley M. DuBose served as a U.S.
Representative from Georgia, and he died on March 2, 1883. **33**

Since the death of Henry Benning, his memory has been honored in
many ways. Officially, by proclamation of the Mayor of Columbus, April
2nd, Benning's birthday, is known as " General Henry L. Benning Day,"
however, its official celebrations have dwindled to small gatherings and
memorials held in Linwood Cemetery. In Columbus, Georgia, until a few
short years ago, a memorial marker honoring Benning, stood near the
location of his home on Broad Street ; however, the marker has been
removed and that section of town is now occupied by a corporate office
complex. Over the years, organizations including the Confederate
Veterans, United Daughters of the Confederacy, and the Sons of
Confederate Veterans have all named camps, chapters and memorial
tributes in honor of Benning. In 1912, the Georgia Division of the United
Daughters of the Confederacy desired to erect a monument to memorialize
the Confederacy. After years of debate, the ladies decided to create a
monument carved from the massive granite on Stone Mountain, just
outside of Atlanta. The project was immensely expensive and at one point
President Calvin Coolidge supported the project by endorsing the sale of
memorial coins. The project was delayed by World War I, but eventually
Augustus Lukeman was hired to carve the largest bas-relief sculpture, the
world had ever seen. Originally, the project was designed to include
Confederate leaders of Georgia. Among those to be carved into the
memorial were Generals Henry L. Benning, John B. Gordon, Ambrose R.
Wright, Thomas R. R. Cobb, and Pierce Young. Over the years, the project
funding waned and the sculptor died, leaving the project unfinished,
however, depictions of three of the primary Confederate leaders were
completed. Thus, President Jefferson Davis, General Robert E. Lee and
General Thomas J. " Stonewall" Jackson now grace the massive memorial
of Stone Mountain. The monument is a glorious work of art and it does not
appear to be unfinished, however, had the project been completed as
planned, it would also honor Henry Benning. **34**

The United States Army bestowed one of the most lasting and well-
known tributes to the memory of Henry Benning. In 1918, as World War I
raged in Europe, General John J. Pershing sent an urgent request to
Washington requesting that troops be thoroughly trained before being
shipped to his command. The U.S. Army responded with the establishment
of several camps of military instruction. During the Spanish-American
War, the army had trained soldiers near Columbus, Georgia, and the area
was selected as an excellent location to train Infantry troops for the

battlefields of Europe. Soon, the lands were secured, facilities erected and troops forwarded for training. The only thing lacking was a name. On October 19, 1918, Camp Benning was officially established, and upon the suggestion of Mrs. J. E. Minter, a member of the Columbus chapter of the UDC, the U.S. Government heartily agreed that the camp should be named in honor of Henry Lewis Benning. In 1918, there were many surviving veterans of the Civil War and none disagreed with the name of Benning. Few men better exemplified the desired traits of an Infantry soldier than General Henry Benning did. Not only was he a military hero, but he had served as a forthright judge, and whether in the courtroom or on the battlefield, he poured his heart into his efforts. Few men better represent the values of honor, integrity, and courage than Henry Benning, and he was respected both north and south for his virtues and his spirit. In tribute to her father, Miss Anna Caroline Benning was selected to hoist the first flag to fly over the newly named military camp of instruction, and with that act, Camp Benning was officially begun. Camp Benning grew and in 1922, became Fort Benning, a permanent military installation and the world's leading institution of professional military instruction. Among the numerous courses taught there, are Infantry tactics and Military History, which includes analytical studies of the battles, fought by Henry Benning. During World War II, a Liberty Ship was named in honor of Benning. The *S.S. Henry L. Benning*, United States Merchant Marine 0946, was built in Baltimore, Maryland and went into service on March 9, 1943. The ship hauled cargo and troops throughout the Pacific theater, but alas, there are only several Liberty Ships still in existence, and Benning's maritime namesake is no more. **35**

In Columbus, Georgia, Henry Benning is regarded as one of the most renowned and revered members of the community. Perhaps the most memorable local tribute to " Old Rock " was the honor and affection displayed by Benning's former servant," Old Billie. " The fact that a man shackled in servitude, when freed, chose to honor the man that bound him reflects a genuine tribute, which no monument can display. An emotional bond of mutual respect existed between these men and their relationship reflects the complexity and passions that wrought the era in which they lived. Since Benning's death, the City of Columbus has continued to officially honor the memory of Henry Benning. Over the years, several establishments and community icons have honored his name and many U.D.C. and S.C.V. camps have been named in his honor. Until a few short years ago, a memorial marker honoring Benning, stood near the location of

his home on 1420 Broad Street ; however, the marker has been removed
and that section of town is now occupied by a modern corporate office
complex.

Through the passage of time, the name and deeds of Henry Benning
have waned in the public eye. However, those who study history have not
forgotten Benning's many contributions to the region he so deeply loved.
On March 29, 1999, a memorial service was held in Linwood Cemetery
honoring General Henry L. Benning. The service was sponsored by the
Columbus Guards, the General Henry L. Benning Camp 517, Sons of
Confederate Veterans, the Lizzie Rutherford Chapter No. 60, United
Daughters of the Confederacy, and the Chattahoochee Valley Area Civil
War Roundtable. While the Mayor did not attend the service, he issued a
proclamation honoring the memory of Henry Benning and it was read
aloud. The service was exemplary, dignified and conducted in period
costumes. 36 These organizations plan to annually conduct a memorial
service for Henry Benning, and maintain public awareness of his
contributions.

While this manuscript was being written, the author was reminded
that a biography is never complete as long as you continue to search and
discover the past. As noted throughout the narrative, the histories of Henry
L. Benning and the city of Columbus, Georgia are inherently entwined.
Recently, the City of Columbus embarked on a civil engineering project
known as the Second Avenue Revitalization Project. An important element
of the project included a complete archaeological survey of the area
undergoing transformation, which just happened to include the remnants of
Benning's former house on Broad Street. The resulting excavations
provided the citizens of Columbus with a unique perspective of the history
and heritage buried beneath the streets of the city. Publicly presented
February 27 through May 7, 2000, an exhibition was held at the Columbus
Museum entitled, *Digging History: The Archaeology of Columbus*. The
exhibit highlighted the archaeological amalgamation of several distinct
cultures, which had previously inhabited the same terrain. Within very
close proximity, items of various social and ethnic groups produced an
interesting study concerning the contrast in various lifestyles. The exhibit
included ancient Indian pottery, antebellum bottles, buttons, belt buckles
and combs, which were all excavated, as the area was prepared for modern
construction. This section of downtown Columbus, located along the east
bank of the Chattahoochee River, was previously inhabited by Indians,
African-American slaves, common mill workers, as well as prominent
families and homes of affluent citizens. Henry L. Benning owned one of
these homes, and the excavation of the area presented many unique and
interesting articles. Among the items discovered and prominently

displayed in the exhibit was a large, polished, white marble urn. This urn was discovered in the ruins of Benning's well. Wells are archaeological treasures because throughout history, humans have always disposed of items within them. Yet, their contents often yield strange items and thus present even greater mysteries concerning the past. Little is known concerning the marble urn (large planter) and its connection with Henry Benning. What is certain however, is that throughout the history of the South, the Indians, slaves, aristocrats, common citizens and the towns in which they lived, are forever entwined and full of mystery. 37

By exploring the people and events of our past, we learn more about our diverse and complex social intricacies that are so uniquely American. The story of Henry Lewis Benning and the time in which he lived continues to intrigue us. In particular, the great conflict of the 1860s lacerated the united body of our nation and the repercussions are still haunting our society today. Moreover, the social and psychological wounds our nation suffered have never fully healed, yet the resulting scars have served to strengthen the heart of this great experiment known as American Democracy. Through the horrible ordeal of war, champions on both sides of the great issues emerged. Among these men were many that history regards as relevant to the story, yet one of the lesser known was Henry L. Benning. His unique legacy belongs to each American citizen, as Benning was a man who was admired and respected by everyone, North or South and black or white. A genuine affection and interest in General " Old Rock " Benning, as well as the society in which he lived continues today.

A visit to Columbus, Georgia to tour the town Henry Benning called home is time well spent. While the city is very progressive and filled with all of the modern amenities, it also contains a beautiful historic district. The city is filled with elegant homes where visitors can " step back into time" and marvel at the beauty of antebellum Georgia. The old mansion," El Dorado " looks just like it did when Henry and Mary Benning lived there, and amazingly, it is still used as a modern, private residence. Many other historic homes and points of interest can be visited while in Columbus. Make sure that you visit historic Linwood Cemetery where you can find the graves of most of the people mentioned in this book. It is here that you will also locate the final resting-place of Henry Benning. He lies in eternal sleep surrounded by his family and friends. As previously stated, Benning's Confederate gray marker well represents the character of " Old Rock " himself. Its angular girth and polished granite effectively express the virtues of honor, strength and durability. While Benning's tomb is handsomely built, there are many others that shoot taller into the sky and cast shadows down below. Some markers are quite elaborate and Linwood Cemetery contains the graves of many exemplary people, including two other Confederate generals. Despite the multitude of graves and ornate markers located within the distinguished garden of stone, Benning's grave is not difficult to locate. Ultimately, his is the only marker that states:

Major General
Henry Lewis Benning
" Old Rock "
" This Was a Man "

Abbreviations Used in the Notes:

B&L - Johnson, Robert Underwood, and Clarence Clough Buel, eds. Battles and Leaders of the Civil War . 4 vols. New York, 1887-88.

BP - Henry L. Benning Papers. Southern Historical Society Collection. Wilson Library. University of North Carolina. Chapel Hill, North Carolina.

CMH - *Confederate Military History: A Library of Confederate States History, Written by Distinguished Men of the South.* Vol. 6, Georgia. Evans, General Clement A. ed. Atlanta, Ga. Confederate Publishing Company, 1899.

CSU - Columbus State University Archives. Chattahoochee Valley Historical Collection. Simon Schwob Library. Columbus, Georgia.

DU - Duke University Archives. Durham, North Carolina.

GA - Georgia Department of Archives and History. Atlanta, Georgia.

LC - Library of Congress. Washington D.C.

NA - National Archives. Compiled Military Service Records (U.S. and Confederate), Confederate States of America Collection and Federal Census Bureau Records. Washington D.C.

OR U.S. War Department. The War of the Rebellion: *A Compilation of the Official Records of the Union and Confederate Armies.* 127 vols., index, and atlas. Washington, D.C., 1880-1901.

UGA - University of Georgia Archives. Hargrett Library. Athens, Georgia.

UNC - University of North Carolina. Wilson Library. Chapel Hill, North Carolina.

End Notes

Introduction

1. *Columbus Daily Enquirer*, July 10, 11, 13 and 17, 1875; *Atlanta Herald*, July 11, 1875; Georgia Reports, Vol. LVI, July term, 1876, pp. 694-99, *Georgia Bar Association, 33rd Annual Meeting Session, June 1-3, 1916.*

2. Northern, *Men of Mark in Georgia*, Vol. 3, pp. 256-66. Avery, *The History of the State of Georgia*, pp. 77 & 215. BP, Benning to E.P. Alexander, notes concerning the Battle of Gettysburg, letter from Henry L. Benning to Edward P. Alexander. OR, Vol. XXVII, parts 1-3 (official reports of Generals Benning, Longstreet and Lee). *Columbus Daily Enquirer-Sun*, July 10, 1875.

3. *Columbus Daily Enquirer*, July 11, 1875; *Atlanta Herald*, July 11, 1875. Northern, *Men of Mark in Georgia*, Vol. 3, pp. 256-66.

4. GA, *Georgia Reports*, Vol. LVI, July term, 1876, pp. 694-99; *Columbus Daily Enquirer*, July 10, 11, 13 and 17, 1875; *Atlanta Herald*, July 11, 1875.

5. Benning family bible, death record of Henry L. Benning, verified with Muscogee County Sexton's office, as well as NA census data. CSU, MC 28, UDC, Lizzie Rutherford Chapter, scrapbook, 1928, description of Mary Howard (Jones) Benning and her contributions to Columbus, Georgia; portrait of Mary Howard (Jones) Benning, private collection of Mr. Henry Spencer.

6. *Columbus Enquirer, Centennial Special*, photo of Benning's home, 1420 Broad Street. Muscogee County deed for Lot 194, John King to Henry L. Benning, June 9 1868; Book R, entry 412, Mary H. Benning (daughter and Administratrix to Louis Garrard, December 7, 1875, county estate record sale, Journal U, 1875-77.

7. Berry, *Records of Marriages, Baptism and Burials from the First Register of Trinity Parish* (1836-1903); *Columbus Daily Enquirer*, July 10, 11, 13 and 17, 1875; *Atlanta Herald*, July 11, 1875. GA, *Georgia Reports*, Vol. LVI, July term, 1876, pp. 694-99. GA, *Georgia Bar Association, 33rd Annual Session*, June 1-3, 1916.

8. CSU archives, Linwood Cemetery records, Columbus, Georgia; death and funeral data concerning Henry L. Benning; *Columbus Daily Enquirer*, July 13, 1875.

9. GA, *Georgia Bar Association, Twelfth Annual Meeting (1895) and Twenty-Sixth Annual Meeting (1909)*, poem by Judge Logan Edwin Bleckley, p. 153; GA, *Georgia Reports*, Vol. LVI, July term, 1876, pp. 694-99.

10. Author's collection, photograph of Benning's tomb. CSU, Linwood Cemetery records; Northern, *Men of Mark in Georgia*, Vol. 3, pp. 256-66; Georgia State Historical Marker of General Henry Lewis Benning, formerly located on the east side of Broadway, between 14th and 15th streets (now the location of Total Systems corporate headquarters), whereabouts of marker, unknown.

11. NA, *Compiled Military Service Records of Volunteer Soldiers Who Served During Indian Wars and Disturbances, 1815--1858*, M629, roll 3 (Benning, Henry L., Private, 66th Georgia Infantry Regiment). UGA, Graduating Class Roster, (1834), *Alumni Sketches* (1901), *Catalogue of Alumni* (1906), letter, Benning to Cobb, dated October, 26, 1846; personal data concerning Benning's education; *Columbus Enquirer*, Franklin College, graduating class roster, August 16, 1834.

12. Harris, *A History of the Supreme Court of Georgia*, pp. 37 & 39; GA, *Georgia Reports*, Vol. XV (1855); Savannah, January term, 1854, (Padelford, Fay & Co. vs. Mayor and Aldermen, City of Savannah), pp. 438-513. Muscogee County Marriage Records, Marriage Book A (Henry L. Benning to Mary Howard Jones, September 12, 1839) marriage of Henry L. Benning and Mary Howard Jones. *Columbus Enquirer*, September 18, 1839, GA, *Georgia Reports*, Vol. LVI, July term, 1876, p. 694.

13. UGA Archives, Howell Cobb papers, letter dated July 1, 1849, Benning to Cobb; Harris, *A History of the Supreme Court of Georgia*, p. 40.

14. Shyrock, *Georgia and the Union in 1850*, p. 296; UGA Archives, Howell Cobb papers, letters dated April 27, 1835, May 18, and September 3, 1840.

15. Barney, *The Road to Secession: A New Perspective on the Old South*, pp. 121-22; Cobb, James C.," The Making of a Secessionist: Henry L. Benning and the Coming of the Civil War," pp. 312 -13, *The Georgia Historical Quarterly*, Volume LX, Number 4, University of Georgia: Athens, 1976.

16. Ibid., p. 321.

17. Benning, *Southern Historical Society Papers*, Vol. 7," Notes on the Final Campaign of April, 1865" , Gen. H.L. Benning, pp. 193-195 and Vol. XIV, Field, Charles," The Campaign of 1864 and 1865" , 1886, pp. 560-561. NA, Compiled Service Records of Confederate General and Staff Officers and non-regimental Enlisted Men, National Archives, microfilm number M331, Compiled Service Records of Confederate Soldiers Who Served in Organizations from the State of Georgia, 17th infantry regiments, microfilm numbers M226 & 319, Confederate Pension Applications, GA, Georgia Department of Archives and History, Atlanta, Georgia; NA, Confederate States of America Collection, War Department, List of Official Communications, box 110, Washington, D.C.

18. Harris, *A History of the Supreme Court of Georgia*, p. 62 (note 59- Park's Code, Vol. 1, Introduction). 1968.

Chapter 1

1. Benning Family Records (Pleasant Benning family Bible, with addenda by his granddaughter, Mary Benning), Personal archives of Mrs. Patti Andrews; Benning, Eva Hardin, Ed., Nita Neblock, *Francois Benin (Francis Benning), His Descendants and Allied Families.*

2. Ibid.; Eckinrode, H. J., *Index of the Revolutionary Records in the Virginia State Archives*, Richmond: 1912, Record of Captain John Benning.

3. Benning Family Records, (Pleasant Benning family Bible, with addenda by his granddaughter, Mary Benning), Personal archives of Mrs. Patti Andrews; Cobb Family-Baldwin County.

4. Columbia County Wills, Book A, Benning and White Families; CSU Archives, Benning-Jones Papers, MC 6, Estate of John Benning, Columbia County, Georgia.

5. CSU Archives, Benning-Jones Papers, MC 6, Estate of John Benning, Columbia County, Georgia; Sorley, *Lewis of Warner Hall: The History of a Family*, Columbia County, Will Book A, John Benning; Butts, *The Mother of Some Distinguished Georgians of the Last Half Century*, p. 56-8.

6. Benning Family Records, (Pleasant Benning family Bible, with addenda by his granddaughter, Mary Benning), Personal archives of Mrs. Patti Andrews.

7. *The Holy Bible*, King James version, established in 1611, modern publication by American Bible Society, New York: 1967 (Quote is from Collossians 4:1. Other passages which highlight and support slavery include: Exodus 21:2-6 and 20-21; Colossians, 3:22; Leviticus 25:44-46; Ephesians 6:5; and 1 Peter, 2:18-21. DeBow, J. D., ed. *DeBow's Review.* " The Churches and Slavery." Volume 1, Number 1 (January 1859)." p. 118. New Orleans, Louisiana.

8. Peterson, *The Portable Thomas Jefferson*, p. 545, letter dated August 25, 1814, Thomas Jefferson to Edmund Cates.

9. Map of the State of Georgia, 1814, GA, University of Georgia Archives, Map Collection.

10. Benning Family Records, (Pleasant Benning family Bible, with addenda by his granddaughter, Mary Benning), Personal archives of Mrs. Patti Andrews.

11. Ibid.

12. Northern, *Men of Mark in Georgia*, Vol. II, pp. 95-9, (Carlisle Pollack Beman).

13. *Union Recorder*, Feb. 7, 1893.

14. Hull, p. 44-45, *A Historical Sketch of the University of Georgia*, and UGA Archives, Catalog of Alumni.

15. Northern, *Men of Mark in Georgia*, Vol. 3, pp. 1-16, Robert Toombs.

16. Hull, p. 44-45, *A Historical Sketch of the University of Georgia*, and UGA Archives, Catalog of Alumni; Northern, *Men of Mark in Georgia*, Vol. 3, pp. 566-81, (Howell Cobb).

17. UGA Archives, M 1376, Howell Cobb Papers, (Academic Report, dated Nov. 1, 1833)

18. Census data 1830, (Cobb-Clarke County and Benning- Columbia County); Northern, *Men of Mark in Georgia*, pp. 566-67 (Howell Cobb); Benning Family Records; Hull, *A Historical Sketch of the University of Georgia*, p. 48.

19. Northern, *Men of Mark in Georgia*, Vol. 3, pp. 566-81 (Howell Cobb). Henry Benning fondly referred to Howell Cobb as " Fatty."

20. Coulter, *College Life in the Old South*, pp. 76-7 and 103-05.

21. CSU Archives, MC 34, Alva C. Smith Collection. Autobiographical material of Raphael Moses (material later published in Marcus, *Memoirs of American Jews*).

22. Ibid., p. 89.

23. Ibid., pp. 102 and 133.

24. Lucas, *Gold Lottery of 1832*, pp. 45, 105-09; Harris County Deed Book 1 (B).

25. *Columbus (Georgia) Enquirer*, August 16, 1834.

26. Northern, *Men of Mark in Georgia,*, Vol. II, pp. 399- 402, (George W. Towns).

27. UGA Archives, M 1376, Howell Cobb papers, Henry Benning to Howell Cobb, letter dated Sept. 5, 1834.

28. Ibid., letter dated Sept. 5, 1834.

29. Ibid., letter dated Nov. 20, 1834.

30. Ibid., letter dated Feb. 2, 1835.

31. Ibid., letter dated March 11 and 29, 1835.

32. Clarke County Marriage Book A, Howell Cobb and Mary Ann Lamar.

33. UGA Archives, M 1376, Howell Cobb Papers, Henry Benning to Howell Cobb, letter dated May 27, 1835.

Chapter 2

1. GA, *Georgia Acts* (1826), pp. 57-58, (1827) pp. 69-71; (1829) pp. 25-30.

2. GA, *Georgia Acts* (1827), pp. 69-70.

3. CSU Archives, MC 36 and 9, *Columbus, 1828, Journal of the Commissioners for Laying Out the Town of Columbus*, Jan. 15, 1828-July 22, 1828, Office of the City Clerk, Columbus, Georgia, p. 1-6; Georgia Acts, 1828, pp. 153-54.

4. Quoted in George G. Smith, *The Story of Georgia and the Georgia People, 1732 to 1862*. Macon, Georgia, 1900, p. 544.

5. UNC Archives, MS 2594, Henry L. Benning to Benjamin C. Yancey, letter dated Feb. 4, 1836; *Catalogue of the Trustees, Officers, Alumni and Matriculates of the University of Georgia at Athens, Georgia, from 1785 to 1906*, p. 35.

6. UGA Archives, M 1376, Howell Cobb, Henry Benning to Howell Cobb, letter dated Feb. 4, 1836 and Dec. 9, 1835.

7. Northern, *Men of Mark in Georgia*, Vol. II, p. 236-237, (Seaborn Jones).

8. CSU, Benning-Jones Papers, MC 6, Folders 57 and 98; Young, p. 105, *Columbus (Georgia) Enquirer* Jan. 21 and 28, 1832.

9. *Columbus (Georgia) Enquirer*, Jan. 25, 1832.

10. UGA Archives, M 1376, Howell Cobb papers, Henry Benning to Howell Cobb, letters dated Feb. 4, 1836 and Jan. 12, 1839.

11. CSU, Benning-Jones Papers (Jones's business affairs were numerous and the archives are filled with transactions), MC 6, Leonard Garrard, data concerning Leonard's Spring, Bullock, *A History of Emory University*, p. 55.

12. Worsley, *Columbus on the Chattahoochee*, p. 245; LC, Map of Columbus, Georgia, 1886; Muscogee County Deed Book 1, Property listings for Jones, Howard, Benning and Evans families; Fidler, pp. 11-14, *Augusta Evans Wilson, 1835-1909;* Martin, *Columbus, Georgia, From Its Selection as a " Trading Town" in 1827, To Its Partial Destruction by Wilson's Raid in 1865.* pp. 22, 58, and 62.

13. Ibid., Augusta Jane Evans was born on May 8, 1835 in the dining room at Wildwood.

14. Ibid.

15. Worsley, *Columbus on the Chattahoochee*, p. 248.

16. Kyle, *Images, A Pictorial History of Columbus*, p. 97.

17. Worsley, *Columbus on the Chattahoochee*, pp. 217-61.

18. CSU Archives, MC 22, UDC Scrapbook, Lizzie Rutherford Collection, Mary Howard (Jones) Benning biography, Portrait, private collection of Mr. Henry Benning Spencer; UGA Archives, Howell Cobb papers, Henry Benning to Howell Cobb, letter dated Jan. 12, 1839.

19. Martin, *Columbus, Georgia, From Its Selection as a " Trading Town" in 1827, To Its Partial Destruction by Wilson's Raid in 1865. Volume 1* ; p. 21, 24, and 29; Fetherstonaugh, *Excursion Through the Slave States*, p. 153.

20. *Macon Messenger* Feb. 4, 1836 and April 14, 1836; Georgia Acts, 1835, pp. 289- 90; Martin, *Columbus, Georgia, From Its Selection as a " Trading Town" in 1827, To Its Partial Destruction by Wilson's Raid in 1865. Volume 1*, p. 58.

21. Martin, *Columbus, Georgia, From Its Selection as a " Trading Town" in 1827, To Its Partial Destruction by Wilson's Raid in 1865. Volume 1*, pp. 60-2.

22. UGA Archives, M 1376, Howell Cobb, Henry Benning to Howell Cobb, letter dated Feb. 4, 1836.

23. NA, Compiled Military Service Records of Volunteer Soldiers Who Served During Indian Wars and Disturbances, 1815--1858. M629, roll 3 (Benning) Military Records of Soldiers Serving in the Creek Indian War, 1836, Georgia Militia, (B), Card No. 36748779, 66th Georgia Infantry Regiment, Captain Phillip Schley's Company, Private Henry L. Benning.

24. Martin, *Columbus, Georgia, From Its Selection as a "Trading Town" in 1827, To Its Partial Destruction by Wilson's Raid in 1865. Volume 1*, p. 59; Worsley, *Columbus on the Chattahoochee*, p. 113.

25. Foreman, *Indian Removal*, p. 145, Chapter XI explains this in detail..

26. *Columbus (Georgia) Enquirer*, Jan. 10, 1836.

27. Ibid., May 13, 1836.

28. Telfair, *A History of Columbus, Georgia, 1828-1928*, p. 55-56; Worsley, *Columbus on the Chattahoochee*, p. 130.

29. CSU Archives, MC 36, T. J. Peddy Collection, Schley to Scott, letter dated May 18, 1836, also appears in *American State Papers, Military Affairs*, Vol. VII, p. 311.

30. Martin, *Columbus, Georgia, From Its Selection as a "Trading Town" in 1827, To Its Partial Destruction by Wilson's Raid in 1865. Volume 1*, pp. 57-63.

31. Elliott, *Winfield Scott: The Soldier and the Man*, p. 313-14.

32. Ibid., p. 315.

33. Ibid., p. 317.

34. Ibid., p. 320.

35. Ibid.

Chapter 3

1. GA, *Executive Minutes Book*, Nov. 5, 1834 to Nov. 6, 1839.

2. Martin, *Columbus, Georgia, From Its Selection as a "Trading Town" in 1827, To Its Partial Destruction by Wilson's Raid in 1865. Volume 1*, p. 87.

3. *Columbus (Georgia) Enquirer*, August 18, 1836.

4. Grice, *Georgia Bench & Bar*, p. 157.

5. GA, *Journal of the House of Representatives*, Nov. 12, 1838, Drawer 295, Box number 4; Executive Minutes Book, November 5, 1834 to Nov. 12, 1838.

6. *Columbus (Georgia) Enquirer*, Dec. 21, 1837.

7. Ibid., July 12, 1838; Martin, *Columbus, Georgia, From Its Selection as a "Trading Town" in 1827, To Its Partial Destruction by Wilson's Raid in 1865. Volume 1*, p. 86. Northern, *Men of Mark*, Vol. 2, p. 78, Reverend Lovick Pierce, also had sons, Lovick Jr., and George, whom also served the Methodist Church as Reverends. George was also a Bishop; Northern, *Men of Mark in Georgia*, Vol. 2, pp. 76-8 (Lovick Pierce).

8. *Columbus (Georgia) Enquirer*, Jan. 15 and Dec. 21, 1837.

9. UGA Archives, M 1376, Howell Cobb Papers, letter dated Jan. 12, 1839.

10. *Columbus Sentinel and Herald*, Sept. 12, 1839; Benning Family Records, (Pleasant Benning family Bible, with addenda by his granddaughter, Mary

Benning), Personal archives of Mrs. Patti Andrews. (Death of Sarah Amanda Benning)

11. *Columbus (Georgia) Enquirer*, Sept. 18, 1839, Muscogee County, Marriage Book A, Henry L. Benning to Mary Howard Jones.

12. CSU Archives, MC 6, Jones-Benning papers; Benning Family Records, (Pleasant Benning family Bible, with addenda by his granddaughter, Mary Benning), Personal archives of Mrs. Patti Andrews.

13. UGA Archives, M 1376, Howell Cobb papers, Henry Benning to Howell Cobb, letter dated June 10, 1840.

14. Benning Family Records, (Pleasant Benning family Bible, with addenda by his granddaughter, Mary Benning), Personal archives of Mrs. Patti Andrews, (Birth of Seaborn Jones Benning).

15. UGA Archives, M 1376, Howell Cobb papers, Henry Benning to Howell Cobb, letter dated Sept. 3, 1840.

16. Murray, *The Whig Party in Georgia, 1825-1853*, p. 3..

17. Martin, *Columbus, Georgia, From Its Selection as a " Trading Town" in 1827, To Its Partial Destruction by Wilson's Raid in 1865. Volume 1*, p. 106.

18. Benning Family Records, (Pleasant Benning family Bible, with addenda by his granddaughter, Mary Benning), Personal archives of Mrs. Patti Andrews, (Birth of Mary Howard Benning).

19. Ibid., Muscogee County Marriage Book A, Marriage of Benjamin Y. Martin to Caroline Matilda Benning; see *The Daily Sun* (Columbus), Dec. 24, 1860, eulogy and description of Benjamin Y. Martin.

20. CSU Archives, Jones- Benning Papers, MC 6 (John A. Jones to Seaborn Jones, letter dated March 30, 1842).

21. UGA Archives, M 1376, Howell Cobb, letter dated May 5, 1842.

22. McCash, p. 13, *Thomas R. R. Cobb (1823-1862): The Making of a Southern Nationalist;* Northern, *Men of Mark in Georgia*, Vol. 3, pp. 155-162 (Thomas R. R. Cobb).

23. UGA Archives, M 1376, Howell Cobb papers, Henry Benning to Howell Cobb, letter dated Oct. 26, 1842.

24. Ibid.

25. Benning Family Records, (Pleasant Benning family Bible, with addenda by his granddaughter, Mary Benning), Personal archives of Mrs. Patti Andrews (birth of Sarah Elizabeth Benning); Muscogee County Marriage Book A & B, Oct. 5, 1843, Marriage of John A. Jones to Mary Leonard; Worsley, *Columbus on the Chattahoochee,* p. 246; Leonard family data, 1850 census, Muscogee County and Worsley, p. 236-37.

26. Ibid.; Harris County Marriage Book A, Marriage of Richard E. Benning to Francis Simpson.

27. UGA Archives, M 1376, Howell Cobb papers, Henry Benning to Howell Cobb, letter dated Dec. 4, 1844.

28. Garrard, Leonard and Mrs. Patti Andrews (Benning family Bible), genealogical notes concerning the birth of Seaborn Leonard Jones, also listed in Allen, Sarah, *Our Children's Ancestors*, p. 397.

29. Martin, *Columbus, Georgia, From Its Selection as a "Trading Town" in 1827, To Its Partial Destruction by Wilson's Raid in 1865. Volume 1*, pp. 124-51.

Chapter 4

1. *Columbus (Georgia) Times*, April 16, 1845.
2. CSU Archives, MC 22, Records of the Anne Elizabeth Shepherd Home, organizational pamphlet, p. 2; Journal entries," Ladies' Education and Benevolent Society of the Methodist Episcopal Church, of the City of Columbus," 1845-1860.
3. Ibid.
4. Ibid.
5. Dudley, *100 Years History of St. Luke Methodist Episcopal Church*, p. 40, 42, and 65.
6. Matthews, *Slavery and Methodism: A Chapter in American Morality, 1780-1845*, p. 62.
7. Ibid., p. 63.
8. Ibid. p. 239.
9. *Slave Narratives*, Part 1, Vol. 2, p. 5, This multi-volume set consists of interviews with former slaves. The program was conducted by the federal government, as part of Roosevelt's Works Progress Administration (W.P.A). There are numerous first-hand accounts provided by former slaves of Georgia, with several from Columbus and surrounding counties. While those interviewed were elderly, their memories of slavery were quite clear.
10. Ibid. p. 2.
11. Dudley, *100 Years History of* St. *Luke Methodist Episcopal Church*, pp. 39-41.
12. Ibid.
13. Benning Family Records, (Pleasant Benning family Bible, with addenda by his granddaughter, Mary Benning), Personal archives of Mrs. Patti Andrews: Benning-Jones clan, births and deaths.
14. National Archives, *Volunteer Soldiers Who Served During the Mexican War*, M-616, Roll # 19.
15. Benning Family Records, (Pleasant Benning family Bible, with addenda by his granddaughter, Mary Benning), Personal archives of Mrs. Patti Andrews: Deaths of Sarah Elizabeth Benning and Eugene Jones; also births of Caroline Matilda Benning and Henry Benning Jones.
16. Muscogee County Land Deeds, Deed Book A.
17. NA, Agriculture Census, 1850, Muscogee County; Muscogee County Probate records, Seaborn Jones estate (slave list); Muscogee County, Deed Book 1, Property listings of Seaborn Jones; Banks, *Economics of Land Tenure in Georgia*, 1850, p. 21-22; Northern, *Men of Mark in Georgia*, Vol. 2, pp. 236-42 (Seaborn Jones).
18. Barfield, *A History of Harris County*, p. 609; Worsley, *Columbus on the Chattahoochee*, p. 240 and 248.

19. CSU Archives, MC 34, autobiographical material of Raphael Moses. (Moses
     was a prominent lawyer, planter, and friend of the Bennings, Jones, Toombs,
     and Crawfords. His plantation called Esquiline, was located on a hill south of
     Columbus. He also served as Toombs and Benning's commissary officer
     during the Civil War.); Northern, *Men of Mark in Georgia*, Vol. 3, p 565
     (Raphael Moses).
20. Banks, *Economics of Land Tenure in Georgia*, pp. 21-2.
21. NA, Agriculture Census, 1850, Muscogee County; Muscogee County Probate
     records, Seaborn Jones estate (slave list); Muscogee County, Deed Book 1,
     Property listings of Seaborn Jones; Banks, *Economics of Land Tenure in
     Georgia*, 1850, p. 21-22; Northern, *Men of Mark in Georgia*, Vol. 2, pp. 236-
     42 (Seaborn Jones); Worsley, *Columbus on the Chattahoochee*, p. 218.
22. UGA Archives, M 1376, Howell Cobb Papers, Henry Benning to Howell
     Cobb, letter dated Jan. 15, 1846. Phillips, p. 97, *Toombs, Stephens, Cobb
     Correspondence*, Henry Benning to Howell Cobb, letter dated, Feb. 23, 1848;
     Northern, *Men of Mark in Georgia*, Vol. 4, pp. 204-07 (Herschel V. Johnson).
23. Ibid.
24. Ibid.
25. Ibid.
26. Ibid.
27. Ibid., p. 168-172, Henry Benning to Howell Cobb, letter dated July 1, 1849.
28. Murray, p. 141, *The Whig Party in Georgia, 1825-1853*. See also James C.
     Cobb's article appearing in the *Georgia Historical Quarterly* concerning
     Benning and his relations with other key Georgia politicians during this era.

Chapter 5

1. *Columbus Times*, Feb. 5, 12, 19, 26; March 5, 12; April 23, 1850.
2. Ibid., June 18, 1850.
3. Shyrock, *Georgia and the Union in 1850*, pp. 270-71.
4. Ibid., p. 272-73.
5. Ibid., p. 276.
6. *Columbus Times*, September 10, 1850.
7. Ibid., September 24, 1850.
8. Shyrock, *Georgia and the Union in 1850*, p. 292.
9. Ibid.
10. Ibid., p. 297 (Governor Towns quoted in); Northern, *Men of Mark in Georgia*,
     Vol. 2, pp. 399- 402 (George W. Towns).
11. Ibid.
12. *Columbus Times*, February 25, 1851.

13. Shyrock, *Georgia and the Union in 1850*, pp. 298-99.
14. *Columbus Times*, July 22, 1851.
15. Benning Family Records, (Pleasant Benning family Bible, with addenda by his granddaughter, Mary Benning), Personal archives of Mrs. Patti Andrews; Birth of Infant Son, October, 1851.
16. Northern, *Men of Mark in Georgia*, Vol. II, p. 301, (Martin J. Crawford); Vol. 4, pp. 204-07 (Herschel V. Johnson).
17. Muscogee County Records, Muscogee County Deed Book 1: I, 664, M. J. Crawford to Henry L. Benning, August 26, 1858.
18. Northern, *Men of Mark in Georgia*, p. 302 and 305 (Joseph H. Lumpkin).
19. Phillips, p. 318, *Toombs, Stephens, Cobb Correspondence*, letter dated Aug. 27, 1852, Howell Cobb to Mary Ann Cobb.
20. Ibid., letter dated September 2, 1852, Henry Benning to Howell Cobb.
21. Ibid.
22. Ibid.
23. Ibid., letter dated September 15, 1852, George D. Phillips to Howell Cobb.
24. Benning Family Records, (Pleasant Benning family Bible, with addenda by his granddaughter, Mary Benning), Personal archives of Mrs. Patti Andrews (Birth of Anna Caroline, June 22, 1853, death of Caroline Matilda and Anna Malinda). Description of Madison L. Patterson appears in *The History of Russell County*, p. F-182.
25. Harris, *A History of the Supreme Court of Georgia*, p. 37; Northern, *Men of Mark in Georgia*, Vol. 4, pp. 204-07 (Herschel V. Johnson).
26. Ibid.

Chapter 6

1. McCash, *Thomas R. R. Cobb (1823-1862): The Making of a Southern Nationalist*, p. 48; Northern, *Men of Mark in Georgia*, Vol. 3, pp. 155-162 (Thomas R. R. Cobb).
2. Ibid., p. 42.
3. Ducat, *Constitutional Interpretation*, p. 7.
4. UGA Archives, MS 192, Lumpkin papers, Henry Benning to Joseph Lumpkin, letter dated Oct. 5, 1856.
5. Harris, *A History of the Supreme Court of Georgia*, p. 48.
6. Avery, *The History of the State of Georgia, From 1850 to 1881*, p. 54.
7. Harris, *A History of the Supreme Court of Georgia*, p. 50.
8. Ibid., (Judge E. A. Nisbet quoted)
9. Strozier, *Report of the 38th Annual Session of the Georgia Bar Association Held at Tybee Island, Georgia, June 2-4, 1921*, p. 101.
10. Ibid., p. 100.; *Georgia Reports*, Vol. 14, p. 438 (1854).
11. Ibid.

12. GA, *Georgia Reports*, Vol. 84, p. 754., Comments of Chief Justice Bleckley.

13. Black, *Black's Law Dictionary*, p. 1072.

14. GA, *Georgia Reports*, Vol. 14, p. 443.

15. Avery, *The History of the State of Georgia, From 1850 to 1881*, p. 77.

16. GA, *Georgia Reports*, Vol. 14, p. 440-41.

17. Ibid.

18. Strozier, *Report of the 38th Annual Session of the Georgia Bar Association Held at Tybee Island, Georgia, June 2-4, 1921*, p. 105.

19. *Georgia Reports*, Vol. 14., p. 443.

20. Strozier, *Report of the 38th Annual Session of the Georgia Bar Association Held at Tybee Island, Georgia, June 2-4, 1921*, p. 105.

21. Ibid. p. 106.

22. GA, *Georgia Reports*, Vol. 14, p. 503.

23. Ibid., p. 106.

24. Ibid.

25. Ibid., p. 506.

26. Ibid., p. 507.

27. Ibid., p. 508.

28. Ibid., 513.

29. Ducat, *Constitutional Interpretation*, p. 59.

30. Strozier, *Report of the 38th Annual Session of the Georgia Bar Association Held at Tybee Island, Georgia, June 2-4, 1921*, p. 113, (quote from Ohio 6, 377, p. 45.)

Chapter 7

1. *Times and Sentinel* (Columbus) Feb. 10, 1857.

2. Muscogee County Property deeds, Seaborn Jones to multiple family members: Deed books G, entries 309, 310, and 311, dated February 12, 1855; I, entry 227; K, entry 178; G, entry 245, dated September 23, 1854.

3. Cobb, p. xxxvi, *An Historical Sketch of Slavery, From the Earliest Periods*.

4. Ibid., p. cix.

5. Faust, *The Ideology of Slavery: Proslavery Thought in the Antebellum South, 1830-1860*, p. 12.

6. Cobb, *An Historical Sketch of Slavery, From the Earliest Periods*, p. ccv.

7. *Slave Narratives*, Part 1, Vol. 2, p. 10.

8. Eaton, *The Mind of the Old South*, p. 312.

9. Kolchin, *American Slavery: 1619-1877.*, pp. 192-93.

10. Jenkins, *Pro-Slavery Thought in the Old South*, p. 262.

11. Faust, *The Ideology of Slavery: Proslavery Thought in the Antebellum South, 1830-1860.*, p. 116.
12. Hollander, *Slavery in America: Its Legal History*, p. 112.
13. DeGregorio, *The Complete Book of U. S. Presidents*, p. 228.
14. Phillips, *Toombs, Stephens, Cobb Correspondence*, Henry Benning to Howell Cobb, letter dated July 1, 1849, p. 168-172.
15. *Reports of Cases of Law and Equity Argued and Determined in the Supreme Court of the State of Georgia*, Vol. 15, No. 72, p. 498 (1855). Hereinafter and commonly referred to as *Georgia Reports*.
16. Ibid., p. 502.
17. Ibid.
18. Ibid., p. 503.
19. Ibid.
20. Ibid., p. 507.
21. Ducat, *Constitutional Interpretation*, p. 59.
22. Benning Family Records, (Pleasant Benning family Bible, with addenda by his granddaughter, Mary Benning), Personal archives of Mrs. Patti Andrews. (Ages and status of Benning and Jones children in 1855)
23. Muscogee County Deeds (Index Book 1: Individual Land purchases listed in: D 174; F 299; 410; 477; 242; 243; 311; 529; and K743); Agriculture Census 1850 & 1860 (Muscogee County, Georgia, Henry Benning; Seaborn Jones; and John Woolfolk).
24. Northern, *Men of Mark in Georgia*, Vol. 3, p. 302, (Martin J. Crawford).
25. Ibid., Vol. 3, p. 576, (Howell Cobb).
26. Harris, *A History of the Supreme Court of Georgia, p. 42.*
27. Ibid., pp. 62 and 64.
28. Grice, *Georgia Bench and Bar*, p. 157.

Chapter 8

1. Avery, *The History of the State of Georgia, From 1850 to 1881*, p. 79.
2. Martin, *Columbus, Georgia, From Its Selection as a " Trading Town" in 1827, To Its Partial Destruction by Wilson's Raid in 1865. Volume 1*, pp. 47, 48, 78, 86, 150.
3. GA, *Georgia Reports*, Vols. 8, 11, 16, 19, 26.
4. Ibid., Vol. 19, pp. 337-341, *Robinson v. Lane.*
5. Fielder, *A Sketch of the Life and Times and Speeches of Joseph E. Brown*, p. 61.
6. Ibid.
7. Ibid., p. 63.
8. Ibid., p. 62, *Georgia Reports*, Vol. 16, *Lane v. Harris*, (Lengthy justification and remarks by Benning).

9. Ibid., *Times and Sentinel* (Columbus), Aug. 28, 1858 (also appears in South
    Western (American) News).

10. GA, *Georgia Reports*, Vol. 26, p.17.

11. Avery, *The History of the State of Georgia, From 1850 to 1881.*, p. 77.

12. Ibid.

13. GA, *Georgia Reports*, Vols. 8, 11, 16, 19, 26: Vol. 8, *Lane v. Morris,
    Hightower v. Thornton, Hightower v. Mustian, Carey v. Jones, Robinson v.
    Carey*; Vol. 11, p. 459, *Thornton v. Lane*, Vol. 16, 217, *Lane v. Harris*; Vol.
    19, 337, *Robinson v. Lane*; Vol. 26, p. 17, *Robinson v. Beall*.

14. Ibid., *The Times*(Columbus), November, 8, 1859.

15. GA, *Georgia Reports*, Vol. 11 and 16. *Ann E. McDougald, et. al. v. William
    Dougherty*, July, 1852 and *Edward Carey v. Thomas Hoxey*. (These cases
    amplify Benning's role)

16. The *Times and Sentinel* (Columbus), August 28, 1858.

17. *The Times* (Columbus), Nov. 8, 1859; Harris, *A History of the Supreme Court
    of Georgia*, p. 65; Northern, *Men of Mark in Georgia*, Vol. 4, pp. 204-07
    (Herschel V. Johnson).

18. Thornton, *A Biographical Sketch of Linton Stephens*, p. 13.

19. *The Times* (Columbus), November 3 and 8, 1859.

20. The *Times and Sentinel*, September 1, 1859.

21. Grice, *Georgia Bench and Bar*, p. 158; Avery, *The History of the State of
    Georgia, From 1850 to 1881*, p. 77.

22. *The Times* (Columbus), Nov. 8, 1859; Harris, *A History of the Supreme Court
    of Georgia*, pp. 41-2.

23. GA, *Georgia Reports*, Vol. 56, p. 693, memorial tribute to Henry L. Benning.

24. *City Directory (Columbus)*, 1859-60.; Census 1860 (Muscogee County);
    Muscogee County Will Book A, p. 26, Benjamin Y. Martin; Benning Family
    Records, (Pleasant Benning family Bible, with addenda by his granddaughter,
    Mary Benning), Personal archives of Mrs. Patti Andrews. (Death of Caroline
    Matilda (nee Martin) Benning).

25. Benning Family Records, (Pleasant Benning family Bible, with addenda by his
    granddaughter, Mary Benning), Personal archives of Mrs. Patti Andrews.
    (Benning and Martin children); Northern, *Men of Mark in Georgia,,* Vol. 3, pp.
    259-67, Henry L. Benning.

26. *Official Register of the Officers and Cadets*, Georgia Military Institute,
    Marietta, Georgia, Atlanta, Ga., J. I. Miller & Company: 1858; *Regulations of
    the Georgia Military Institute, Marietta, Georgia*. Atlanta: C. R. Hanleiter,
    1857.

27. UGA Archives, Benning, Henry Lewis (M 2601), Box No. 1, Item 1, letter
    dated Feb. 1, 1858, Henry L. Benning to Mary Benning.

28. Benning Family Records, (Pleasant Benning family Bible, with addenda by his granddaughter, Mary Benning), Personal archives of Mrs. Patti Andrews; Benning Estate Records; CSU Archives, Ladies Society Journal, MC 22 and MC 28, Anne Elizabeth Shepherd Home, 1859.

29. Martin, *Columbus, Georgia, From Its Selection as a " Trading Town" in 1827, To Its Partial Destruction by Wilson's Raid in 1865. Volume 1*; pp. 113-14; Worsley, *Columbus on the Chattahoochee*, p. 138.

30. Fidler, *Augusta Jane Evans*, pp. 68-9; Derby, *Fifty Year Among Authors*, op. cit. p. 391.

31. Ibid.

32. Ibid., pp. 78-9.

33. *Columbus Daily Times*, December 22, 1859; Avery, *The History of the State of Georgia, From 1850 to 1881*, p. 108.

34. Eaton, *History of the Southern Confederacy*, pp. 13-5.

35. Phillips, *Toombs, Stephens, Cobb Correspondence*, pp. 168-72, Henry Benning to Howell Cobb, letter dated July 1, 1849.

Chapter 9

1. McGinnis, *Muscogee County, Georgia, 1860 Census Index*; p. x; Federal Census 1860; Muscogee County, Georgia, Census 1860 (Conflicting data exists between the federal and local census data. The McGinnis tabulation addresses a more detailed schedule, an index, and serves as a valuable genealogical tool).

2. Ibid.; Federal Slave Schedule, 1860, Muscogee County, Georgia, (Henry Benning; Seaborn Jones; and John Woolfolk).

3. Ibid.; *City Directory, Columbus, Georgia*, 1859-60.

4. McGinnis, *Muscogee County, Georgia, 1860 Census Index*, p. xii (valuable Muscogee County historical overview provided by Columbus State University, Professor John S. Lupold).

5. *Columbus (Georgia) Enquirer*, April 10, 1860; Martin, *Columbus, Georgia, From Its Selection as a " Trading Town" in 1827, To Its Partial Destruction by Wilson's Raid in 1865. Volume 1*, p. 118.

6. *The Daily Sun* (Columbus), March 16, 1861; April 8, 1863; Standard, *Columbus, Georgia in the Confederacy: The Social and Industrial Life of the Chattahoochee River Port*, pp. 28-9, (detailed narrative of Georgia's war time industrial production).

7. Olmstead, I, *Journeys and Explorations in the Cotton Kingdom*, p. 273; *Columbus Daily Sun*, April 18, 1863.

8. *City Directory, Columbus, Georgia, 1859-60*; *Columbus Daily Sun*, April 18, 1863.

9. *Columbus Daily Times*, March 17, 1860; Avery, *The History of the State of Georgia, From 1850 to 1881, p. 114;* Pickett, *History of Alabama*, p. 707.

10. Ibid., May 1, 4, 5, 1860; Avery, *The History of the State of Georgia, From 1850 to 1881*, p. 115.

11. Ibid.

12. Ibid.

13. Ibid., May 15, 16, 18, 31, 1860.

14. Ibid., May 11, 1860.

15. Ibid., May 3, 8, 1860.

16. Ibid., June 6, 7, 14, 1860.

17. Ibid., June 23, 25, 26, 28, 1860; Avery, *The History of the State of Georgia, From 1850 to 1881*, pp. 122-23.

18. Ibid., August 27, October 24, and November 5, 1860.

19. Avery, *The History of the State of Georgia, From 1850 to 1881*, p. 125.

20. DeGregorio, *The Complete Book of U. S. Presidents*, p. 234.

21. Candler, *The Confederate Records of the State of Georgia*, pp. 19-57; (Governor Brown's original executive message is housed in the Georgia Archives).

22. Ibid., pp. 92-3. GA, *House Journal*, Drawer 295, Box 9, Senate Journal, Drawer 295, Box 55, (Original messages from various counties concerning Federal Relations).

23. *Columbus Daily Times*, March 17, 1860; Avery, p. 114, *The History of the State of Georgia, From 1850 to 1881.* (accurate, insightful and encompassing survey of antebellum, Civil War and post-bellum Georgia history); Northern, *Men of Mark in Georgia*, Vol. 4, pp. 204-07 (Herschel V. Johnson).

24. Candler, p. 158 and 176, *The Confederate Records of the State of Georgia.* (Edited version also appears in Freehling's *Secession Debated*, both versions are transcribed from " Substance of Remarks Made by Thomas R. R. Cobb, Esq. In the Hall of the House of Representatives, Monday evening, Nov. 12, 1860" ; Northern, *Men of Mark in Georgia*, Vol. 3, pp. 155-162 (Thomas R. R. Cobb).

25. Ibid.

26. Freehling, *Secession Debated: Georgia's Showdown in 1860*, pp. 32-50.

27. Pamphlet entitled " Speech of Honorable Robert Toombs, on the Crisis, Delivered Before the Georgia Legislature. Lemuel Towers, Washington D.C.: 1860; Toombs' speech is also recorded in Freehling, *Secession Debated: Georgia's Showdown in 1860*, p. 50.

28. Candler, *The Confederate Records of the State of Georgia*, p. 183.

29. Ibid., p. 203.

30. " Speech on Federal relations...Delivered in the Hall of the House of Representatives," University of Georgia Archives; Benning's speech is also

recorded in its entirety in Freehling, *Secession Debated: Georgia's Showdown in 1860*, pp. 116-144.

31. Ibid., p. 118.
32. Ibid.
33. Ibid., p. 119.
34. Ibid., p. 122
35. Ibid., p. 127.
36. Ibid., pp. 129-30.
37. Ibid., p. 131.
38. Ibid., p. 144.
39. Avery, *The History of the State of Georgia, From 1850 to 1881*, p. 131.
40. Candler, *The Confederate Records of the State of Georgia*, pp. 206-09.
41. Phillips, *Toombs, Stephens, Cobb Correspondence, p. 524;* Arthur Hood (statesman from Cuthbert, Georgia) to Howell Cobb, letter dated December 19, 1860.
42. Quote appears in *Columbus Daily Sun, Nov. 26, 1860;* Other pertinent articles concerning the hysteria during this time in Columbus appear in: *Columbus Daily Times*, Dec. 24, 1860; *Columbus Daily Sun*, Nov. 23, 27, 28, Dec. 12, 17, and Jan. 3 & 14, 1861. Martin, *Columbus, Georgia, From Its Selection as a "Trading Town" in 1827, To Its Partial Destruction by Wilson's Raid in 1865. Volume 1*, pp. 120-127.
43. Ibid.
44. Eaton, *The History of the Confederacy*, pp. 22-31.

Chapter 10

1. *The Daily Sun* (Columbus) ran numerous articles espousing independence throughout November, and December, 1861. (Both Benning's and Cobb's speeches mentioned the fight for independence, as experienced by their forefathers. Both speeches also culminate with appeals for independence.)
2. Freehling, *Secession Debated: Georgia's Showdown in 1860*, Benning's speech, p. 120.
3. Williams, *Diary From Dixie*, p. 20 (Mary Boykin Chestnut's diary spans the era prior to and during the civil war, providing an excellent, Southern primary source with a unique, feminine perspective).
4. CSU Archives, MC 2, Augusta Evans letter to Henry Benning, dated January 13, 1861; Fidler, pp. 11-14, *Augusta Evans Wilson, 1835-1909*. (Evans wrote several best-selling books, including *St. Elmo, Macaria*, and *Beulah*).
5. Ibid., Augusta Evans letter to Mrs. Seaborn Jones, dated December 4, 1860.
6. Ibid., Augusta Evans letter to Mrs. G. Virginia French, dated January 13, 1861.

7. Avery, *The History of the State of Georgia, From 1850 to 1881, p. 150*; Mosocco, *The Chronological Tracking of the American Civil War per the Official Records of the War of the Rebellion*, p. 5.

8. Candler, *The Confederate Records of the State of Georgia*, (Secret Proceedings), pp. 212-18.

9. *The Daily Times* (Columbus), January 21, 1861; Avery, *The History of the State of Georgia, From 1850 to 1881*, p. 155.

10. Candler, *The Confederate Records of the State of Georgia*, (Secret Proceedings) pp. 229-75; Avery, *The History of the State of Georgia, From 1850 to 1881*, p. 155.

11. Ibid., pp. 272-74; *The Daily Times* (Columbus), January 21 and 22, 1861.

12. Ibid., pp. 294-95.

13. Ibid., pp. 329-30; Phillips, *Toombs, Stephens, Cobb Correspondence*, p. 554, Howell Cobb to his wife, letter dated February 20, 1861.

14. Mosocco, *The Chronological Tracking of the American Civil War per the Official Records of the War of the Rebellion*, p. 6 (excellent reference source for accurate dates of events during the Civil War).

15. *The Daily Times* (Columbus), January 13, 1861; Worsley, p. 272, *Columbus on the Chattahoochee*.

16. Ibid., February 21, 1861.

17. *The Daily Sun* (Columbus), April 17, 1861; Worsley, *Columbus on the Chattahoochee*, p. 272.

18. *Columbus (Georgia) Enquirer*, January 2, 3, 1861, March 20, 1862; *The Daily Sun*, January 1 and 31, 1861, April 1, 1861.

19. CSU Archives, MC 9, Box 2, Folder 1, unpublished Blanchard diary, entries in February 16 and 18, 1861; Also appears in Worsley, *Columbus on the Chattahoochee*, p. 274.

20. Quote is from Henry Benning's speech, published in *Addresses Delivered Before the Virginia State Convention*, p. 42; *The Daily Times* (Columbus), February 27, 1861; Candler p.259, *The Confederate Records of the State of Georgia*; Dumond, *The Secession Movement: 1860-1861*, pp. 256-57.

21. Pollard, *The Lost Cause*, p. 161; OR, Series, IV, Vol. 1, p.223.

22. OR, Series IV, Vol. 1, pp. 136-147; Candler, *The Confederate Records of the State of Georgia*, pp. 422-446. (Copies of original Constitution of the Confederate States of America are located in the Georgia Department of Archives and History, Atlanta, Georgia, and in the University of Georgia Archives, Athens, Georgia.

23. Ibid., p. 459.

24. Pollard, *The Lost Cause*, p. 105 quote; OR, Series I, Vol. LI, p.8, (appointment of special commissioners to U. S. Government).

25. Ibid., p. 106.

26. Ibid.
27. OR, Series IV, Vol. 1, pp. 250-51, 261-63, 266. (Fort Sumter); Pollard, *The Lost Cause*, pp. 110-11.
28. NA, CSA Records, Compiled Service Records of Confederate General and Staff Officers and non-regimental Enlisted men, microfilm number M 331, Paul Semmes; *The Daily Sun* (Columbus), April 17, 1861.
29. *The Daily Times* (Columbus), October 1, 1861; *The Daily Sun* (Columbus), June 10, 1861.
30. Ibid., October 2, 1861; *The Daily Sun* (Columbus), April 28, 1863; *Columbus (Georgia) Enquirer*, September 26, 1862 and November 4, 1864.
31. *The Daily Times (Columbus)*, March 26 and July 19, 1861.
32. *Columbus (Georgia) Enquirer*, quote appears in August 3, 1861; *The Daily Times* (Columbus), June 4 and July 19, 1861.
33. Ibid.
34. Ibid.
35. NA, CSA Record, Howell Cobb; Northern, *Men of Mark in Georgia*, Vol. 3, pp. 566-81.
36. CSU Archives, Jones- Benning Papers, MC 6; NA, CSA Record, Compiled Service Records of Confederate General and Staff Officers and non-regimental Enlisted men, microfilm number M 331, Compiled Service Records of Confederate Soldiers Who Served in Organizations from the State of Georgia, 17th Infantry Regiment, Henry L. Benning; Northern, Vol. 3, pp. 259-67, Henry L. Benning.
37. NA, CSA Record, Compiled Service Records of Confederate Soldiers Who Served in Organizations from the State of Georgia, 17th Infantry Regiment, Seaborn Jones Benning; Benning Family Records.
38. Ibid., Compiled Service Records of Confederate Soldiers Who Served in Organizations from the State of Georgia, 20th Infantry Regiment, John Abraham Jones; Benning Family Records.
39. Ibid., *Compiled Service Records of Confederate Soldiers Who Served in Organizations from the State of Georgia*. National Archives, M266: 3d Cavalry, rolls 16-19; 1st. Georgia Regulars (Ramsey's), Rolls 143-45; 2nd Georgia Infantry, Rolls 152-56; 15th Georgia Infantry, Rolls 290-96; 17th Georgia Infantry, Rolls 303-07; 20th Georgia Infantry, Rolls 325-32; Index, M266, Georgia, Rolls 1-67.
40. *Columbus Daily Enquirer*, July 10, 11, 13 and 17, 1875. " Old Billie" was just one of the many Negro men that diligently served the Confederacy.
41. Ibid., Peyton Colquitt, Alfred Iverson Jr., Beverly A. Thornton; Northern, Vol. 3, pp. 301-07, Martin J. Crawford, Vol. 3, pp. 561-66, Raphael Moses, and Vol. 3, pp. 251-53, Paul Semmes; Worsley, pp. 494-95 contains information about John S. Pemberton's military service and the invention of Coca-Cola.
42. Ibid., Northern, Vol. 3, 43-7, (Linton Stephens), and Vol. 3, pp. 155-162, (Thomas R. R. Cobb); Yancey, Catalogue of the University of Georgia, 35;

Compiled Service Records of Confederate Soldiers Who Served in
Organizations from the State of Georgia (Cobb's Legion).

43. Ibid., Vol. 3, pp. 1-16, Robert Toombs.
44. Avery, *The History of the State of Georgia, From 1850 to 1881*, p. 225.
45. Phillips, *Toombs, Stephens, Cobb Correspondence*, p. 168, Henry Benning to
Howell Cobb, letter dated July 1, 1849; Columbus Times, February 25, 1861.

Chapter 11

1. *Columbus Daily Enquirer*, June 20, 1861.
2. Ibid.
3. Northern, *Men of Mark in Georgia*, Vol. 3, pp. 10-11, Robert Toombs.
4. *The Daily Sun* (Columbus), February 6 and 7, 1861.
5. *Columbus (Georgia) Enquirer*, June 10 and 18, 1861; November 21, 1862.
6. *The Daily Sun* (Columbus), May 26 and 27, 1861.
7. CSU Archives, MC 28, UDC records; notes of Anna Caroline and Mary
Benning concerning the " Ladies Society" ; Uzar," Confederate Hospitals in
Columbus, Georgia."
8. Ibid., comments by Mary Benning.
9. Ibid.
10. *The Daily Sun* (Columbus), April 27, June 6 and 10, July 2, September 11,
1861; *Columbus (Georgia) Enquirer*, July 12 and 20, 1861; Martin, *Columbus,
Georgia, From Its Selection as a " Trading Town " in 1827, To Its Partial
Destruction by Wilson's Raid in 1865. Volume 1*, p. 143.
11. *Columbus Daily Enquirer*, June 28, 1861.
12. Pollard, *The Lost Cause*, pp. 127 and 129. Quotes are from the *Philadelphia
Press* and the *New York Times*.
13. *Columbus (Georgia) Enquirer*, August 9, 1861.
14. NA, M861, rolls 2 and 16, Benning's Brigade- Company Returns, (Aug.- Sept.
1861) and Compiled Service Rosters; *Columbus Daily Enquirer* and *Columbus
Daily Sun*, June-Aug., 1861; NA, Microfilm Rolls 290-296, (Muster Rolls).
15. OR, Series IV, Vol. 1, pp. 446 and 1095-99. Act of Congress, dated March 20,
1863, Section 10, specified that regimental promotions would no longer be
filled by elections, but by seniority up to and including the rank of colonel.
16. NA, Compiled Military Service Records of Volunteer Confederate Soldiers,
M374, rolls 242 and 255; M861, rolls 2, 15 and 16, Company Returns/ Muster
Rolls: Aug.- Sept. 1862); OR, Series 1, Vol. LI, part II, p. 349; *CMH*, Vol. VI,
Biographical sketch of Robert Toombs, Henry L. Benning, and Dudley M.
DuBose, pp. 395-396; 414-415, and 446-448.
17. Ibid., Service record of Seaborn Jones Benning, Roll 121.

18. Ibid., Rolls 242 and 255; See Appendix B for detailed data.

19. UNC Archives, Southern Historical Society Collection, Stephens, Alexander Hamilton, Correspondence with his brother, Judge Linton Stephens, Benning's Brigade, 1861, Wilson Library, Chapel Hill, N.C.; Ware, (Dec. 1861-Jan. 1862),Vol. 1, pp. 49-74; NA, M861, rolls 2, 15 and 16, Muster Rolls.

20. See Chart, Appendix B for detailed data.

21. BP, Letter to Edward Porter Alexander, 1866; NA, M861, rolls 2, 15 and 16, Microfilm Rolls 290-296, (Aug. - Nov. 1861.)

22. NA, Compiled Military Service Records of Volunteer Confederate Soldiers, M374, rolls 242 and 255, Company Returns/ Muster Rolls: Aug.- Sept. 1862); *CMH*, Vol. VI, Biographical sketch of Robert Toombs, Henry L. Benning, and Dudley M. DuBose, pp. 395-396; 414-415, and 446-448.

23. NA, Compiled Military Service Records of Volunteer Soldiers Who Served During Indian Wars and Disturbances, 1815--1858. M629, rolls 3 (Benning) & 38 (Toombs), American State Papers, Military Affairs, Vol. VII, pp. 309-339, Various letters appearing in this volume between Georgia Governor Schley, General Jessup and General Winfield Scott concerning the Creek uprising of 1836.

24. Stovall, quoted by in *Robert Toombs: Statesman, Speaker, Soldier, Sage*, p. 331.

25. NA, Compiled Military Service Records of Volunteer Confederate Soldiers, M374, rolls 242 and 255, M861, rolls 2, 15 and 16, Company Returns/ Muster Rolls: Aug.- Sept. 1862); *CMH*, Vol. VI, Biographical sketch of Robert Toombs, Henry L. Benning, and Dudley M. DuBose, pp. 395-396; 414-415, and 446-448.

26. *Columbus (Georgia) Enquirer*, September 19, 1861.

27. NA, M861, rolls 2, 15 and 16, Company Returns, (Dec. 1861- Jan. 1862); Ware, Vol. 1, pp. 60-61; Rozier, John, Ed., The Granite Farm Letters, The Civil War Correspondence of Edgeworth & Sallie Bird, Athens & London, 1988, pp. 51-53, letter dated: Jan. 10, 1862; Longstreet, *From Manassas to Appomattox*, pp. 59-63; Allen, *Our Children's Ancestry, pp. 399-400* (Letter from Captain Van A. Leonard to Dolly Whitaker).

28. Ibid., UDC, Vol. VII, p. 169, letter dated August 22, 1861. Ware, Vol. 1, pp. 61-77; *The Granite Farm Letters, The Civil War Correspondence of Edgeworth & Sallie Bird*, pp. 57-58, letter dated: Jan. 12, 1862.

29. NA, CSA Record, Compiled Service Records of Confederate General and Staff Officers and non-regimental Enlisted men, microfilm number M 331, NA, Compiled Military Service Records of Volunteer Confederate Soldiers, M374, rolls 242 and 255, M861, rolls 2, 15 and 16, Company Returns/ Muster Rolls: March.- April, 1862); *CMH*, Vol. VI, Biographical sketch of Paul Semmes and William Duncan Smith.

30. UNC Archives, SHSC, Ware Diary, Vol. 1, October, 1861. Private Ware was a member of the 15th Georgia. Ware recorded poignant and insightful

observations in a personal diary, until his death at the Battle of Gettysburg, July, 2, 1863. His brother Robert, brought the diary home, and it now resides in the archives of the University of North Carolina.

31. Benning Papers UNC Archives, Letter to Edward Porter Alexander, 1866 (In 1866, Edward Porter Alexander, former Artillery commander in Lee's Army of Northern Virginia, solicited data from Benning concerning unit strength movements, battles, and reports as source material for two books, *Military Memoirs of a Confederate, by Alexander*, and *Fighting For the Confederacy*, which was edited by historian Gary Gallagher.); See Chart, Appendix B for detailed data. The Official Appomattox Roster lists Benning's Brigade as surrendering 812 officers and enlisted men, however, there are discrepancies, which show the total varied between 785 to 812 men reported as present and paroled on August 10-11, 1865.

Chapter 12

1. Ware, Vol. 2, (March 8 & 9, 1862), pp. 87 & 88; NA, M861, rolls 2, 15 and 16, Company Returns: (Mar. - May 1862); Longstreet, *From Manassas to Appomattox*, page 64; Wiley, p. 53, *Recollections of a Confederate Staff Officer*, (Sorrel's candid observations of Longstreet's corps, his command and staff and their respective traits, provide a unique and insightful source).

2. OR, Vol. II, Part 1, pp. 943-946; Vol. XI, part 3, pp. 444-445; Ware, Vol. 2, (April 17-20, 1862), pp. 120-125.

3. B&L, Johnston, Joseph E., Gen.(CSA)," Manassas to Seven Pines" , Vol. 2, pp. 202-219; Longstreet, *From Manassas to Appomattox*, pp. 68-71; Ware, Vol. 2, (May 1862), pp. 135-163.

4. Ibid.

5. Ware, Vol. 2, (March-April 1862), pp. 81-134; *Southern Historical Society Papers,,* Vol. 1, Alexander, E.P., Gen. Chief of Artillery, Records of Longstreet's Corps, A.N.V.," The Seven Days Battle" , Jan. to June 1876, pp. 61-65.

6. CSU Archives, MC 34, autobiographical material of Raphael Moses. (Moses was a prominent lawyer, planter, and friend of the Bennings, Jones, Toombs, and Crawford. His plantation called *Esquiline*, was located on a hill south of Columbus. He also served as Toombs and Benning's commissary officer during the Civil War.); Northern, *Men of Mark in Georgia*, Vol. 3, pp. 561-66 (Raphael Moses).

7. Northern, *Men of Mark in Georgia*, Vol. 3, pp. 10-11, (Robert Toombs).

8. Stovall, quoted by in *Robert Toombs: Statesman, Speaker, Soldier, Sage,* p. 331.

9. Ibid., p. 242, Robert Toombs to his wife, letter dated, March 22, 1862.

10. Benning Papers, UNC Archives, Robert Toombs to Henry Benning, letter dated December 10, 1862; *Southern Historical Society Papers,,* Vol. XVI, *Notes by General Benning Concerning the Battle of Sharpsburg*, pp. 393-94.

11. OR, Series 4, Vol. 2, pp. 1095-99 and p. 446. (Elections of officers, regimental and below.); BP, Henry McCauley to Secretary of War Randolph, letter dated June 23, 1862; NA, M861, rolls 2, 15 and 16, company returns, Company F, 17th regiment, March-April, 1862.

12. Benning Papers UNC Archives, McCauley to Secretary of War Randolph, letter dated June 23, 1862.

13. Ibid., letter dated July 17, 1862.

14. Ibid.

15. Ibid.

16. Ibid.

17. NA, Compiled Military Service Records of Volunteer Confederate Soldiers, M374, rolls 242 and 255, Company Returns/ Muster Rolls: May-June, 1862; *CMH*, Vol. VI, Biographical sketch of Robert Toombs, Henry L. Benning, and Dudley M. DuBose, pp. 395-396; 414-415, and 446-448.
18. OR, Series 1, Vol. XI, pp. 720 and 723.
19. Ibid., Vol. XI, pp. 699-700, Report of Lieutenant Colonel Holmes, Second regiment; *CMH*, Battles of Garnett's Farm and Malvern Hill, pp. 172-176; Ware, Vol. 2, (June 1862), pp. 155-182; OR, Vol. XXIII, pp. 701-704.
20. Ibid., pp. 701-02, Report of Colonel Millican, Fifteenth regiment.
21. Ibid., pp. 702-03, Report of Colonel Benning, Seventeenth regiment.
22. Ware, Vol. 2, (June 1862), pp. 155-182; OR, Vol. XXIII, pp. 701-704; NA, M861, rolls 2, 15 and 16, Company Returns: June- August 1862).
23. OR, Series 1, Vol. XI, pp. 700-01.
24. GA, Georgia Division, UDC, *Confederate Reminiscences and Letters 1861-1865, Volume VII*, p. 181, William Terrell Millican to his wife, letter dated July 11, 1862.
25. OR, Series, 1, Vol. XI, pp. 703-04, Report of Colonel Benning, Seventeenth regiment.
26. Ibid., pp. 697-98, Report of General Toombs, commanding brigade at Malvern Hill.
27. Ibid., p. 700, Report of Lieutenant Colonel Holmes, Second regiment.
28. Ibid., pp. 697-98, Report of General Toombs, commanding brigade at Malvern Hill.
29. GA, Georgia Division, UDC, *Confederate Reminiscences and Letters 1861-1865, Volume VII*, p. 181, William Terrell Millican to his wife, letter dated July 11, 1862; OR, Series, 1; Ware, Vol. 2, (June 1862), pp. 155-182; NA, M861, rolls 2, 15 and 16, Company Returns: June- August, 1862.
30. OR, Series, 1, Vol. XI, pp. 703-04, Report of Colonel Benning, Seventeenth regiment.
31. NA, Compiled Military Service Records of Volunteer Confederate Soldiers, M374, 20th regiment, Company I, Lieutenant Van A. Leonard, NA; M861, roll 16, company returns, Company I, 20th regiment, June-July, 1862.

Chapter 13

1. OR, Series 1, Vol. XI, part 2, p. 628. (Report of General Daniel Harvey Hill, Battle of Malvern Hill); Stovall, p. 255, quoted by in *Robert Toombs: Statesman, Speaker, Soldier, Sage*.
2. Ibid.

3. BP & AP, (Various reports concerning troop movements, August, 1862); Ware, Vol. 3, (Aug. 12, 1862), page 211; Longstreet, *From Manassas to Appomattox*, page 158; NA, M861, rolls 2, 15 and 16, Company Returns: August, 1862.
4. CSU Archives, MC 34, autobiographical material of Raphael Moses. (Moses was a prominent lawyer, planter, and friend of the Bennings, Jones, Toombs, and Crawford. His plantation called Esquiline, was located on a hill south of Columbus. He also served as Toombs/ Benning's commissary officer during the Civil War.)
5. BP, (Benning notes concerning the arrest of Toombs, and his assumption of command); Phillips, pp. 603-04, *Toombs, Stephens, Cobb Correspondence*, Robert Toombs to Alexander Stephens, letter dated Aug. 22, 1862; Longstreet, *From Manassas to Appomattox*, page 161.
6. Stovall, p. 246, Toombs and his impulsive nature was displayed throughout his life; Phillips, *Toombs, Stephens, Cobb Correspondence*, letter from Robert Toombs to Alexander H. Stephens, dated August 22, 1862.
7. NA, M861, rolls 2, 15 and 16, Company Returns, July 1862; *CMH*, 2nd. Manassas, page 182; DU, Tondee, Robert P. Jr., letter to his sister, September 3, 1862, events occurring in the 17th. Georgia regiment, at Thoroughfare Gap, August 28, 1862.
8. OR, Series 1, Vol. XII, part 2, p. 586, Report of Captain Abner McLewis, Second regiment.
9. Ibid., pp. 580-81, Report of Colonel Henry L. Benning, commanding brigade.
10. Ibid., pp. 590-91, Report of Major Waddell, Twentieth regiment.
11. Andrews, p. 61, *Footprints of a Regiment*; NA, M861, rolls 2, 15 and 16, Company Returns, July 1862; *CMH*, 2nd. Manassas, page 182.
12. Longstreet, James, Lt. Gen. (CSA)," Our March Against Pope" , Vol. 2, pp. 512-526; Longstreet, *From Manassas to Appomattox*, pp. 174-175; DU, Tondee, Robert P. Jr., letter to his sister, Sept. 7, 1862, events occurring in the 17th. Georgia regiment.
13. OR, Series 1, Vol. XII, part 2, pp. 583-85, Report of Colonel Henry Benning, commanding brigade at Battle of Second Manassas.
14. Ibid.
15. Ibid.
16. Ibid., pp. 591-92, Report of Major J. D. Waddell, Twentieth regiment.
17. Ibid., pp. 584, Report of Colonel Henry Benning, commanding brigade at Battle of Second Manassas.
18. Ibid.
19. Ibid., pp. 590, Report of Captain Hiram French, Seventeenth regiment.
20. Ibid., p. 592, Report of Major J. D. Waddell, Twentieth regiment.
21. DU, Tondee, Robert P. Jr., letter to his sister, Sept. 7, 1862, events occurring in the 17th. Georgia regiment.

22. OR, Series 1, Vol. XII, part 2, pp. 584, Report of Colonel Henry Benning, commanding brigade at Battle of Second Manassas; Stovall, p. 261, quoted by in *Robert Toombs: Statesman, Speaker, Soldier, Sage.*

23. Ibid., p. 560, Surgeons report of casualties, Battle of Second Manassas, Benning's Brigade; *CMH*, 2nd Manassas, p. 182.

24. DU, Tondee, Robert P. Jr., letter to his sister, Sept. 7, 1862, events occurring in the Seventeenth Georgia regiment.

25. Ware, Vol. 3, (July 1-3), 1862, pp. 183-187; Buel, *Battles & Leaders*, Longstreet, James, Lt. Gen. (CSA)," The Invasion of Maryland" , Vol. 2, pp. 662-665; Longstreet, *From Manassas to Appomattox*, pp. 201-205; NA, M861, rolls 2, 15 and 16, Company Returns, Sept. 1862.

26. Longstreet, *From Manassas to Appomattox*, pp. 239-254.; OR, Series 1, Vol. LI, part 1, pp. 160-168.

27. OR, Series 1, Vol. LI, part 1, pp. 161-65, Colonel Henry Benning's report, Battle of Sharpsburg. (commanding brigade).

28. Terrill, Section I, p. 278, *History of Stewart County, Georgia.* Letters of Charles Frederick Terrill, Second Georgia regiment, letter dated September 25, 1862.

29. Ibid., p. 165, Report of Captain Abner McLewis, commanding Second regiment, Battle of Sharpsburg.

30. Ibid., pp. 161-65, Colonel Henry Benning's report, Battle of Sharpsburg. (commanding brigade).

31. Ibid., Vol. XIX, pp. 888-893, General Robert Toomb's report, Battle of Sharpsburg. (commanding division).

32. Ibid., pp. 161-65, Colonel Henry Benning's report, Battle of Sharpsburg. (commanding brigade).

33. Ibid., p. 167-68, Report of Major McGregor, commanding Seventeenth regiment, Battle of Sharpsburg.

34. Ibid., pp. 161-65, Colonel Henry Benning's report, Battle of Sharpsburg. (commanding brigade).

35. Ibid., p. 166, Report of Captain Thomas Jackson, commanding Fifteenth regiment, Battle of Sharpsburg.

36. NA, CSA Record, Compiled Service Records of Confederate Soldiers Who Served in Organizations from the State of Georgia, 17th Infantry Regiment, Seaborn Jones Benning; GDAH, Compiled Records of General and Staff Officers and non-regimental enlisted men, Box 277, roll 28, Seaborn Benning, CSU Archives, MC 28, UDC records; comments by Anna Caroline concerning her mother Mrs. Mary Benning during the Civil War; Mr. Henry Benning Spencer to author, letter dated April 24, 1999, Mr. Spencer is the great-great grandson of Henry L. Benning, (incidentally, both he and his father were lawyers too). Mr. Spencer kindly filled in several gaps concerning details of

the Benning family, which included the health of Seaborn Benning, his war wounds, and his death at the age of thirty-four, due to complications of his wounds.

37. Ibid., pp. 161-65, Colonel Henry Benning's report, Battle of Sharpsburg. (commanding brigade).

38. Ibid., Vol. XIX, pp. 888-893, General Robert Toomb's report, Battle of Sharpsburg. (commanding division).

39. Houghton, p. 182, *Two Boys in the Civil War and After.* (1st Sergeant Houghton was from Columbus, Georgia, and he was a member of the " Columbus Guards," Company G, Second regiment). There are numerous references to Benning's nickname of " Old Rock," and his daughters had it etched in his tombstone. Several veterans writing in post war narratives alluded that perhaps they were the first to use the name. Regardless of whoever was first, it stuck. The title " Old Rock," combined with the affection and respect that Benning won from his men, his peers, his superiors, and his opponents, all validate his sobriquet.

40. Longstreet, *From Manassas to Appomattox*, pp. 256-259. (On page 257, Longstreet commends Benning and Toombs for their work at the Battle of Sharpsburg.); OR, Official Report from Longstreet also contains a formal commendation for Benning.

41. NA, (Company Returns: Aug.- Sept. 1862); B&L," With Burnside at Antietam" , D.L. Thompson, Co. G, 7th New York Volunteers, page 662.

42. BP, Notes concerning the Battle of Sharpsburg written by Henry L. Benning, 1869. Later published in *Southern Historical Society Papers,*, Vol. XVI, p. 393.

43. Stovall, p. 268, *Robert Toombs: Statesman, Speaker, Soldier, Sage.*

44. Ibid.

45. Longstreet, *Manassas to Appomattox*, p. 262.

46. NA, CSA Record, Compiled Service Records of Confederate Soldiers Who Served in Organizations from the State of Georgia, 17th Infantry Regiment, Seaborn Jones Benning; Northern, *Men of Mark in Georgia*, Vol. 3, pp. 566-81 (Howell Cobb), Vol. 3, pp. 155-162 (Thomas R. R. Cobb); Longstreet, *Manassas to Appomattox*, p. 290. Terrill, Section I, p. 278, *History of Stewart County, Georgia.* Letters of Charles Frederick Terrill, Second Georgia regiment, letter dated September 25, 1862; Irwin, Richard B., Col. (U.S.)," The Removal of McClellan" , pp. 102-104. NA, M861, rolls 2 and 16, Benning's Brigade- Company Returns Oct. 1862); Ware, Vol. 4, (Oct. 30 & 31,1862), pp. 1&2; *CMH*, Vol. VI, pp. 194-195.

Chapter 14

1. Buel, *Battles & Leaders*, Longstreet, James, Lt. Gen. (CSA)," Burnside at Fredericksburg" , pp. 70-85; OR, Series 1, Vol. XXI, pp. 555-626, (Battle of Fredericksburg, Virginia, December 13, 1862).

2. OR, Series 1, Vol. XXI, p. 173, Colonel Benning's report of the Battle of Fredericksburg.

3. Ibid.

4. Ibid.

5. McCash, *Thomas R. R. Cobb (1823-1862): The Making of a Southern Nationalist* p. 317; Northern, *Men of Mark in Georgia*, Vol. 3, pp. 155-162 (Thomas R. R. Cobb).

6. Longstreet, *Manassas to Appomattox*, pp. 323-24.

7. BP, General Robert Toombs to Colonel Henry Benning, letter dated December 10, 1862.

8. Ibid.

9. Ware, Vol. 4, (Dec. 16 & 17, 1862); *CMH*, p. 198.

10. Ibid., (Jan. 1-2, 1863); NA, Company Returns: January, 1863.

11. OR, Series 1, Vol. XXI, p. 1009, Colonel Benning's promotion to Brigadier-General; CSU Archives, Jones- Benning Papers, MC 6; (Benning's original promotion orders); NA, CSA Record, Compiled Service Records of Confederate General and Staff Officers and non-regimental Enlisted men, microfilm number M 331, Compiled Service Records of Confederate Soldiers Who Served in Organizations from the State of Georgia, 17th Infantry Regiment, Henry L. Benning (contain copies of orders assigning Benning to Semmes brigade, and then back to take command of his former brigade); Northern, Vol. 3, pp. 259-67, Henry L. Benning.

12. CSU Archives, MC-9, Box 2, Folder 3, letters of Confederate soldiers of the 20th regiment, Benning's brigade, J. A. Maddox to Miss Jennie Smith, letter dated February 5, 1863.

13. Confederate Veteran," Accurate Historic Records" , by John H. Martin, pp. 114-115; Ware, Vol. 4, (March 6, 1863), page 66.

14. *CMH*, Biographical sketch of Henry L. Benning,(CSA), pp. 395-396; Sorrell, General G. Moxley, *Recollections of a Confederate Staff Officer*, p. 96.

15. Ware, Vol. 4, (Jan. 1-2, 1863); NA, Company Returns: January- March 1863).

16. Houghton, *Two Boys in the Civil War and After*, p. 181. (1st Sergeant Houghton was from Columbus, Georgia, and he was a member of the " Columbus Guards," Company G, Second regiment).

17. Ware, Vol. 4, (Feb.-April, 1863; NA, Company returns, February-April, 1863).

18. NA, Company Returns: April, 1863); Ware, Vol. 5, (April 13-16,1863); Longstreet, *Manassas to Appomattox*, pp. 323-324.

19. Lokey, J. W. Typed manuscript entitled " My Experiences in the War Between the States". (Private, Co. B, 20th regiment). W. C. Bradley Library Archives, Columbus, Georgia. (Gift of Ray Lokey, great-grandson).

20. Houghton, *Two Boys in the Civil War and After*, p. 181. (1st Sergeant Houghton was from Columbus, Georgia, and he was a member of the " Columbus Guards," Company G, Second regiment).

21. Lokey, J. W. Typed manuscript entitled " My Experiences in the War Between the States". (Private, Co. B, 20th regiment). W. C. Bradley Library Archives, Columbus, Georgia. (Gift of Ray Lokey, great-grandson).

22. BP, (Various papers, reports and correspondence concerning details of his brigade during the Suffolk Campaign); AP, (Various papers, reports and correspondence concerning the 1st Corps events during the Suffolk Campaign); Ware, Vol. 5, (May 3, 1863).

23. Ware, Vol. 5, (May 4, 1863); DU, Tondee, Robert P. Jr., letter to his sister, May 6, 1863, concerning events occurring in the 17th Georgia regiment.

24. Ibid., Vol. 5, (May 10, 1863); OR, Vol. XXV, parts 1&2.

25. Ibid., Vol. 5, (May 27, 1863); OR, Vol. XVIII (Suffolk) and XXV, part 1 and 2 (Battle of Chancellorsville); NA, (Company Returns: May-June 1863).

26. NA, CSA Record, Compiled Service Records of Confederate Soldiers Who Served in Organizations from the State of Georgia, 17th Infantry Regiment, Seaborn Jones Benning; Benning Family Records; Ibid., Compiled Service Records of Confederate Soldiers Who Served in Organizations from the State of Georgia, 20th Infantry Regiment, John Abraham Jones; Benning Family Records; NA, (Company Returns: May-June 1863); *(Columbus) Weekly Enquirer*, May 26, 1863 (quote concerning Colonel Jones).

27. Ware, Vol. 5, (15 June- July 1, 1863); NA, (Company Returns: June and July, 1863); OR, Vol. XXVII, parts 1-3.

28. Ibid., Longstreet, *Manassas to Appomattox*, pp. 341-47.

29. Ibid.

30. Houghton, *Two Boys in the Civil War and After*, p. 67. (1st Sergeant Houghton was from Columbus, Georgia, and he was a member of the " Columbus Guards," Company G, Second regiment); quote of Hood's Foot Cavalry appears in *(Columbus) Weekly Enquirer*, May 26, 1863.

31. Hunt, Henry J., Brevet Maj. Gen. (U.S.)," The First Day at Gettysburg" , Vol. 3, pp. 255-290.

32. Longstreet, *Lee & Longstreet*, Chapter II, pp. 40-49; *Battles & Leaders*, Law, E.W., Maj. Gen. (CSA)," The Struggle for Round Top" ; OR, Vol. XXVII, part 2, pp. 392-395.

Chapter 15

1. Longstreet, *Manassas to Appomattox*, p. 361; OR, Series 1, Vol. XXVII, part 1, pp. 414-27.

2. OR, Series I, Vol. XXVII, part 1, pp. 424-25, Report of Major Wesley Hodges, Seventeenth Georgia regiment.

3. Houghton, *Two Boys in the Civil War and After*, p. 34. (1st Sergeant Houghton was from Columbus, Georgia, and he was a member of the " Columbus Guards," Company G, Second regiment).

4. OR, Series I, Vol. XXVII, part 1, pp. 414-19, Report of Brigadier General Henry Benning, Benning's brigade. Perry, W. F., *Confederate Veteran*," The Devil's Den," Vol.,XI, p. 161-62.

5. OR, Series I, Vol. XXVII, part 1, pp. 414-19, Report of Brigadier General Henry Benning, Benning's brigade.

6. McGregor, John A., Papers. (Captain E, 17th Georgia regiment), Private collection of Mr. Blaine Walker, Cornelia, Georgia; Quote by OR, Series I, Vol. XXVII, part 1, pp. 424-25, Report of Colonel Wesley C. Hodges, commander of the Seventeenth regiment.

7. Houghton, *Two Boys in the Civil War and After*, pp. 220-21. (1st Sergeant Houghton was from Columbus, Georgia, and he was a member of the " Columbus Guards," Company G, Second regiment).

8. Perry, W. F., *Confederate Veteran*," The Devil's Den," Vol. XI, p. 161-62.

9. OR, Series I, Vol. XXVII, part 1, pp. 424-25, Report of Major Wesley Hodges, Seventeenth Georgia regiment.

10. Polley, Joseph Benjamin, *Hood's Texas Brigade. Its Marches, Its Battles, Its Achievements*. p. 168.

11. Hatchett, Pinkney G., (First Lieutenant, Co. E, 20th Georgia regiment). Private Collection of Mr. David Cress, Charlotte, North Carolina.

12. OR, Series I, Vol. XXVII, part 1, pp. 414-19, Report of Brigadier General Henry Benning, Benning's brigade; Longstreet, *Manassas to Appomattox*, pp. 346-84; 36. Longstreet, Helen, *Lee & Longstreet at High Tide*, Chapter II, pp. 40-49; Buel, *Battles & Leaders*, Law, E.W., Maj. Gen. (CSA)," The Struggle for Round Top" ; OR, Vol. XXVII, part 2, pp. 392-395; 420-426; Norton, Oliver Wilcox, *The Attack and Defense of Little Round Top, Gettysburg, July 2, 1863*, pp. 167-171 and 227-233, New York, 1913; BP, Benning mentioned in his memoirs that his units fought in the Devils Den and in the Plum Run Valley and that although they never received any special recognition for their efforts, his men had captured the only Federal artillery pieces north of the Potomac River.

13. Ibid., pp. 425-27, Report of Lieutenant-Colonel James D. Waddell, Twentieth regiment.

14. Bowden, p. 6, Reverend John Malachi Bowden's unpublished journal, MSS number 537f, Atlanta History Center. (John Malachi Bowden served in Company G, Second regiment).

15. OR, Series I, Vol. XXVII, part 1, pp. 420-21, Report of Lieutenant-Colonel William S. Shepherd, Second regiment.

16. Houghton, *Two Boys in the Civil War*, p. 236.

17. *Confederate Veteran*, Vol. XXII, Number 8, August, 1914, p. 400," Wounded at Gettysburg," by J. W. Lokey. (Private John W. Lokey was present at Gettysburg and a member of Company B, 20th regiment); NA, Company Returns, Juy-August, 1863.

18. OR, Series I, Vol. XXVII, part 1, pp. 414-19, Report of Brigadier General Henry Benning, Benning's brigade.

19. Ibid., See also pp. 421-24, Report of Colonel Dudley M. DuBose, Fifteenth regiment.

20. Ibid., NA, CSA Record, Compiled Service Records of Confederate Soldiers Who Served in Organizations from the State of Georgia, 17th Infantry Regiment, Seaborn Jones Benning; Benning Family Records.

21. OR, Series I, Vol. XXVII, part 1, pp. 414-19, Report of Brigadier General Henry Benning, Benning's brigade.

22. Longstreet, *Manassas to Appomattox*, p. 361; OR, Series 1. Vol. XXVII, part 1, Longstreet's official report of the Battle of Gettysburg.

23. Ibid., pp. 414-19, Report of Brigadier General Henry Benning, Benning's brigade.

24. Hunt, Henry J., Brevet Maj. Gen. (U.S.)," The Third Day at Gettysburg" , Vol. 3, pp. 369-384; OR, Vol. XXVII, parts 1-3, A compilation of the dead at Gettysburg is staggering. In the aftermath of the battle, there were approximately 6,000 men and an almost equal number of horses which littered the fields surrounding Gettysburg; OR, Series I, Vol. XXVII, part 1, pp. 421-24, Report of Colonel Dudley M. DuBose, Fifteenth regiment; Smith, *The Life and Times of George F. Pierce*, 481-82; Duggan Papers, Special Collections, Robert Woodruff Library, Emory University, (Private Ivy Duggan, Company K, 15th regiment was a friend of Major Edgeworth Bird and his company was from Hancock County).

25. Ibid.; Bowden, Rev. John Malachi, p. 8, unpublished journal, MSS number 537f, Atlanta History Center. (John Malachi Bowden served in Company G, Second regiment).

26. OR, Series I, Vol. XXVII, part 1, p. 340, (Official casualty report); NA, Company Returns: July-August, 1863; See Appendix B for casualty data compiled from individual records.

27. NA, CSA Record, Compiled Service Records of Confederate Soldiers Who Served in Organizations from the State of Georgia, 17th Infantry Regiment, Seaborn Jones Benning; GDAH, Compiled Records of General and Staff Officers and non-regimental enlisted men, Box 277, roll 28, Seaborn Benning,

CSU Archives, MC 28, UDC records; comments by Anna Caroline concerning her mother Mrs. Mary Benning during the Civil War; Mr. Henry Benning Spencer to author, letter dated April 24, 1999, Mr. Spencer is the great-great grandson of Henry L. Benning, (incidentally, both he and his father were lawyers too). Mr. Spencer kindly filled in several gaps concerning details of the Benning family, which included the health of Seaborn Benning, his war wounds, and his death at the age of thirty-four, due to complications of his wounds. Benning Family Records, Death of Colonel John A. Jack Jones, (Pleasant Benning family Bible, with addenda by his granddaughter, Mary Benning), Personal archives of Mrs. Patti Andrews; Muscogee County probate records, Estate papers of Seaborn Jones reflects that after the war, John Jones son, Seaborn Leonard Jones went to Gettysburg and retrieved his father's body.

28. OR, Series 1, Vol. XXX, pp. 260-261 and 517-520. 36. Longstreet, Helen, *Lee & Longstreet at High Tide*, pp. 191-194; NA, (Company Returns: Aug.- Sept. 1863).

29. *CMH*, p.252, Hood's wound was originally believed to be mortal, however, he survived with an arm that was nearly useless.

30. *The North Carolina Standard*, October 2 and 27, 1863.

31. Ibid., October 2, 1863.

32. BP, Brigadier-General Henry L. Benning to Adjutant Inspector General, S. Cooper, letter dated September 23, 1863; OR, Series 1, Vol. LI, part II, pp. 768-71, correspondence between Benning, his officers, and the Adjutant and Inspector General's office, S. Cooper.

33. *The North Carolina Standard*, October 2, 1863.

34. Ibid.

35. Governor Zebulon B. Vance to President Jefferson Davis, message dated September 10, 1863, printed in *The North Carolina Standard*, October 27, 1863.

36. Ibid.

37. Ibid.

38. BP, Brigadier-General Henry L. Benning to Adjutant Inspector General, S. Cooper, letter dated September 28, 1863; OR, Series 1, Vol. LI, part II, pp. 768-71, correspondence between Benning, his officers, and the Adjutant and Inspector General's office, S. Cooper.

39. Ibid.

40. *The North Carolina Standard*, October 27, 1863.

41. Ibid.

42. Lieutenant-Colonel William S. Shepherd to Adjutant Inspector General, S. Cooper, letter dated Oct. 6, 1863, printed in *The North Carolina Standard*, October 27, 1863; OR, Series 1, Vol. LI, part II, pp. 768-71, correspondence

between Benning, his officers, and the Adjutant and Inspector General's office, S. Cooper.

43. BP, Governor Zebulon B. Vance to Colonel John Whitford, letter dated November 10, 1863.

44. Lieutenant E. M. Seago to William Holden, letter printed in *The North Carolina Standard*, October 27, 1863.

45. OR, Vol. XXX, part 4, p. 652; James A. Maddox to Miss Jennie Smith, letter dated September, 1863, CSU Archives, MC-9, Columbus Museum of Arts & Sciences Collection, Box 2, Folder 3. (Maddox was a Second Lieutenant in Company E, 20th regiment, and a resident of Harris County. Miss Jennie Smith was a popular young belle and collected letters, throughout the war, from several soldiers in Benning's brigade.)

46. Longstreet, Helen, *Lee and Longstreet at High Tide*, p. 194; Buel, *Battles & Leaders*, Vol. III, Hill, Daniel H., Gen. (CSA)," Chickamauga, The Great Battle in the West", pp. 638-661; Sorrell, General G. Moxley, *Recollections of a Confederate Staff Officer*, p. 194; OR, Vol. XXX, part 4, pp. 260-261, 517-520, and 652; *Confederate Veteran*," Longstreet's Forces at Chickamauga", Vol. 20, Number 12, December 1912, Captain J. H. Martin, Hawkinsville, Georgia, page 564; Longstreet, *Manassas to Appomattox*, p. 448.

47. Houghton, p. 141, *Two Boys in the Civil War and After*. (1st Sergeant Houghton was from Columbus, Georgia, and he was a member of the " Columbus Guards," Company G, Second regiment).

48. OR, Series I, Vol. XXX, part 4, pp. 517-19, Report of Brigadier General Henry Benning, Benning's brigade.

49. Ibid.

50. *Confederate Veteran*," Longstreet's Forces at Chickamauga", Vol. 20, Number 12, p. 564, December, 1912, Captain J. H. Martin, Hawkinsville, Georgia; Hays, J. E., comp., *Reminences of Confederate Soldiers and Stories of the War, 1861-1865, Vol. 1*, pp. 2-3.

51. OR, Series I, Vol. XXX, part 4, pp. 517-19, Report of Brigadier General Henry Benning, Benning's brigade.

52. *Confederate Veteran*," Longstreet's Forces at Chickamauga", Vol. 20, Number 12, p. 564, December, 1912, Captain J. H. Martin, Hawkinsville, Georgia; Hays, J. E., comp., *Reminences of Confederate Soldiers and Stories of the War, 1861-1865, Vol. 1*, pp. 2-3.

53. Mills, Lane, ed., *Dear Mother: don't Grieve about Me...Letter from Georgia Soldiers in the Civil War*, p. 275; Polley, Hood's Texas Brigade, pp. 210-11.

54. Ibid.

55. OR, Series I, Vol. XXX, part 4, pp. 517-19, Report of Brigadier General Henry Benning, Benning's brigade.

56. Ibid.

57. Captain J. H. Martin, Hawkinsville, Georgia; Hays, J. E., comp., *Reminences of Confederate Soldiers and Stories of the War, 1861-1865, Vol. 1*, pp. 2-3.

58. Longstreet, *Manassas to Appomattox*, p. 448.
59. Sorrell, *Recollections of a Confederate Staff Officer*, p. 194.
60. Longstreet, *Manassas to Appomattox*, p. 448.
61. OR, Series I, Vol. XXX, part 4, pp. 517-19, Report of Brigadier General Henry Benning, Benning's brigade.
62. Mills, Lane, ed., *Dear Mother: don't Grieve about Me...Letter from Georgia Soldiers in the Civil War*, p. 276.
63. Fidler, William, *Augusta Evans Wilson*, pp. 84-114.

Chapter 16

1. Alexander, E. P., Notes concerning events leading up to Battle at Wauhatchie. (Later published as *Military Memoirs of a Confederate* by Edward Porter Alexander, pp. 467-473, New York, 1907, Reprinted by the De Capo Press, Inc., New York, 1993. Alexander was the artillery commander of the 1st Corps. His detailed memoirs contain valuable insight into why certain events occurred as they did, including his personal feelings about key members of the command and their actions.)

2. OR, Series 1, Vol. LII, part 1, supplement, General Benning's report of battle of Wauhatchie, Tennessee. NA, company returns, October, 1863.

3. NA, Company Returns: October - November, 1863; AP, (Notes concerning occurrences between the Battle of Chickamauga and Knoxville.); DU, Tondee, William H. (2d Lt., Co. B, 17th Georgia), letter, Nov. 7, 1863, concerning events occurring in the 17th Georgia regiment.

4. OR, series 1, Vol. 31, part 1, p. 475, report of General Benning concerning the battle of Knoxville and pp. 524-31, Jenkins report.; NA, Company Returns: Oct. - Nov. 1863; Buel, *Battles & Leaders*, Vol. III, Alexander, E.P., Gen., (CSA)," Longstreet at Knoxville", pp. 745-752.

5. OR, Vol. XXXI, part 2, Vol. XXXV, part 1; AP, Notes concerning events at Knoxville and East Tennessee Campaign, Vol. 42 and 51. 36. Longstreet, Helen, *Lee & Longstreet at High Tide*, pp. 195-204; *CMH*, Chapter 14, pp. 264-268; Longstreet, *From Manassas to Appomattox*, pp. 504, 511 and 521.

6. Houghton, *Two Boys in the Civil War and After*, p. 67; NA, (Company Returns: April 1864); Evans, *Confederate Military History*, Volume 6, pp. 395-396; Longstreet, *From Manassas to Appomattox*, pp. 512-516.

7. Alexander, *Military Memoirs of a Confederate*, p. 491.

8. Houghton, *Two Boys in the Civil War and After*, p. 68.

9. Ibid., p. 182.

10. NA, Company returns, December, 1863)

11. Houghton, *Two Boys in the Civil War and After*, p. 69.

12. OR, series 1, vol. LII, part 2, p. 634.

13. Ibid., XXXI, part 1, pp. 500-01 and 505-06.

14. *Columbus Daily Enquirer*, December 20, 1863; CSU Archives, MC 22, UDC Scrapbook, Lizzie Rutherford Collection, efforts of Mary Benning and the Soldiers' Friend Society" during the war.

15. *Columbus Daily Enquirer*, September 13, 1862.

16. CSU Archives, MC 34, autobiographical material of Raphael Moses.

17. Houghton, *Two Boys in the Civil War and After*, p. 71.

18. CSU Archives, MC 22, UDC Scrapbook, Lizzie Rutherford Collection, letter dated December 24, 1864.

19. Longstreet, Helen,, *Lee and Longstreet at High Tide*, pp. 205-208; *CMH*, Chapter 15, pp. 290-293; OR, Vol. XXXIII, XXXVI, parts 1&2.

20. CSU Archives, MC-9, Box 2, Folder 3, letters of Confederate soldiers of the 20th regiment, Benning's brigade, J. Alexander Maddox to Miss Jennie Smith, letter dated February 7, 1864.

21. Benning Family Records, (Pleasant Benning family Bible, with addenda by his granddaughter, Mary Benning), Personal archives of Mrs. Patti Andrews; CSU Archives, MC-9, Columbus Museum of Arts & Sciences Collection (Linwood Cemetery records).

22. Longstreet, Helen, *Lee & Longstreet at High Tide*, p. 208.

23. *Columbus Times*, March 19, 1864; Benning Family Records, (Pleasant Benning family Bible, with addenda by his granddaughter, Mary Benning), Personal archives of Mrs. Patti Andrews; CSU Archives, MC-9, Columbus Museum of Arts & Sciences Collection (Linwood Cemetery records); MC 6, Benning-Jones papers.

24. Buel, *Battles & Leaders*, Vol. IV, Law, E.M.," From the Wilderness to Cold Harbor", pp. 118-144; *Southern Historical Society Papers,*, Vol. XIV, Field, Charles," The Campaign of 1864 and 1865", 1886, pp. 542-546.

25. NA, (Company Returns: Apr. - May 1864); AP, (Notes concerning the Battle of the Wilderness.)

26. Alexander, E. P, (Notes concerning the battle of Cold Harbor and the Union movements toward Richmond & Petersburg, Va.); NA, (Company Returns & Muster Rolls: June 1864); *Southern Historical Society Papers,*, Vol. XIV, Field, Charles," The Campaign of 1864 and 1865", 1886, pp. 548-549.

27. Longstreet, *From Manassas to Appomattox*, p. 568.

28. Ibid., page 570, (Longstreet survived his wound, but he was incapacitated for the next six months.); *Southern Historical Society Papers,*, Vol. XIV, Field, Charles," The Campaign of 1864 and 1865", 1886, pp. 545.

29. NA, Company returns, May, 1864; See Appendix B.

30. NA, CSA Record, Compiled Service Records of Confederate General and Staff Officers and non-regimental Enlisted men, microfilm number M 331, Compiled Service Records of Confederate Soldiers Who Served in Organizations from the State of Georgia, 17th Infantry Regiment, Henry L. Benning; Northern, Vol. 3, pp. 259-67, Henry L. Benning.

31. Alexander, E. P, (Notes concerning the 1st. Corps data, commanded by Gen. R.H. Anderson, dates: June 12-19, 1864.); NA, (Company Returns & Muster Rolls: June 1864).15. AP, (Notes concerning the battle of Cold Harbor and the Union movements toward Richmond & Petersburg, Va.); *Southern Historical Society Papers,*, Vol. XIV, Field, Charles," The Campaign of 1864 and 1865", 1886, pp. 548-549.

32. Rozier, *The Granite Farm Letters*, p. 164 (Edgeworth Bird to Sallie Bird, letter dated May 6, 1864).

33. CSU Archives, MC 22, UDC Scrapbook, Lizzie Rutherford Collection, notes concerning Mary (Jones) Benning trip to Virginia to retrieve her husband; *(Columbus) Daily Sun*, May 11, 25 & 26, 1864.

34. CSU Archives, SMC-16, Post Register of Sick & Wounded in Hospitals, Columbus, Georgia, 1864-1865 (Henry Benning).

35. Uzar, *Muscogiana*, Volume 3, Numbers 1 & 2, (Spring 1992)," Confederate Hospitals in Columbus, Georgia," pp. 16-21.

36. UNC Archives, Benning Papers, microfilm number M-2225, Captain Herman H. Perry to General Henry L. Benning, letter dated June 22, 1864.

37. *Compiled Records Showing Service of Military Units in Confederate Organizations.* National Archives, Seventeenth Georgia Infantry, Roll 16 (Colonel Wesley C. Hodges); Muscogee County probate records (estate record of Seaborn Jones reflects business arrangements between Hodges and Benning); CSU Archives, MC 22, Anne Elizabeth Shepherd Home pamphlet, p. 2; Journal entries," Ladies' Education and Benevolent Society of the Methodist Episcopal Church, of the City of Columbus," 1845-1860 (several female members of the Hodges served as officers on the staff of the Girls' Asylum along with the Jones and Benning families).

38. Muscogee County probate records (estate of Seaborn Jones, Journal O, p.415), Muscogee County property deeds (Benning and Jones families); Benning Family Records (Pleasant Benning family Bible, with addenda by his granddaughter, Mary Benning), Personal archives of Mrs. Patti Andrews.

39. Standard, *Columbus, Georgia in the Confederacy: The Social and Industrial Life of the Chattahoochee River Port*, p. 53-5.

40. *Columbus Daily Sun*, July 11, 1863.

41. *Columbus Daily Enquirer*, February 5, 1864.

42. Ibid., April 7, 1864.

43. Martin, *Columbus, Georgia, From Its Selection as a Trading Town in 1827, To Its Partial Destruction by Wilson's Raid in 1865*, pp. 16-68.

44. *Columbus Daily Sun*, October 13, 1863; David William's book *Rich Man's War: Class, Caste, and Confederate Defeat in the Lower Chattahoochee Valley*, provides the definitive work concerning the vast disparity between the rich and poor as experienced by the people of the lower Chattahoochee Valley, during the Civil War.

Chapter 17

1. Buel, *Battles and Leaders*, Vol. IV, Grant, U.S., Gen. (U.S.)," General Grant on the Siege of Petersburg", pp. 574-579; Alexander, E. P., (Letter from Dudley M. DuBose to E.P. Alexander, dated Aug. 23, 1866 and 1st Corps data, June 12-19, 1864.)

2. NA, (Company Returns: June - July 1864); Fuller, Joseph P. (2d Corporal, Co. B, 20th Georgia), Diary, May-Sept. 1864, Miscellaneous Collection of Civil War materials, Diaries, Georgia Archives.

3. Alexander, E. P., (Notes concerning life in the breastworks during the siege of 1864.)*; The Granite Farm Letters, The Civil War Correspondence of Edgeworth & Sallie Bird*, Athens & London, 1988, page 176, Edgeworth Bird to Sallie Bird, letter dated: July 17, 1864; Longstreet, *From Manassas to Appomattox*, pp. 580-581.

4. OR, Vol. XLII, part 1, pp. 761, 764-765; *Southern Historical Society Papers,*, Vol. XIV, Field, Charles," The Campaign of 1864 and 1865", 1886, pp. 552-554.

5. *Richmond Enquirer*, Article entitled " Field's Division", August 31, 1864.

6. OR, Vol. XL, parts 1-3, Vol. XLII, parts 1-3.

7. Evans, Clement. *Confederate Military History*. Vol. 6, Chapter 27, p.353; NA, (Company Returns: Sept. 1864).

8. OR, Vol. XL, pp. 474-478; AP, (Notes concerning the Fall of 1864.) *Southern Historical Society Papers,*, Vol. XIV, Field, Charles," The Campaign of 1864 and 1865", 1886, pp. 552-555.

9. *Southern Historical Society Papers,*, Vol. XIV, Field, Charles," The Campaign of 1864 and 1865", 1886, page 556; Vol. II, McCabe, W. Gordon," Defense of Petersburg", 1876, pp. 257-306.

10. Alexander, E. P, (Notes concerning the Fall of 1864; NA, (Company Returns: Sept. 1864.); *Confederate Veteran*, Vol. 13, No. 9, Moore, James B.," The Attack of Fort Harrison", 1905, pp. 418-420; Allen, Cornelius Tacitus," Fight at Chaffin's Farm, Fort Harrison".

11. *Confederate Veteran*, Vol. 12, No. 12, May, T.J., The Fight at Fort Gilmer, 1904, pp. 587-588; Vol. 13, No. 6, Martin J.H., The Assault on Fort Gilmer, 1905, pp. 269-270; Vol. 13, No. 9, Granberry, J.A.H., That Ft. Gilmer Fight, 1904, pp. 587-588.

12. Ibid.

13. Alexander, E. P, (Letter from Dudley M. DuBose to E.P. Alexander, dated Aug. 23, 1866 and 1st Corps data, Sept. 1864.)

14. OR, Vol. 42, part 1, p. 934, Report of General Gregg.

15. OR, Vol. 42, part 2; p. 875, 877; NA, (Company Returns: Oct. 1864).
16. *Southern Historical Society Papers*, Field, Charles, Vol. XIV," The Campaign of 1864 and 1865", page 558; Alexander, E. P., Notes concerning 1st Corps data, Oct. 1864.
17. NA, (Company Returns: Sept..- Oct. 1864); Alexander, E. P., Notes concerning the fall of 1864 and letter: D.M. DuBose to E.P. Alexander, dated 1866.
18. UNC, John Bratton letters, MS # 2216 (General John Bratton to his wife, letter dated November 23, 1864).
19. Ibid.
20. NA, Company Returns, May-November, 1864.
21. Cleveland, *Reminiscences of Confederate Soldiers and Stories of the War, 1861-1865, Vol. 1*, p. 146.
22. Houghton, *Two Boys in the Civil War*, p.80; Polley, *Hood's Texas Brigade*, p. 261.
23. Ibid., Nov. 1864; Buel, *Battles & Leaders*, Vol. IV, Sherman, William T., Gen.(U.S.)," The Grand Strategy of the Last Year of the War", pp. 247-259.
24. *The Granite Farm Letters, The Civil War Correspondence of Edgeworth & Sallie Bird*, pp. 194-196, letter dated: Sept. 3, 1864; Wiley, Letter to his parents, dated Nov. 26, 1864.
25. Ibid; Smith, *The History of Hancock County, Georgia*; Smith, *The Life and Times of George F. Pierce.*
26. Wiley, letter to his parents, dated Nov. 26, 1864.
27. Lane, *Marching Through Georgia: William T. Sherman's Personal Narrative of His March Through Georgia*, p. 145. (General Sherman's orders to his army, dated November 9, 1864, pp. 144-46).
28. Ibid., p. 173 (General Sherman to his wife, Ellen, letter dated December 16, 1864).
29. Ibid., p. 186 (General Sherman to his wife, Ellen, letter dated December 25, 1864).
30. NA, Microfilm copy 331, No. 60, Military service record of Dudley M. DuBose (CSA). (DuBose was appointed to the position of Brigadier-General in Nov. of 1864, but officially promoted in January of 1865.)
31. *(Columbus) Daily Sun*, March 21 and 22, 1865.
32. NA, (Company Returns: Jan. - Feb. 1865 reflect 50 deserters); Buel, *Battles & Leaders*, Vol. IV, Slocum, Henry W.," Sherman's March From Savannah to Bentonville", pp. 681-700; *The Granite Farm Letters, The Civil War Correspondence of Edgeworth & Sallie Bird*, pp. 203-206, letter dated: Sept. 22, 1864; Houghton, *Two Boys in the Civil War*, p.79.
33. Benning, *Southern Historical Society Papers*, Vol. 7," Notes on the Final Campaign of April, 1865", pp. 193-195; Vol. 14, Field, Charles," The Campaign of 1864 and 1865", 1886, pp. 560-561; Longstreet, *From Manassas to Appomattox*, page 606.

34. Ibid.
35. Booklet entitled," Thirty-Six Hours Before Appomattox: April 6 and 7, 1865" , Christopher M. Calkins, 1980, Chapter 3, Farmville & Cumberland Church; Buel, *Battles & Leaders*, Vol. IV, Porter, Horace, Gen. (U.S.)," Five Forks and the Pursuit of Lee" , pp. 708-722; OR, Vol. XLVI, Chapter 58," Lee's Report of the Appomattox Campaign" , pp. 1264-1270.
36. Longstreet, Helen, *Lee & Longstreet at High Tide*, pp. 209-210.
37. Alexander, E. P., Notes concerning the fall of 1864, (which include the retreat and surrender in 1865.); The *Century Illustrated Monthly Magazine*, Vol. LXIII, Alexander, E.P.," Lee at Appomattox" , pp. 921-931.
38. CSU Archives, Benning-Jones Papers, MC 6, (hand written letter (orders of General U.S. Grant) explaining the arrangements for surrendering commands to U. S. officials- Document signed by the Adjutants of: Longstreet's corps, Colonel Latrobe; Field's division, Jonathan Stephenson; and Seaborn Benning, Benning's brigade.
39. *Southern Historical Society Papers*, Vol. XX, Perry, Herman H., Col. (CSA)," Account of the Surrender of the Confederate States of America, April 9, 1865" , 1892; Benning, *Southern Historical Society Papers*, Vol. 7," Notes on the Final Campaign of April, 1865" , pp. 193-195.
40. CSU Archives, Benning-Jones Papers, MC 6, (hand written letter (orders of General U.S. Grant) explaining the arrangements for surrendering commands to U. S. officials- Document signed by the Adjutants of: Longstreet's corps, Colonel Latrobe; Field's division, Jonathan Stephenson; and Seaborn Benning, Benning's brigade.
41. Longstreet, *From Manassas to Appomattox*, (quote) p. 629.
42. Houghton, *Two Boys in the Civil War*, p. 80.
43. Lokey, J. W. Typed manuscript entitled " My Experiences in the War Between the States," p. 24.(Private, Co. B, 20th regiment). W. C. Bradley Library Archives, Columbus, Georgia. (Gift of Ray Lokey, great-grandson).
44. Northern, *Men of Mark*, Vol. 3, pp. 259-67, (biographical sketch of Henry L. Benning by his daughter, Anna C. Benning); Knight, *A Standard History of Georgia and Georgians*, Vol. 2, p. 749.
45. Benning, *Southern Historical Society Papers*, Vol. 7," Notes on the Final Campaign of April, 1865" , pp. 193-195;
46. *Columbus Enquirer*, July 17, 1875 (memorial tribute to Henry L. Benning, written by James D. Waddell; also appeared in the Atlanta Herald, July 11, 1875); Northern, *Men of Mark*, Vol. 3, pp. 259-67, (biographical sketch of Henry L. Benning by his daughter, Anna C. Benning).
47. Houghton, *Two Boys in the Civil War*, pp. 182 and 235; CSU Archives, Benning-Jones Papers, MC 6 (Parole passes of General Henry L. Benning and Captain Seaborn Benning); Lokey, J. W. Typed manuscript entitled " My

Experiences in the War Between the States," p.26. (Private, Co. B, 20th regiment). W. C. Bradley Library, Columbus, Georgia. (Gift of Ray Lokey, great-grandson).

48. Dameron, *Benning's Brigade*, pp. 108-114; Wounded soldiers joined the units as they passed through Richmond only to drop out again several days later. Official records reflect inaccuracies, as do individual service records, and various accounts of the surrender, such as Benning, *Southern Historical Society Papers*, Vol. 7," Notes on the Final Campaign of April, 1865" , pp. 193-195; Vol. 14, Field, Charles," The Campaign of 1864 and 1865" , 1886, pp. 560-561. (See Appendix C for detailed list of soldiers paroled from Benning's brigade).

Chapter 18

1. *Columbus Daily Enquirer*, July 10, 11, 13 and 17, 1875; *Atlanta Herald*, July 11, 1875 (comments made by Benning's friend and commander of the Twentieth regiment, Colonel James D. Waddell); Northern, Men of Mark in Georgia, Vol. 3, pp. 259-67; Knight, Vol. 4, p. 749, *A Standard History of Georgia and Georgians*; OR, series 1, Vol. 46, part 2, pp. 1256 and 1269 (Benning's assignment as the division commander of Field's division, Feb. 24 and 28, 1865); Henry L. Benning tombstone in Linwood Cemetery, Columbus, Georgia, states Major General, C.S.A.

2. OR, series 1, Vol. 49, part 2, p. 383. Report from Brevet Major General Wilson to Major General Canby, message dated April 17, 1865.

3. Martin, *Columbus, Georgia, From Its Selection as a " Trading Town" in 1827, To Its Partial Destruction by Wilson's Raid in 1865*, p. 185.

4. OR, series 1, part 1, pp. 486-87. Report of Brigadier General Edward Winslow, dated April 18, 1865.

5. Worsley, *Columbus on the Chattahoochee*, p. 297.

6. Barfield, *History of Harris County, Georgia*, 1827-1961, p. 684.

7. Martin, *Columbus, Georgia, From Its Selection as a " Trading Town" in 1827, To Its Partial Destruction by Wilson's Raid in 1865*, pp. 183-86.

8. Muscogee County probate records (the records of the estate of Seaborn Jones contains detailed financial transactions for 1864, 1865 and 1866 of both the Jones and Benning families). Copy of letter from W. J. Coffield to Mary Benning, letter dated May 12, 1865, located in the estate record on p. 419.

9. Northern, *Men of Mark in Georgia*, Vol. 3, pp.259-67 (Henry L. Benning).

10. Muscogee County probate records (the records of the estate of Seaborn Jones contains detailed financial transactions for 1864, 1865 and 1866 of both the Jones and Benning families); CSU Archives, Benning-Jones Papers, MC 6; City Directory, 1873-74.

11. Ibid., quote is in the Jones estate record, p. 393.

12. Ibid.
13. Ibid.
14. Northern, *Men of Mark in Georgia*, Vol. 3, 212-20 (Alexander Stephens); pp. 1-16 (Robert Toombs); Stovall, *Robert Toombs*; Avery, *Recollections of Alexander H. Stephens;* Evans, *Confederate Military History,* Vol. 6, pp. 414-15, 446-48.
15. Andrews, *The Wartime Journal of a Georgia Girl*, p. 354.
16. Ibid.
17. Avery, *The History of the State of Georgia*, p. 341; Columbus Daily Enquirer, September 9, 1865 (Croxton in command of Columbus); Ibid., November 1, 1865, (Idle Negroes on the chain gang).
18. *Columbus Daily Sun,* September 14, 1865 (quote), other newspaper articles, which reflect similar situations, include: *Milledgeville Federal Union*, October 17, 1865; *Savannah Herald*, January 3, 1866; and the *Macon Telegraph*, January 13, 1866.
19. Avery, *The History of the State of Georgia*, p. 341.
20. Telfair, *A History of Columbus, Georgia, 1828-1928*, pp. 140-41.
21. Avery, *The History of the State of Georgia*, p. 356.
22. *Columbus Daily Sun,* December 13 and 15, 1865.
23. Muscogee County probate records (the records of the estate of Seaborn Jones contains detailed financial transactions for 1864, 1865 and 1866 of both the Jones and Benning families); Muscogee County Census, 1870; City Directory, 1873-74 include the names and occupations of several black entrepreneur laborers named Benning.
24. UGA Archives, Howell Cobb Papers, MSS 1376, Martin J. Crawford to Howell Cobb, letter dated September 29, 1865.
25. Thompson, *Reconstruction in Georgia*, p. 117 (Copy of letter dated November 24, 1865, Howell Cobb to his wife).
26. UGA Archives, Howell Cobb Papers, MSS 1376, Martin J. Crawford to Mrs. Howell Cobb, letter dated November 30, 1865.
27. Ibid.
28. Thompson, *Reconstruction in Georgia*, p. 130.
29. *(Columbus) Daily Sun*, December 15, 1865.
30. Avery, *The History of the State of Georgia*, p. 357.
31. Thompson, *Reconstruction in Georgia*, p. 127.
32. *Testimony Taken by The Joint Select Committee to Inquire into The Condition of Affairs in The Late Insurrectionary States, Georgia, Volume I*, pp. 182-89 (Testimony of Henry L. Benning, July 18, 1871).
33. Thompson, *Reconstruction in Georgia*, p. 131 (quote is from *New York Herald*, June 18, 1866).

34. Ibid., p. 53 (letter dated June 14, 1865, Howell Cobb to General James Wilson), also published in Fleming, documentary History of Reconstruction, vol. I, pp. 128-131.

35. *Testimony Taken by The Joint Select Committee to Inquire into The Condition of Affairs in The Late Insurrectionary States, Georgia, Volume I*, pp. 182-89 (Testimony of Henry L. Benning, July 18, 1871).

36. *Macon Telegraph*, January 24, 1866.

37. CSU Archives, MC 22, UDC Scrapbook, Lizzie Rutherford Collection Benning, Anna Caroline and Mary Jones Benning., MC-28, United Daughters of the Confederacy Collection, Lizzie Rutherford Chapter, (journals, pictures, medals, pins, scrapbooks, and reminiscences.) This collection also includes material from the Ladies' Aid Society and the post-war, Ladies Memorial Society.

38. Ibid., Confederated Southern Memorial Association. *History of the Confederated Memorial Associations of the South, pp. 126-34.*

39. Ibid., p. 126.

40. Muscogee County probate records (the records of the estate of Seaborn Jones contains detailed financial transactions for 1864, 1865 and 1866 of both the Jones and Benning families).

41. Ibid.

42. Fidler, William, *Augusta Evans Wilson*, pp. 128-44.

43. Ibid., CSU Archives, MC 22, UDC Scrapbook, Lizzie Rutherford Collection Benning, Anna Caroline and Mary (Jones) Benning., MC-28, United Daughters of the Confederacy Collection, Lizzie Rutherford Chapter, (journals, pictures, medals, pins, scrapbooks, and reminiscences.) This collection also includes material from the Ladies' Aid Society and the post-war, Ladies Memorial Society; Confederated Southern Memorial Association. *History of the Confederated Memorial Associations of the South, pp. 126-34.*

44. *Testimony Taken by The Joint Select Committee to Inquire into The Condition of Affairs in The Late Insurrectionary States, Georgia, Volume I*, p. 184 (Testimony of Henry L. Benning, July 18, 1871).

45. Ibid.

46. *State Agricultural Society of Georgia Proceedings*, pp. 44-5 (Yancey's quote); Banks, *The Economics of Land Tenure in Georgia*, pp. 63-4 (acreage in Georgia owned by blacks); Thompson, *Reconstruction in Georgia*, p. 294-95 (post-war division of lands in Georgia).

47. Muscogee County Property Deeds (former Benning lot number 95, Thomas Narrymore to " Society of Friends of Zion," Gardner Williams, R. B. Bell, Jacob Hardaway, 1887).

48. *Testimony Taken by The Joint Select Committee to Inquire into The Condition of Affairs in The Late Insurrectionary States, Georgia, Volume I*, p. 184 (Testimony of Henry L. Benning, July 18, 1871).

49. Ibid.

50. Ibid.

51. Worsley, *Columbus on the Chattahoochee*, p. 308; Avery, *The History of the State of Georgia*, p. 357-84; Thompson, *Reconstruction in Georgia*, p. 181; Lamar, A Standard History of Georgia and Georgians, Volumes 2 and 4 (quotes are from Worsley and background data is from Avery, Thompson and Lamar). Phillips, *Annual Report of the American Historical Association for the Year 1911, Vol. II, The Correspondence of Robert Toombs, Alexander H. Stephens, and Howell Cobb* (Howell Cobb to his wife, letter dated September 1, 1867).

Chapter 19

1. Worsley, *Columbus on the Chattahoochee*, p. 308-09; *(Columbus) Daily Sun*, March 15, 1868.

2. *Columbus Enquirer*, March 1, 1868; Telfair, *A History of Columbus, Georgia, 1828-1928*, p. 156.

3. *(Columbus) Daily Sun*, March 21, 1868; Worsley, *Columbus on the Chattahoochee*, p. 308-09.

4. Avery, *The History of the State of Georgia*, p. 386; Lamar, A Standard History of Georgia and Georgians, Volumes 2 and 4.

5. UGA Archives, M 1376, Howell Cobb Papers, Henry Benning to Howell Cobb, letter dated Mar. 27, 1868.

6. Worsley, *Columbus on the Chattahoochee*, p. 310; *Testimony Taken by The Joint Select Committee to Inquire into The Condition of Affairs in The Late Insurrectionary States, Georgia, Volume I*, p. 184 (Testimony of Henry L. Benning, July 18, 1871); *(Columbus) Daily Sun* reported the Ashburn murder and subsequent trial throughout the months of April-July, 1868.

7. Ibid.

8. Telfair, *A History of Columbus, Georgia, 1828-1928*, p. 159.

9. Ibid., p. 161.

10. Avery, *The History of the State of Georgia*, p. 387; Telfair, *A History of Columbus, Georgia, 1828-1928*, p. 163.

11. Worsley, *Columbus on the Chattahoochee*, p. 311.

12. Confederated Southern Memorial Association. *History of the Confederated Memorial Associations of the South*, pp. 127-28; CSU Archives, MC 22, UDC Scrapbook, Lizzie Rutherford Collection Benning, Anna Caroline and Mary (Jones) Benning., MC-28, United Daughters of the Confederacy Collection, Lizzie Rutherford Chapter, (journals, pictures, medals, pins, scrapbooks, and reminiscences.) This collection also includes material from the Ladies' Aid Society and the post-war, Ladies Memorial Society.

13. Ibid.

14. Ibid.

15. Ibid.

16. Ibid., p. 129.

17. Ibid.

18. *(Columbus) Daily Sun* (April-July, 1868: Trial transcripts appearing in); Avery, *A History of the State of Georgia*, pp. 386-87; Worsley, *Columbus on the Chattahoochee*, p. 312; Telfair, *History of Columbus, Georgia, 1828-1928*, pp. 164-65.

19. Ibid.

20. *Atlanta Constitution*, July 25, 1868.

21. Avery, *The History of the State of Georgia*, pp. 386-87.

22. Ibid., p. 388.

23. CSU Archives, MC 28, UDC records; notes by Anna Caroline concerning the move from " El Dorado" to 1420 Broad Street; Muscogee County Superior Court Minutes, Volumes Q, R, S (1867-1877).

24. Columbus City Directory, 1873-74, W. C. Bradley Library Archives.

25. Garrard, Leonard, Personal archives, genealogical notes, family papers, and interview with author. Mr. Garrard is the grandson of Louis F. Garrard and Anna Foster (Leonard) Garrard. Allen, Sarah, *Our Children's Ancestors*, pp. 401-03; Worsley, *Columbus on the Chattahoochee*, pp. 237, 290-91.

26. Muscogee County Deed Book 1, Benning's purchase of home at 1420 Broad Street, deed recorded June 9, 1868; Map of Downtown Columbus (1861-1865) by George J. Burrus, 1928, W. C. Bradley Library Archives.

27. *(Columbus) Daily Sun* (April-July, 1868: Trial transcripts appearing in); Avery, *A History of the State of Georgia*, pp. 386; Worsley, *Columbus on the Chattahoochee*, p. 312; Telfair, *History of Columbus, Georgia, 1828-1928*, pp. 164.

28. CSU Archives, MC 28, UDC records; notes by Anna Caroline concerning the move from " El Dorado" to 1420 Broad Street.

29. *Atlanta Herald*, July 11, 1875; Northern, Men of Mark in Georgia, Vol. 3, pp. 259-67 (Henry L. Benning).

30. *(Columbus) Daily Sun,* July 1, 1868.

31. *Atlanta Constitution*, December 20, 1925.

32. UGA Archives, M 1376, Howell Cobb papers, Henry Benning to Howell Cobb, letters dated Feb. 4, 1836 and Jan. 12, 1839.

33. *(Columbus) Daily Sun,* July 2, 1868.

34. *(Columbus) Daily Sun* (April-July, 1868: Trial transcripts appearing in); Avery, *A History of the State of Georgia*, pp. 386-89; Worsley, *Columbus on the Chattahoochee*, p. 312-13; Telfair, *History of Columbus, Georgia, 1828-1928*, pp. 168-69.

35. *Atlanta Constitution*, July 22-26, 1868 (quote appears on the front page of July 25th issue); Worsley, *Columbus on the Chattahoochee*, pp. 313-14.

36. Worsley, *Columbus on the Chattahoochee*, p. 314.

37. *Atlanta Constitution*, July 22-26, 1868.

38. DeGregorio, *The Complete Book of U. S. Presidents, pp.* 265-66.

39. Northern, *Men of Mark in Georgia*, Vol. 3, pp. 566-81 (Howell Cobb).

40. Benning Family Records (Pleasant Benning family Bible, with addenda by his granddaughter, Mary Benning), Personal archives of Mrs. Patti Andrews.

41. *Columbus Enquirer-Sun*, November 11 and 12, 1869.

42. Northern, *Men of Mark in Georgia*, Vol. 3, pp. 559-67 (Henry Benning).

43. Benning Family Records (Pleasant Benning family Bible, with addenda by his granddaughter, Mary Benning), Marriage of Reese Crawford and Augusta Jones Benning, Personal archives of Mrs. Patti Andrews; Muscogee County Marriage Book A.

44. Federal Census 1870 (Muscogee County); Benning Family Records, (Pleasant Benning family Bible, with addenda by his granddaughter, Mary Benning), Personal archives of Mrs. Patti Andrews.

45. Ibid.

46. Avery, *The History of the State of Georgia*, p. 466-67.

47. *Testimony Taken by The Joint Select Committee to Inquire into The Condition of Affairs in The Late Insurrectionary States, Georgia, Volume I*, pp. 182-89 (Testimony of Henry L. Benning, July 18, 1871).

48. Ibid., (quote is from page 182).

49. *Savannah News*, November 9, 1871.

50. Ibid.

51. Knight, *A Standard History of Georgia and Georgians*, Volume 4, p. 1237 (DuBose entered the 42nd U.S. Congress); Avery, *The History of the State of Georgia*, pp. 468-69.

52. Avery, *The History of the State of Georgia*, p. 498.

53. Benning Family Records (Pleasant Benning family Bible, with addenda by his granddaughter, Mary Benning), Marriage of Samuel Spencer to Louisa Vivian Benning, Personal archives of Mrs. Patti Andrews; Muscogee County Marriage Book A.

54. Avery, *The History of the State of Georgia*, p. 502.

55. Private collection of Henry Benning Spencer, Seaborn Jones Benning to Louisa Vivian (Benning) Spencer, letter dated June 23, 1872.

56. *(Columbus) Daily Sun*, January 12, 1873.

57. Ibid.

58. Ibid.

59. Ibid., January 19, and 23, 1873; Knight, *A Standard History of Georgia and Georgians*, Volume 4, p. 1241.

60. Avery, *The History of the State of Georgia*, p. 77.

61. Private collection of Henry Benning Spencer, Seaborn Jones Benning to Louisa Vivian (Benning) Spencer, letter dated April 16, 1872.

62. Ibid., letter dated April 7, 1872.

63. Ibid.

64. Benning Family Records (Pleasant Benning family Bible, with addenda by his granddaughter, Mary Benning), Personal archives of Mrs. Patti Andrews (death of Seaborn Jones Benning); MC-9, Columbus Museum of Arts & Sciences Collection (Linwood Cemetery records: Seaborn Jones Benning, death listed as Consumption); Northern, *Men of Mark in Georgia*, Vol. 3, p. 262 (Henry Benning), Anna C. Benning recorded that Seaborn died from effects of his wounds; CSU Archives, MC 28, UDC records; notes of Anna Caroline Benning state that Seaborn died from " effects of wounds received."

65. Private collection of Henry Benning Spencer, Seaborn Jones Benning to Louisa Vivian (Benning) Spencer, letter dated April 7, 1872; Tomb of Seaborn J. Benning, Linwood Cemetery, Columbus, Georgia.

66. Benning Family Records (Pleasant Benning family Bible, with addenda by his granddaughter, Mary Benning), Personal archives of Mrs. Patti Andrews (death of Mary Louisa Jones).

67. Muscogee County Superior Court Minutes, Volumes Q, R, S (1867-1877).

68. *Columbus Enquirer-Sun*, July 17, 1875; *Baldwin County News*, July 13, 1875.

69. Muscogee County Probate records, Henry Benning estate; *Columbus Sunday Enquirer*, July 11, 1875.

70. GA, *Georgia Reports*, Vol. LVI, July term, 1876, pp. 694-99.

71. *Columbus Daily Enquirer*, July 10, 11, 13 and 17, 1875; *Atlanta Herald*, July 11, 1875. GA, *Georgia Reports*, Vol. LVI, July term, 1876, pp. 694-99, *Georgia Bar Association, 33rd Annual Meeting Session*, June 1-3, 1916.

72. GA, *Georgia Reports*, Vol. LVI, July term, 1876, pp. 694-99. ND, *Columbus Daily Enquirer*, July 10, 11, 13 and 17, 1875; *Atlanta Herald*, July 11, 1875.

73. *Atlanta Herald*, July 11, 1875.

74. *Columbus Enquirer, Centennial edition*, photo of Benning's home, 1420 Broad Street. Muscogee County deeds, deed for Lot 194, John King to Henry L. Benning, June 9, 1868; Book R, entry 412; Mary H. Benning (daughter and Administratrix), to Louis Garrard, December 7, 1875, county estate record sale, Journal U, 1875-77.

75. Berry, Mary Kent, compiler, *Records of Marriages, Baptism and Burials from the First Register of Trinity Parish* (1836-1903). ND, *Columbus Daily Enquirer*, July 10, 11, 13 and 17, 1875; *Atlanta Herald*, July 11, 1875. GA, *Georgia Reports*, Vol. LVI, July term, 1876, pp. 694-99. *Georgia Bar Association, 33rd Annual Session*, June 1-3, 1916.

76. CSU Archives, MC-9, Columbus Museum of Arts & Sciences Collection (Linwood Cemetery records), Columbus, Georgia, death and funeral data concerning Henry L. Benning; *Columbus Daily Enquirer*, July 13, 1875.

77. *Georgia Bar Association, Twelfth Annual Meeting (1895) and Twenty-Sixth Annual Meeting (1909)*, poem by Judge Logan Edwin Bleckley, p. 153, GA, *Georgia Reports*, Vol. LVI, July term, 1876, pp. 694-99.

78. Northern, *Men of Mark in Georgia*, Vol. 3, pp. 256-66; Avery, *The History of the State of Georgia*, pp. 77 & 215. BP, notes concerning the Battle of Gettysburg, letter from Henry L. Benning to Edward P. Alexander. OR, Vol. XXVII, parts 1-3 (official reports of Generals Benning, Longstreet and Lee); *Columbus Daily Enquirer-Sun*, July 10, 1875.

79. Photograph of Benning's tomb, Author's collection; CSU, Linwood Cemetery records. Northern, William J., ed., *Men of Mark in Georgia*, Vol. 3, pp. 256-66. Georgia State Historical Marker of General Henry Lewis Benning, formerly located on the east side of Broadway, between 14th and 15th streets (now the location of Total Systems corporate headquarters), whereabouts of marker, unknown.

Chapter 20

1. Muscogee County Probate records, Estate of Henry Lewis Benning, Journal U, Wills and Estates (1875-1877).

2. Ibid., Estate of Seaborn Jones, Journal O, Wills and Estates (1864-1866).

3. Muscogee County Property Deeds, Record Book V, p. 141.

4. Ibid., (sale of former Seaborn Jones residence," El Dorado," Lot #51 and part of #70) Record Book S-135, Mary Benning to Louis F. Garrard, and S-141, Louis F. Garrard to Lelia B. Slade; *Columbus Ledger, 75th Anniversary Special*," Greek Fire Burned Brightly in Columbus" ; Whitehead, *City of Progress, A History of Columbus, Georgia*, p. 338.

5. Muscogee County Probate records, Estate of Henry Lewis Benning, Journal U, Wills and Estates (1875-1877); Estate of Seaborn Jones, Journal O, Wills and Estates (1864-1866); Muscogee County Property Deeds, Record Books R through Z (entries listed as FROM: Benning, Mary H, Adm., TO: various purchasers).

6. Muscogee County Probate records, Estate of Henry Lewis Benning, Journal U, Wills and Estates (1875-1877), voucher numbers 2 through 5.

7. Muscogee County Property Deeds, Record Book R, p. 412 (Mary Benning to Louis Garrard).

8. Ibid. Record Book R, p. 415 (Louis Garrard to Mary, Anna and Sarah Benning).

9. Ibid., Record Book S, p. 135 (Mary Benning to Louis Garrard).

10. Benning Family Records (Pleasant Benning family Bible, with addenda by his granddaughter, Mary Benning), Personal archives of Mrs. Patti Andrews (Marriage of Herbert Ladson Hull to Sarah Jones Benning).

11. CSU Archives, MC 22, UDC Scrapbook, Lizzie Rutherford Collection Benning, Anna Caroline and Mary Jones Benning., MC-28, United Daughters of the Confederacy Collection, Lizzie Rutherford Chapter, (journals, pictures, medals, pins, scrapbooks, and reminiscences.) This collection also includes material from the Ladies' Aid Society and the post-war, Ladies Memorial Society.

12. Benning Family Records (Pleasant Benning family Bible, with addenda by his granddaughter, Mary Benning), Personal archives of Mrs. Patti Andrews (Marriage of Herbert Ladson Hull to Sarah Jones Benning); CSU Archives, MC-9, Columbus Museum of Arts & Sciences Collection (Linwood Cemetery records); *(Columbus) Daily Sun*, February 6, 1927.

13. Worsley, *Columbus on the Chattahoochee*, pp. 456 and 466.

14. Northern, *Men of Mark in Georgia*, Vol. 4, pp. 367-70. (Samuel Spencer); Davis, *The Southern Railway: Road of the Inventors*, pp. 19-20.

15. Ibid., Southern Railway, In Memoriam, Samuel Spencer.

16. Jones Benning., MC-28, United Daughters of the Confederacy Collection, Lizzie Rutherford Chapter, (journals, pictures, medals, pins, scrapbooks, and reminiscences.) Quotes are from biographical data concerning members of the UDC. This collection also includes material from the Ladies' Aid Society and the post-war, Ladies Memorial Society; Benning Family Records (Pleasant Benning family Bible, with addenda by his granddaughter, Mary Benning), Personal archives of Mrs. Patti Andrews (Marriage of Louisa Vivian Benning and Samuel Spencer).

17. Ibid. (death of Louisa Vivian (Benning) Spencer).

18. Benning Family Records (Pleasant Benning family Bible, with addenda by his granddaughter, Mary Benning), Personal archives of Mrs. Patti Andrews (Death of Anna Caroline Benning); CSU Archives, MC-9, Columbus Museum of Arts & Sciences Collection (Linwood Cemetery records), Columbus, Georgia, death and funeral data concerning Anna Caroline Benning; *Columbus Enquirer*, February 9, 1935;

19. Georgia Division UDC, *The History of the United Daughters of the Confederacy, 1895-1995*, pp. 214-17; DeLamar, *History of the Georgia State Society of the National Society of the Daughters of the American Revolution* " Anna Caroline Benning."

20. Ibid., quote is from the *Constitution and By-Laws of the Women's Reading Club of Columbus, Georgia, 1888*, which are housed in the Columbus State University Archives, MC-79, Edith Kyle Crawford Collection.

21. Ibid.

22. Ibid.

23. Confederated Southern Memorial Association, *History of the Confederated Memorial Associations of the South*, pp. 129-30.
24. Worsley, *Columbus on the Chattahoochee*, p. 421.
25. *Columbus Enquirer*, February 9, 1935.
26. Benning Family Records (Pleasant Benning family Bible, with addenda by his granddaughter, Mary Benning), Personal archives of Mrs. Patti Andrews (Death of Sarah (Sallie) Jones (Benning) Hull); *Columbus Enquirer*, May 17, 1949.
27. Benning Family Records (Pleasant Benning family Bible, with addenda by his granddaughter, Mary Benning), Personal archives of Mrs. Patti Andrews (Death of Richard Edwin Benning).
28. Ibid., (birth, marriage and deaths of Augusta Palmyra (Benning) Patterson and her family); Russell County Historical Commission, *The History of Russell County, Alabama*, p. F266 (Madison L. Patterson).
29. Fidler, William, *Augusta Evans Wilson*, pp. 145-215.
30. Data concerning Louis F. Garrard and " Wildwood" provided by interview with Mr. Leonard Garrard, Muscogee County records and CSU archives, Linwood Cemetery records, Columbus, Georgia; Allen, Sarah, *Our Children's Ancestors*, pp. 401-03.
31. Northern, *Men of Mark in Georgia*, Vol. 3, pp. 561-66 (Raphael Moses); Worsley; *Columbus on the Chattahoochee*, p. 240-41, CSU archives, autobiography of Raphael Moses.
32. Ibid., Vol. 3, pp. 301-07 (Martin J. Crawford), CSU archives, Linwood Cemetery records.
33. Ibid., Vol. 3, pp. 212-20 (Alexander Stephens); pp. 1-16 (Robert Toombs), Dameron, *Benning's Brigade*, p. 94 (Dudley M. DuBose), Knight, *A Standard History of Georgia and Georgians*, Vols. 2 and 4.
34. *Atlanta Constitution*, December 20, 1925; Garrett, Atlanta and Environs, Vol. II, pp. 591-95.
35. *Columbus Enquirer Sun*, October 19 and 20, 1918, Whitehead, *City of Progress: A History of Columbus, Georgia*, p. 249.
36. Author's notes, photographs and observations; pamphlet entitled *General Henry Lewis Benning Memorial Service, March 29, 1999*.
37. The Columbus Museum newsletter, *The News,* " Digging History: The Archeology of Columbus," p. 4, The Columbus Museum: Columbus, Georgia, Spring 2000.

Bibliography

UNPUBLISHED MANUSCRIPTS AND ARCHIVAL RECORDS
GOVERNMENT DOCUMENTS:
Acts of the General Assembly of Georgia. Milledgeville: Published
   annually by the State Printers, 1825-1841, biennially, 1843-1853.
Candler, Allen D. comp. *The Confederate Records of the State of Georgia.*
   6 vols. (vol. 5 never published). Atlanta: State Printing Office, 1909-
   11.
Compiled Military Service Records of Volunteer Soldiers Who Served
   During Indian Wars and Disturbances. National Archives, 1815-
   1858, M629, rolls 3 and 38.
Compiled Military Service Records of Volunteer Soldiers Who Served
   During the Mexican War. National Archives, 1846-1848,
   M616.
Compiled Service Records of Confederate Soldiers Who Served in
   Organizations from the State of Georgia. National Archives, M266:
   3d Cavalry, rolls 16-19; 1st. Georgia Regulars (Ramsey's), Rolls 143-
   45; 2nd Georgia Infantry, Rolls 152-56; 15th Georgia Infantry, Rolls
   290-96; 17th Georgia Infantry, Rolls 303-07; 20th Georgia Infantry,
   Rolls 325-32; Index, M266, Georgia, Rolls 1-67.
Compiled Records Showing Service of Military Units in Confederate
   Organizations. National Archives, M861: 1st. Georgia Regulars and
   2nd Georgia Infantry, Roll 14; 15th, 17th, and 20th Georgia Infantry,
   Roll 16.
Confederate General Staff Officers and non-Regimental Enlisted Men.
   National Archives, M331, Roll 22.
Confederate List of Volunteer Companies (Georgia). Georgia Department
   of Archives and History, Miscellaneous, Drawer 283, Roll 58.
Confederate States of America Collection. War Department, List of
   Official Communications, box 110, maps, Library of Congress,
   Washington, D.C.
Fort Benning, National Infantry Museum, United States Army Infantry
   School. Personal artifacts and portraits of Henry L. Benning
   contributed by his grandsons, Henry Benning Spencer, Henry
   Benning Crawford, and Benning Hull in 1940.

Georgia House Journal. Georgia Department of Archives and History.
Drawer number 295, Boxes 1 through 12 (1821-1875).

Georgia Senate Journal. Georgia Department of Archives and History.
Drawer number 295, Boxes 47 through 60 (1821-1875).

Governor Joseph E. Brown 's Incoming Correspondence, 1861-1865.
Georgia Department of Archives and History, Atlanta, Georgia.

Journal of the State Convention Held in Milledgeville in December, 1850.
Milledgeville: R. M. Orme, 1850.

Journal of the Lower House of the General Assembly of Georgia.
Milledgeville: Published Annually by the State Printers, 1825-1841.
biennially, 1843-1853.

*Journal of the Public and Secret Proceedings of the Convention of the
People of Georgia, 1861.* Milledgeville, Georgia: Boughton, Nisbet,
Barnes, and Moore, 1866.

Records of Baldwin County, Georgia. (Census, Marriage and Deeds)

Records of Clarke County, Georgia. (Census and Marriage)

Records of Colombia County, Georgia. (Census, Marriage, Birth, Deeds)

Records of Harris County, Georgia. (Census, Marriage, Birth, Deeds)

Records of Muscogee County, Georgia. (Census, Marriage, Birth, Court,
Deeds, Estates, city of Columbus)

*Reports of Cases of Law and Equity Argued and Determined in the
Supreme Court of the State of Georgia,* Vols. VIII - XXVI, Various
State Publishers, Atlanta: 1852-1875 (Reprint Edition annotated by
Howard Van Epps), The Harrison Company, State Publisher: 1932.

*Testimony Taken by The Joint Select Committee to Inquire into The
Condition of Affairs in The Late Insurrectionary States, Georgia,
Volume I,* (Testimony of Henry L. Benning, July 18, 1871),
Government Printing Office, Washington D. C., 1872.

United States Census Bureau. *Agricultural Census of 1850.* Georgia
Department of Archives and History. Drawer 331, Roll 70, Muscogee
County.

_____. *Agricultural Census of 1860.* Georgia Department of Archives and
History. Drawer 332, Roll 43, Muscogee County.

_____. *Fifth Census of the United States, 1830.* Microfilm number M19,
Georgia: Roll 16, Clarke, Columbia, and Baldwin Counties.

_____. *Sixth Census of the United States, 1840.* Microfilm number M704, Georgia: Roll 39, Clarke and Columbia Counties; Roll 43, Harris County ; Roll 47, Muscogee County.

_____. *Seventh Census of the United States, 1850.* Microfilm number M432, Georgia: Roll 66, Columbia County; Roll 73, Harris County; Roll 79, Muscogee County ; Slave Schedules: Roll 89, Columbia County; Roll 91, Harris County; Roll 93, Muscogee County.

_____. *Eighth Census of the United States, 1860.* Microfilm number M653 Georgia: Roll 118, Columbia County; Roll 116, Clark County; Roll 126, Harris County; Roll 132, Muscogee County ; Slave Schedules: Roll 144, Clarke and Columbia Counties; Roll 146, Harris County; Roll 149, Muscogee County.

_____. *Ninth Census of the United States, 1870.* Microfilm number M593, Georgia: Roll 145, Columbia County; Roll 156, Harris County; Roll 167, Muscogee County.

U.S. War Department, *The War of the Rebellion: A Compilation of the Official Records of the Union and Confederate Armies.* 127 Volumes, index and atlas. Washington D.C., 1880-1901.

ARCHIVAL DOCUMENTS:

Andrews, Patti Mrs. (Wife of Mote Andrews Jr., great-great-grandson of Pleasant Moon Benning). Personal archives, photographs, extensive genealogical notes and interview with author. Benning family Bible , genealogical records and papers of Pleasant Moon Benning (Henry L Benning's father), Miss Mary Benning (Henry Benning 's daughter), and Augusta (Benning) Patterson.

Alexander, Edward Porter. Papers, (correspondence with Benning, Toombs, DuBose, McLaws , Longstreet and other key members of the Army of Northern Virginia gathered for a history of Longstreet's corps. Data includes regimental and brigade rosters, statistics, descriptions of battles, maps, and a manuscript copy of *Military Memoirs of a Confederate*). Southern Historical Society Collection, Wilson Library, University of North Carolina, Chapel Hill, North Carolina.

Benning, Anna Caroline and Mary (Jones) Benning. MC-28, United Daughters of the Confederacy Collection, Lizzie Rutherford Chapter, (journals, pictures, medals, pins, scrapbooks, and reminiscences.) This collection also includes material from the Ladies' Aid Society and the postwar, Ladies Memorial Society. Columbus State

University (CSU) Archives, Simon Schwob Library, Chattahoochee Valley Historical Collection, Columbus, Georgia.

Benning, Mary Howard (Jones), Mrs. John A. Jones , and Mrs. Seaborn Jones, MC-22; Anne Elizabeth Shepherd Orphans Home Records (journal of the Ladies' Education and Benevolent Society of the Methodist Episcopal Church, of the City of Columbus). CSU Archives, Simon Schwob Library, Chattahoochee Valley Historical Collection, Columbus, Georgia.

Benning, Henry L. Papers, microfilm number M-2225, Southern Historical Society Collection, Wilson Library, University of North Carolina, Chapel Hill, North Carolina.

_____. (also Seaborn Jones). Henry Lewis Benning - Seaborn Jones Collection, MC 6. This collection includes business, legal, and official documents of both Henry L. Benning and Seaborn Jones. CSU Archives, Simon Schwob Library, Chattahoochee Valley Historical Collection, Columbus, Georgia.

_____. Papers. Manuscript number 2601(m), (General Henry L. Benning papers) Hargrett Rare Book and Archives Collection, University of Georgia, Athens, Georgia.

_____. SMC-16, Post Register of Sick & Wounded in Hospitals, Columbus, Georgia, 1864-1865. CSU Archives, Simon Schwob Library, Chattahoochee Valley Historical Collection, Columbus, Georgia.

Bratton, John. (Brigadier General) Manuscript number 2216, (Bratton letters). Southern Historical Society Collection, Wilson Library University of North Carolina, Chapel Hill, North Carolina.

Childs, Mimi Pease Mrs. (Descendant of John A. Jones) Personal archives, photographs, interview, and extensive genealogical notes concerning the Benning, Jones and Pease families.

Cobb, Howell. Manuscript number 1376, (Howell Cobb papers). Hargrett Rare Book and Archives Collection, University of Georgia, Athens, Georgia.

Bowden, John Malachi. (Private, 2nd Georgia), Unpublished Journal, MSS collection, MSS 537f, Atlanta History Center, Atlanta, Georgia.

Catalogue of the Trustees, Officers, Alumni and Matriculates of the University of Georgia at Athens, Georgia, from 1785 to 1906. Athens, Georgia: The E. D. Stone Press, 1906.

Cleveland, Reuben Weston, *Reminiscences of Confederate Soldiers and Stories of the War, 1861-1865, Vol. 1*, Georgia Division, United Daughters of the Confederacy. Central Research Library, Georgia Department of Archives and History, Atlanta, Georgia, 1940.

Crawford, Edith Kyle Collection. MC-73. (Her husband was Henry Benning Crawford, Columbus City Manager and the grandson of Henry L. Benning). CSU Archives, Simon Schwob Library, Chattahoochee Valley Historical Collection, Columbus, Georgia.

DeLapp, Larry Russell. Genealogical notes concerning the Benning, Cobb and Russell family.

Dougherty, William. (Pamphlet- privately printed) and entitled, *Bank Cases and Decisions in Macon*, 1859, University of Georgia Archives.

Duggan, Ivy. Papers, (Private, 15th Georgia regiment), Special Collections Robert W. Woodruff Library, Emory University, Atlanta, Georgia.

Evans, Augusta Jane. Letters. MC-2, Louise Gunby Jones DuBose Papers. (Evans was a popular writer and cousin of Mrs. Henry L. Benning) CSU Archives, Simon Schwob Library, Chattahoochee Valley Historical Collection, Columbus, Georgia.

Fluker, W. T., Papers, (Private, Co. D, 15th Georgia regiment, 1861-1865) Special Collections Department, Duke University, Durham, North Carolina.

Fuller, Joseph Pryor. (Private, Co. B, 20th Georgia regiment), Diary, May-Sept. 1864, Miscellaneous Collection of Civil War Material, sub-file " Diaries," Georgia Archives.

Garrard, Leonard. (Grandson of Louis F. Garrard and Anna Leonard Garrard) Personal archives, photographs, genealogical notes, family papers, and interview with author.

Hatchett, Pinkney G. Papers. (First Lieutenant, Co. E, 20th Georgia regiment). Private Collection of Mr. David Cress, Charlotte, North Carolina.

Langford, Thomas. Papers, (Private, 17th Georgia regiment), Private collection of Mrs. Patti L. Parrish, Fitzgerald, Georgia.

Lokey, J. W. Typed manuscript entitled " My Experiences in the War Between the States". (Private, Co. B, 20th regiment). W. C. Bradley Library Archives, Columbus, Georgia. (Gift of Ray Lokey, great-grandson).

Lumpkin, Joseph H. , Manuscript number 192, (Joseph Henry Lumpkin papers). Hargrett Rare Book and Archives Collection, University of Georgia, Athens, Georgia.

Martin, John H. (Captain, 17th Georgia), *Reminences of Confederate Soldiers and Stories of the War, 1861-1865*, Vol. 1, Georgia Division, United Daughters of the Confederacy. Central Research Library. Georgia Department of Archives and History, Atlanta, Georgia, 1940.

McGregor, John A. A. Papers. (Captain E, 17th Georgia regiment), Private collection of Mr. Blaine Walker, Cornelia, Georgia.

Millican, William Terrell. (Colonel, 15th Georgia), *Reminences of Confederate Soldiers and Stories of the War, 1861-1865*, Vol. VII, Georgia Division, United Daughters of the Confederacy. Central Research Library. Georgia Department of Archives and History, Atlanta, Georgia, January 1998.

Moses, Raphael. (Major, Toombs-Benning brigade), MC 34, Alva C. Smith Collection. Autobiographical material and journal of Raphael Moses. (Moses was a prominent lawyer, planter, and friend of the Bennings, Jones, Toombs, and Crawfords. His plantation called Esquiline, was located on the outskirts of Columbus, on property purchased by the federal government and incorporated into Fort Benning . CSU Archives, Simon Schwob Library, Chattahoochee Valley Historical Collection, Columbus, Georgia.

Official Register of the Officers and Cadets, Georgia Military Institute, Marietta, Georgia. Atlanta: J. I. Miller & Co., 1858.

Pease, William. (Descendant of John A. Jones) Personal papers and genealogical notes of the Benning, Jones, and Pease families.

Peddy, Thomas J. MC-36 (Thomas J. Peddy Collection, notes and material related to early Columbus history) CSU Archives, Simon Schwob Library, Chattahoochee Valley Historical Collection, Columbus, Georgia.

Regulations of the Georgia Military Institute, Marietta, Georgia. Atlanta: C. R. Hanleiter, 1857.

Smith, Jenny, MC-9, Box 2, Folder 3, Columbus Museum of Arts & Sciences Collection (letters of Confederate soldiers of the 20th regiment, Benning's brigade) CSU Archives, Simon Schwob Library Chattahoochee Valley Historical Collection, Columbus, Georgia.

Spencer, Henry Benning. Personal archives and papers. (Portraits of Mr. and Mrs. Henry L. Benning ; letters of their children Seaborn Jones Benning and Louisa Vivian (Benning) Spencer).

Tondee, Robert P. Jr., Papers, (Captain, 17th Georgia regiment), Special Collections Department, Duke University, Durham, North Carolina.

Waddell, James D. , Papers, (Colonel, Twentieth regiment) Special Collections, Robert W. Woodruff Library, Emory University, Atlanta, Georgia.

Ware, Thomas L. , Diary, (1861-1863, Sergeant, 15th Georgia regiment) Southern Historical Society Collection, Wilson Library, University o North Carolina, Chapel Hill, North Carolina.

Wiley, Samuel H., Diary, (Sergeant, 15th Georgia regiment), Southern Historical Society Collection, Wilson Library, University of North Carolina, Chapel Hill, North Carolina.

Yancey, Benjamin C., Papers, Southern Historical Society Collection, Wilson Library, University of North Carolina, Chapel Hill, North Carolina.

NEWSPAPERS

Atlanta (Georgia) *Constitution*
Atlanta (Georgia) *Herald*
Atlanta (Georgia) *Journal*
Columbus (Georgia*)* *Daily Enquirer*
Columbus (Georgia) Daily Sun
Columbus (Georgia) *Weekly Enquirer*
Columbus (Georgia) Times and Sentinel
Macon Messenger (Georgia)
Macon Telegraph (Georgia)
Milledgeville Federal Union (Georgia)
North Carolina Standard , Raleigh, North Carolina
Richmond *Enquirer* (Virginia)
Savannah Herald (Georgia)
Savannah News (Georgia)
Southern Recorder, Milledgeville, Georgia
Union Recorder, Milledgeville, Georgia

PUBLISHED CAMPAIGN AND BATTLE NARRATIVES

Allen, Cornelious Tacitus. " Fight at Chaffin's Farm, Fort Harrison," Confederate Veteran, Vol. XIII, No. 9 (1905), p. 418.

Benning, General H. L. " Notes on the Final Campaign of April, 1865,"
    Southern Historical Society Papers, Vol. VII, pp. 193-195.
Benning, General H. L. " Notes on the Battle of Sharpsburg," *Southern
    Historical Society Papers*, Vol. XVI, pp. 393-397.
Bowden, Reverend John Malachi. (Private, Company G, Second
    regiment) Unpublished Manuscript, Atlanta History Center,
    MSS 537f.
DuBose, Dudley McIver. " Fifteenth Georgia at Gettysburg. " *Southern
    Historical Society Papers*, Vol. XVIIII (1891), pp. 179-183.
Field, Charles W. " The Campaign of 1864 and 1865: The Narrative of
    Major General C.W. Field," *Southern Historical Society Papers*, Vol.
    XIV, pp. 542-563.
Flanigan, W.A. " That Fight at Fort Gilmer," *Confederate Veteran*, Vol.
    XIII, No. 3 (1905), p. 123.
Granberry, J.A.H. " That Fort Gilmer Fight," *Confederate Veteran*. (1904),
    pp. 587-588.
Howard, James McHenry. " Closing Scenes of the War About Richmond,"
    Southern Historical Society Papers, Vol. XXXI, pp. 129-145.
Johnson, Robert Underwood and Clarence Buel. eds. *Battles and Leaders
    of the Civil War*. 4 vols., New York, 1887-1888.
Johnston, Charles. " Attack on Fort Gilmer, September 29th, 1864,"
    Southern Historical Society Papers, Vol. I (1876), pp. 438-442.
Longstreet, James. *From Manassas to Appomattox*. Reprint ed. New York:
    Smithmark Publishers Inc., 1994.
Lokey, J. W. " Wounded at Gettysburg," *Confederate Veteran*, Vol. XXII,
    Number 8, August, 1914, p. 400.
Martin, J. H. "The Assault on Fort Gilmer," *Confederate Veteran*, Vol.
    XIII, No. 6, (1905), pp. 269-270.
May, T.J. " The Fight at Fort Gilmer," *Confederate Veteran*, Vol. XII, No.
    12 (1904), pp. 587-588.
Moore, James B. " The Attack of Fort Harrison," *Confederate Veteran*,
    Vol. XIII, No. 9 (1905), pp. 418-420.
Norton, Oliver Wilcox. *The Attack and Defense of Little Round Top*,
    Gettysburg, July 2, 1863, New York, The Neale Publishing
    Company, 1913.
Perry, Herman H. " Assault on Fort Gilmer," *Confederate Veteran*, Vol.
    XIII, No. 9 (1905), pp. 413-415.

_____. Colonel (CSA). " Account of the Surrender of the Confederate States of America, April 9, 1865, *Southern Historical Society Papers* Vol. XX, 1892.

Winder, J. R. " Judge Martin's Report Approved," *Confederate Veteran*, Vol. XIII, No. 9 (1905), p. 417.

PUBLISHED SOURCES

Alexander, Edward Porter. *Military Memoirs of a Confederate*. Bloomington, Indiana: Indiana University Press, 1962.

Allen, Sarah Cantey Whitaker. *Our Children's Ancestry*. Atlanta, Georgia: Curtis Printing Company, 1938.

American State Papers, Volume VII, Military Affairs. Washington: Gales and Seaton, 1798-1838.

Andrews, Eliza Frances. *The War-Time Journal of a Georgia Girl, 1864-1865*. New York: D. Appleton Company, 1908.

Anderson, Fulton, Henry Benning and John S. Preston. *Addresses Delivered Before the Virginia State Convention*. Richmond, Virginia: Wyatt M. Elliott, 1861.

Avery, Isaac W., *The History of the State of Georgia, From 1850 to 1881*. New York: Brown & Derby Publishers, 1881.

Banks, Enoch Marvin, Ph.D. *The Economics of Land Tenure in Georgia*. New York: The Columbia University Press, 1905.

Barfield, Louise Calhoun. *History of Harris County, Georgia, 1827-1961*. Columbus, Ga.: Columbus Office Supply Company, 1961.

Barney, William L., *The Road to Secession: A New Perspective on the Old South*. New York: Praeger Publishing, 1972.

Benning, Eva Hardin. *Francois Benin (Francis Benning): His Descendants and Allied Families*. Independence, Missouri: Eva Hardin Benning, 1981.

Berry, Mary Kent. comp., *Records of Marriages, Baptism and Burials from the First Register of Trinity (1836-1903)*, Columbus, Georgia: Muscogee Genealogical Society, 1985.

Black, Henry. *Black's Law Dictionary*. 6th. Edition. St. Paul, Minnesota: West Publishing Co., 1990.

Butts, Sarah Harriet. comp. *The Mother of Some Distinguished Georgians of the Last Half Century*. New York: J. J. Little & Co., 1902.

Cobb, James C. " The Making of a Secessionist: Henry L. Benning and the Coming of the Civil War. " *Georgia Historical Quarterly* 60, Numbe 4, (1976): 313-323.

Cobb, Thomas R. R. *An Historical Sketch of Slavery, From the Earliest Periods*. Savannah: W. Thorne Williams, 1858.

_____. comp. *New Digest Laws of Georgia*, Milledgeville: State of
   Georgia, 1851.

Confederated Southern Memorial Association. *History of the Confederatec
   Memorial Associations of the South.* New Orleans: The Graham
   Press, 1904.

Coulter, Merton. *College Life in the Old South.* Athens, Georgia:
   University of Georgia Press, 1964.

Derby, J. C. *Fifty Years Among Authors, Books, and Publishers.* New
   York: G. W. Carleton & Co., 1884.

Ducat, Craig R., and Harold W. Chase. *Constitutional Interpretation.* St.
   Paul, Minnesota: West Publishing Co., 1992.

Dudley, F. J. *100 Years History of St. Luke M.E. Church, South.*
   Columbus, Georgia: Columbus Office Supply, 1929.

Faust, Drew Gilpin. *The Ideology of Slavery: Proslavery Thought in the
   Antebellum South, 1830-1860. Baton Rouge:* Louisiana State
   University Press, 1981.

Freehling, William M., and Craig Simpson. eds. *Secession Debated:
   Georgia's Showdown in 1860.* New York: Oxford University Press,
   1992.

Houghton, W. R., and M. B. Houghton, *Two Boys in the Civil War and
   After.* Montgomery, Alabama : The Paragon Press, 1912.

Jones, J. William, et al., eds. *Southern Historical Society Papers.* 52 Vols.
   Virginia Historical Society:[etc.], 1876-1959.

Telfair, Nancy.[Louise Gunby Jones DuBose]. *A History of Columbus,
   Georgia, 1828-1928.* Columbus, Georgia: The Historical Publishing
   Company, 1919.

Uzar, Sandra White. *Muscogiana*, Volume 3, Numbers 1 & 2, (Spring
   1992)," Confederate Hospitals in Columbus, Georgia," pp. 16-21.

Worsley, Etta Blanchard. *Columbus on the Chattahoochee.* Columbus,
   Georgia: Columbus Office Supply Company, 1951.

Young, Mary. *Redskins, Ruffleshirts and Rednecks: Indian Allotments in
   Alabama and Mississippi, 1830-1860.* Norman, Oklahoma:
   University of Oklahoma Press, 1961.

INDEX

INDEX

Brussels, Belgium, 278
Buchanan, James, 49, 77
Buckingham County, Virginia
Buena Vista, 45
Bullock, Rufus B., 245, 254
Burch, John E., 123
Burnside, Ambrose, 151, 155, 156, 158, 193, 194, 195, 203
Burnside's Bridge, 270
Burnside's IX corps, 153
Burnside's Bridge, 156
Bush Arbor, 254, 255
Butler, Benjamin, 211
Butt, Edgar M., 122, 136
cabinet, 109, 111, 230, 246
Cade, A. B., 123
Calhoun, John C., 32, 51, 52
California, 52, 93
camp, 126, 127, 143, 157, 165, 193, 281
Camp Benning, 276, 279, 281
Camp Georgia, 125
Camp Lookout, Maryland, 201
Campbell, Charles G., 120
Campbell, W. A., 122
Candler, D. G., 122
Capitol building, 5
captain of industry, 274
Cardinal Richelieu, 1
Carey v. Jones, 80
Carey, Edward, 20, 82, 83
carpetbagger, 243, 245, 255
carpetbaggers, 255
Carroll County, Georgia, 30
Carswell, Reuben, 116
Cass, Lewis, 49
Catharpin Road, 202
Catoosa Station, 186
cavalry units, 169, 218
cemetery, 33, 44, 201, 249, 266, 268, 277, 279
Cemetery Ridge, 170
Cenotaph, 249
Census, 285, 337, 338
Centreville, Virginia, 125, 149
Cerro Gordo, 45
Chaffin, Thomas, 267
Chaffin's Farm, 212, 342
Chancellorsville, Virginia, 166, 181, 202
Chapel Hill, North Carolina

INDEX

Georgia politics, 35, 249, 260, 261
Georgia regiments, 116, 126, 213, 215
Georgia Reports, 74
Georgia State Militia, 24, 110
Georgia Supreme Court, 61, 63, 76, 78
Georgia troops, 27, 108, 221
Germanna Ford, 202
Gettysburg, Battle of, 127, 170, 172, 173, 179, 180, 181, 182, 240, 248, 343
Gilbert, James F., 12
Girard, Alabama, 229
Girls' Asylum, 42, 207
Gittinger, Phillip, 134
Gladdy, Mary, 71
Glen Lora, 23
Glenn, Jesse A., 122
Glover, Henry S., 12
Gold Lottery, 11
gold rush, 36
Goldsboro, North Carolina, 184
Gone with the Wind, 252, 253
Goochland Artillery, 214
Goochland County, Virginia, 2
Gordon, John B., 116, 243, 254, 261, 262, 280
Gordonsville, Virginia, 143
government of Georgia, 258
Governor Brown, 79, 95, 96, 99, 102, 108, 109, 120, 134
Governor Bullock, 255, 258, 260
Governor Fitzpatrick, 95
Governor of Georgia, 8, 24, 42, 55, 77, 103, 234, 249, 262
Grand Divisions, 158, 159
Grant Factory, 92
Grant, U. S., 203
Grant, Ulysses, 92, 193, 194, 199, 202, 203, 204, 205, 206, 208, 211, 212, 213, 214, 217, 218, 220, 223, 224, 225, 226, 227, 228, 243, 247, 249, 255, 261
grape shot, 139, 189
graybacks, 212
Great Britain, 5
Great Compromiser, 52
Greeley, Horace, 261
Green Island Hills, 272
Greencastle, Pennsylvania, 168, 169
Gregg, John, 213, 214, 215, 216, 217, 218, 224
Guinea Station, Virginia, 162
gunboat, 229
habeas corpus, 258

INDEX

Missouri Compromise, 52, 53, 73, 76
Mitchell, Peggy (Margaret), 28, 120, 252, 253
Mobile, Alabama, 86, 87, 209, 232, 277
Monacan Towne, 1
Montgomery, Alabama, 27, 110, 231, 345
Moore, James B., 343
Morgan County, Georgia, 38
Morristown, Tennessee, 197
Moses plantation, 279
Moses, Raphael J., 23, 47, 116, 132, 158, 198, 206, 223, 239, 249, 251, 252, 253, 254, 267, 272, 278, 279, 341
Moses, Stanford E., 279
Mother of Patriotic Organizations, 275
Mott, John, 115
Mott, John R., 178, 205
Mott, Randolph, 229, 257
Mt. Zion Academy, 7
Mule Shoe, 204
Muscogee Blues, 24, 27
Muscogee County, Georgia, 16, 34, 52, 53, 89, 96, 102, 103, 115, 209, 234, 243, 271, 277, 337, 338
Muscogee Mounted Rangers, 109
Muscogee Southern Rights Association, 52
Muscogiana, 345
Mustian, John, 90
Nashville, 53, 54, 250
National Archives, 285, 336
National Infantry Museum, 336
Negro, 22, 43, 70, 71, 72, 73, 74, 75, 111, 214, 217, 220, 239, 241
Negro Loyal League, 241, 246
Negroes, 63, 69, 70, 71, 72, 100, 131, 158, 214, 217, 221, 230, 233, 235, 237, 238, 239, 241, 242, 253, 256, 257
Nelson's Rangers, 250
Nestor of Education, 7
Nestor of Southern Methodism, 32
New Hope Church, 225
New Market Heights, Battle of, 127
New Market Road, Battle of, 138, 213
New Market, Battle of, 127, 138, 213, 214, 215, 216
New Orleans, Louisiana, 41, 242, 345
New York, 8, 41, 47, 49, 86, 87, 100, 108, 216, 245, 274, 285, 343, 344, 345
Nisbet, Eugenius A. (Judge), 59
Norfolk, Virginia, 132
North and South, 52, 54, 72, 73, 94, 96, 112, 114, 119, 131, 157, 171, 228, 237
North Anna River, 204

INDEX

369

Petersburg, Siege of, 127, 182, 204, 205, 206, 211, 212, 213, 214, 218, 220, 221, 223, 224, 228
Phenix City, Alabama, 229
Phi Kappa Society, 10, 61
Phillips House, 215
Philo Kosmean, 10
Phoenix Bank of Columbus, 39, 80
picket duty, 125, 135
Pickett, George E., 179
Pickett, John H., 120
Pierce, Lovick, 21, 23, 32, 38, 40, 42, 44, 86, 121, 180, 251
Pigeon Roost Mining Company
plantation, 3, 4, 6, 9, 11, 35, 46, 47, 56, 58, 77, 85, 206, 207, 230, 235, 242, 253, 272, 277, 279, 341
Plantation owners, 257
planters, 34, 46, 47
Planters' and Merchants Bank, 82
platform, 49, 52, 53, 54, 55, 88, 93, 94, 255
Plum Run Valley, 175, 180
pneumonia, 273, 276
Pond Mountain, 144
Poole, William R., 123
Pope, John, 143, 144, 145, 146, 233
Portsmouth, Virginia, 132
Potomac River, 150, 168
POW (Prisoners of War), 201
practice of law, 15, 16, 29, 34, 35, 38, 56, 255, 263
President Davis, 110, 112, 117, 129, 133, 134, 135, 142, 184, 185, 193, 195, 230
President Jackson, 26, 27, 29
President Johnson, 234, 236, 237, 238, 242, 245
President Lincoln, 119, 129, 158, 161, 190
President LincolnSee Lincoln, Abraham, 119
President of the United States, 45, 95
presidential election, 35, 77, 88, 95, 254, 255
Primus, 12
prison camps, 201
pro, 51, 53, 54, 56, 97, 229
properties, 14, 19, 207, 231, 232, 240, 271, 272, 279
prosecution team, 249, 253
prosecutor, 30, 249
prostitutes, 246, 247
Protestants, 1
provisional government, 110
Provisional Governor, 8, 234
public library, 31

ABOUT THE AUTHOR

J. DAVID DAMERON JR. was born in Washington, D.C., and raised in Virginia. He holds advanced degrees in history and education and he is an alumnus of Campbell University, the University of North Carolina and Troy State University. He is also a graduate of the U.S. Army, John F. Kennedy Special Warfare School, where he specialized in Unconventional Warfare. He is a combat veteran and served in the Special Forces. With twenty-four years of federal service, Dave now works as a civilian research specialist in the Concepts and Analysis Division of the U.S. Army Infantry Center, Fort Benning, Georgia. Dave serves on several museum history advisory committees and he has authored several articles as well as non-fiction history books, which include *A History and Roster of the Fifteenth Georgia*, *General Henry Lewis Benning*, *King's Mountain: The Defeat of the Loyalists*, and a forthcoming biography of Horace King. He is a member of the Veterans of Foreign Wars, the American Legion, the Special Forces "Decade" Association, and the Organization of American Historians. Dave is married to the former Pamela Gail Brown of Kingsport, Tennessee, and they have two children, Kevin and Christina.

www.ingramcontent.com/pod-product-compliance
Lightning Source LLC
Chambersburg PA
CBHW071826270326
41929CB00013B/1909